A Court Divided

DEBORAH J. BARROW · THOMAS G. WALKER

A COURT DIVIDED

The Fifth Circuit
Court of Appeals
and the Politics
of Judicial Reform

Yale University Press
New Haven and London

Published with assistance from the Louis Stern Memorial Fund.

Designed by Nancy Ovedovitz and set in Baskerville with Gill Sans type by Rainsford Type. Printed in the United States of America by Braun-Brumfield, Inc., Ann Arbor, Michigan.

Library of the Congress Cataloging-in-Publication Data
Barrow, Deborah J., 1952–
A court divided: the Fifth Circuit Court of Appeals and the politics of judicial reform / Deborah J. Barrow, Thomas G. Walker.
    p. cm.
    Bibliography: p.
    Includes index.
    1. United States. Court of Appeals (5th Circuit)—History.
2. Judicial process—Southern States—History. 3. Civil rights—Southern States—History. 4. United States. Court of Appeals (11th Circuit)—History. I. Walker, Thomas G., 1945– . II. Title.
KF8752 5th.B27 1988
347.73'24—dc19
[347.3073]   88–2045
                                                                         CIP
ISBN: 0-300-04165-9 (cloth)
          0-300-04896-3 (pbk.)

The paper in this book meets the guidelines for permanence and durability of the Committee on Production Guidelines for Book Longevity of the Council on Library Resources.

10   9   8   7   6   5   4   3   2

To my parents, Emma and Gene Barrow
D. J. B.

To Aimee and Emily, for their spirit and their love
T. G. W.

Contents

Preface

This study is based upon the reality that federal judges in the United States are by nature and necessity politicians. The courts on which they serve constitute a separate and coequal branch of government, sharing responsibility with the legislative and executive branches for exercising political authority over the nation. While the trappings, procedures, and roles of the judicial branch may vary from those of the more outwardly political institutions, it would be a mistake to forget that whenever governmental power is wielded politics is present.

"A judge," as one scholar of the courts has observed, "is a black-robed homo sapiens."[1] As such, the federal jurist is subject to the same forces that influence the behavior of other individuals. Judges have attitudes, values, and political opinions. They share with other citizens the preference to see their own values and priorities prevail over competing policy interests. Accepting a judgeship does not carry with it a forfeiture of political ideology. Quite the contrary, individuals are customarily chosen for federal judgeships precisely because of their political philosophies and prior involvement in the political process. The selection system is tilted toward judicial candidates who have led active lives in partisan affairs. A judge must always be cognizant of the obligations and responsibilities of the judicial role, but putting on the black robe cannot be expected to neutralize an individual's political nature.

Federal judges are entrusted with the duty of managing the United States court system. They not only perform an adjudicative function but also act as professional administrators of their own branch of the government. Individual judges have clear opinions, often strongly held and actively pursued, about how the judiciary should be run, and, as in any organization, they do not always agree. In much the same way that Congress has developed ways to settle internal conflicts, the judiciary has arrived at its own system for making

1. S. Sidney Ulmer, "Dissent Behavior and the Social Background of Supreme Court Justices," *Journal of Politics* 32 (August 1970): 580–98, at 580.

administrative decisions. These mechanisms for identifying problems and recommending solutions constitute a political process of their very own. How courts arrive at policy conclusions can be understood only by examining the internal, and largely private, world of politics within the Third Branch.

In determining public policy for the nation's court system, the Constitution has given each of the three branches of government an appropriate role. It is an example of what Richard Neustadt has called "separated institutions sharing powers."[2] Changes in the structure, jurisdiction, and procedures of the judiciary generally require the approval of Congress, subject to a presidential veto. Levels of financial support and staffing must go through the same political process. To obtain favorable action from the legislature, federal judges must first use their own internal political process to arrive at official policy preferences and then engage in effective political lobbying with Congress. By necessity, therefore, federal judges participate in politics. The welfare of the institution requires it.

The legislative and judicial branches exercise cooperative oversight to keep the court system functioning effectively. The judges know what conditions face them in the daily exercise of their judicial powers. They possess the expertise to identify problems and recommend solutions. The legislature receives their recommendations and places them in the broader perspective of an institution that must deal with the entire gamut of governmental affairs. Congress often defers to the expertise of the judiciary, especially when there is consensus among the judges and no objections are raised by nonjudicial interests. But it is not uncommon for the legislature and the judiciary to clash. There is inevitable tension between the two branches. Elected legislators are accountable to the people at regular intervals and respond to different forces than those that motivate the appointed and life-tenured judges. The offsetting grants of authority provided for in the Constitution allow one branch to check the other and add to the process competition for political power. Through this system of cooperation and competition, policy for the judicial branch is determined.

The story of the splitting of the Fifth Circuit Court of Appeals into two courts is much more than the mere chronicling of routine administrative reform. The events from 1963 to 1981 highlight the way in which the judicial and legislative branches interact politically. They reveal the formal and informal aspects of interinstitutional politics, as competing approaches to managing the court system contend for approval. The saga of the Fifth Circuit demonstrates the inextricable relationship between a federal court and the sociopolitical milieu of its jurisdiction. It shows how questions of administration can become far-reaching political conflicts involving a host of public and private institutions and how seemingly neutral structural changes can result in an alteration in substantive policy. And finally, the history of the Fifth

2. Richard E. Neustadt, *Presidential Power* (New York: John Wiley and Sons, 1960).

Circuit allows us to examine the rarely documented activities of federal judges outside their adjudicative responsibilities: We see how they arrive at policy positions within the confines of their own institution and how they interact with the decision-making centers of other political agencies.

In conducting this research we generally relied on three sources of information. First, we examined the public record. The publications, reports, records, and files maintained by the Administrative Office of United States Courts, the Federal Judicial Center, the various courts of appeals, and both houses of Congress were extremely helpful. These materials, coupled with information reported in newspapers and other media outlets, provided the factual basis for reconstructing the formal stages through which the realignment issue passed. Second, we interviewed as many participants as possible. Most responded generously to our invitation to discuss the subject. Those who declined usually did so because of health considerations or because they claimed to have no recollection whatsoever of the specific events in which we indicated an interest. (See the appendix for a complete list of those interviewed.) Judges, of course, were our most frequent subjects. We held open-ended discussions with federal appellate court personnel from five different circuits, including seven former or current chief judges. From the executive branch, President Carter and Justice Department officials from the Kennedy, Johnson, and Carter administrations were willing to share their knowledge and opinions. Members of the House and Senate as well as key legislative staff also contributed their time and information. From the private sector, interest-group representatives, attorneys, and scholars who had been drawn into the debate shared their accounts of what transpired. As a group, the subjects represented every perspective and institution involved in the issue. Almost all interviews were face-to-face, although a small number were conducted by telephone. With few exceptions, the sessions were recorded, with the permission of the subjects. Interviews ranged from approximately thirty minutes to two full days. Several key figures consented to more than one interview. The interviews supplied much information that was unavailable in public sources.

Third, we obtained access to the private papers of certain individuals who were active at various stages of the controversy. This was particularly valuable in reconstructing the events of the earlier years of the dispute and the roles played by persons who are no longer living. The memoranda, notes, speeches, draft documents, and correspondence in these collections allowed us to flesh out the skeleton assembled from the public record and to verify some of the information recalled in the interview sessions. The attitudes and motivations of the participants became clearer. Public events took on greater meaning, and activities not documented in the public record began to fill in vital gaps in the research.

Among the collections consulted, the judicial papers of Judge John Minor

Wisdom, which have been deposited in the special collections of the Tulane University Law Library, deserve particular mention. The Wisdom papers, extensive in coverage and varied in nature, provide a rich source of information on the more than three decades of Judge Wisdom's service as an active and senior member of the Fifth Circuit Court of Appeals. Splitting the court ran counter to Wisdom's strongly held convictions on the proper role of the courts of appeals. He consequently devoted a substantial amount of his time and energy to opposing the division. His papers, to which we were given access prior to official cataloguing, contain not only his perspectives on the issue, but also the views of many individuals who took an active interest in the Fifth Circuit Court.

Acknowledgments

Throughout the course of this research we encountered many persons who gave generously of their time, effort, criticism, and guidance. Although none of these individuals bears responsibility for the shortcomings of the study, they all share in whatever contribution it makes.

We are grateful for the special efforts expended by many already busy staff members who went out of their way to help us locate important information in the files and records of the Administrative Office of the United States Courts, the Federal Judicial Center, the Courts of Appeals for the Fifth, Ninth, and Eleventh Circuits, the National Archives, and the Senate and House Judiciary Committees. Similarly, a number of research librarians were most gracious in their response to our needs. We extend a special thanks to the staffs of the manuscript division of the Library of Congress, the Tulane University Law Library, the Robert W. Woodruff Library for Advanced Studies at Emory University, the Carter Presidential Library, and the Emory University Law Library.

The individuals who participated in our interviews were generous with their time and willingness to discuss the issues and events recounted in this study. Several aided the project immeasurably by referring us to other significant participants or directing our attention to relevant records and files. All were courteous and accommodating, and many went to great lengths to extend hospitality to us.

Without necessary financial support provided by the Carter Center of Emory University, the Emory University Research Committee, and the Emory University Graduate School of Arts and Sciences the project could not have been completed. We are also indebted to the Engineering Learning Resource Center of Auburn University, and especially to Violet Erdey, for valuable technical assistance. In addition, Deborah McBride of Representative Bill Nichols's (D-AL) office was particularly helpful in locating important research materials.

This volume profited immeasurably from the care and attention given it by the editorial staff at Yale University Press. We are particularly indebted to Eric L. Van Horne, into whose hands the manuscript fortunately fell, and to Barbara W. Folsom and Caroline Murphy, who shepherded it through the editorial stages. We thank Marian Neal Ash for her continued confidence in this project and her patience throughout. We also appreciate the assistance given to the whole project by Leslie Nelson.

A number of people made significant professional and personal contributions to our research and writing. We offer a special expression of gratitude to Judge John Minor Wisdom and his staff. Without Judge Wisdom's commitment to the preservation of the history of the Fifth Circuit, some lessons of judicial reform might have been lost. J. Woodford Howard, Jr., and Jack Bass, whose scholarly works on the federal judiciary serve as models, generously provided us with research materials, information, and insights. David J. Danelski read the entire manuscript and offered welcome suggestions for its improvement. Dr. Edward Holladay's assistance at the earliest stages of our research was very important. Emory University professors Kenneth W. Stein and Eleanor C. Main not only provided personal encouragement but also were instrumental in helping us obtain necessary institutional support. Special thanks go to our families and close friends, who patiently and optimistically endured the time and effort we expended on this project. Finally, we feel particularly grateful for the efforts of Gerard S. Gryski. His substantive comments were of great value and his devotion to the completion of this study was unsurpassed.

A Court Divided

1

The Fifth

On October 15, 1980, President Jimmy Carter expressed his pleasure at signing into law the Fifth Circuit Court of Appeals Reorganization Act.[1] The president's approval signaled the end of the federal judiciary's venerable Fifth Circuit, a jurisdictional unit consisting of the six states of the Deep South. The legislation receiving Carter's blessing realigned the old Fifth into two jurisdictional areas: a new Fifth Circuit composed of Texas, Louisiana, and Mississippi and a new Eleventh Circuit containing the states of Florida, Georgia, and Alabama. This split was dictated by the region's rapid caseload growth, which had come to necessitate periodic creation of additional court of appeals judgeships. When the authorized size of the Fifth Circuit Court of Appeals reached twenty-six judges in 1978, Carter explained, the result was an unwieldy bench, one that was beset with management problems and that found it difficult to preserve consistency and predictability in the law. The active judges on the court had thus unanimously petitioned Congress to divide the region into two autonomous circuits in order "to enhance the court's ability to deliver consistent, fair, and expeditious justice." The president concluded his public statement by commending Congress "for having acted so promptly in response to the needs of our Federal courts."[2]

On the face of it, then, the realignment appeared to be a simple administrative reform based on the need for efficient management of a rising caseload. The active judges of the circuit had requested the legislation with one voice, and Congress had responded with dispatch. The bill had moved through the legislative maze and had been signed into law just five months after receipt of the judges' request.

The gloss of simple administrative change, judicial unanimity, and prompt congressional response, however, masks the reality of a long and often bitter

1. Public Law 96–452, enacted from H.R. 7665.
2. Public statement of President Jimmy Carter upon signing into law the Fifth Circuit Court of Appeals Reorganization Act of 1980, October 15, 1980.

eighteen-year controversy. In fact, the complex political history of the Fifth
Circuit offers us a rich lesson in the functioning of American political
institutions.

THE NEED FOR JUDGES AND THE RULE OF NINE

Chief Judge Elbert Parr Tuttle of the United States Court of Appeals for
the Fifth Circuit arrived in Washington for the September 1963 meeting of
the Judicial Conference of the United States with the clear mission to plead
the case of his court for additional judges. Only if he could convince the
conference to endorse such an expansion would Congress seriously entertain
the possibility of passing the necessary legislation. Tuttle realized that his task
would not be easy. Only two years before, in 1961, the Fifth Circuit had
expanded from seven to nine, and now Tuttle was coming to the Judicial
Conference arguing for more judgeships.

As a member of the Judicial Conference, Tuttle met twice a year with
twenty-four other judges to set policy for the federal court system. The 1963
meetings were chaired by Earl Warren, who, by virtue of his office as Chief
Justice of the United States, headed the conference. Each of the eleven regional circuits sent two representatives—the chief judge of the court of appeals
and one elected district court judge. Tuttle's Fifth Circuit contained the six
states of the Deep South (Texas, Louisiana, Mississippi, Alabama, Georgia,
and Florida) and the Canal Zone.[3] In addition to the regional court representatives, the Court of Claims and the Court of Customs and Patent Appeals
were entitled to send their respective chief judges to the conference meetings.

Chief Judge Tuttle, along with another member of the Fifth Circuit, Judge
John Brown, had been laying the groundwork for securing the additional
judges since May, when the members of the court had met in council in New
Orleans to discuss, among other matters, the escalating caseload levels facing
them. At that meeting the judges present unanimously "agreed that the problem had reached emergency proportions and that it was incapable of solution
by the present judge personnel."[4] During the summer months, Tuttle and
Brown took their case to the meetings of two important committees of the
Judicial Conference—the Committee on Court Administration and the Committee on Judicial Statistics. Favorable reports from both were crucial to Tuttle's efforts.

Tuttle, a member of the conference's Court Administration Committee,
advanced a compelling rationale for an expansion in the court's judgeships.
He concentrated on the particular conditions existing in the region, including

---

3. Federal jurisdiction over the Canal Zone continued until March 1982, as stipulated
in the Panama Canal Treaty.

4. Minutes of the meeting of the Judicial Council of the Court of Appeals for the Fifth
Circuit, New Orleans, May 29 and 31, 1963.

its geography, population, commercial activity, and especially the growth of its litigation rates. Judge Brown articulated the court's position before the conference's Committee on Judicial Statistics.[5]

The Fifth Circuit Court of Appeals had been created by an act of Congress in 1891 to hear disputes arising from the federal trial courts of the six southeastern states.[6] Although the territory covered was immense, its population at the time numbered only 8.3 million. It was a region of rural agriculture, small towns, and port cities. New Orleans, with 242,000 residents, was the only city of major consequence. The circuit's caseload was modest in the early years, as could be expected in a largely rural culture and agrarian economy. From the very beginning, however, the court developed an expertise in certain areas of the law. Paramount among these was maritime law, which evolved from disputes involving the Gulf of Mexico and southern Atlantic ports.

By 1963, the region had undergone substantial change, most of it occurring after 1950, and all of it a modest prelude to the great expansion that was yet to come. In population, the Fifth Circuit states had grown to over twenty-nine million, an increase of one-third over the 1950 census figures—this compared to a 25 percent increase for the nation as a whole over the same period.[7] The states of Florida and Texas were growing at a particularly fast rate. Although still a relatively poor region, the Fifth Circuit area showed a 54 percent increase in per capita income between 1950 and 1960, outdistancing all of the other judicial regions.[8] Retail sales and commercial activity blossomed. Industrial plants were being built at a brisk pace as new companies formed and expanded in the South or migrated from the North in order to reduce their costs and avoid strong unions. With increased industrialization, the South's cities began to flourish. Each of the six states witnessed an acceleration in urbanization and a decrease in acreage devoted to farming. Dallas, Houston, Miami, and Atlanta joined New Orleans as major regional centers. The South was no longer the homogeneous region it once had been. The Fifth Circuit now encompassed the oil fields of west Texas, the cotton plantations of Mississippi, the mountains of North Georgia, and the seaports of Savannah, Mobile, Jacksonville, Miami, New Orleans, and Houston. From El Paso to Atlanta to Key West, the Sun Belt was clearly emerging from the old Confederacy.

With these progressive changes an increase in federal law suits was inevi-

5. Letter from Chief Judge Elbert Tuttle to Judges Joseph C. Hutcheson, Jr., Richard T. Rives, John R. Brown, and John Minor Wisdom, March 25, 1964.

6. For a discussion of the historical development of the Fifth Circuit, see Harvey C. Couch, *A History of the Fifth Circuit, 1891–1981* (Washington, D.C.: Government Printing Office, under the auspices of the Bicentennial Committee of the Judicial Conference of the United States, 1984).

7. Department of Commerce, Bureau of the Census.

8. *Statistical Abstract of the United States* (Washington, D.C.: United States Bureau of the Census, 1962), p. 319.

table, which naturally added to the workload of the Fifth Circuit Court of Appeals.[9] In 1950, with seven authorized judges, the Fifth Circuit received 408 appeals. By 1960, still with seven judges, the court's docket had increased by 41 percent to 577 appeals, more than any other circuit except the Second (New York, Connecticut, and Vermont). By the time Tuttle made his pleas to the conference committees in the summer of 1963, however, the Fifth Circuit was completing a year in which it had received 874 appeals, an increase of 51 percent over a three-year period. The Fifth Circuit was now the busiest in federal appellate court history. It was not to relinquish the distinction of having the largest docket of all circuit courts over the next two decades.

More important to the case Tuttle presented were the statistics for workload per judge. Throughout the decade of the 1950s, the Fifth Circuit had ranked either first or second of all circuits for number of appeals commenced per judgeship. By 1963, however, the judges of the Deep South carried by far the heaviest workload. The national average for federal appellate courts for that year was sixty-nine cases filed per judge. In the Fifth Circuit, the figure was ninety-seven cases per judge, 41 percent higher than the national average and 11 percent higher than the second-ranking workload of eighty-seven cases per judge in the District of Columbia circuit. Clearly, the expansion of the Fifth Circuit from seven to nine judges in 1961 had not kept pace with the rising caseloads generated from the region. To exacerbate matters, the docket of the Fifth Circuit was now plagued with difficult administrative agency cases and publicly explosive civil rights issues.

Tuttle's arguments for additional judgeships took on a special urgency because of certain particular conditions facing his court. Two of its nine judges were in failing health and could not carry full caseloads. Another two had only recently been added and were still becoming accustomed to their duties. Internal conflict over the handling of civil rights cases had sapped the time and strength of the judges. The forces generating rising caseloads were un-relenting. Every prediction of future trends indicated that the situation in the Fifth Circuit would only deteriorate.[10] Because its usual procedure was to

9. The caseload data presented here are taken from various annual reports of the Administrative Office of the United States Courts.

10. Predicting caseloads is not an exact science even today; and in 1963 the state of the art was not well advanced. In that year, the Judicial Conference of the United States was asked to comment on the probable impact of a civil rights bill that President Kennedy had transmitted to Congress. At its September meeting, the conference endorsed a report on this proposed legislation prepared by its Revision of the Laws Committee. The report concluded that "the volume of civil rights litigation would not be substantially increased under the proposed legislation, although there will undoubtedly be additional injunction suits under the public accommodations sections and that, therefore, the provisions...will not impose an unreasonable burden on the federal courts or unduly increase the amount of time now required by the courts to deal with civil rights cases." *Report of the Proceedings of the Judicial Conference of the United States*, September 17–18, 1963, p. 74. The legislation in question became the Civil Rights Act of 1964!

consider cases by dividing them up among three-judge panels, additional personnel would expand the court's decision-making capacity by allowing it to create more panels.[11] Additional judgeships were needed to cope with the workload, and they were needed immediately.

Both the Court Administration and the Judicial Statistics committees were receptive to Tuttle's plea and were sympathetic to the court's plight. They were convinced that increased resources in the form of additional judgeships were necessary. However, several of the judges were fearful of expanding the Fifth Circuit as it was then constituted. Many jurists adhered to the theory that no court could operate efficiently with more than nine judges. Beyond this maximum, they believed, a court would become too cumbersome: collegiality would diminish; the sessions of the important en banc court procedure would become unwieldy;[12] free and full deliberative exchange would become impossible; and the logistics required for the members of the court to keep abreast of one another's opinions would be burdensome. In short, a court of more than nine would cease to exhibit those necessary attributes of a properly functioning collegial tribunal and would begin to take on the characteristics of a legislature or a political convention. The large geographical expanse of the Fifth Circuit imposed the additional burden of travel. Unfortunately for Tuttle, Chief Judge John Biggs, Jr., of the Third Circuit and Chief Judge Harvey M. Johnsen of the Eighth Circuit were strong advocates of this "Rule of Nine" theory. Biggs chaired the Court Administration Committee and Johnsen, the Judicial Statistics panel.

To jurists like Biggs and Johnsen, who recognized the need for additional judges but also adhered to the nine-judge limit, only one alternative appeared feasible: divide the circuit. Consequently, the two committees discussed the possibility of splitting the Fifth Circuit into two separate courts and adding the number of judges necessary to manage the caseload demands of each. For those jurists who subscribed to the nine-judge maximum, this proposal had the dual advantage of providing sufficient judge power to the southern states while keeping the size of each circuit court at a level below the nine-judge limit.

The suggestion to split the Fifth Circuit was not warmly received by its

11. The panel procedure is practiced by each of the courts of appeals. In the Fifth Circuit, a panel sits for a period of four to five days hearing arguments and reaching decisions on a group of assigned cases. Panel memberships are rotated throughout the year. When a panel issues a ruling, it speaks with the authority of the entire court. The ruling becomes part of the "law of the circuit" and is binding on all other members of the court. This procedure requires a judge to be constantly aware of the decisions handed down by each of his or her colleagues.

12. Upon majority vote of the judges, the court may sit en banc, with all its members participating in the disposition of a particular appeal. An en banc session is considered an extraordinary procedure, generally reserved for particularly important or novel legal questions. When sitting en banc, the court has the authority to reconsider cases previously decided by a panel.

members, but neither was it unexpected. The idea had been advanced as early as 1950.[13] No circuit had been divided since the huge Eighth Circuit, encompassing thirteen states from the Mississippi River to the Rocky Mountains of Utah and Wyoming, was split in 1929.[14] The lack of experience with this unconventional measure and its unknown costs and consequences led some judges to view this solution with suspicion. The prospects of circuit realignment had been discussed by the judges of the Fifth Circuit both formally and informally. They hoped that additional judges might be obtained without it. In fact, at their May meeting they had decided not to include any mention of redrawing circuit boundaries in petitioning for additional judgeships;[15] but realizing that the issue might be raised, the council gave Tuttle "an open proxy to discuss splitting the circuit should it become necessary to get the additional judges."[16] As feared, the advocates of the nine-judge maximum rule were not willing to act on any expansion of the Fifth Circuit, no matter how badly additional judges were needed, without serious consideration of realignment.

Not all the members of the conference committees were convinced that a court could not function well with more than nine judges. To several judges, an increase to thirteen positions seemed reasonable. At the very least, they thought, a court larger than customary might be tried before turning to the drastic alternative of dividing the circuit. Furthermore, the judges of the Fifth Circuit had not formally petitioned to be divided into two courts. The policy of the conference was to consider changes affecting a particular circuit only if the judges of that circuit expressed support for them. Imposing circuit division on the Fifth might touch off a series of similar heretofore unrequested actions in other circuits that were beginning to experience large increases in caseloads. Finally, there was substantial sentiment in both committees that the subject of realignment had not yet received adequate study and that to recommend such a course of action was premature.

Despite considerable deliberation, the Court Administration and Judicial Statistics committees were unable to agree on a recommendation. Although both committees clearly saw the need for additional judgeships, they were deadlocked on the question whether to expand the court beyond its membership of nine judges or to require circuit division as a prerequisite for additional judgeships. More for political than for administrative reasons, the

13. John H. Wahl, Jr., "The Case for an 11th Court of Appeals (For a Circuit Embracing Florida, Georgia, Alabama, Puerto Rico and the Virgin Islands)," *Florida Law Journal* 24 (July 1950): 233–35.

14. Denise Bonn, *Geographical Division of the Eighth Circuit Court of Appeals: An Historical Analysis* (Washington, D.C.: The Federal Judicial Center, 1974).

15. Letter from Chief Judge Elbert Tuttle to Judges Joseph C. Hutcheson, Jr., Richard T. Rives, John R. Brown, and John Minor Wisdom, March 25, 1964.

16. Minutes of the meeting of the Judicial Council of the Court of Appeals for the Fifth Circuit, New Orleans, May 29 and 31, 1963.

committees could report to the United States Judicial Conference, when it convened in September of 1963, only that they "were in agreement on the need for additional judgeships in the United States Court of Appeals for the Fifth Circuit, but were divided on the question of geographical division of the Circuit."[17]

THE BIGGS COMMITTEE

Tuttle feared that the committee deadlock would jeopardize his court's chances of receiving the immediate help it so badly needed. The Judicial Conference was generally reluctant to transmit recommendations to Congress without support from its relevant committees. These committees were treated with considerable deference because of their recognized expertise and influential makeup. Committee service was not restricted to members of the Judicial Conference but might be drawn from the ranks of the judiciary, bar associations, universities, and government service. Tuttle also had reason to worry that by raising the issue of circuit division the conference committees might open a Pandora's box of troubles for his court.

Tuttle realized that this was not a time for precipitous action. He was confident that his case for more judges was a sound one, but he also knew that circuit realignment was an uncharted course. He opted for the strategy of convincing the conference to appoint a special ad hoc committee to assess the Fifth Circuit's needs and the impact that realignment might have. This option would mean a delay in getting the needed judges for his court, but it would insure that the conference would proceed only after having made a more complete appraisal of the issues. Tuttle also needed time to consult with the members of his court. In order to achieve these goals, the chief judge contacted Earl Warren prior to the convening of the September meeting of the conference.

Any request from the Fifth Circuit was certain to receive special attention from Earl Warren. Like Warren, over half of the Fifth Circuit judges had been appointed by Dwight Eisenhower. Several had histories of Republican activism similar to that of the chief justice. But perhaps what most linked the Fifth Circuit to Warren was the decision-making role of the court. A liberal faction on the Fifth Circuit shared Warren's views on civil rights and formed a majority on many panels that rendered trailblazing civil rights decisions. Warren needed the support of the Fifth Circuit if his mandate in *Brown v. Board of Education* was to be enforced in the Deep South; and the Fifth Circuit, in turn, needed the reinforcement of Warren's court when its own directives were challenged on appeal. In this sense, Warren and the Fifth Circuit judges were mutually dependent in the handling of civil rights matters.

These common political and judicial interests paved the way for effective

17. *Report of the Judicial Conference*, p. 65.

communications between Tuttle and Warren. Although the kinds of administrative matters that concerned the Fifth Circuit were not Warren's forte, Tuttle was able to convince the chief justice that a special committee to consider the needs of the circuit was necessary, and he secured Warren's promise that such a committee would be appointed at the September meeting.[18]

The judges who assembled for the meeting were aware that the Fifth Circuit was experiencing internal strife over civil rights cases. They also knew that the court had aroused the ire of Mississippi Senator James O. Eastland, who believed his state was suffering unduly at the judicial hands of the Fifth Circuit. Any legislative recommendation of the conference would necessarily undergo Eastland's scrutiny because of his position as head of the Senate Judiciary Committee. The conference members nonetheless seemed receptive to Tuttle's argument for additional judges.

The conference was similarly concerned about the growing caseload problems of the Ninth Circuit. Although its caseload lagged behind that faced by the Fifth (ninety-seven cases per judge in the Fifth Circuit in 1963 versus eighty in the Ninth), the Pacific Coast region was also experiencing rapid growth and covered an enormous geographical area. A split of the Ninth Circuit had been suggested several times in the past, and legislation had been introduced as early as 1940. Efforts to divide the Ninth were generated by the desire of the Pacific Northwestern states to have a circuit of their own, independent of the growing presence of the state of California. It became clear that the Ninth Circuit issue would have to be included in any special committee study of the Fifth Circuit's problems.[19] Similarly, advocates of the nine-judge limit were demanding that any such committee fully address the relationship between court size and judicial efficiency.

As Warren had promised, the conference authorized the appointment of a special Committee on the Geographical Organization of the Courts. Though the committee's title was inclusive, its mandate was specific. First, it was directed to study and report on whether there should be a division of circuits covering a large geographical area or burdened with a heavy caseload, in particular the Fifth and Ninth Circuits. Second, the members were to report specifically on the number of judges needed to handle the caseload in the Fifth Circuit. Third, the committee was asked to report "its judgment as to the maximum number of judges which could be authorized for the court of appeals of any circuit without impairing its efficiency."[20] Finally, it was charged with the responsibility to report on the Senate bill that had been introduced

---

18. Interview with Judge Elbert P. Tuttle, Atlanta, Georgia, October 20, 1982.

19. A bill to divide the Ninth Circuit (S. 1876) was pending before Congress in 1963, an additional factor mandating that the conditions of Pacific Coast states be studied along with the Fifth Circuit issue.

20. *Report of the Judicial Conference*, p. 65.

in July to divide the Ninth Circuit. The committee was asked to report back to the conference at its next meeting, scheduled for March 1964.

As head of the Judicial Conference, Chief Justice Warren was empowered to appoint members of all committees. His eleven assignments to the geographical organization committee indicated a concern for staffing the panel with judges who had particular expertise in administrative matters.[21] He included all the members of the Court Administration Committee. They had given attention to the geographical organization question for several years and were generally oriented to the problems connected with the issue. Warren added two important conference committee chairs, Judge Harvey Johnsen of the Judicial Statistics Committee and Judge Albert Maris, who headed the Committee on the Revision of the Laws. He also provided for broad geographic representation, appointing members from eight of the nation's eleven circuits, and including the chief judges of five circuits. Three of his appointees were federal trial court judges and eight served on courts of appeals. Finally, he chose Elbert Tuttle, chief judge of the Fifth Circuit, and, as chair, John Biggs, chief judge of the Third Circuit.

The appointment of Judge Biggs to head the special committee was to have a profound effect on the contours of the controversy that was about to envelop the Fifth Circuit. The sixty-eight-year-old Biggs, educated at Princeton and Harvard, was a formidable force among the nation's judges. A native of Delaware, born into a family with a long history of government service, he had been nominated for the Third Circuit Court of Appeals by Franklin D. Roosevelt in 1937 at the relatively young age of forty-one. Two years later he became chief judge of the court and retained that position until he retired from active service in 1965, at the age of seventy. His twenty-six years as a member of the Judicial Conference was the second longest tenure in the history of that institution. This seniority endowed Biggs with substantial power and respect.

Having long chaired the Judicial Conference Committee on Court Administration, John Biggs had developed great expertise in the field of judicial administration. He devoted large amounts of time to conference affairs and had the ability to recognize court problems before they reached a crisis point.[22] He was intensely involved in drafting proposed legislation for submission to

21. The members of the special Committee on the Geographical Organization of the Courts were: Senior Judge Orie L. Phillips (Tenth Circuit), Senior Judge Albert P. Maris (Third Circuit), Chief Judge Harvey M. Johnsen (Eighth Circuit), Judge Charles Fahy (District of Columbia Circuit), Chief Judge Elbert P. Tuttle (Fifth Circuit), Chief Judge J. Edward Lumbard (Second Circuit), Chief Judge John S. Hastings (Seventh Circuit), Chief Judge Ben Connally (Southern District of Texas), Chief Judge Edward J. Devitt (District of Minnesota), Judge William T. Sweigert (Northern District of California), and Chief Judge John Biggs, Jr. (Third Circuit)

22. Interview with Judge David W. Dyer, Highlands, North Carolina, June 14, 1983.

Congress and became known among federal judges as the lobbyist for the federal courts. Biggs frequently found himself in Congress advocating improvements in judicial machinery. He had well-developed relationships with the judiciary committees of both houses.

That Warren appointed Biggs to chair the special committee was no surprise. The chief justice once declared that there had not been one advance made in the administration of justice in the United States for over a quarter of a century "that does not have the fingerprints of John Biggs all over it." Warren was known to have described Biggs as a "one-man ministry of justice."[23]

John Biggs was a vital, energetic man who approached life with zest.[24] He had a particular love for the written word, undoubtedly reinforced by F. Scott Fitzgerald, his college roommate at Princeton. He approached his judicial administration responsibilities with intensity and strength. He enjoyed the politics of the judiciary and exercised control over the committees he chaired. In fact, a colleague once claimed that Biggs had the only vote on the Court Administration Committee.[25]

Warren's appointments to the special Committee on the Geographical Organization of the Courts gave Biggs substantial influence over its activities. The assignment of the members of Biggs's own court administration committee enhanced his potential for control. The addition of Judge Albert Maris, a man of considerable judicial reputation, added to Biggs's influence. Maris had served with Biggs on the Third Circuit Court of Appeals since 1938, and the two were close friends.[26] Maris once said that they were "as closely associated as two men could be." He had great respect for Biggs's efforts on behalf of the federal courts, claiming that his "dogged perseverance in pressing for the improvement of judicial administration has never been equalled by any other federal judge in the history of the country."[27] In Biggs and Maris, then, Warren selected judges in whom he had deep confidence. Warren gratefully acknowledged that, when he first became chief justice, two men taught him about the intricacies of the Judicial Conference when he knew practically

23. Chief Justice Earl Warren, Comments to the Third Circuit Judicial Conference, September 9, 1965. 355 F.2d., page 43 of special proceedings; quoted by Vincent A. Theisen, president of the Delaware State Bar Association, October 7, 1965, in ceremonies on the retirement of John Biggs, Jr., 355 F.2d., page 7 of special proceedings.

24. Interview with Judge Clement F. Haynsworth, Jr., Greenville, South Carolina, August 9, 1983.

25. Peter Graham Fish, *The Politics of Federal Judicial Administration* (Princeton, N.J.: Princeton University Press, 1973), p. 294.

26. Interview with Judge J. Skelly Wright, Washington, D.C., May 22, 1985.

27. Judge Albert Maris, Comments to the Third Circuit Judicial Conference, September 9, 1965. 355 F.2d., page 30 of special proceedings. Chief Justice Warren echoed this sentiment, likening Biggs and Maris to the "Gold Dust twins" and noting, "When I thought of one, I thought of the other." Comments to the Third Circuit Judicial Conference, September 9, 1965. 355 F.2d., page 40 of special proceedings; Maris, Comments, p. 30.

nothing about the organization: "These two men were John Biggs and Al Maris."[28]

So, through his expertise, seniority, and political powers, John Biggs was a dominant force on the special committee. It was little wonder that the special committee quickly became known as the "Biggs Committee." Perhaps unwittingly, Earl Warren had predetermined the outcome of the committee's deliberations when he appointed Biggs as its leader, for the head of the newly installed committee was a vocal proponent of the view that no federal appellate court should exceed nine judges.

Issues pertaining to the administration of justice were of paramount concern to the judges who attended Judicial Conference sessions. The members were aware, however, that politics external to their organization could enter into the deliberations. Never far beneath the surface of the realignment debate was an especially traumatic series of civil rights appeals that the Fifth Circuit had faced in the aftermath of *Brown*. These political undertones became more apparent as events unfolded during 1963 and 1964, as the various participants took their stands.

THE JUDGES

Elbert Tuttle returned to his home in Atlanta following the September conference meeting with mixed feelings. He had pressed his case with the other members of the conference and was pleased with the generally sympathetic attitudes his fellow jurists held toward the conditions facing the Fifth Circuit. He was happy that the conference had not acted in haste, either by rejecting the court's petition for more judgeships or by recommending a division of the circuit without sufficient study. Yet Tuttle knew that the appointment of the Biggs Committee would complicate matters tremendously. The Fifth Circuit issue was now being combined with the problems facing the Ninth, and the question of circuit division was inextricably tied up with the special committee's mandate to discuss the question of maximum court size. Tuttle had hoped that the staffing needs of his court would be considered on their own merits without the confusion introduced by these additional issues. The creation of the Biggs Committee also meant delay. The Fifth Circuit needed immediate help, but now that might take years to get. The special committee would require about six months to make general recommendations, and then perhaps another six months would be needed for the Judicial Conference to turn the committee's recommendations into proposed legislation. Any bill to authorize additional judgeships would then have to be maneuvered successfully through Congress before the president could even begin to consider candidates for the new positions.

Although the future of the court was uncertain, it was clear that the coming

28. Warren, Comments, p. 42.

months would be difficult ones. The judges were severely overworked in terms of sheer volume of cases. The civil rights issue was becoming an overwhelming problem. The Supreme Court's *Brown* decision, if effectively enforced, meant massive changes for the South—changes that were not welcomed by the majority of the region's residents. It was left to the Fifth Circuit Court of Appeals to insure that the *Brown* mandate be faithfully implemented by state and local officials and by the federal trial court judges. This task was made more difficult by the lack of unanimity among the judges on the meaning of *Brown* or how it should be implemented. Nor was there consensus on the most appropriate way to deal with the increasingly hostile public opposition to desegregation. The impending battle for more judges and the debate over circuit division would only exacerbate the situation.

Because the Biggs Committee would expect formal recommendations from the Fifth Circuit Council regarding the judgeship and circuit division questions, Tuttle had to consult with his eight colleagues. The Judicial Conference normally gives great weight to the views of the judges when a policy consideration affects a single circuit. Consequently, if the court reached a consensus, its decision would likely be supported by the Biggs Committee and the conference. The fate of the Fifth Circuit would in large measure depend upon the views held by the nine judges who comprised the institution.

In Tuttle, however, the Fifth Circuit had a chief judge who was capable of effectively leading the court through trying times. The sixty-six-year-old Atlantan had been a member of the Court of Appeals since July of 1954. He became chief judge in 1960, selected, as dictated by federal statute, on the basis of seniority. As chief judge, Tuttle was the administrative head of the circuit and the presiding officer of his court. He was responsible for insuring that the court ran efficiently and for representing his judges in communications with Congress, the bar, and the various units of the federal judicial system. Under applicable law at that time, Tuttle would retain his leadership position until he voluntarily relinquished it or reached the age of seventy.[29]

Tuttle was a most unlikely person to head the federal judiciary in the Deep South. He had been born in Pasadena, California, in 1897, but moved to the territory of Hawaii at a young age when his father took a position with the Hawaiian Sugar Planters Association. The multiethnic climate of the Pacific Islands had a major impact on the development of Tuttle's views on race relations. When it came time to attend college, he selected Cornell, where he studied journalism and edited the school's newspaper. Following his graduation in 1918 the future judge worked as a journalist for two years. While visiting in Florida during this time, Tuttle met William Sutherland, a recent

29. Chief Judges Resignation Act of 1958, 72 Stat. 497. Further restrictions were placed on the office of chief judge by Congress in the 1982 Federal Courts Improvement Act (Public Law 97–164). This statute retained seniority as the basis for selection, but the office could be held no longer than seven years.

Harvard Law School graduate. This association also had a crucial impact on his life. Sutherland and Tuttle became close friends, and as a result Tuttle became attracted to the law and decided to leave journalism, returning to Cornell for legal studies. During this same period, he courted and married Sutherland's sister, Sara.

Tuttle excelled in law school. He served as editor-in-chief of the law review and was elected to the prestigious Order of the Coif. Upon his graduation in 1923, he joined Sutherland in law practice. The two young attorneys decided that Atlanta offered a promising environment for their new law firm. Tuttle received his greatest acclaim when he represented a man accused of counterfeiting and tried in federal court without the assistance of an attorney. His arguments before the Supreme Court in this case led to a major precedent: the Sixth Amendment's requirement that indigent criminal defendants be provided counsel in federal criminal cases.[30] When World War II broke out, Tuttle joined the army and saw action in the Pacific. He remained in the army reserve after hostilities ceased, eventually attaining the rank of brigadier general.

Tuttle returned to Atlanta after the war with politics on his mind. He was a lifelong Republican and decided that the postwar period offered an opportunity to begin building the party in the Democratic South. He took the lead in organizing the few Republicans who could be found in Georgia. He became aligned with the Eisenhower forces and was a delegate pledged to the general at the 1952 national convention. Following Eisenhower's nomination, Tuttle campaigned hard for the Republican ticket in his home state. Although Eisenhower did not carry Georgia, the president rewarded Tuttle's efforts by naming him general counsel of the Treasury Department in 1953.

In 1954, Congress passed legislation expanding the number of federal judges. One of the new seats went to the Fifth Circuit Court of Appeals, raising its number from six to seven judges. Eisenhower was relatively unrestrained in his selection of an individual to fill this position. As a Republican, he was not bound by the rules of senatorial courtesy, since the South had no Republican senators. As each of the six states in the Fifth Circuit already had one judge sitting on the court, no state could lay claim to the seat—although Texas, by far the largest state in the circuit, thought it deserved the next appointment. Eisenhower preferred to nominate a Republican, but there were few loyal party members in the South. The choice finally fell on Elbert Tuttle. Although he had never held elective office and lacked judicial experience, he brought to the court twenty-five years of private law practice and fine legal credentials. The new federal judge was confirmed by the Senate during the summer of 1954. Tuttle is reported to have told friends that he was leaving Washington to return home and "retire" on the court of appeals. His confirmation, however, came only a few short weeks after the Supreme Court

30. *Johnson v. Zerbst*, 304 U.S. 458 (1938).

announced the *Brown* decision, and Tuttle's career on the court was to be anything but a retirement.[31]

Judge Tuttle's personal qualities made him an exceptional leader. He was a deeply religious man of the highest integrity. Although he possessed strong views on the civil rights question, he elicited great respect even from those attorneys who appeared before the court to argue for continuation of the status quo of the Old South. Tuttle was a person of unfailing fairness who combined strength with modesty and courtesy. His opinions were always clearly written and fully developed, leaving little room for misinterpretation. In this ambience of respect, Tuttle led the court through difficult years. John Minor Wisdom, who served with Tuttle during this time, characterized his leadership as "shepherding a court of very unsheeplike judges at a time of social ferment, when the court, as an institution, was exposed to severe stresses and strains."[32]

In both age and seniority, eighty-four-year-old Joseph Hutcheson was the most senior member of the court. He had been a federal judge for forty-five years, having first been appointed to the district court bench in 1918 by President Wilson and later, in 1931, elevated to the court of appeals by Herbert Hoover. Hutcheson was a lifelong resident of Houston, born to a former Confederate army captain and his wife. Following his mother's death when he was only two years old, Hutcheson was raised by his father. The two later practiced law together. Hutcheson left Texas to obtain his undergraduate education at the University of Virginia but returned to his home state for law school. He graduated first in his class at the University of Texas and received several academic honors. After a period of private practice, Hutcheson became mayor of Houston in 1917, but he resigned the next year in order to accept Wilson's nomination to become a federal trial court judge.

Small in stature, Hutcheson was a vigorous, active man. He is reported to have been both temperamental and quick-tempered, but he also showed a certain sensitivity to the needs of people. He was a strong believer in the dignity of the law and of the individual. Politically, Hutcheson classified himself as a Jeffersonian Democrat, perhaps because of the rich heritage of that philosophy to which he was exposed at the University of Virginia. He was generally conservative on crucial civil rights issues. A true son of Texas, he was not immune to the racial attitudes of his generation. Yet Hutcheson's strong belief in individualism and essential fairness would not allow him to

31. See Frank T. Read and Lucy S. McGough, *Let Them Be Judged: The Judicial Integration of the Deep South* (Metuchen, N.J.: Scarecrow Press, 1978); Jack Bass, *Unlikely Heroes* (New York: Simon and Schuster, 1981); Couch, *A History.* Each of these works contains a rich source of information on the backgrounds of the judges during this period and provided relevant material for the analysis presented here.

32. John Minor Wisdom, "Chief Judge Tuttle and the Fifth Circuit," *Georgia Law Review* 2 (1967): 4.

tolerate flagrant violations of civil rights. Above all else, Hutcheson believed in judicial restraint. This philosophy kept him from joining the liberal bloc on the court with any consistency. He valued stability and predictability in the law; once a precedent was set, Hutcheson believed in following it. Consequently, he tended to reject doctrines of judicial activism that civil rights liberals thought necessary to effect change in the South.

In 1963, Judge Hutcheson was in declining health. He was no longer the strong, stern taskmaster who had served from 1947 to 1959 as the court's domineering chief judge. Nor did he still possess the intellectual strength of the man who had been Hugo Black's primary competition for a seat on the Supreme Court in 1937. Hutcheson's poor physical condition was contributing to the court's workload problem. Because infirmity no longer allowed him to endure the burdens of travel, his responsibilities were reduced. He had served on the court for almost thirty-three years, and would serve one additional year before retiring in November of 1964. His tenure was the longest in the history of the court.

Hutcheson's position on the administrative questions now facing the court was uncertain, or at least not strongly held. He would surely be an advocate for additional judges, but the circuit division issue would pose difficulties for him. He loved his court and its rich history. It would not be easy for him to see his circuit carved into two separate pieces. Yet workload problems were a major concern for the former chief judge; and if circuit division was to be the price for additional judges, Hutcheson might well agree to pay it.

Richard T. Rives, a gentlemanly Alabama native, ranked second to Hutcheson in seniority. Rives was one of the last federal judges to receive his education by "reading the law" under the tutelage of an experienced attorney rather than attending a formal law school. Rives's family had been landowners of considerable wealth but lost their fortunes as a result of the Civil War. Consequently, when Rives was born in 1895 it was into a poor family. He grew up close to the people and soil of Alabama. Although he attained a high judicial position, Rives never lost sight of his roots. He was educated in a one-room schoolhouse during his elementary years and performed so well in high school that he was awarded an academic scholarship to Tulane University in New Orleans. In spite of this financial assistance, young Rives was forced to borrow living-expense money from his sister. After one year at Tulane, he decided for financial reasons that he could not continue. Upon his return to Montgomery, he began to study under Wiley Hill, a successful local attorney and friend of Rives's father. In this way he quickly acquired a sufficient mastery of the law to be admitted to the bar at the age of nineteen.

Rives immediately began practicing law as a member of Hill's firm. The firm not only provided general legal services but was also heavily involved in Democratic party politics and bar association activities. Rives soon found himself taking a major role in various political campaigns and also served as president of the local and state bar associations. For thirty-seven years he worked behind the scenes, exercising a great deal of political influence. He directed three successful gubernatorial campaigns and Hugo Black's successful bid for the U.S. Senate. He was closely aligned with those Democrats who considered themselves part of the national Democratic party. This more moderate wing of the organization often engaged in political battle with those Democrats who held fiercely to states' rights and segregationist views.

Judge Rives changed his racial attitudes substantially over the course of his adult life. Although never a confirmed segregationist, he was very much a product of his Alabama heritage. Perhaps what kept him from joining the segregationist forces in his state was a profound commitment to basic human fairness. Although some students of Alabama politics thought Rives could have been elected governor, the stands he took on racial issues were not always popular and would have been a major political liability in any attempt to attain statewide office. In 1946, for example, Rives publicly attacked passage of the Boswell amendment, which granted local registrars the authority to withhold the right to vote from anyone who did not have sufficient "understanding" to be an intelligent elector. The unabashed purpose of the amendment was to provide an effective barrier to black political participation. The amendment was ratified by the state's voters, but was later declared unconstitutional by the courts.

Of considerable importance in the moderating of Rives's racial views was his close relationship with his only son, Richard, Jr. The elder Rives was committed to providing his son the advantages of a formal education that he himself had been denied. He sent his son to Exeter Academy and then to Harvard. When war broke out, Richard, Jr., served as a lieutenant in the navy, and on his return enrolled in law school at the University of Michigan. Throughout these years the two had a number of discussions on the subject of civil rights. The younger Rives brought back to his father much of the social philosophy to which he had been exposed in the North and talked about the associations he had had with blacks while serving in the military. He also introduced his father to Gunnar Myrdal's *An American Dilemma*, a two-volume work on the plight of blacks in the United States. Rives's study of this scholarly classic influenced his thinking in a fundamental way.

Rives's fondest dream was to practice law with his son. In preparation for this professional association, he left the Hill law firm and set up in practice alone. On spring vacation in 1949, however, Richard, Jr., was killed in a tragic automobile accident in Florida. Rives was grief-stricken.

Had the younger Rives lived, his father might never have accepted a position on the court of appeals; he probably would have been content to live out his dream of practicing law with his son. In 1951, however, Judge Leon McCord announced his retirement from the bench. McCord held Alabama's informal seat on the Fifth Circuit Court of Appeals. He had known Richard Rives as a friend and political ally for many years, and it was his wish that

Rives be appointed to succeed him. McCord made his views known to Senators Lister Hill and John Sparkman, and Rives also approached Alabama's two senators. Hill and Sparkman, of course, knew Rives well and endorsed his candidacy. With the support of Hill and Sparkman, President Truman submitted Rives's name to the Senate as his nominee for the McCord vacancy. Rives received word of the nomination while in Washington arguing a case before the Supreme Court. Before leaving the capital, he paid a visit to his old friend Hugo Black to seek advice on whether he should accept the nomination. Rives questioned his own ability because of his lack of formal education and his inexperience in such areas of the law as admiralty, patents, and labor. But Black assured his fifty-six-year-old friend that he was indeed fully capable of executing the responsibilities of the office. With that encouragement, Rives accepted the nomination and took his place on the bench.

Rives's career on the court was indeed a distinguished one. Although he was not an intellectual leader, he had a keen sense of fairness and justice. Philosophically, he was an activist, believing that the courts of appeals should do more than just march lockstep with precedent. He was a creative judge, who held to the notion that judicial innovation is to be valued. On questions of social change Rives was a liberal. He was a solid supporter of civil rights and became noted for his rulings desegregating public accommodations and juries. He was best known for his majority opinion in the case of *Browder v. Gayle*, a 1956 decision that desegregated public transportation in his hometown of Montgomery.[33] That decision was notable because it ruled that the Supreme Court's 1954 precedent of *Brown v. Board of Education* was not confined to public schools but extended to other government facilities as well. Because of decisions like this, Richard Rives became the target of public abuse. Segregationist forces in Alabama were particularly enraged about his role in desegregation because he came from a poor white Alabama family. They had considered him a friend of the people of Alabama; now he was viewed as a traitor. Members of his own Presbyterian church ostracized him. Longtime friends refused to speak to him. On one occasion his son's grave was heaped with garbage. None of this deterred Rives. He remained a sturdy defender of civil rights.

Richard Rives was one of the most respected members of the court. His colleagues enjoyed his quiet strength, courtesy, and integrity. Even those who did not join in his resolute defense of civil rights admired the courage it took to hold that position in the face of public contempt. Because of his background, Rives understood the people's reaction to the court's civil rights rulings, and he fashioned judicial remedies with a deep appreciation for how the public would react to them. Rives was a modest man, always willing to defer to those whose abilities he deeply respected. This trait came to the fore when he relinquished the position of chief judge in 1960. He had assumed

33. *Browder v. Gayle*, 142 F.Supp. 707 (M.D. Ala., 1956). Affirmed, 352 U.S. 903 (1956).

this post less than two years earlier, when Chief Judge Hutcheson was forced to step down because of age. Rives did not particularly enjoy the administrative aspects of the position and desired to be free of its time-consuming obligations in order to devote more attention to his wife, who was ill. But another important reason for stepping down from the chief judgeship several years before he was required to do so was to allow Elbert Tuttle, next in line of seniority, to take the reins of the court. Rives simply thought that Tuttle would be the ideal court leader and saw no reason to postpone his promotion to that position. Jack Bass has reported that an additional motive for Rives's stepping aside was his hope that Tuttle's elevation to the chief judgeship would give his Georgia friend sufficient exposure to be considered for a Supreme Court appointment.[34]

Rives's stance on the division of the Fifth Circuit was unequivocal. He would oppose it, and his opposition would be strong. He was simply too committed to the ongoing legal battles over civil rights issues to support any change that might have an adverse impact on the rights of minorities. The Fifth Circuit as then constituted comprised a fragile coalition devoted to the enforcement of constitutional guarantees. To Rives, any circuit division would jeopardize the continuation of progress in civil rights.

Judge Benjamin Franklin Cameron was a very different sort of person. An advocate of states' rights and a vocal supporter of segregation, he was the court's chief opponent of the civil rights movement. His conservative views on social and legal policy were consistent with his personal background. Born in 1890 in Meridian, Mississippi, Cameron was a patrician of the Old South. He attended prep school in Virginia and then received his undergraduate education at the University of the South in Tennessee, followed by law school at Cumberland University. The tall, slim Cameron was deeply involved in athletics and community affairs in his hometown of Meridian.

Cameron's appointment to the court of appeals was, strangely, due to his views on alcohol. Although an Episcopalian, Cameron was a strict prohibitionist. In 1928, when Al Smith, the Democratic party's nominee for president, advocated the repeal of prohibition, Cameron immediately decided to join the Republican party. He volunteered to work in Herbert Hoover's campaign in Mississippi. Following Hoover's election, Cameron was repaid for his services by being named United States Attorney for the Southern District of Mississippi. When the Democrats captured the White House in 1932, Cameron entered a long period of private law practice.

Twenty-two years later, Fifth Circuit Judge Edwin Holmes of Mississippi retired. Eisenhower was searching for a member of his own party to assume the Holmes seat. In 1954, however, prominent Republicans were a rare breed

34. Bass, *Unlikely Heroes*, pp. 136–37.

in Mississippi. Cameron's name began to surface because of his reputation as an excellent lawyer and his experience as U.S. attorney during the Hoover administration. All of the relevant organizations and officials found Cameron to be acceptable. James O. Eastland, the Mississippi senator who headed the Judiciary Committee, endorsed the nomination, as did the American Bar Association. Ironically, even the NAACP approved the Cameron appointment when it was learned that he had made financial contributions to a local black college. Of additional importance was the support of John Minor Wisdom, a New Orleans attorney with considerable influence in Republican circles. Wisdom, himself only two years away from joining the court, was prominent in building the Republican party in Louisiana. Since there was no Republican party structure of substance in Mississippi, Wisdom was often consulted by the Eisenhower administration on appointments for his neighboring state.[35] In 1955, when Eisenhower first met Cameron, the president remarked: "Mr. Cameron, you are the only lawyer I know of in the South nominated to the federal bench who has the endorsement of both Senator Eastland and the NAACP."[36] As the years passed, Eastland found much more pleasure in recalling his support of Cameron than did the NAACP.

Cameron's record on the court was one of staunch conservatism. He was a very well-read man with an academic bent. Even the most liberal members of the court respected his legal abilities. One referred to the Mississippian as a "cracking-good lawyer" and another praised Cameron's writing abilities and educational qualifications.[37] During his first five years on the court, Cameron's opinions were conservative in outcome but moderate in tone. They were well researched and developed, without the rigid dogmatism that was to come. Some observers ranked the scholarship of his work as second only to Wisdom's.[38] After 1960, however, Cameron began to change. He constantly found himself in the minority on civil rights questions. As these issues became increasingly visible and controversial, Cameron became more and more frustrated by consistently losing to the dominant liberal faction on the court.[39] His steadfast, almost religious advocacy of states' rights made it very difficult for him to accept the legal doctrine that the court was developing. Southern culture was undergoing change, and he resisted it.

The 1962 legal controversy over the integration of the University of Mississippi finally pushed Cameron over the edge. His dissents became strongly worded, biting attacks on his colleagues. He questioned the personal integrity of some of his fellow judges and charged publicly that judicial panels hearing

35. Interview with Judge John Minor Wisdom, New Orleans, Louisiana, May 28, 1985.
36. Quoted in Read and McGough, *Let Them Be Judged*, p. 267.
37. Confidential interview; Wisdom interview, May 28, 1985.
38. Read and McGough, *Let Them Be Judged*, p. 47.
39. See Cameron's dissent in *Boman v. Birmingham Transit Co.*, 292 F.2d 4 (1961), and *United States v. Wood*, 295 F.2d. 722 (1961).

civil rights cases in Mississippi were being stacked to ensure liberal outcomes.[40] Cameron had become a bitter champion of a losing cause. Increasingly he became an isolate on the court. By the time he died in April 1964, his relationship with his colleagues had become so strained that only two members of the court (Walter Gewin and John Wisdom) attended his funeral.[41]

Cameron would endorse a split of the circuit. The reasons were twofold. First, the Mississippi judge had severe heart problems and was experiencing difficulty carrying a full caseload. A division of the circuit plus additional judges would reduce the court's workload and limit the amount of necessary travel. Second, a realignment of the circuit would also alter the balance of power on the court and offered Cameron hope of slowing the advance of liberal activist policies. Depending upon the geographic contours of the division and the ideological positions of the new judges appointed, the resulting court with jurisdiction over Mississippi cases might have a conservative majority. Even if these hopes were not fully realized, in Cameron's mind any change would be a change for the better. His reasons for supporting the split were thus much the same as Rives's reasons for opposing it.

Eisenhower's third appointment to the Fifth Circuit was Warren L. Jones, who took office in 1955 at the age of sixty. Jones had been born in Nebraska but spent his young adult years in Denver where he attended law school after a stint in the army in World War I. After being awarded a law degree with honors from the University of Denver in 1924, he began private practice. Only two years later Jones was lured away from Colorado by the growth potential of Florida and moved to Jacksonville to continue his legal career. He became senior partner in one of the more successful corporate law firms in the state. He was elected president of the local chamber of commerce and of the Jacksonville and Florida state bar associations. Outside his law practice, Jones involved himself in a number of community activities and became moderately active in the fledgling Republican party in Florida. He was a student of American history and was particularly intrigued by the presidency of Abraham Lincoln.

When Florida's Louis Strum died in 1954 after having served only four years on the Fifth Circuit, the Eisenhower administration initiated the search for a replacement. Once again, the number of loyal Republicans available was small. Jones's name was discussed for the vacancy, but the Justice Department was not convinced that he was the appropriate person for the judgeship. At a crucial point in these deliberations, Elbert Tuttle interceded in support of Jones. Tuttle considered the Jacksonville lawyer to be an exceptionally well-qualified attorney who would make an excellent addition to the court.

40. See Cameron's dissent in *Armstrong v. Board of Education in the City of Birmingham*, 323 F.2d. 333, 352 (1963).

41. Read and McGough, *Let Them Be Judged*, p. 48. Wisdom interview, May 28, 1985.

Jones's judicial record would place him firmly among the conservative judges. His conservatism, however, was not similar to the states' rights and segregationist views of Ben Cameron. Jones was motivated primarily by the philosophy of judicial self-restraint. He did not believe that the judges should readily impose their will on the actions of popularly elected leaders. In this vein, his views were quite close to those of Judge Hutcheson. Jones had great difficulty agreeing with the path-breaking work of the liberal activists on the court. He was clearly not an innovator. He would be better described as a strict constructionist who held social and political views that were consistent with his background as a very successful corporate attorney. Yet he was a firm advocate of *stare decisis*, and once a new precedent was set he followed it.

Jones would support the division of the circuit if a split was necessary to gain additional judgeships. Workload considerations were important to the then sixty-eight-year-old Floridian, but he had also expressed dissatisfaction with the activist way in which the court was being administered. Jones would be eligible for retirement in just two years, and it was unlikely that additional judges would be in place before he stepped down. Nonetheless, he had become so disgruntled with the court's activist orientation that he would likely support a reorganization of the circuit.

Judge John R. Brown, Eisenhower's fourth appointment to the circuit bench, was, like Warren Jones, a Nebraska native who had migrated to an urban center in the South and had joined a corporate law firm. But there the similarities between the two ended. Brown was a legal innovator, a liberal activist. He joined with Tuttle and Rives as champions of civil rights in the South. He was an intelligent, well-educated judge who demanded not only correct legal rulings but also the implementation of those rulings. His opinions were well crafted and colorfully written.

Brown was born in 1909 in a small Nebraska town. He graduated from the University of Nebraska in 1930 and immediately enrolled in law school at the University of Michigan. In recalling his Ann Arbor years, he reminisced that he "studied like hell and got drunk once a month."[42] The result was a distinguished academic record and a law degree awarded in 1932.

Following graduation, Brown sought out job opportunities in Texas, a state he predicted would undergo substantial growth and prosperity. He affiliated himself with a distinguished Houston law firm, later advancing to senior partner. From 1932 to 1955, he developed great expertise in admiralty and transportation law, specialties that were to serve him well in his judicial career. World War II interrupted Brown's law practice. He joined the air force in 1942 and served in the Pacific until 1946, leaving with the rank of major. Upon returning to Texas, Brown set about to help organize a viable Repub-

42. Quoted in Bass, *Unlikely Heroes*, p. 101.

lican party. He became a supporter of Dwight Eisenhower and was one of the general's delegates to the 1952 convention. Following Eisenhower's nomination, Brown directed the campaign in the Houston area and became head of the Republican party in Harris County.

In 1955, death ended the career of Judge Robert Russell, the brother of powerful Senator Richard Russell of Georgia. With Russell's death, the court was left with six judges, one from each state in the circuit. It was generally conceded that Texas, which made the largest contributions to the circuit's docket, deserved a second "seat." Once more Eisenhower had to find a qualified Republican attorney to fill a vacancy on the court. John Brown sought the post. His expertise in maritime law and administrative regulatory activity was much needed on the court, and his Republican credentials were in order. At forty-five, he was young, active, and highly respected. So Eisenhower sent John Brown's name to the Senate for confirmation. The congressional process went smoothly until a newspaper column by Drew Pearson charged that Brown had acted unethically in a claims case involving the explosion of two ships loaded with ammonium nitrate that had resulted in the deaths of almost six hundred persons.[43] Brown was able to present sufficient documentation to the Senate Judiciary Committee to rebut the charges. He was confirmed and took office in July of 1955, at the time the youngest judge ever appointed to the Fifth Circuit Court of Appeals.

Brown proved to be a forceful member of the court. He was known for his sharp questioning of attorneys, his direct and clear opinions, and his flamboyant personal style. He also became a valuable administrative resource for the circuit. Chief Judge Hutcheson recognized early that the young judge had a knack for administrative detail. Because both Brown and Hutcheson were stationed in Houston, it was quite convenient for the chief to assign certain administrative duties to Brown. Most important, he put Brown in charge of assigning other judges to the panels that heard and decided cases. As Brown enjoyed the administrative role, and especially his position as assignment judge, he continued to perform this duty during the leadership tenures of Rives and Tuttle.

John Brown's reaction to the proposal to split the circuit would be more tentative and pragmatic than that of other members of the court. He would hold many of the same reservations as Rives as to the impact a split might have on civil rights cases and would probably reject the idea that nine judges were the absolute maximum a court should have. But Brown was also a practical man and realized the clear need for more judges. Rather than engage in a philosophical debate over maximum court size, he might well support a split to get the additional help.

---

43. For a more thorough discussion of this incident see ibid., pp. 102–04.

Eisenhower's fifth and final appointment to the court was John Minor Wisdom, an aristocratic Louisiana attorney. Wisdom was born into wealth in the city of New Orleans in 1905. The family pressure to obtain a proper education instilled in him a zest for scholarly pursuits that later earned him the reputation of the Fifth Circuit's intellectual leader. As a young man Wisdom attended his father's alma mater, Washington and Lee University in Virginia. His close association with that institution is confirmed by his membership on the board of trustees and the prominent display of his father's diploma, signed by Robert E. Lee, in his New Orleans chambers. Following his graduation in 1925, Wisdom began graduate studies in English at Harvard. During this time, however, he developed a strong attraction to the law and returned to New Orleans to pursue legal studies at Tulane, where his grandfather had been a member of the law school's first graduating class. Wisdom's command of the law manifested itself as early as 1929, when he graduated first in his class and was elected to the Order of the Coif. Wisdom's association with Tulane continued as he became a part-time lecturer on trusts and estates, specialties he later pursued during his long and prosperous law partnership with classmate Saul Stone.

John Wisdom's devotion to scholarship continued throughout his years in private practice. Widely read in the fields of literature, history, American political thought, and the social sciences, and a self-described "frustrated historian," Wisdom acquired a rich knowledge of Louisiana history and an impressive command of the state's unique civil law code. He later put this expertise to good use in his thoroughly researched and skillfully crafted majority opinion in *United States v. Louisiana*,[44] which helped to eliminate black disenfranchisement by barring the use of understanding tests in voter registration. Wisdom still considers this his most significant opinion.

When war erupted, Wisdom joined the army at the rank of captain. He served for four years, leaving in 1946 as a lieutenant colonel. He was assigned to the Office of Legal Procurement, an experience that was to serve him well for the rest of his years in both public and private life. He worked closely there with an extraordinary group of young attorneys who later held crucial positions in party politics, government, and academic life. These associations formed the basis of a political network that he used effectively in subsequent years. When he returned to New Orleans after the war, Wisdom had the same goal in mind as Tuttle and Brown—to build a viable Republican party organization in the South.

Wisdom's desire to contribute to the creation of a two-party system in his home state was based in large measure on his philosophy that the political process functions best when it enjoys widespread participation and the ventilation of a spectrum of robust viewpoints. When Wisdom was unsure about

44. *United States v. Louisiana*, 225 F.Supp. 353 (1963).

the best way of initiating a party structure in Louisiana, he contacted his friend Herbert Brownell, later a member of Eisenhower's cabinet, for advice. Brownell instructed Wisdom to contact a man named Elbert Tuttle in Atlanta who had already started organizational efforts on behalf of the Republican party in Georgia. Unknown to Tuttle and Wisdom, this first communication was the beginning of a friendship and professional association that would last for decades. Wisdom labored hard to develop the party in Louisiana and also devoted some effort to Republican organizational attempts in Mississippi. In 1952, he joined Tuttle and Brown as southern delegates to the Republican National Convention committed to Eisenhower. Following the election, Wisdom was chosen Republican National Committeeman from Louisiana, a position he held from 1952 to 1957. He considers his efforts to help establish the first viable Republican party organization in the post–Civil War South one of his most important accomplishments.

Some people might think John Wisdom led a paradoxical life during his years in private practice. He maintained the life-style of a southern aristocrat, marrying New Orleans socialite Bonnie Matthews, whose grandfather, as presiding judge of the Louisiana Supreme Court in the mid-1800s, had rendered a civil rights decision favorable to a black plaintiff. The couple moved in wealthy circles and held memberships in exclusive clubs and organizations that discriminated on the basis of race and ethnic background. Yet in spite of his elitist connections, Wisdom consistently spoke out against racism and bigotry. He strongly opposed the segregationist laws of the South and was active in such liberal organizations as the Urban League. He later explained that he had refused to relinquish his associations with exclusive clubs because his fellow members were his lifelong friends and, besides, they had always known where he stood on racial matters.

On December 31, 1956, Judge Wayne G. Borah of Louisiana retired from his position on the Fifth Circuit Court of Appeals. After thirty years in private practice, Wisdom was eager to pursue a career in the judiciary. There was formidable competition for the Borah vacancy, but eventually Wisdom received the nod from President Eisenhower, reportedly because his record as an attorney was superior to those of the other candidates. His cause was advanced substantially when he received the recommendation of Herbert Brownell, his friend and the president's attorney general.

But Wisdom's nomination ran into trouble in the Senate because of his liberal political views. The New Orleans attorney's record on matters of race relations caused alarm among some of the more conservative members of the Senate Judiciary Committee, especially Senator James Eastland. Wisdom's association with the Urban League, his service on the President's Committee on Government Contracts, and his work with various social agencies in New Orleans all led to this suspicion. Supporters of racial segregation certainly did not want to contribute further to the liberal presence of Rives, Tuttle, and Brown. Wisdom answered the committee's questions adeptly and the senators were at least partially satisfied,[45] but it also took the endorsement of conservative Louisiana District Judge Ben Dawkins, Jr., and the direct intercession of Fifth Circuit Judge Ben Cameron to ease Senator Eastland's fears. Wisdom eventually took his seat on the court in June of 1957, at the age of fifty-two.

Once he was on the bench, Wisdom's record was everything that the segregationist forces had dreaded. The New Orleans judge quickly aligned himself with the court's integrationist bloc. Furthermore, he became the intellectual leader of the court. His opinions consistently demonstrated scholarship of high quality, containing rich, clear legal and historical analyses. The combination of Tuttle's leadership, Brown's energy, Rives's knowledge of the southern people, and Wisdom's scholarship created an activist force for civil rights that had a far-reaching impact on the South.

John Wisdom's record both as a party activist and as a judge reflects his political personality. His positions on issues were always strongly held and defended with great zeal. His Republican affiliation and his views on civil rights often placed him among a small minority in his native region, yet he was never reluctant to go against the grain of southern opinion. Once he took a stand, he pursued it with tenacity and panache, generally preferring to win or lose on its merits rather than to compromise. Both as a politician and later as a judge, Wisdom was results-oriented. He used his scholarship and intellectual ability to promote his policy viewpoints. This trait caused one judge who found himself on the losing side of a Wisdom-led majority in a civil rights case, though marveling at the scholarship contained in the Wisdom authored opinion, to charge that it read like a brief for the plaintiff.[46]

For those who knew Wisdom, his reaction to the circuit division proposal was easy to predict. He would be strongly opposed and would most likely be relentless in his opposition regardless of the odds of success. Although he fully recognized the need for additional judges to cope with the court's caseload, he would consider splitting the circuit an unjustifiable price to pay. Wisdom, more than any other judge on the court, had a firm philosophical notion of what the courts of appeals should be. He believed that the circuit courts perform a critical role in the political system—a role he called the "federalizing function."[47] This function included the responsibility for insuring that local legal policies remain consistent with national policy, and for supervising the lower courts in such a way that this consistency is achieved. Wisdom strongly advocated that circuits be as large as practicably possible so that the courts of appeals reflect diverse interests and values. Splitting the Fifth Circuit, regardless of which geographical configuration was imposed,

45. A good account of the Wisdom confirmation can be found in Read and McGough, *Let Them Be Judged*, esp. pp. 54–56.

46. Judge Dozier A. DeVane dissenting in *Meredith v. Fair*, 305 F.2d 343 (1962).

47. John Minor Wisdom, "The Frictionmaking, Exacerbating Political Role of Federal Courts," *Southwestern Law Journal* 21 (1967): 411–28, at 411.

would create two relatively small circuits that might have a dangerous tendency toward parochialism. Consequently, for the same reason that John Wisdom fought the provincialism of a one-party South, he later opposed the provincialism he saw as the inevitable result of circuit realignment.

The two most junior members of the court obtained their positions as a result of the Omnibus Judgeship Act of 1961. This legislation was passed immediately after the elections of 1960 that saw the Democrats gain control of both the White House and the Congress. The statute created additional judgeships across the nation, including two badly needed positions on the Fifth Circuit. This brought the court's staff level to nine judges. The appointment calculus, however, had now changed. Although John Kennedy was generally regarded as more liberal on economic and social issues than his predecessor, he did not have the latitude of appointment in the South that Eisenhower had enjoyed. The reason for this was the tradition of senatorial courtesy. Southern Democratic senators held the informal power to block any nomination from their home states made by a Democratic president. As all of the southern states had Democratic senators, the Kennedy administration was forced to clear with them all judicial selections for the Fifth Circuit appellate and trial courts. The ultimate choices for the two new seats on the court were Walter Pettus Gewin of Alabama and Griffin B. Bell of Georgia.

Walter Gewin shared many background characteristics with his fellow Alabama judge, Richard Rives. Like Rives, Gewin was born into a small-town family that had long since lost most of its economic assets. The family atmosphere was one of middle-class values and an appreciation for learning and the arts, but also one in which money was in scarce supply. Gewin had been educated in a one-room schoolhouse and was able to attend Birmingham Southern College only on borrowed funds. Following his 1930 graduation with honors, he moved to Atlanta to do postgraduate work in library science at Emory University. This educational experience reflected his love of books and gave him a certain mastery over research techniques, but it was not sufficiently strong to alter his growing love for the law. After receiving his library degree in 1932, Gewin immediately began legal studies at the University of Alabama.

In private practice Gewin was a general practitioner. His legal career spanned twenty-five years, the first fifteen in Greensboro and the final ten in Tuscaloosa. He was quite active in Democratic politics as a party worker and public official, serving both as a local prosecutor and state legislator. During World War II he was a member of the army's Judge Advocate Corps. His legal career also included election to the presidency of the Alabama State Bar Association.

According to an account provided by Jack Bass, Gewin's appointment to the Fifth Circuit was due directly to the death of his law partner, Marc Ray

(Foots) Clement.[48] Clement, John Kennedy's Alabama campaign director, was very influential in the state party and was close to both of the state's senators, Lister Hill and John Sparkman. Clement had a legitimate political claim to one of the new seats on the court. Before he could be appointed, however, Clement died and on his deathbed reportedly expressed the wish that his good friend and associate Walter Gewin be selected to fill the position. Hill and Sparkman urged that Clement's request be honored. After the Kennedy administration had investigated and found him acceptable, Gewin's name was submitted to the Senate.

Gewin brought to the court a gentle manner and a capacity for thorough research. He always considered himself a man of the Alabama people and readily mixed with blue-collar workers and people on the street. Gewin was politically and socially conservative. He strongly resisted change and espoused the principles of judicial restraint that Jones and Hutcheson also advocated. He had an abiding faith in the states. Gewin was not comfortable with the liberal activism of Tuttle, Wisdom, Rives, and Brown, and often joined Cameron's attacks on his liberal colleagues. As the years passed, however, Walter Gewin moderated his views substantially, and his sympathy for the civil rights struggle grew.

Kennedy's appointment to fill the second new position was Griffin Bell. Bell was born in 1918 in the south Georgia city of Americus, not far from the birthplace of Jimmy Carter, who much later would name Bell attorney general of the United States. Bell attended college at Georgia Southwestern in his hometown. He joined the army in 1941, serving until the end of hostilities. Upon his discharge at the rank of major, Bell began legal studies at Mercer University in Macon, Georgia, and graduated with honors in 1948. For five years he practiced law in Savannah and Rome, Georgia, finally accepting a position with the prestigious law firm of King and Spalding in Atlanta. During these years, he was involved in bar association activities and Democratic party politics.

Bell's appointment to the court was in great measure a return of political favors. In 1959 and 1960, he had served as chief of staff for Governor Ernest Vandiver. Bell and Vandiver both worked for John Kennedy during the 1960 campaign. Bell directed the election effort in Georgia for the Massachusetts senator. Vandiver was instrumental in gathering the support of other southern governors for Kennedy. The governor also played a major role in obtaining the release of Martin Luther King, Jr., who had been jailed in Atlanta and then moved to the state prison.[49] Kennedy made tremendous political gains in the black community as a result of his actions in this incident. The new president was grateful to the governor for his efforts, and when Vandiver

48. Bass, *Unlikely Heroes*, pp. 158–59.
49. See Theodore H. White, *The Making of the President 1960* (New York: Pocket Books, 1961), pp. 385–87; Bass, *Unlikely Heroes*, pp. 161–62.

suggested Bell for the Fifth Circuit vacancy, Kennedy was receptive. The administration did not investigate Bell's record on civil rights because he was being rewarded as a political loyalist.[50] Georgia's powerful senators Russell and Talmadge expressed their support for Bell, and the administration submitted his name to the Senate for confirmation.

Griffin Bell was a valuable addition to the court, although his judicial philosophy differed markedly from that of his colleagues. He emphasized the role of the judge as accommodator. He had the ability to bring together opposing sides, to find a common ground, and to reconcile differences. He was brilliant in the use of compromise. One member of the court later described Bell's negotiating abilities as being so effective that when the two of them went hunting Bell could "talk the birds out of the trees to sit on his shoulder."[51] Bell was a pragmatist whose detractors considered him more a political wheeler-dealer than a judge. Individuals like John Wisdom, who put a premium on legal principle, sometimes found it difficult to deal with Bell, whose goal often seemed to be to reach an acceptable resolution without showing strong allegiance to any particular ideology.

Bell also possessed a knack for administration. It was no accident that the members of his large law firm had made him its managing partner or that Governor Vandiver had called upon him to head his gubernatorial staff. As the caseload problems of the Fifth Circuit grew, Bell was often the one who could suggest innovative methods of dealing with the management problems. Bell, then, brought to the court many problem-solving capabilities, both judicial and administrative.

Bell's judicial positions fluctuated during his tenure on the court. He described himself as a middle-of-the-road jurist, although at times he joined the civil rights activists and authored progressive opinions. He remained steadfast in his supervision of school desegregation plans when recalcitrant district judges were trying to delay implementation of the *Brown* mandate. He even wrote the court's final opinion in *United States v. Lynd*,[52] the lengthy voting-rights litigation involving Mississippi District Judge Harold Cox's outright defiance of Fifth Circuit orders. Yet, when the time came to fashion the remedial aspects of school desegregation (busing), Bell led the court's conservative forces against Wisdom and the more results-oriented judges who held that busing was a legitimate and necessary means to achieve integration. Bell, however, expressed the opinion, held by other members of the court, that to classify the judges of the Fifth Circuit as being in either "liberal" or "conservative" camps on the civil rights issue was unfortunate. It distorted reality and prompted many to leap to the conclusion that the liberals were for integration and the conservative judges for segregation. Although a judge like Bell was to the right of his four liberal associates, his decisions were

50. Victor Navasky, *Kennedy Justice* (New York: Atheneum, 1971), p. 272.
51. Interview with Judge Thomas Gibbs Gee, Austin, Texas, March 18, 1983.
52. *United States v. Lynd*, 349 F.2d 785 (1965).

unquestionably more progressive than the majority of the southern electorate would have preferred.

President Kennedy finalized his choices for the newly created seats in the fall of 1961. The Senate was not then in session, but because the president was keenly aware of the circuit's mounting caseload problems, he did not wait until the Senate reconvened to take action on the nominations of Gewin and Bell. As a result of being appointed immediately, the two new federal judges were able to begin their service as recess appointees. The fifty-two-year-old Gewin and forty-two-year-old Bell were adding much needed assistance to the court when they assumed their seats on October 6, 1961. Four months later, on February 9, 1962, the Senate confirmed them to life-time appointments.

The two junior members had been sitting on the court for only two years when the circuit division controversy became an immediate issue. Both were concerned about the growing volume of court business and saw no indication that the trend was going to abate. In addition, Gewin had a visual handicap that made the efficient handling of excessive workloads somewhat difficult. Concerns other than caseload were also involved. Like Jones, Judges Bell and Gewin were to be increasingly distressed by the court's activism. Both men would conclude, not surprisingly, that if a split of the circuit was the prereq-uisite for obtaining more judges, then the action to divide the court should be immediate.

THE COURT'S POSITION

Following his return from the September 1963 meeting of the Judicial Conference, Tuttle reported to the members of the court what had transpired and told them of the appointment of the Biggs Committee. Most seemed receptive to the idea that the needs of the circuit were to be analyzed, although the inevitable delay that such a study would entail meant that obtaining judicial help was perhaps years away.

Tuttle needed the Fifth Circuit Judicial Council to take a formal position on the questions surrounding the issue so that the preferences of the circuit could be transmitted to the Biggs Committee. The council was entrusted with making administrative and policy decisions for the circuit. Its membership included all active judges in regular service on the court of appeals.[53] As such,

---

53. The circuit councils were first recognized by Congress in 1939 as bodies to conduct the administrative affairs of the various circuits (28 U.S.C.332). Recent amendments to federal law, however, require district judge representation on the circuit councils and allow the number of members on a circuit's council to be determined by a majority vote of the active appellate judges. (See Public Law 96–458, The Judicial Councils Reform and Judicial Conduct and Discipline Act of 1980.) For an analysis of this legislation, see Michael J. Remington, "Circuit Council Reform: A Boat Hook for Judges and Court Administrators," *Brigham Young University Law Review* (1981): 695–736; Steven Flanders and John T. McDermott, *Operation of the Federal Judicial Councils* (Washington, D.C.: The Federal Judicial Center, 1978).

it was identical to the court sitting en banc. When convened as a circuit council, however, the judges did not engage in adjudicative actions but dealt exclusively with administrative and policy questions.

Tuttle put three questions to the judges. First, were additional judgeships necessary? Second, should additional judgeships be added to the circuit as presently constituted? And third, if a division of the circuit had to be a condition for receiving the added judgeships, should the court be split?

As expected, the judges were unanimous in their view that additional judges were necessary. The data on current and projected caseloads were overwhelming, to say nothing of alarming. The general view was that expansion of the court from nine to thirteen positions would be a reasonable staff increment.

The members of the court were also of similar mind on the issue of maintaining the circuit intact if possible. In spite of their past and continuing internal conflicts on judicial questions, the judges were trying hard to retain a level of collegiality. All had an emotional attachment to the history and traditions of the Fifth Circuit, but they differed over which course to follow. Several judges were uneasy about the prospect of such a large court, but they did agree that if additional judgeships could be obtained an expanded court should be tried before adopting the more radical alternative of dividing the circuit. Others had no concerns at all about a court of thirteen judges. John Brown, for one, characterized the conventional wisdom that no appellate court should be larger than nine judges as "hogwash."[54]

The final question was the most crucial. If either the Judicial Conference or Congress balked at the notion of a court with more than nine members, did the Fifth Circuit so badly need increased staff that the judges would be willing to divide? Judges Jones, Cameron, Gewin, and Bell voted to split the circuit if necessary. Somewhat surprisingly, even Hutcheson, Brown, and Tuttle agreed that division was perhaps the only pragmatic means of getting the additional judges. All were convinced that the authorization of additional judgeships was absolutely essential to the welfare of the court. If, as a last resort, no method of gaining the new positions could be successful other than realignment, then a split should not be rejected out of hand.

Rives and Wisdom objected vehemently. They insisted that circuit division would not produce the desired efficiency but would only lead to two small circuits inevitably characterized by excessive parochialism. They thought alternatives to realignment should be studied first, with the goal of finding creative ways to handle caseload growth. Underlying this contention was their fear, particularly held by Rives, of the impact that circuit splitting might have on the development of civil rights law. The legal struggle for racial equality in the South was still in its infancy, and Rives worried about any structural change that would adversely affect the continuation of this progress.

It was unusual for Brown and Tuttle to disagree with Wisdom and Rives

54. Interview with Judge John R. Brown, Houston, Texas, August 10, 1983.

over judicial decisions. The former, however, found themselves in a particularly strained position on this administrative matter. While in Washington pressing the need for additional judges during the summer of 1963, both had recognized the nature and magnitude of the political and administrative obstacles to be overcome. It was this realization that led them to take a pragmatic position toward circuit division.

Chief Judge Tuttle was especially torn. When discussed in terms of caseload only, the proposal appeared to be a neutral administrative issue, but Tuttle knew well that the issue carried all the potential of a major political battle. Had he not been in a position of formal leadership, he might have followed his deep feelings and voted against the realignment option. As chief judge, however, he had an acute sense of responsibility for administrative matters. He realized the magnitude of the caseload problem and was desperate for assistance to deal with it. Resources were already stretched to the limit. Tuttle's sense of the leadership role included a representational component. If a majority of the court agreed on a particular course of action on nonadjudicative matters, then Elbert Tuttle believed it was his responsibility as chief judge to articulate that position. Consequently, in the fall of 1963 the Judicial Council of the Fifth Circuit, by a seven-to-two vote, agreed to accept circuit reorganization if it was the sole avenue for obtaining the needed judgeships.

From its earliest stages the Fifth Circuit realignment issue highlighted certain principles of judicial reform politics. First, in matters affecting a single circuit, formal demands for change are initiated at the circuit council level. The requests are communicated upward to the Judicial Conference of the United States for committee study and final recommendations. If legislation is necessary, the conference addresses proposals to Congress. Thus, it was the Fifth Circuit Council that initiated the request for additional judgeships. Because of the decentralized nature of the federal judiciary, great weight is given to the wishes of the judges to be affected. Change is rarely imposed on an unreceptive circuit. Second, widely held principles on the proper operation of the judiciary can have a powerful effect on judicial reform issues. The "Rule of Nine," for example, immediately came into play when the Fifth Circuit made its request for additional judgeships. Third, the likelihood that proposals for reform will be considered favorably rises dramatically if the change is perceived as politically neutral. In other words, Congress is most receptive to deferring to the desires and expertise of the judiciary if the requested legislation is purely technical or administrative. If, on the other hand, the proposed change is seen as having a possible impact on the substantive decisions of the courts with consequences to interests outside the judiciary, then Congress will move with caution. Mindful of these realities, the Judicial Conference is always concerned about the political ramifications of the issues with which it deals. Thus, the prospect that civil rights might play a role in the Fifth Circuit proposal caused considerable uneasiness.

2

The Trial of
Civil Rights

The national policy process and attendant politics of the initial proposal to split the Fifth Circuit Court of Appeals were played out during one of the most controversial periods in American political history. Between 1961 and 1963, the civil rights movement achieved many of its historic milestones. The movement's strategy of nonviolent protest heightened public awareness and focused government attention on racial discrimination, paving the way for enactment of the Civil Rights Act of 1964 and the Voting Rights Act of 1965. The Fifth Circuit Court of Appeals was often entangled in the civil rights conflicts of the period, as the movement relied heavily on it for vindication. These events are crucial to understanding the political pressure placed on the court by its environment. Perhaps of even greater consequence for the realignment controversy, the character of this period places the court's internal relationships in perspective and allows us to see the genesis of its clash with Senator Eastland. The legal issues brought to the Fifth Circuit by the civil rights movement were to alter the circuit's role in history.

SOCIAL CHANGE AND THE LAW:
FREEDOM RIDES AND VOTER RIGHTS

By 1961, the civil rights movement could claim legal and statutory victories that barred racial discrimination in public schools, public transportation, public accommodations, and voting. To the extent that progress had been made at all, it was through federal action, usually in spite of the states. In *Brown v. Board of Education*, the United States Supreme Court had renounced its 1896 "separate but equal" doctrine, and subsequently showed its displeasure with virtually any form of state-supported segregation. Congress, through enactment of the Civil Rights and Voting Rights acts of 1960, also registered its support for the principle of equal protection under the law. Moreover, President Kennedy was perhaps the most sympathetic friend the movement ever had in the Oval Office. But despite these apparent national endorsements for the principle of equality between the races, southern blacks had gained few tangible benefits.

Against this backdrop, leading civil rights activists concluded that before further progress could be made the movement would have to activate the federal government in its behalf. Almost one hundred years of post–Civil War social and legal separation of the races in the South made it obvious that a massive voluntary change of attitude would not be forthcoming. The objective for the movement, and one for which it was well suited, was to bring this harsh reality to Washington and in so doing to spur the federal government to action. Thus began the movement's determination to draw attention to the plight of blacks, and consequently to their status in the South.

As a first-line tactic, civil rights leaders in 1961 decided to challenge segregation laws and customs throughout the South. Despite Supreme Court decisions, integration of public transportation facilities and accommodations was virtually nonexistent. None of the southern states had laws barring discrimination in such places but, on the contrary, had laws—and, more importantly, attitudes—mandating separation of blacks and whites.

Only a year earlier, in 1960, spontaneous public demonstrations originating in North Carolina in the form of "sit-ins" met with immediate success in spite of periodic violence. These student-initiated protests were the stimuli for the tactical use of nonresistant direct action. The movement's central leader, the Reverend Martin Luther King, Jr., consistently advocated the use of pacifist principles borrowed from the teachings of Mahatma Ghandi. Their success during the sit-ins encouraged other civil rights leaders to adopt pacificist methods in their all-out strategic attack on segregation laws.[1]

The first advocate to step forward with a well-developed strategy was James Farmer, head of the Congress of Racial Equality (CORE). A small and until then relatively obscure organizational arm of the civil rights movement, CORE embarked upon what became known as the "Freedom Rides," which were joined immediately by the Student Nonviolent Coordinating Committee (SNCC), responsible for many of the earlier sit-ins, and the Southern Christian Leadership Conference (SCLC). Dr. King, SCLC's president, chaired the Freedom Ride Coordinating Committee. The Freedom Rider strategy consisted of a racially integrated group traveling by bus along a planned route, with Washington as the starting point and New Orleans the destination.[2] Intending to make periodic stops to challenge segregated bus terminal facilities, the

    1. Anthony Lewis and the *New York Times, Portrait of a Decade* (New York: Random House, 1964), pp. 85–87; Alan F. Westin and Barry Mahoney, *The Trial of Martin Luther King* (New York: Thomas Y. Crowell Co., 1974), pp. 31–38.
    2. Lewis, *Portrait*, pp. 87–88; Carl M. Brauer, *John F. Kennedy and the Second Reconstruction* (New York: Columbia University Press, 1977), pp. 99–108.

group made arrangements to travel through Virginia, the Carolinas, Georgia, Alabama, Mississippi, and Louisiana. The protesters wanted "to dramatize Southern noncompliance with Supreme Court rulings outlawing segregation in interstate transportation and terminal facilities."[3]

The Freedom Rides began on May 4, 1961. Ten days into the excursion the first serious violence occurred. Once the riders reached Alabama they separated into two groups, one bound for Anniston, the other for Birmingham. At both locations a mob of angry white segregationists had gathered and, upon the protesters' arrivals, proceeded to beat the Freedom Riders with pipes, baseball bats, and bicycle chains. An enraged white mob burned one of the buses just outside Anniston, descended upon another as it arrived, attacked its passengers, and followed the shaken riders to their next stop. When they arrived in Birmingham, the Ku Klux Klan, promised a fifteen-minute moratorium by the police, inflicted probably the most vicious violence up to that point.[4]

Alerted to these violent actions, Attorney General Robert F. Kennedy devised a contingency plan for federal protection of the Freedom Riders. Once he and his top aides had warned the Justice Department of more violence in Alabama, an effort was made to insure the orderly conduct of the demonstrations and safe continuation for the Riders. After considerable segregationist rhetoric, negotiations with Alabama governor John Patterson resulted in the eventual safe departure of the wounded Birmingham Freedom Riders via air transportation to New Orleans.[5]

Having escorted the Freedom Riders to New Orleans, John Seigenthaler, a personal representative of President Kennedy, negotiated the safe continuation of yet another group of protesters who had assembled in Birmingham. These particular Riders were bound for Jackson, Mississippi, via Montgomery, Alabama. The ride was quickly transformed into a nightmarish odyssey that resulted in beatings, federal court orders, deployment of special U.S. marshals and the national guard, and ultimately jail for the protesters.

Traveling under the protection of sixteen Alabama state highway patrol cars and one airplane, the Freedom Riders were escorted hastily to the outskirts of Montgomery. Later that Saturday morning (May 20), when the bus arrived at the Montgomery depot, the protesters realized that they had been abandoned by the Montgomery police. Nor did any other law enforcement personnel come to protect them. Instead, a mob of one thousand angry whites attacked the Riders as they disembarked from the bus. According to one

3. Westin, *The Trial*, p. 39.

4. Arthur M. Schlesinger, Jr., *Robert Kennedy and His Times* (Boston: Houghton Mifflin Co., 1978), pp. 294–300; Brauer, *Kennedy*, p. 100; Victor S. Navasky, *Kennedy Justice* (New York: Atheneum, 1971), pp. 20–21, 124–25.

5. Schlesinger, *Kennedy*, pp. 294, 297; Brauer, *Kennedy*, pp. 99–101; Westin and Mahoney, *The Trial*, pp. 39–40.

observer, the protesters were beaten with clubs, pipes, and fists.[6] Even by-standers with no apparent connection to the demonstration were injured: one young man's leg was broken and another person was doused with flammable liquid and set on fire. Reporters and photographers were assaulted as well. One blow, however, went directly to Washington. Seigenthaler, who had been the voice of moderation and mediation throughout, was struck from behind while trying to help a young female protester under attack. He lay unconscious on the ground for almost half an hour before police took him to the hospital. Ambulances were either allegedly out of commission or chased from the scene. Although some police arrived approximately fifteen minutes after the rioting began, an hour and fifteen minutes elapsed before law enforcement officers trained for riot control appeared and gained control of the crowd. Agents of the FBI were present but only took notes recording their observations.[7]

President Kennedy issued a concerned statement about the Montgomery incident and unleashed the Justice Department by advising them to take all necessary steps to return Montgomery to order and peace. Robert Kennedy dispatched Deputy Attorney General Byron White to the city with instructions to organize a specially deputized group of U.S. marshals, recruited nation-wide, and have them in Montgomery as soon as possible. The attorney general then directed John Doar, chief assistant to Burke Marshall (head of the Justice Department's Civil Rights Division), to file for a federal court injunction re-straining the Ku Klux Klan, the National States Rights party, and the Bir-mingham and Montgomery police from interfering with interstate travel.[8]

The plea fell on a sympathetic ear. At that time Judge Frank Johnson, Jr., was the U.S. District Court for the Middle District of Alabama. Johnson had already gained national attention for his liberal activist decisions in the area of civil rights, most notably when he joined Fifth Circuit Judge Rives to form the majority opinion in the landmark decision *Browder v. Gayle*.[9] Doar had the injunction prepared by Saturday afternoon, May 20. Judge Johnson signed it, and by late evening White had many of the notified marshals pa-troling Montgomery.[10]

By Sunday (May 21), five hundred U.S. marshals were waiting at nearby Maxwell Air Force Base, and a few in Montgomery. Almost fifty marshals were sent to the airport to meet and escort Martin Luther King, who had come to address an evening rally at the First Baptist Church in support of the beleaguered Freedom Riders. Tension mounted throughout the day, as fifteen hundred blacks assembled for the Sunday night service. During the

6. Navasky, *Kennedy*, p. 124.
7. Lester A. Sobel, *Civil Rights 1960–1966* (New York: Facts on File, 1967), pp. 60–61, 65–66.
8. Sobel, *Civil Rights*, pp. 62–63; Schlesinger, *Kennedy*, p. 297; Westin and Mahoney, *The Trial*, pp. 40–41; Brauer, *Kennedy*, pp. 101–02.
9. 142 F.Supp. 707 (M.D. Ala., 1956).
10. Westin and Mahoney, *The Trial*, p. 41.

meeting a mob of several thousand angry whites gathered across the street. They hurled rocks, destroyed a car, and threatened to burn the church next. When the U.S. marshals tried to disperse them with tear gas, they threw the gas bombs back.[11] The confrontation lasted all night. Finally, at daybreak, the church members were able to leave.[12]

Although worried that more violent outbreaks would result, Justice officials seemed to accept, if not endorse, the Freedom Riders' determination to continue into Mississippi. In preparation for moving the protesters quickly out of Alabama and safely into Mississippi, Burke Marshall telephoned Mississippi Attorney General Joe Patterson on Monday after the incident at the First Baptist Church. Patterson was generally uncooperative, and Marshall was left with the impression that if by chance no violence occurred, arrests surely would. Former Mississippi governor and attorney general James P. Coleman, a political rival of Governor Ross Barnett and his allies, warned Marshall not to trust Barnett.[13] Coleman believed the Riders would be killed before they reached Jackson, and his belief apparently alarmed Justice officials enough to prompt a call to Senator James O. Eastland (D-MS) from Robert Kennedy. Burke Marshall later explained that "there was considerable evidence that there would be violence in Mississippi."[14] Kennedy sought Eastland's opinion of what actions the state authorities were likely to take against the Freedom Riders. Despite their differences on civil rights, Eastland had been a loyal party supporter in 1960, and the Kennedys believed he was someone whose word could be trusted.[15]

Eastland promised that although there would be no violence the Riders would be arrested in Jackson. Relieved that there would be no further beatings and also having no apparent alternative, Kennedy acquiesced. After similar assurances from Governor Barnett and Jackson mayor Allen Thompson, two buses of Freedom Riders left Montgomery on Wednesday May 24, flanked inside and out by the state patrol and National Guard reinforcements. Even the highway from Montgomery to Jackson was lined with the National Guard, as U.S. aircraft hovered above. In the caravan there were almost as many members of the media as there were law enforcement officers; twenty cars of reporters trailed sixteen state highway patrol cars, and aboard the bus were seventeen reporters and six armed members of the National Guard.[16] True to promise, James Farmer and the Freedom Riders were arrested within

11. Sobel, *Civil Rights*, p. 62.

12. Brauer, *Kennedy*, pp. 102–04; Lewis, *Portrait*, pp. 88–89; Navasky, *Kennedy*, p. 24; Schlesinger, *Kennedy*, pp. 297–99.

13. Schlesinger, *Kennedy*, p. 299.

14. Navasky, *Kennedy*, p. 170.

15. Schlesinger, *Kennedy*, pp. 234, 299.

16. Sobel, *Civil Rights*, pp. 65–66.

minutes of their arrival in Jackson, as soon as the activists tried to use the "whites only" facilities.

Once arrested, the Freedom Riders would not post bond and leave jail. When the attorney general insisted to King that the protesters leave without incident, the civil rights leader explained that, given the amount of official protection, the trip had not been a valid test of segregation laws. The Riders, King told Kennedy, were staying in jail as a "matter of conscience and morality."[17] James Farmer issued appeals from his jail cell in Jackson to challenge segregation laws in rail and air terminal facilities throughout the South.[18] Despite pleadings from the administration and a federal court injunction from Judge Frank Johnson to halt interstate travel in Alabama for purposes of testing segregation laws (*United States v. U.S. Klans, Knights of Ku Klux Klan, Inc.*),[19] the Freedom Rides continued to expand throughout the South. By the end of summer 1961, more than three hundred protesters had been arrested in Jackson alone. Only two weeks after the initial arrests, so many Freedom Riders had descended upon Jackson that the Hinds County jail was filled to capacity and state officials began transferring the protesters to the Mississippi State Penitentiary.[20]

Ultimately, the attorney general persuaded Martin Luther King to accept a "temporary lull" in the tactical use of nonviolent direct action.[21] Civil rights leaders considered the Freedom Rides an enormous success and a crucial step forward in the movement's progress. The major reason for their positive attitude about such painful incidents was Robert Kennedy's rather novel executive action. Five days after the Jackson arrests, the Justice Department formally petitioned the Interstate Commerce Commission (ICC) to promulgate regulations barring segregation in interstate bus terminals and provided the agency with a plan.

Recalcitrance in Mississippi, however, necessitated federal court intervention. In November, on the effective date of the order, officials in Jackson simply moved segregation signs to the sidewalk in front of the terminal. These actions by Mississippi state authorities spawned two suits (*Bailey v. Patterson,* and *United States v. City of Jackson, Mississippi*),[22] which epitomized the legal difficulties facing the Freedom Riders as they sought vindication of their constitutional rights.

The first case (*Bailey*) was a class-action suit in which the civil rights plaintiffs asked a three-judge federal district court to enjoin state authorities and transportation carriers from maintaining segregated terminal facilities in violation

17. Quoted in Schlesinger, *Kennedy*, p. 299.
18. Sobel, *Civil Rights*, p. 66.
19. 194 F.Supp. 897 (1961).
20. Sobel, *Civil Rights*, p. 66.
21. Brauer, *Kennedy*, p. 107; Schlesinger, *Kennedy*, p. 302.
22. 199 F.Supp. 595 (1961); 206 F.Supp. 45 (1962).

of the ICC order.[23] U.S. District Judge Sidney C. Mize of the Southern District of Mississippi and Claude F. Clayton of the Northern District of Mississippi formed the majority opinion, with Fifth Circuit Judge Richard T. Rives dissenting. Basing their decision on the equitable abstention doctrine, the majority ruled against the black plaintiffs. The abstention doctrine prevents federal courts from intervening in a state's judicial process "until potentially controlling questions of state law have been answered by the state judiciary."[24] In civil rights cases, it often became a dilatory tactic used by recalcitrant federal circuit and district judges in the South. Because the black plaintiffs were challenging the constitutionality of Mississippi's segregation laws, the *Bailey* majority held that the statutes in question should first be interpreted by the Mississippi Supreme Court. At that time, to demand that black plaintiffs challenging Mississippi laws file their civil rights claims in state court, and further constrain them by requiring the exhaustion of all state judicial remedies, inevitably meant interminable delays and adverse decisions.

When black plaintiffs met with Judge Mize's tactics in the *Bailey* case, they immediately appealed directly to the U.S. Supreme Court, which had exclusive mandatory appellate jurisdiction over most appeals from three-judge district courts. The petitioners requested the Court to enjoin city and state officials in Mississippi from enforcing segregated terminal facilities. While the justices still refused to intervene in criminal prosecutions pursuant to breach of peace statutes, the Court, in a per curiam decision, called the use of the abstention doctrine patently frivolous in light of well-settled precedents in the area.[25] The ICC order notwithstanding, the Court already had established a doctrinal lineage in the realm of public desegregation. Two prior Court decisions—*Boynton v. Virginia* and *Morgan v. Virginia*—even addressed the specifics in the *Bailey* case.[26] On remand Judge Mize declared the Mississippi statutes unconstitutional, just as he had been ordered. Twice, however, he refused injunctive relief to the plaintiffs because the signs and practices were isolated and had been corrected. Ultimately, the black plaintiffs were granted injunctive relief in a subsequent appeal to the Fifth Circuit, two years after the claim was initiated.[27]

Filing civil rights claims in southern federal trial courts rather than Mississippi state courts was only a small improvement. Unless the civil rights claim

23. Three-judge district courts were created pursuant to the Three-Judge Court Act of 1910. Usually comprised of two district and one circuit judge, these unique tribunals hear reapportionment and certain civil rights issues. Appeals from them go directly to the Supreme Court, which has mandatory jurisdiction. See Thomas G. Walker, "Behavioral Tendencies in the Three Judge District Court," *American Journal of Political Science* 17 (1973): 407–13.

24. "Judicial Performance in the Fifth Circuit, *Yale Law Review* 73 (1963): 96.

25. *Bailey v. Patterson*, 369 U.S. 31 (1962).

26. 364 U.S. 454 (1960) and 328 U.S. 373 (1946). "Judicial Performance," pp. 102–03, n. 73; Navasky, *Kennedy*, p. 205.

27. *Bailey v. Patterson*, 323 F.2d 201 (1963).

was filed with a liberal appellate panel, the results were commensurately damaging. In their legal quest to invoke federal jurisdiction in Mississippi, Freedom Riders faced two of the most notoriously recalcitrant federal jurists in the South. The ability of U.S. District Judges Sidney C. Mize (Biloxi) and William Harold Cox (Jackson), both of the Southern District of Mississippi, to circumvent a liberal majority opinion from either the U.S. Supreme Court or the Fifth Circuit through procedural delays was unsurpassed. Both jurists repeatedly refused even to grant federal jurisdiction over the Freedom Rider cases. Judge Mize denied writs of habeas corpus on grounds of exhaustion of state remedies and defended the arrests as preventing more violence.[28] In *United States v. City of McComb*,[29] when a majority of a three-judge district court comprised of Fifth Circuit judges Elbert P. Tuttle (Atlanta) and Richard T. Rives (Montgomery) granted injunctive relief to black plaintiffs and ordered McComb authorities to comply with the ICC order, Mize (also a member of the panel) refused to sign the decision.[30] A few days later Judge Mize retaliated by granting McComb authorities a temporary injunction prohibiting further Freedom Rides in the city. In another Freedom Ride suit, *Brown v. State*,[31] Judge Cox not only refused to grant federal jurisdiction over the civil rights claims, but also made disparaging remarks from the bench about the character of the civil rights plaintiffs, as he lauded segregationist views.[32]

In *United States v. City of Jackson, Mississippi*,[33] Judge Mize refused the government's petition to enjoin Jackson authorities from placing the segregation signs on the pavement outside the terminal. Again Judge Mize was reversed on appeal to the Fifth Circuit. In this instance, however, he fell prey to a much more harshly worded and directly leveled reversal written for a panel of the Fifth Circuit by Judge John Minor Wisdom. Citing Mize for "abuse of judicial discretion," Wisdom rebuffed the city's defense that the signs were there merely to "assist members of both races in *voluntary* separation" as "disingenuous quibble" that "must rest on the assumption that federal judges are more naive than ordinary men.... Perhaps they are." Wisdom continued, "We again take judicial notice that the State of Mississippi has a steelhard, inflexible, undeviating official policy of segregation."[34] It was not the first nor the last confrontation between these two federal jurists. This case was merely a sideswipe compared to the head-on collision they had over the three-year

28. Sobel, *Civil Rights*, p. 67.

29. 6 *Race Rel. L. Rep.* 780 (S.D. Miss. 1961).

30. "Judicial Performance," p. 116; Sobel, *Civil Rights*, p. 68.

31. 6 *Race Rel. L. Rep.* 780 (S.D. Miss. 1961).

32. "Judicial Performance," p. 101. See also Mary H. Curzan, "A Case Study in the Selection of Federal Judges: The Fifth Circuit, 1953–1963" (Ph.D. diss., Yale University, 1968).

33. 206 F.Supp. 45 (1962).

34. *United States v. City of Jackson, Mississippi*, 206 F.Supp.5 (1962); *United States v. City of Jackson, Mississippi*, 318 F.2d 5 (1963).

(1961–63) battle to integrate the University of Mississippi. The *Jackson* and *Bailey* cases were by no means the only major litigation to emerge from the Freedom Riders conflicts. In every respect, however, the path of this litigation and the manner in which all the political actors related (ill or otherwise) to one another comprised a typical pattern in the civil rights disputes of the early sixties.

Unbeknownst to the public, the Freedom Riders episode had touched off a significant internal clash among members of the Fifth Circuit. In the early summer of 1961, when Freedom Rider litigation appeared certain, Judge Ben Cameron wrote to Chief Judge Tuttle advising him that he was fully prepared to participate in any special three-judge district court case arising in Mississippi from these civil rights protests.[35] Tuttle's response came one week later. He informed Cameron that because the Mississippian was behind in his opinion-writing duties, "I think I shall not trouble you to participate in any three-judge courts that may need to be appointed during this summer."[36] Instead, Tuttle appointed himself to sit with Mississippi District Judges Sidney Mize and Claude Clayton to hear the first of the Freedom Rider cases requiring a three-judge district court.[37]

Cameron was outraged. Responding to Tuttle ten days later, the conservative Mississippi jurist claimed that the action of the chief judge constituted "one of the greatest surprises of my experience" and that he was "embarrassed" by Tuttle's "unjustified" exercise of the assignment powers.[38] In Cameron's view, Tuttle had violated one of the cardinal norms of judicial procedure: that circuit court judges are entitled to sit on special three-judge district court cases arising from their home states.

Rather than escalate the level of hostilities, Tuttle ended his exchange with Cameron by writing: "I am sorry you feel as you do about the matter. I simply handled it in the way I thought was best under the circumstances."[39] But the issue was not to disappear so easily. Cameron was not placated, nor did he consider Tuttle's action an isolated incident. To him, this was only one example of how the court's liberal members dominated the conservative, states' rights–oriented judges. Cameron was not about to let the matter die, but continued to monitor Judge Tuttle's three-judge district court assignment behavior, as well as the assignments made by Judge Brown to court of appeals panels. He was not reluctant to reargue his position when he thought such assignments

35. Letter from Judge Ben F. Cameron to Chief Judge Elbert P. Tuttle, June 10, 1961.
36. Letter from Chief Judge Elbert P. Tuttle to Judge Ben F. Cameron, June 19, 1961.
37. Later Tuttle withdrew from this case (*Bailey v. Patterson*, 199 F.Supp. 595), when Mississippi District Judges Mize and Clayton outvoted the chief judge and rescheduled a hearing at a time when Tuttle was committed to being on the West Coast. Tuttle appointed Judge Richard Rives to take his place, once again bypassing Judge Cameron.
38. Letter from Judge Ben F. Cameron to Chief Judge Elbert P. Tuttle, June 29, 1961.
39. Letter from Chief Judge Elbert P. Tuttle to Judge Ben F. Cameron, June 30, 1961.

constituted "panel stacking." This issue would drive a wedge through the court for some time to come.

Throughout the summer and fall of 1961 the Justice Department applied many of its efforts to redirecting the overall strategy of the civil rights organizations. In June, Robert Kennedy met with Dr. King in an attempt to convince him that a larger, more important battle could be won on the enfranchisement front. Rather than continue the direct-action strategy and run the risk of more violence, Kennedy urged King to focus attention on a voter registration drive. A peaceful resolution of the South's racial discrimination problems became a top priority for many federal officials. Soon the Justice Department was joined by Judge Frank Johnson. Johnson blamed the Klan and the police for the violence but enjoined every organization involved in the Freedom Ride episode to cease agitation, whether or not it was "within the law," so that the public could be granted complete relief.[40] This perspective very adequately reflected the shock and dismay felt by federal officials who had witnessed in Montgomery the "most serious racial disturbance . . . in the postwar era." Besides aversion to violence, the Justice Department strongly held the view, "litigate to enfranchise the Negro and all else will follow."[41]

Voter registration statistics indicated that Mississippi and Alabama were the most blatant violators of black voting rights. Based upon its voting rights litigation strategy, the Justice Department believed both states posed severe problems and thus chose to file its first voting rights suits there. Indeed, after months of investigation the Civil Rights Division in July 1961 targeted seven counties in Mississippi where deprivation of the vote was so grave that suits were filed in each county.[42] No voting rights cases had ever been filed against Mississippi, and a total of only twelve voting suits had been pursued during the entire Eisenhower administration.[43]

Civil rights leaders were equally concerned about voting discrimination and violations in Mississippi. Robert Moses issued warnings that economic reprisals, evictions, and physical violence warranted the filing of a "broad" federal government suit. He noted that "widespread publicity" of the violations in Sunflower County (home of James O. Eastland) would probably have to occur before the federal government would act.[44] Although the Civil Rights Division was diligently forging ahead with its right-to-vote litigation strategy, Moses' assessment was largely accurate. Yet Justice officials were reluctant to initiate voter intimidation suits.

40. *United States v. U.S. Klans, Knights of Ku Klux Klan, Inc.*, 194 F.Supp. 897 (1961).

41. Foster Rhea Dulles, *The Civil Rights Commission, 1957–1965* (East Lansing: Michigan State University Press, 1968), p. 95; Navasky, *Kennedy*, p. 207.

42. Frederick M. Wirt, *Politics of Southern Equality* (Chicago: Aldine Publishing Co., 1970), pp. 76–77, 95; Commission on Civil Rights, *Voting* (Washington, D.C.: U.S. Government Printing Office, 1961), pp. 31–32.

43. Theodore C. Sorenson, *Kennedy* (New York: Harper & Row, 1965), p. 479.

44. Brauer, *Kennedy*, p. 165.

In the few voter intimidation cases eventually initiated by the Justice Department, the results were mixed, and the gains were very narrowly tied to specifics.[45] At one point in the spring of 1963, conditions turned so violent in Greenwood, Mississippi, threatening the lives of Robert Moses and two other voter registration workers, that the Justice Department was prompted to file a petition to enjoin state authorities from interfering with voter registration. Under the threat of a crisis and the refusal of the federal court injunction, Justice was cornered into a position of dropping the suit in exchange for the release of eight civil rights workers who were jailed following the violence.[46] In one of the rare Justice Department suits that occurred at this time, however, the Fifth Circuit made known its position on this issue. Although the appeal was highly unusual, the violence surrounding the case and the Fifth Circuit's opinion both had a familiar ring.

In July 1961, members of SNCC began to organize the first voter registration drives in Mississippi. By August, one black student member, John Hardy, began a voter education school in Walthall County, one of the counties in which the Justice Department had filed a voter discrimination suit. Of the 2,490 voting-age blacks in Walthall County, not one was registered. In an effort to solve this obvious problem, Hardy and his fellow civil rights workers opened classes to teach eligible blacks how to register pursuant to Mississippi's "interpretation tests" procedure. After about two weeks of classes, eleven blacks had sought registration, and all had been refused. When the last of the applicants, two black farm owners in their early sixties, accompanied Hardy to the registrar's office, they were met by violence and harassment. John Q. Wood, the registrar, picked up a pistol, pointed it toward the door, and ordered Hardy out of the office. As Hardy agreeably turned and approached the door, the registrar struck him in the back of the head, exclaiming, "Get out of here you damn son-of-a-bitch and don't come back in here."[47] The elderly black applicants helped Hardy as they rushed out of the office. When the three tried to report the incident to the sheriff, Hardy was arrested for a breach of peace violation. Two days before Hardy's trial, Burke Marshall and John Doar filed a petition with District Judge William Harold Cox for a temporary restraining order. The government contended that Hardy's prosecution, whether or not he was acquitted, would irreparably injure blacks in the county who wished to register. Late in the afternoon on the day before Hardy's scheduled trial, Judge Cox denied the government's plea. That evening attorneys from both sides flew to Montgomery and at 10:30 P.M. met with Fifth Circuit Judge Richard T. Rives at his home to file an appeal.

Rives expedited the appeal, held the hearing on October 3, and a panel of Judges Rives, John R. Brown, and Ben F. Cameron rendered a two-to-one

45. Commission, *Voting*, pp. 91–97.
46. Sobel, *Civil Rights*, pp. 192–93; Navasky, *Kennedy*, pp. 217–18.
47. *United States v. Wood*, 295 F.2d at 776 (1961).

decision on October 27, reversing Judge Cox and restraining the justice of the peace from prosecuting Hardy until a full hearing could be held on the government's petition for a preliminary injunction against the discriminatory voting procedures in Walthall.

Writing the panel's majority opinion in *United States v. Wood*,[48] Judge Rives agreed with the government's "irreparable harm" contention. He noted that not one black resident had sought an application to vote since Hardy's arrest, whereas eleven blacks had made an attempt to register during the registration drive. The opinion was sharply worded and directly to the point. Rives, obviously appalled by the behavior of the local Mississippi authorities, wrote: "The blunt truth is that it can really not be expected that Negroes who have lived all their lives under the white supremacy conditions which exist in that area of Mississippi will continue their efforts to register ... if in addition to being threatened and beaten, they will also be prosecuted in state court with all that such a prosecution entails."[49] He went on to refer to those who interfere with another person's right to vote as "political termites" who had to be eradicated, or at least whose activities had to be checked "to prevent irreparable damage to our Government."[50] Rives used two extraordinary procedures: the expedited appeal, moving the case forward on the docket ahead of its chronological order; and the offshoot exception to the final judgment rule, which construes the lower-court decision as final when it technically does not meet the final judgment requirements.[51] The Fifth Circuit gained a widespread and controversial judicial reputation (as well as internal problems later on) as an activist court as a result of its use of a whole battery of extraordinary procedures directed at bringing recalcitrant district court judges in line with the law of the circuit.

The majority opinion drew immediate fire from the Fifth Circuit's most conservative member, Judge Ben Cameron. Referring to Judges Rives and Brown as "bent upon the exaltation of federal sovereignty" and the "debasement of state sovereignty," he accused Rives of depicting elected Mississippi officials as "unworthy of trust." Cameron did not agree with the majority that the Fifth Circuit had jurisdiction over the issue because Cox's order was nonreviewable. But more than legal procedure irritated Cameron. In his dissent he frequently quoted from another of his dissents on similar grounds, *Boman v. Birmingham Transit Co.*:[52]

> It is to me a saddening spectacle to witness the publishing of decisions such as that of the majority here, which can have no other effect than to cause the people of the southland to look upon federal functionaries ... as alien intruders.

48. 295 F.2d at 772.
49. *Wood*, 295 F.2d at 781.
50. Ibid. at 785.
51. "Judicial Performance," p. 127.
52. 292 F.2d 4 (1961). Also quoted in *Wood*, 295 F.2d at 788.

... It is the universal conviction of the people of the conquered provinces also that the judges who function in the circuit should render justice in individual cases against a background of, and as interpreters of, the ethos of the people whose servants they are.

Referring to the voter registration volunteers as "outsiders" and "agitators," Cameron contended that they had "set neighbor against neighbor" over an issue that could "best be worked out if they [whites and blacks] were left alone to continue the unbroken improvement in relationships which has taken place in the last eight decades."[53] Cameron's dissents in subsequent civil rights cases became even more vehement, to the point that the court's internal strife made headlines.

Agreement on a more peaceful resolution of racial discrimination through the use of litigation meant interminable delays for civil rights groups. Gains in the number of black voters had been limited, and voting rights litigation moved extraordinarily slow, despite the efforts of the Fifth Circuit. Direct confrontations over voting registration did not generate the media or institutional attention produced by the Freedom Rides. The Justice Department was determined to grind on in the federal courts over substantive issues, as opposed to issues or incidents of local breach, as in the *Woods* case. But even the voting discrimination issues were eventually resolved by civil rights leaders' return to direct action—for example, the events involved in "Bloody Sunday" in Selma, Alabama, which precipitated enactment of the 1965 Voting Rights Act.

Although Justice officials and the Fifth Circuit were making their most concerted efforts in late 1962 and 1963 to "bear down" on obdurate southern officials, civil rights leaders ultimately returned to a more frequent use of direct means to raise the nation's consciousness. This strategy took its toll on all the institutions involved. Before the resurgence of direct confrontation, however, protesters witnessed another example of the agonizing delay inherent in litigation. The conflict over the integration of the University of Mississippi ushered in the convergence of strategies, attitudes, and political reactions that led to the passage of the Civil Rights Act of 1964. One black man "in search of an education"[54] triggered events that changed the course of institutional activity.

THE MEREDITH EPISODE

With a recently elected president whose campaign stumping had been laced with statements of support for civil rights, the time seemed ripe for desegregating one of the last vestiges of racial separation in higher education. James H. Meredith, a twenty-eight-year-old former staff sergeant, proceeded on this

53. *Wood*, 295 F.2d at 788.
54. *Meredith v. Fair*, 298 F.2d 696 (1962).

assumption and applied for admission to the University of Mississippi on January 21, 1961, the day after John F. Kennedy was inaugurated. For the next four months Meredith met with avoidance and evasion, and finally, as Judge Wisdom later wrote: "The axe fell on May 25, 1961. On that date the Registrar closed his correspondence file on the application and returned the money Meredith had deposited."[55] Meredith's request for admission to Ole Miss led instead to his entry into the southern federal courts. At the outset he was joined by a battery of capable legal counselors. On the advice of Medgar Evers of Mississippi's NAACP, who himself had tried unsuccessfully to enter Ole Miss in 1954, Meredith sought and received legal aid from Thurgood Marshall and Constance Baker Motley, both of whom then worked for the NAACP Legal Defense Fund.

Less than a week after the outright denial of his application, Meredith filed an appeal that led to an exasperating nine-month encounter with U.S. District Judge Sidney C. Mize. True to form, Meredith's initial hearing had scarcely been in progress for a full day when Mize rescheduled it for a month later due to his crowded docket. Judge Mize already had declined a temporary restraining order that would have given Meredith immediate relief by permitting his enrollment in the first summer semester session scheduled to begin on June 8. Instead, Mize set the case for hearing on June 12, four days after summer school commenced. By then Meredith had missed the spring semester he initially applied for and the beginning of the summer semester as well. When he first applied for admission, Meredith, who had been attending Jackson State University with the financial aid of his military benefits, had a year and a half of course work remaining to complete his degree. A third of that time had already been consumed by state officials enforcing segregationist policies.[56]

On July 10, the rescheduled date for Meredith's hearing for a preliminary injunction,[57] the proceedings were again postponed until the following day because of a docket conflict. That same day, because of illness, Mississippi's counsel was granted a delay until July 19, in order to allow him time to answer a second motion for a preliminary injunction Meredith had filed on June 29, seeking admission to the second session of summer school, which was to begin on July 17. As Judge Wisdom noted, the "possibility of attending the second summer session had gone winging." Also in the interim Constance Baker Motley was five times denied permission, at Judge Mize's discretion, to take

55. *Meredith v. Fair*, 305 F.2d 348 (1962).
56. Eleven years prior to Meredith's federal suit to enter a state university as an undergraduate, the Supreme Court had already begun to be more receptive to the attempts of blacks to enroll in state-supported law schools and graduate schools. See *Sweatt v. Painter*, 339 U.S. 629 (1950) and *McLaurin v. Oklahoma State Regents*, 339 U.S. 637 (1950).
57. A favorable ruling on the preliminary injunction would have permitted Meredith's entrance until the issue could have been settled on its merits.

the registrar's deposition. Later, in the Fifth Circuit's final opinion, this was called a "clear abuse of judicial discretion."[58]

The hearing recessed in June and resumed for one day on August 10, was recessed on August 11 due to a court schedule conflict, resumed on August 15, concluded on August 16, and permitted another month's delay for the filing of each litigant's brief. Fall semester began on September 28. Judge Mize denied Meredith's petition for a preliminary injunction on December 14, 1961, and set January 15, 1962, for a final hearing on the merits of the case. Mize's reasoning was: "The Registrar swore emphatically and unequivocally that the race of plaintiff or his color had nothing in the world to do with the action of the Registrar in denying his application.... The burden of proof, of course, is upon the plaintiff to prove by a preponderance of the evidence that his admission was denied because of his race or color and this the plaintiff has utterly failed to do."[59]

With the spring semester date of February 5 approaching, Meredith petitioned the Fifth Circuit for the extraordinary remedy of a preliminary injunction pending appeal and for this current appeal to be expedited. A panel of Judges Wisdom, Tuttle, and Rives expedited the appeal, hearing it three weeks after Meredith's request was filed, December 18, a week before the holiday recess. Although the panel took judicial notice that Mississippi's schools were segregated by state action, noted five specific observations for guidance at the trial, and requested that Mize set an earlier date for the trial and issue his decision promptly, the panel unanimously denied Meredith's interlocutory appeal, explaining that the case needed a full trial on the merits to clear the "muddy record."[60] Mize's exclusion of evidence and the severe limitation placed on inspection of the records for Meredith's counsel made a determination of the case difficult.

Once again Meredith stood before Judge Mize. The trial started a day late. Then, due to the illness of the Mississippi assistant attorney general and the inability of the two special assistants to continue without him, it was postponed for a week and concluded after three days. About a week later Mize issued an order denying all relief to Meredith.

Again Meredith petitioned the Fifth Circuit to grant the injunction before the case had a full hearing in the appellate court. Meredith maintained that his case would be moot unless he was permitted to enter spring semester, 1962, because he could graduate from Jackson State if he continued his course work there. In a sympathetic tone, the panel, with Chief Judge Tuttle dissenting, explained that it wanted a full appellate hearing before issuing an injunction to permit Meredith's entry.[61] It was almost as if Wisdom wanted

58. *Meredith*, 305 F.2d at 349.
59. *Meredith v. Fair*, 199 F.Supp at 754 (1962).
60. *Meredith*, 298 F.2d at 703.
61. *Meredith*, 305 F.2d at 341.

to ensure proper procedural completeness and to bring the controversy to a head before he landed a final heavy blow in what he called the "showdown fight."[62] At least his opinion in June could easily point to this conclusion.

On June 25, 1962 (Meredith's twenty-ninth birthday), a Fifth Circuit panel of Judges Wisdom (who authored the opinion), Brown, and Senior District Judge Dozier A. DeVane of Tallahassee rendered a two-to-one decision (DeVane dissenting) supporting Meredith's entry into the University of Mississippi. *Meredith v. Fair*[63] was a sharply worded, point-by-point reversal of the university's defense. Countering the Board of Trustees' claim that Meredith's credits were not transferable, Wisdom wrote, "We draw the inference again that the assigned reason for rejecting Meredith was a trumped-up excuse without any basis except to discriminate."[64] Using words such as *frivolous* and *trivial* throughout the opinion to describe the university's various contentions, Wisdom was most vitriolic when he began to rebut the complaints against Meredith's moral character. He claimed that the trustees were "scraping the bottom of the barrel in asserting that the University should not now admit Meredith because he is a bad character risk."[65] The university had produced air force transcripts in an attempt to prove that Meredith was a troublemaker. Wisdom began his opinion by lauding Meredith's air force background and responding in an offended tone: "One short answer to the defendants' contention is the Good Conduct Medal. Another short answer is that Meredith's record shows just about the type of Negro who might be expected to try to crack the racial barrier at the University of Mississippi: a man with a mission and with a nervous stomach."[66] Wisdom's opinion was a resounding victory for Meredith. But it was Judge DeVane's dissenting opinion that proved prophetic.

DeVane praised Judge Wisdom's opinion, calling it a masterpiece and admitting that he agreed with almost everything Wisdom had to say and indeed believed that university officials had never accepted the Supreme Court's *Brown* public school desegregation decision. He concluded, however, with an admonition that ran completely contrary to the earlier portions of the opinion. The court, he wrote, did not have a right to ignore the consequences of its decision for the "citizens of Mississippi," but did have a "duty" to avoid incidents comparable to Little Rock. He continued: "Integration is not a question that can ever be settled by Federal Judges. It is an economic, social and religious question and in the end will be amicably settled on this basis." Noting that he considered Meredith to be a troublemaker, DeVane warned that his entry would be "nothing short of a catastrophe."[67]

62. Ibid. at 351.
63. Ibid. at 343.
64. Ibid. at 354.
65. Ibid. at 358.
66. Ibid.
67. Ibid. at 362.

In the three months preceding Meredith's October enrollment for fall semester, 1962, defiance of the Fifth Circuit's orders came from every sector—public, private, and official. Less than three weeks after the orders were issued, Fifth Circuit Judge Ben F. Cameron took extraordinary steps to prevent Mize from having to issue the injunction that would permit Meredith's admission to the university. From July 18 through August 6, 1962, Cameron, though not a member of the panel, issued four separate stays of the Fifth Circuit's decision. The first three were promptly set aside by the court. The fourth, however, was voided by Supreme Court Justice Hugo Black, who as circuit justice for the Fifth retained responsibility for any emergency matters arising from the circuit's judicial proceedings. Upon consultation with the Justice Department, which was asked to intervene in the case with an amicus curiae brief, and after discussions with the other justices, Black voided Cameron's stay on September 10 and ordered that the Fifth Circuit's decision be expedited. Three days later Mize signed the injunction. That evening, in a statewide radio and television address, Mississippi Governor Ross Barnett invoked the doctrine of interposition, proclaiming state sovereignty between the citizens and the federal government. He announced that the schools were operating under state supervision and thus were answerable only to state law.[68]

For the next two weeks Attorney General Kennedy openly communicated with Governor Barnett through a series of some twenty telephone conversations. Negotiations notwithstanding, Meredith unsuccessfully attempted to register four times from September 20 through September 26. Barnett flew to Oxford to block Meredith's first registration attempt on September 20. This prompted the Fifth Circuit to order a contempt hearing for the university's top three officials and the board of trustees. The following day Judge Mize dismissed contempt charges against the board of trustees because Barnett had taken over its authority and even had the trustees appoint him special registrar for Meredith. The Fifth Circuit, sitting en banc with Cameron absent because of ill health, agreed to issue orders restraining Barnett from interfering with Meredith's enrollment while holding in abeyance the contempt charges against the university officials.[69]

The same day (September 24), Barnett ordered the summary arrest of any official "who sought to arrest or fine any Mississippi official for defying court desegregation orders."[70] Barnett flagrantly defied the Fifth Circuit the following day by again physically blocking Meredith's entrance, this time at the college board office in Jackson, and by refusing to accept a summons from the Fifth Circuit.[71] In a conversation with Robert Kennedy that day, Barnett

68. Sobel, *Civil Rights*, p. 114; Read and McGough, *Let Them Be Judged*, pp. 222–23; Brauer, *Kennedy*, pp. 181–82; "Judicial Performance," pp. 90–92.

69. Sobel, *Civil Rights*, pp. 113–16; Schlesinger, *Kennedy*, pp. 318–20; Lewis, *Portrait*, pp. 216–18.

70. Sobel, *Civil Rights*, p. 115.

71. Lewis, *Portrait*, p. 217; Sobel, *Civil Rights*, p. 115.

fumed that he would rather spend the rest of his life in the penitentiary than permit Meredith to enter Ole Miss.[72] Later that evening, the Justice Department obtained an order against Barnett from the Fifth Circuit requiring him to show cause why he should not be held in contempt. He was to appear in court three days later, on September 28.[73]

Meredith, escorted by Chief U.S. Marshal James P. McShane, made his third attempt to enter Ole Miss the following day. McShane, a former prize-fighter, doubled up his fist and tried to push through the group led by Lieutenant Governor Paul Johnson that was blocking the doorway. Later in the day the Fifth Circuit issued show-cause contempt orders against the lieutenant governor and sent a U.S. marshal in another attempt to issue its summons to Barnett at his Jackson office. The marshal, however, was blocked by state police.[74] After Meredith's fourth attempt to enter failed, events became more volatile. From Thursday, September 27, through Monday, October 1, everyone appeared to lose control of the situation.

On Friday, September 28, while Attorney General Kennedy met with the head of the joint chiefs of staff and the secretary of the army, the Fifth Circuit convened in New Orleans for the show-cause contempt hearing.[75] Barnett and Johnson refused to appear. Burke Marshall did attend, however, and was confronted by queries from several of the judges as to the intentions of the executive branch to enforce the court's orders. Marshall assured them that it would in fact enforce the court's rulings. The court then found Barnett guilty of contempt and ordered him to purge himself by discontinuing his own interference with Meredith's enrollment and by ordering Mississippi officials to end theirs, or face arrest and a $10,000 per day fine. The same decree applied to Johnson, with the fine reduced to $5,000 per day. Both officials were given until Tuesday, October 2, to comply.[76]

Until Saturday, September 29, President Kennedy had maintained a low profile on the Meredith issue. The president had had a series of conversations with Barnett, explaining that he did not know Meredith and had not enrolled him in the University but warning that he was going to carry out the court's orders and wanted Barnett's cooperation. At midnight on Saturday, Kennedy federalized Mississippi's national guard. On Sunday evening, September 30, the president appeared on national television to announce Meredith's arrival at the university.

James Meredith was ushered onto campus during the late afternoon by McShane and John Doar, while Nicholas deB. Katzenbach, deputy attorney general, supervised the area and about three hundred marshals. Minutes

72. Schlesinger, *Kennedy*, p. 319.
73. Brauer, *Kennedy*, pp. 184–85.
74. Navasky, *Kennedy*, p. 208; Lewis, *Portrait*, p. 217; Sobel *Civil Rights*, pp. 115–16.
75. Schlesinger, *Kennedy*, p. 320.
76. Read and McGough, *Let Them Be Judged*, pp. 234–36; Sobel, *Civil Rights*, pp. 121–22.

before the president's address a crowd of spectators of about one hundred that had increased to approximately two and a half thousand grew violent, and the tear gas discharged at Katzenbach's order was not enough to subdue it. Katzenbach began to call for troops that had been taken off alert status after the president's speech. By midnight, a full-fledged riot had broken out, with gunfire and reports of deaths. There was a crucial delay in deploying the military, and when they did arrive the situation was well beyond what they had expected. Katzenbach and the troops began opening crates of guns in the dark with a flashlight.[77]

By mid-morning (October 1), fifteen hours after the first incident, the campus returned to calm and Meredith was registered with the aid of 3,500 federal soldiers, a number that increased to 13,000 by the next day—twice the population of Oxford. On October 2, 1962, Meredith began classes for the fall semester, almost two years after his first application. The Justice and Defense departments, in early December, released estimates of the costs of enforcing the court-ordered entrance of Meredith. The combined estimate revealed that the executive branch had spent well over four million dollars to integrate Ole Miss.[78] In September 1963, James Meredith wrote to Attorney General Kennedy: "I am a graduate of the University of Mississippi. For this I am proud of my country—the United States of America."[79]

Although the legal battle had ended for Meredith, the judicial showdown between the Fifth Circuit and Governor Barnett and Lieutenant Governor Johnson had just begun. It raged for another year and a half, threatening the internal functioning of the court. The political fallout from the Meredith case, moreover, had repercussions for the court for the next twenty years. Charges against university officials were dropped the day that Meredith started class. The court refused to dismiss Barnett's and Johnson's contempt citations, despite the Justice Department's belief that the imposition of a $100,000 fine and an additional $10,000 per day until Barnett disavowed his statements of defiance would end the dispute. By the end of the year the Justice Department had made its position clear on the Barnett issue; the attorney general was not interested in pressing the matter through the courts.

The incensed Fifth Circuit judges, however, in November ordered the Justice Department to file criminal contempt charges against Barnett and Johnson for defying the court's orders. As requested, the Justice Department filed charges in New Orleans on December 21, 1962. The immediate legal proceedings surrounding Barnett's contempt culminated in an evenly and

77. Sobel, *Civil Rights*, pp. 111–24; Schlesinger, *Kennedy*, pp. 316–25; Navasky, *Kennedy*, pp. 208–34; Brauer, *Kennedy*, p. 194.

78. Sobel, *Civil Rights*, pp. 110–13, 118–21; Read and McGough, *Let Them Be Judged*, p. 255.

79. Schlesinger, *Kennedy*, p. 325.

bitterly divided court in the spring. With Judge Hutcheson absent for health reasons, the remaining eight judges, sitting en banc, divided four-to-four on the question of whether or not Barnett was entitled to a jury trial. Every judge wrote an opinion on the case. Four (Wisdom, Rives, Brown, Tuttle) contended that the Fifth Circuit's September 25 temporary restraining order had been defied, and therefore a jury trial was not in order. These judges, the four most liberal on civil rights issues, believed that Barnett would be acquitted if tried by a federal jury of Mississippi citizens. The other four (Gewin, Bell, Jones, Cameron) maintained that after Justice Black vacated the fourth stay, the status of the case reverted back to District Judge Mize's September 13 injunction, which had been remanded upon the orders of Judge Wisdom in the June 25 decision. Under this status, Barnett statutorily would be entitled to a jury trial. Cameron also rumbled in his dissent that the judges comprising the panels in the Meredith proceedings had been drawn disproportionately from the liberal ranks.[80] Cameron's expressed discontent over panel assignments was the second in his series of unconventional behavior displays.

Because of the impasse the Fifth Circuit made the unusual (and for them unprecedented) move of certifying the Barnett jury-trial issue to the U.S. Supreme Court, a means of asking for its legal advice on the case. Almost a year later to the day, and three days after Judge Cameron's death, the Supreme Court also rendered a divided (5–4) decision against Barnett's right to a jury trial.[81] The High Court, however, cautioned the Fifth Circuit in a footnote that any serious penalty (by implication, confinement) would require a jury trial. Ironically, the more liberal justices (Warren, Black, Douglas, Goldberg) disagreed with their usual compatriots on the Fifth Circuit. Finally, in the summer of 1965, the Fifth Circuit dismissed the charges against Barnett in a four-to-three decision (at the time there were only seven members on the court). Although Wisdom, Brown, and Tuttle dissented, Rives decided that the Fifth Circuit had to be free of the divisive matter and voted with Gewin, Bell, and Jones to dismiss the charges. The per curiam opinion noted that a majority of the court would not grant a jury trial and that it was doubtful that the defendants could receive a fair hearing because of the sentiment toward their guilt.[82]

MOMENTUM BUILDS

On the heels of the Meredith affair, civil rights events took yet another turn. A wave of demonstrations spread throughout the southern states while federal officials were still reeling from the events of the previous months. The Kennedy administration had yet to recover from the episode in Mississippi, which had rekindled thoughts of Little Rock; the necessity of deploying fed-

80. Sobel, *Civil Rights*, p. 122; Read and McGough, *Let Them Be Judged*, pp. 257–65.
81. 376 U.S. 681 (1963).
82. Read and McGough, *Let Them Be Judged*, pp. 254–65.

eral troops in domestic actions had sparked feelings of failure. Whether spontaneous or strategic, the nationwide demonstrations throughout the spring and summer of 1963 significantly aided the movement's momentum.

Throughout April, May, and June the nation witnessed one violent scene after another in the South—particularly in Birmingham, Alabama. Most of these incidents were the consequences of plans initiated in December 1962 by Dr. King and his chief strategists. The leaders were gravely concerned about the complete lack of progress in school desegregation.[83] Almost ten years had elapsed since the Supreme Court's *Brown* decision, yet over 90 percent of southern schools were still operating on a segregated basis. Of the states in the Fifth Circuit, neither Alabama nor Mississippi had any desegregated school districts; Georgia and Louisiana each had desegregated only one. Only Florida and Texas had over 10 percent of their school districts desegregated, and even so, fewer than 1 percent of Florida's black children attended the desegregated schools; the respective figure for Texas was 2 percent.[84] Above all, civil rights leaders were concerned that "the impetus provided by the direct-action programs of the early 1960s was being lost."[85]

To broaden the scope of conflict, Dr. King defiantly focused on Birmingham, the reasons for which strategem he later described in his letter from his jail cell there: "Birmingham is probably the most thoroughly segregated city in the United States. Its ugly record of police brutality is known in every section of this country. . . . We can never forget that everything Hitler did in Germany was legal. . . . But I am sure that, if I had lived in Germany during that time, I would have aided and comforted my Jewish brothers even though it was illegal."[86]

Justice officials protested that the Birmingham campaign was ill-timed, unwise, and posed difficulties in the Barnett case: Justice would be placed in the untenable position of defending King's defiance of a state court injunction while reluctantly pressing criminal contempt charges against Barnett for defying a federal injunction. Also, Justice officials cautioned King that he was confronting one of the most difficult of all segregationists, Police Commissioner Eugene "Bull" Connor.[87]

Despite the Justice Department's admonitions, protests and demonstrations began in early April, highlighted by King's infamous Good Friday march, which resulted in his arrest and detainment in the Birmingham jail for defying the state court injunction, and by subsequent "kneel-ins" throughout Easter weekend. The situation turned ugly in early May, when Bull Connor and his

83. Westin and Mahoney, *The Trial*, pp. 47–48, 59–61.

84. Commission on Civil Rights, *Civil Rights* (Washington, D.C.: U.S. Government Printing Office, 1963), pp. 64–65.

85. Westin and Mahoney, *The Trial*, p. 47.

86. *A Letter from Birmingham Jail*, quoted in Westin and Mahoney, *The Trial*, pp. 131, 135.

87. Westin and Mahoney, *The Trial*, pp. 60–61, 86–87.

police force turned powerful fire hoses and vicious police dogs on thousands of black elementary and secondary schoolchildren who had joined King in protesting the operation of Birmingham's segregated schools. The media captured these events in pictures of blacks—many of them youths—being clubbed, attacked by fierce dogs, and knocked down by the pressure from the hoses. The photographs had worldwide circulation. These incidents precipitated intervention from Justice Department officials, who were able to allay the situation through skillful negotiations between the white business community and civil rights leaders. The Birmingham board of education's announcement that more than a thousand black schoolchildren who participated in the march would be expelled, however, required Fifth Circuit involvement in late May. The resulting *Armstrong* case led directly to Judge Cameron's final and most vehement attack on his brethren.[88]

The summer, however, ended on a more uplifting note for the civil rights movement when Dr. King led the most famous of all his marches and gave his historic "I Have a Dream" speech. On August 28, 1963, a quarter of a million people gathered outside the Washington Monument while thirteen civil rights leaders met with members of Congress. Then, in an orderly manner, they proceeded to the Lincoln Memorial where seventy-five members of Congress joined them. After King's speech some of the leaders met with the president, who praised their behavior.[89] The movement thus demonstrated the degree of public support it had and both literally and symbolically left its request on the doorstep of the Capitol.

No single episode, from the Freedom Rides to the March on Washington, evoked graver institutional reactions than the repeated confrontations, violence, and intransigent official behavior in the South that occurred from September 1962 to June 1963. A comprehensive response from the president on civil rights came two and one half years after his inauguration, when Kennedy proposed a civil rights package to Congress that essentially passed intact as the Civil Rights Act of 1964.

Throughout this period the Justice Department played a critical role. Few government officials responded as frequently and directly as Robert Kennedy, along with his staff and the entire Civil Rights Division. Scholars have noted that the Justice Department during this period consisted of one of the brightest groups of young individuals ever to serve in government.[90] It reacted on many fronts and always operated on the "negotiation first" principle. Former Deputy Attorney General Katzenbach recalled that the department's negotiation principle started with the proposition that, although law and judicial process could aid in curing the ills of racial discrimination, there was no

88. Ibid., pp. 141–50; Navasky, *Kennedy*, pp. 208–18; Schlesinger, *Kennedy*, pp. 328–29; Sobel, *Civil Rights*, pp. 179–86.

89. Sobel, *Civil Rights*, pp. 170–73.

90. Brauer, *Kennedy*, p. 93; Navasky, *Kennedy*, pp. 322–23.

substitute for the people and the states solving the problem. This was a "responsible" position for which no one ever gave "credit" to Robert Kennedy, he explained.[91]

Some of the Justice Department's more successful and important negotiations occurred behind the scenes with members of the other branches of government. Justice officials conducted a substantial amount of business with Congress during this period. Officially, they often testified on pending legislation. Marshall and Katzenbach spent especially long hours in the spring of 1963 drafting the administration's civil rights proposal and then entering into lengthy negotiations with congressional leaders to mobilize support. In this context the Justice Department, primarily through Katzenbach, played an especially ameliorative role throughout the civil rights crises by its ability to "do business" with Senator James Eastland. Eastland was civil rights' greatest stumbling block in Congress, because it was through his judiciary committee that any civil rights legislation had to pass—and none did.[92]

Eastland derived power from having served as a senator from Mississippi for twenty years by 1963, a total that reached thirty-six before his retirement in 1979. The Senate's seniority norm placed him in charge of the Senate Judiciary Committee in 1956. He quite often combined this powerful position with those of his fellow southerners in similar positions to block legislation. In every sense, Eastland was a true product of the Mississippi Delta from which he hailed, a region of rich farmland, huge plantations, and black sharecroppers. His Sunflower County home, owned by his family for three generations, was a 5,800-acre cotton plantation staffed by black tenant farmers. As one of the first organizers of the White Citizens Council, his stance on civil rights was etched in stone. He quite often spoke publicly in very abrasive rhetoric about communists and civil rights activists. According to one account, Lyndon Johnson once described Eastland in this way: "Jim Eastland could be standing right in the middle of the worst Mississippi flood ever known, and he'd say the niggers caused it, helped out by the Communists—but, he'd say, we gotta have help from Washington."[93]

Although Eastland rarely fared well in comparison with Mississippi's more reserved junior senator, John Stennis, his manner was said to have struck an oddly likable note with Robert Kennedy, who had an "Irish weakness for rogues."[94] Katzenbach also got along very well with Eastland because he found the senator to be honest and straightforward: "He never, never misled me about anything." But neither did the deputy attorney general try to persuade Eastland to change his mind; they understood each other's positions. Having

91. Interview with Nicholas deB.Katzenbach, May 8, 1985.
92. Navasky, *Kennedy*, p. 195; Schlesinger, *Kennedy*, pp. 348–50; Brauer, *Kennedy*, pp. 280–83.
93. Schlesinger, *Kennedy*, p. 234.
94. Ibid.

worked with him for many hours on such matters, Katzenbach developed the perspective that Eastland "did what you did if you were a senator from Mississippi," and that he cared more for his duties on the Agriculture and Forestry Committee than for civil rights, which was more of a "political or constituency matter."[95] This mutual understanding between Justice officials and Eastland kept open a critical line of communication during various crisis situations in Mississippi. The attorney general tolerated Eastland's public statements and delaying actions for constituency consumption, but Justice officials expected an honest evaluation in private meetings and conversations. From 1961 to 1963, Mississippi was rarely out of public scrutiny, a condition that was wearing down any patience Eastland may have had.

EFFECTS ON THE FIFTH CIRCUIT

Of all the institutions involved, the Fifth Circuit sustained the heaviest blow from the civil rights battles fought between 1961 and 1963. Internally, the court was deeply divided. The four liberal activists (Tuttle, Rives, Brown, and Wisdom) were not about to concede anything to public opinion, the white citizens councils, recalcitrant district judges, or even the more conservative members of their own court. Tuttle often resorted to extraordinary procedural maneuvers to insure that the Supreme Court's *Brown* mandate was diligently enforced. The less activist members of the Fifth Circuit frequently chafed under these tactics, and none more so than Judge Ben Cameron, who saw the ways of the Old South dying at the hands of liberal federal court rulings.

Cameron was unwilling to let the situation continue unchallenged. He had already taken vigorous exception to Tuttle's three-judge district court assignments in the aftermath of the Freedom Riders cases during the summer of 1961. Cameron's continued surveillance of Tuttle's and Brown's assignments confirmed his belief that they were stacking the panels that reviewed civil rights cases, especially those arising in Mississippi. Since there had been no change in the court's panel assignment patterns, Cameron once again sharply questioned the way in which the circuit was being administered.

This time Cameron's attack on Tuttle's leadership came in the form of an internal letter addressed to the entire court membership in November 1962.[96] Cameron's letter first reviewed the initial charges he had made against Tuttle's Mississippi court assignments in the summer of 1961 and then cited five additional three-judge district court cases that had occurred since his original objections had been filed. All five were Mississippi cases, and four centered

95. Katzenbach interview.

96. Letter from Judge Ben F. Cameron to Chief Judge Elbert P. Tuttle and Judges Joseph C. Hutcheson, Jr., Richard T. Rives, Warren L. Jones, John R. Brown, John Minor Wisdom, Walter P. Gewin, and Griffin B. Bell, November 23, 1962.

on civil rights issues. In each case Tuttle had failed to appoint Cameron to the panel, instead assigning two members of the court's liberal bloc to sit with a single Mississippi district judge.

According to Cameron's analysis, in the preceding eighteen years there had been only one case in which a majority of the judges in a three-judge district court case had not been residents of the state in which the case was filed. Cameron further charged that an additional six civil rights cases heard by Fifth Circuit panels from 1961 to November 1962, including *United States v. Wood* and *Meredith v. Fair*, were decided by panels dominated by a majority of "dedicated integrationist" judges. Cameron, Mississippi's only circuit judge, had not been appointed to any of these cases. The imputation of this stinging attack was clear: Chief Judge Tuttle was using his appointment powers over three-judge district court cases to stack panels in order to insure a victory for civil rights proponents. John Brown, Tuttle's panel assignment judge, was following the same policy in appointing judges to court of appeals panels hearing civil rights cases. So Cameron was being selectively eliminated from participating in any race relations cases originating in his home state, an improper and unprecedented slight, in his view.

Tuttle defended the way in which he was exercising the office of chief judge in a seven-page letter sent to all members of the court.[97] He justified his continual refusal to appoint Cameron in race relations cases in two ways. First, he cited concern over Cameron's health, reminding the court that Cameron's heart condition had forced him to request a reduced caseload. Tuttle considered such a health-related request legitimate and expressed the view that it was inappropriate to assign the Mississippian to the extra burden of hearing demanding three-judge district court civil rights cases, given his medical condition and his opinion-writing backlog.

Tuttle's second reason for bypassing Cameron was more to the point. He asked the other members of the court to reread Cameron's dissent in the case of *Boman v. Birmingham Transit*, in which he had stated: "It is the universal conviction of the people of the conquered provinces also that the judges who function in this circuit should render justice in individual cases against a background of, and as interpreters of, the ethos of the people whose servants they are."[98] Tuttle stated that, although this pronouncement was Cameron's earnest attempt to articulate his view of the proper decision-making role of the southern courts, he found the posture unacceptable because it served only as "an open invitation to all of the district courts in the Circuit to ignore and circumvent the decisions of the United States Supreme Court on racial matters." Tuttle considered Cameron's philosophy to have a "legitimate and

97. Letter from Chief Judge Elbert P. Tuttle to Judges Joseph C. Hutcheson, Jr., Richard T. Rives, Ben F. Cameron, Warren L. Jones, John R. Brown, John Minor Wisdom, Walter P. Gewin, and Griffin B. Bell, November 28, 1962.

98. *Boman v. Birmingham Transit Co.*, 292 F.2d 4 (1961).

proper bearing on the basis on which I determine what judges are to be assigned to special three-judge courts."

According to Tuttle, the accusation of judge-stacking in regular court of appeals panels was misplaced. Though he did not deny that at least two of "the four" liberals were assigned to each Mississippi civil rights case, he asserted that this was largely due to special circumstances facing the court. Of its nine members, two (Cameron and Hutcheson) were in ill health and unavailable for full-time duty. Two others (Bell and Gewin) had been serving under recess appointments. Tuttle wrote: "I considered it entirely appropriate not to assign any civil rights cases to a panel on which they were sitting. I may have been wrong in this attitude, but I felt that they were entitled to be confirmed in their positions and hold life tenure before they were called upon to participate in any such actions by the Court." This left Tuttle with five judges fully available for duty. Of the five, only Warren Jones was not a member of the four-judge liberal bloc. Consequently, it should not be surprising that at least two of the activists were appointed to each Mississippi civil rights case heard.

Throughout his correspondence, Tuttle expressed dismay over Cameron's attitudes toward the liberal members of the court. His letter reflected personal disappointment over Cameron's expressed disdain for the acclaim awarded the activist judges by the national media and at his public dissents, which criticized the opinions of civil rights liberals as "blind and witless," "intemperate," and "ill-considered." Tuttle emphasized that, contrary to Cameron's claims, he was not a "dedicated integrationist" but only a dedicated judge. In the end, Tuttle was certainly not willing to apologize for the way in which he exercised the powers of his office; nor did he express any intention to alter his policies. He concluded by repeating a passage from his June 30, 1961, letter to Cameron: " 'I simply handled it in the way I thought was best under the circumstances.' I know of no other way to do it."

In late May 1963, Cameron and his colleague Walter Gewin of Alabama became irate over Tuttle's direct issuance of yet another preliminary injunction. This time the chief judge's actions prohibited suspension of more than a thousand black high school students who had participated in the spring Birmingham demonstrations. When District Judge Clarence Allgood (Northern District of Alabama) refused to issue an injunction to prevent expulsion, Judge Tuttle heard the students' appeal as an emergency request and issued the injunction himself. This provoked Cameron and Gewin to challenge Tuttle's methods of expedited procedures at a May 29 circuit council meeting. Cameron and Gewin were joined by Judges Jones and Bell. These four conservative, restraint-oriented judges were philosophically opposed to the use of the activist and extraordinary procedures that Tuttle was invoking with increasing frequency. Bell and Gewin were further upset by Tuttle's admission that without their knowledge they had been excluded from hearing civil rights cases during the period in which they served as recess appointees.

Judge Tuttle's actions were supported against these charges by three of his brethren—Judges Wisdom, Rives, and Brown—whose judicial positions on civil rights issues were in accord with his. Considered a "hard-core" group of pro–civil rights jurists, the four created a four-to-four deadlock at the council meeting, leaving the charges unresolved. The ninth member who could have broken the impasse (Judge Hutcheson) was not in attendance because of ill health.

Cameron's dissatisfaction with the unresolved issue was heightened in July, when a panel of Tuttle, Rives, and Gewin decided (2–1) to issue a preliminary injunction (previously refused by Seybourne Lynne, chief judge of the Northern District of Alabama) that ordered Birmingham to cease operating its officially segregated school system. It was this judicial action that had prompted the schoolchildren's protests and threat of expulsion. When the Fifth Circuit subsequently refused on July 22, by a five-to-four vote, to hold a rehearing en banc on *Armstrong v. Board of Education of the City of Birmingham, Alabama*,[99] Judge Cameron issued a dissent which was a blistering attack on Chief Judge Tuttle, claiming that for two years Tuttle had assigned some combination of "the Four" (Tuttle, Wisdom, Brown, Rives) as a majority in civil rights case panels. Angered over his exclusion from three-judge district court cases arising in Mississippi, Cameron wrote: "The idea that the Chief Judge may thus gerrymander the United States Judges of a State in order to accomplish a desired result is, I think, entirely foreign to any just concept of the proper functioning of the judicial process." Cameron further emphasized that the court had not vested in any one judge, including the chief judge, authority to assign judges or cases.[100]

Cameron's public outburst obviously erupted from his accumulated frustration of two years of unsuccessful internal attempts to convince Tuttle to alter his court assignment policies. Now that Cameron had gone public so dramatically, the issue could no longer be contained. A major confrontation was inevitable.

When the other Fifth Circuit judges became aware of Cameron's case-by-case list of what he maintained were violations of the court's assignment process, they too were irate. Bell warned the clerk that there would be "deep trouble" if he discovered any irregularities in case assignments that violated court procedures. Jones took immediate action and sought the Fifth Circuit files. As Tuttle was out-of-town, the clerk refused to release them until Jones obtained permission from former Chief Judge Rives, still an active member of the court. Rives rescinded his release of the files upon examining the problematic information they contained. But when Jones issued a threat to call Senator Eastland about the matter, the files were produced.[101]

99. 323 F.2d. 333 (1963).
100. *Armstrong*, 323 F.2d at 359 and 357.
101. Read and McGough, *Let Them Be Judged*, p. 269.

Two days after Judge Cameron issued his assault on Chief Judge Tuttle, Senator Eastland ordered a Senate "staff study" to investigate the panel-stacking charges. Three-inch headlines streamed across the *Houston Chronicle* on August 2, reading, "SENATOR TO SEE IF COURT STACKED IN INTEGRATION CASES.[102] In Eastland's press statement revealing his intent to investigate Cameron's charges that Tuttle was "loading" the panels, he stated:

> The stark, naked reality of the charge of Judge Cameron is that the citizens of Texas, Louisiana, Mississippi, Alabama, Georgia and Florida have not and are not receiving fair trials in the courts of the United States.... The dissent covers a spectrum of manipulations by Chief Judge Tuttle to prevent judges who might entertain a different view to the proper application of the Constitution and statutes of the United States from having an opportunity to participate in this character of cases. The import of the Cameron charges is that rules of the court over which Congress has jurisdiction have been abused by the chief judge of the 5th Circuit in order to circumvent due process and arrive at manipulated decisions. The gravity of these charges needs no comment.[103]

In a final warning statement Eastland contended that, although the Senate could not initiate action against a federal judge, it did have control over the Fifth Circuit's rules and mechanisms.

Although Cameron's dissent drew congressional attention to the Fifth Circuit by prompting Senator Eastland's threat, the investigation was never conducted. Instead, a historic two-day meeting (August 22–23) of the Fifth was held in Judge Tuttle's Houston chambers to resolve the charges. When the judges assembled, the ailing Cameron was the only member missing but was contacted by telephone during the deliberations.

At the emergency meeting in Houston, the status of Judges Bell and Gewin became one of the central issues. The clerk of the court's files revealed that Chief Judge Tuttle had indeed requested that the assignment judge, John Brown, not place civil rights cases on Gewin's and Bell's calendars. Tuttle, however, once again said that he believed it best to wait until the two recess appointees were formally confirmed by the Senate before assigning them to such controversial and significant cases in the event that the decisions might be challenged. At this point, however, what aroused the ire of Bell and Gewin was learning that after their confirmations Brown had failed to relay to the court's clerk another Tuttle message lifting this restriction. As a consequence, they had been assigned to only a fraction of civil rights cases from June 1961 to June 1963. At the conference, Bell expressed just how disappointed and insulted he was to learn that Gewin and he had been treated as less than full-fledged members of the court. Judge Jones, who had initially requested the

102. Sidney Friedman, "Jurist Says Every Case Loaded," *Houston Chronicle*, August 2, 1963, pp. 1, 20.
103. "Eastland Calls for Probe of Federal Court," *New Orleans States-Item*, August 2, 1963.

clerk's files, reportedly was so incensed by their contents that he threw them onto the floor and challenged the integrity of the liberal activist judges.[104]

The judges adjourned the Houston conference after having reached administrative decisions that were to have long-term consequences for their internal judicial process. The judges eventually agreed that the chief judge be permitted to continue delegating the panel assignment responsibility to Judge Brown but restricted communication among Tuttle, Brown, and the court's clerk. In effect, the clerk would have no knowledge of panel composition until after cases had been calendared for each sitting. Also, a consensus was reached which prohibited a judge from requesting that he not sit with another member of the court. Finally, an interim panel was established to hear the kind of emergency matters that had prompted the dissent. At the conclusion of the meeting, the court issued the following brief, unanimous press statement: "The problems alleged to exist in this Court have been considered by the Court. The Court believes that in no given case has there been a conscious assignment for the purpose of accomplishing a desired result. Action has been taken to avoid any appearance of inconsistency in the assignment of judges or the arrangement of the docket."[105] As Cameron indicated to Eastland that he was satisfied with the results of the Houston conference, Eastland abandoned his threatened investigation.[106]

Following the meeting, Judge Wisdom stepped down from his assignment on the three-judge district court, comprised of Fifth Circuit Judge Brown and District Judge Cox, that was scheduled to hear challenges on the constitutionality of Mississippi's election laws. Wisdom was replaced by Judge Cameron, who subsequently wrote the opinion in the two-to-one decision (Judge Brown dissenting) denying the claim of voter discrimination.[107]

Judge Wisdom later expressed the opinion that Cameron's charges with respect to the three-judge district courts in Mississippi were probably accurate, but not with respect to panels of Fifth Circuit judges. He was quick to defend Tuttle, however, by explaining that the chief judge had been forced to stack the panels to ensure a fair trial in accordance with the Constitution: assigning two Mississippi district judges and Ben Cameron to a civil rights case would be the equivalent of deciding it for the defense.[108]

These tumultuous years created a divisive political environment and contentious attitudes about civil rights issues among key policymakers. In a fundamental way, this period shaped the manner and even the direction of intra- and intergovernmental relationships among the major decision makers on

104. Read and McGough, *Let Them Be Judged*, pp. 270–80; Bass, *Unlikely Heroes*, pp. 235–47.

105. Minutes of the Houston meeting of the Judicial Council of the Court of Appeals for the Fifth Circuit, August 23, 1963.

106. Read and McGough, *Let Them Be Judged*, p. 278.

107. *United States v. Mississippi*, 229 F.Supp 925 (1964).

108. Wisdom interview, May 28, 1985.

civil rights for years to come. It was in this political climate that the Civil Rights Act of 1964 was introduced in Congress on behalf of the Kennedy administration. Moreover, these were the conditions under which the geographical split of the Fifth Circuit was proposed. Three weeks after the Houston meeting, Chief Judge Tuttle made his court's request for more judges without a split of the circuit. Both Tuttle and the conference knew, based on these events, that this proposal was quite possibly unrealistic. And so the conference set out, through the Biggs Committee, to see if a consensus could be reached, at least within the federal judiciary, on the issue of dividing the court.

3

The Battle
Is Joined

The issue of circuit division merely simmered among the members of the Fifth Circuit Court of Appeals during the fall of 1963. Keeping pace with the court's caseload was sufficiently taxing to command the full attention of the judges. The deteriorating health of Joseph Hutcheson and Ben Cameron and the lack of senior-status judges to help shoulder the burden made matters even more difficult.[1] Routine litigation continued to pour into the clerk's office at record rates, civil rights appeals were growing in number and complexity, and the court was still trying to put itself back together in the aftermath of the Houston conference. The Biggs Committee was scheduled to meet in January, and the judges appeared content to let it conduct a full study of the Fifth Circuit's problems. The tragic news of John Kennedy's assassination further deflected their attention; the impending possibility of circuit division seemed insignificant in comparison to the nation's grief. Yet the problems facing the court were not about to disappear.

On December 2, 1963, Chief Judge Tuttle wrote to the members of the court about three major points. First, he carefully explained that case filings for the fall months were growing at least as fast as earlier projections had anticipated. Second, he informed them that the Biggs Committee was scheduled to meet during the first week of January and encouraged any member

1. Since 1919, federal judges who qualify for retirement have been able to take "senior status" (40 Stat. 1156). This allows the judge to receive full retirement benefits while continuing to serve as a federal jurist on a part-time basis. The retiring judge's vacancy is filled by a new appointee. A judge who moves from "active" to "senior" status may accept, with the court's approval, any size workload he or she desires. Senior judges normally do not sit on en banc sessions and are not members of the circuit council. Some choose to give up the judicial function altogether whereas others assume caseloads similar to those carried by their colleagues in active service. Courts of appeals that have contributing senior judges enjoy a welcome source of judge power to complement the authorized number of judges in active service.

of the court to express his individual views either to himself or to John Biggs directly. Finally, and most importantly, the chief judge again stated his understanding of the mandate the Fifth Circuit Council had given him: to express to the committee the urgent need for additional judges and the hope that an increase in judge power could be obtained without dividing the circuit. If the latter course was not acceptable, the court still needed the additional judges, regardless of how this was to be accomplished.[2] "I have, of course," Tuttle wrote, "expressed the deep emotional attachment we all have for the Fifth Circuit as now constituted and have expressed the hope that our problem can be solved without dividing the circuit."[3] Tuttle later recalled that he received only one response to his letter encouraging the judges to register their individual views.[4] It came from Griffin Bell, who reiterated his position that more judges were desperately needed and that the most pragmatic way to obtain them was through a division of the circuit.

The quiet atmosphere that surrounded the realignment issue as 1963 drew to a close was, in retrospect, the calm before the gale. Although the judges had no reason to predict it, 1964 was to be a year in which the court was drawn into intense political controversy. The particular personalities and political rivalries activated in the battle over the Biggs Committee recommendations permanently shaped the contours of the realignment debate.

THE BIGGS COMMITTEE: DIVIDE AT THE RIVER

The Biggs Committee convened in Washington on January 7, 1964. In addition to the committee members, four key officials of the Administrative Office of the United States Courts and Chief Judge Richard Chambers of the Ninth Circuit were present. The administrative office personnel were armed with statistical and technical information collected for the committee's use, and Judge Chambers appeared to press his court's opposition to any plan that would divide the Ninth Circuit.

Of the three issues on the committee's agenda, two were handled with dispatch. First, the committee concluded, at Judge Chambers's urging, that the Judicial Conference of the United States should oppose passage of S. 1876, the legislation that would have carved a new Pacific Northwest circuit out of the Ninth.[5] Although the Ninth Circuit had a growing caseload and covered a large geographical area, it was coping with its problems relatively well, and circuit splitting did not seem to offer a means of improving the administration of justice.

2. Interview with Judge Elbert P. Tuttle, Atlanta, Georgia, October 20, 1982.
3. Letter from Chief Judge Elbert P. Tuttle to all Circuit Judges of the Fifth Circuit, December 2, 1963.
4. Letter from Chief Judge Elbert P. Tuttle to Judges Joseph C. Hutcheson, Jr., Richard T. Rives, John R. Brown, and John Minor Wisdom, March 25, 1964.
5. *Report of the Special Committee on the Geographical Organization of the Courts*, 1964.

Second, the committee overwhelmingly adopted a resolution that nine judges be considered the maximum recommended number for any federal appellate court. It was the consensus of the members that any more than that would impair the efficiency of the court's operations and, furthermore, a larger court would begin to lose its unity as a judicial institution.[6] Clearly, John Biggs and the other "Rule of Nine" advocates had dominated the committee's deliberations on the issue.

The questions facing the Fifth Circuit commanded most of the committee's attention. Statistics supplied by the administrative office only verified what Tuttle had been arguing for months. The Fifth Circuit Court of Appeals was badly understaffed for its caseload, and those docket demands were only going to increase at a more rapid rate in the future. Caseload data were so compelling that the special committee agreed with the view of Chief Judge Harvey Johnsen (who chaired the Judicial Statistics Committee) that the circuit needed an even greater enlargement than the four additional positions recommended by the Circuit Council and the Conference's Court Administration Committee. The Biggs Committee concluded with Johnsen that fifteen judges were required to meet the needs of the six Southern states.

The solution of circuit division, of course, had become the product of a logical syllogism. If nine was the maximum number of judges recommended for any court, and the Fifth Circuit required fifteen to cope with its appellate business, then the circuit would have to be divided. In the face of this inescapable conclusion, the committee members turned their attention to ways of reshaping the boundaries of the circuit so that the needed judgeships could be added without either of the resulting circuits' exceeding the nine-judge maximum. Although a number of alternatives were suggested, including moving Texas into the adjacent Tenth or Eighth circuits, the most parsimonious method was simply to divide the Fifth Circuit in two. This would solve the problem without directly affecting any other existing circuit.

A split of the Fifth Circuit into eastern and western halves appealed to the committee as the most logical and efficient move. The only question remaining was where to draw the line and, more specifically, what to do with the state of Mississippi, which contributed the smallest number of appeals to the Fifth Circuit—only forty-three cases in 1962 and seventy-eight in 1963—and had one judge informally allocated to it. The circuit that absorbed Mississippi would be gaining judge power in excess of caseload contribution, but this administrative advantage would be offset by that state's continuing and troublesome civil rights problems.

The Biggs Committee advised that Mississippi be placed in a circuit with her sister states to the east. The committee report made special notice of this action by saying: "This seems to be a natural territorial division in view of the fact that it [Mississippi] lies east of the Mississippi River. The natural and

6. Ibid.

inherent interests, including transportation facilities and communications, seem to indicate that the State of Mississippi should be in a circuit east of the river."[7]

The final recommendation of the Biggs Committee was to add six judgeships to the Deep South and split the Fifth Circuit into two parts at the Mississippi River. The resulting two circuits would contain the following geographical and judicial alignments:

The New Fifth Circuit
    States: Alabama, Florida, Georgia, Mississippi
    Judges:
    Elbert P. Tuttle, Georgia, Chief Judge
    Richard T. Rives, Alabama
    Ben F. Cameron, Mississippi
    Warren L. Jones, Florida
    Walter P. Gewin, Alabama
    Griffin B. Bell, Georgia
    Two new judges

The New Eleventh Circuit
    States: Louisiana, Texas, Canal Zone
    Judges:
    John R. Brown, Texas, Chief Judge
    Joseph C. Hutcheson, Jr., Texas
    John Minor Wisdom, Louisiana
    Four new judges

In this geographical configuration, Judges Rives's and Wisdom's worst fears were realized. At that time, to divide east and west of the Mississippi River meant that the Fifth Circuit's four staunch pro–civil rights jurists (Wisdom, Rives, Brown, and Tuttle) would be separated. Any influence the four wielded as a subgroup on the court would thus be substantially undermined. Equally significant, Mississippi's civil rights cases henceforth would be filed in the new eastern circuit (Mississippi, Alabama, Georgia, Florida), which would have a distinctly more conservative orientation. Although it would include liberals Tuttle and Rives, they would be joined by Ben Cameron, Warren Jones, Walter Gewin, and Griffin Bell, who formed the bloc in opposition to Wisdom, Rives, Brown, and Tuttle deadlocking the court's decision in the Barnett contempt trial case. Also, under the Biggs plan the proposed eastern circuit was scheduled to receive two additional judgeships. As Florida and Mississippi each had only one judge, those two states would probably be the beneficiaries of those additions. And considering Eastland's substantial influence over the judicial nomination process in the Senate and his virtual control over his own state's

7. Ibid.

judicial appointees, the new additions would most likely enhance that court's conservative bent.

Further underscoring the conservative bent of the proposed eastern circuit was the impending change in the court's leadership. Elbert Tuttle, who would continue as chief judge in this circuit, would be forced by law to give up his leadership post in three years. When he stepped down in 1967, his successor would be Walter Gewin of Alabama, who possibly could serve as chief until 1978. Gewin had been on the court only two years, but his civil rights stance was closer to Cameron's than that of any other judge then serving on the Fifth Circuit. By the time the split of the circuit was implemented, Tuttle in all probability would have served his entire term as chief judge, thus insuring Gewin's immediate leadership of the new court. Another factor increasing the conservative slant of the proposed eastern circuit was Judge Rives's prospective retirement. While Tuttle was three years from eligibility for retirement, Rives, at sixty-nine, was only one year away from possible senior status. Replacements for Rives and Tuttle could hardly be more liberal than their predecessors.

On the western side of the Mississippi River, with a bench of seven, Judge Brown would take up the leadership reins and could hold them for sixteen years. A combination of Brown's administrative abilities and Wisdom's scholarly power would set the tone for liberal leadership on the western court. Although this circuit would need four new judges and undoubtedly a replacement for the ailing Judge Hutcheson, these personnel changes were not likely to dictate a conservative direction. Because of its size and contribution to the caseload, Texas was entitled to most of the new appointees. President Johnson would most likely claim special latitude in selecting judges from his home state, who would undoubtedly be moderate-to-liberal in political orientation.[8] In sum, the western judges would probably continue the liberal civil rights rulings of the parent court. On the other hand, the new circuit's impact would be lessened considerably, as its geographical jurisdiction would cover only two states. Also, drawing boundary lines to create a circuit of only two states was unprecedented in the history of the courts of appeals.

---

8. This assumption about President Johnson's appointment policies was borne out by subsequent judicial voting behavior research. Johnson's appointees to the courts of appeals rendered decisions favorable to the civil rights claim at a higher rate than judges appointed by Presidents Kennedy, Nixon, and Ford. Only Jimmy Carter–appointed circuit judges have exhibited civil rights support scores as high as Johnson's appointees. These differences also hold for district judges. For a more detailed discussion, see Jon Gottschall, "Carter's Judicial Appointments: The Influence of Affirmative Action and Merit Selection on Voting on the U.S. Courts of Appeals," *Judicature* 67 (October 1983): 164–73; Robert A. Carp and C. K. Rowland, *Policymaking and Politics in the Federal District Courts* (Knoxville: University of Tennessee Press, 1983); Neil D. McFeeley, *Appointment of Judges: The Johnson Presidency* (Austin: University of Texas Press, 1987).

As a member of the Biggs Committee, Chief Judge Tuttle found himself in an unenviable—and untenable—position. If he supported the committee's recommendation, he would place himself in direct opposition to his two closest colleagues, Rives and Wisdom. As a consistent member of the court's liberal voting bloc, Tuttle found Rives's and Wisdom's arguments against splitting persuasive. He knew that progress in civil rights policy depended on the continuing existence of an activist circuit court. Tuttle also understood the price that civil rights litigants would have to pay if left subject to recalcitrant district judges, especially those in Mississippi, without constant supervision from the appellate courts. Yet the spiraling caseload and the majority of the court were demanding additional judges. So, hoping that his two judicial brothers would understand, Tuttle reluctantly joined the Biggs Committee recommendation.

Following the announcement of the committee's decision, Elbert Tuttle explained to Wisdom and Rives why he had felt compelled to support the recommendation. As chief judge, Tuttle told them, his duty was to follow the Circuit Council's mandate to obtain additional judges however that could be accomplished. He further emphasized that when the special committee made clear its overwhelming opposition to increasing the court beyond nine judges without a split, he was forced to support its decision in order to get the needed help. This position, Tuttle concluded, he intended to maintain at the Judicial Conference's March meeting.

What Elbert Tuttle was not at liberty to discuss with Rives and Wisdom at the time was the latent threat lurking behind his decision. From the time the Biggs Committee was established until it rendered a decision, Tuttle had become increasingly concerned that the court was heading toward a clash with Mississippi's senior senator, James O. Eastland. Such a confrontation could jeopardize gaining the desperately needed additional judicial help. Tuttle's apprehensions grew substantially during the fall of 1963 when he received a message from Eastland relayed by Judge Warren Jones. The content of that message was clear and direct: "the only way additional judges would be obtained for the six southern states was if the circuit were divided along the lines of east and west of the Mississippi River."[9] As Tuttle later explained to the opponents of division, when he learned that Eastland's stance was firm— no split, no judges—he accepted this as a major political obstacle. And, to avoid flying in the face of a seemingly unsurmountable political reality, he succumbed to Eastland's ultimatum.

9. Letter from Chief Judge Elbert P. Tuttle to Judges Joseph C. Hutcheson, Jr., Richard T. Rives, John R. Brown, and John Minor Wisdom, March 25, 1964. The Eastland/Jones communications link is also referred to in a letter from Judge John Minor Wisdom to Justice William J. Brennan, Jr., July 16, 1964. Additional information was provided in interviews with Judge Elbert P. Tuttle, Atlanta, Georgia, August 9, 1982, and October 20, 1982.

THE EASTLAND STRATEGY

The Eastland message conveyed the disquieting news that the senator from Mississippi was not going to stay on the sidelines of the Fifth Circuit predicament. Not only was Eastland demanding a split of the circuit, he was dictating the terms of division. Furthermore, the senator was willing to hold the needed judgeships in ransom to achieve his ends. The Biggs Committee was handing Eastland exactly what he needed to dismember the Fifth Circuit's liberal bloc of judges. What disturbed these judges was that Eastland was not acting out of concern for judicial administration or philosophical advocacy of the "Rule of Nine"; had that been the case, he would not have demanded a particular geographical configuration. He clearly had other goals in sight. Two factors motivated Eastland to take an active interest in what would usually be considered a rather sedate issue of judicial administration. The first concerned the changing attitudes toward civil rights in the nation in general and in the Senate in particular. The second involved Eastland's own view of the judges on the Fifth Circuit and the decisions they were rendering.

Eastland's positions on race were consistent with those of his white constituency. He was an avowed segregationist and opposed for both representational and personal reasons the decisions of the Warren Court.[10] He used his position as head of the Senate Judiciary Committee to block civil rights bills and to deter or delay confirmation of nominees holding liberal civil rights views.

Eastland had a reputation for being forthright in his direct political dealings but was never eager to explain his motives publicly when not required to do so.[11] The senator was a smart legislative poker player. He knew there was nothing to be gained from revealing a weak hand. He was able to bluff with the best, leaving opponents wondering what his hand really contained. Eastland understood that how people perceived him and what they feared he might do could be just as effective as what he was actually willing to do. This was particularly important to a legislator who frequently took policy positions not supported by a majority of his Senate colleagues. Eastland's skills as a legislative strategist were ideally suited to the dilatory tactics he would have to employ as a leader of the shrinking minority of Senate segregationists. As

10. James O. Eastland, *Is the Supreme Court Pro-Communist? Here Are the Facts as Disclosed by United States Senator James O. Eastland* (Richmond, Va.: Patrick Henry Group, 1962).

11. Attempts to interview Senator Eastland for this book were unsuccessful. At first he declined to be interviewed in person because of health problems but agreed to respond to written questions. (Letter from James O. Eastland to authors, April 21, 1983.) When he received a list of written questions, however, the senator responded, "I am very sorry but I cannot recall the answers to your questions." (Letter from James O. Eastland to authors, May 26, 1983.) Eastland died on February 19, 1986.

a result, his Senate Judiciary Committee became "infamously known as the graveyard of civil rights legislation."[12]

Such strategy, however, would soon be inadequate. Eastland was shrewd enough to realize what the future had in store for the South. The decisions of the Fifth Circuit enforcing *Brown* were but a prelude to what was to come. The assassination of President Kennedy delivered a sharp blow to those who wanted to slow down the progress of civil rights in the South. Although Kennedy was committed to civil rights, he had been willing (or compelled) to cooperate with the southern white power structure to further his other legislative objectives. The president submitted civil rights legislation to Congress but had difficulty getting his bills passed. Eastland and other conservative senators were more than up to the task of blocking or delaying his proposals. But the assassination changed everything. The nation's public opinion had turned toward support of the Kennedy legacy. Lyndon Johnson was riding this political tide. He, too, was a master legislative strategist and was committed to seeing that the civil rights legislation was passed. Johnson was extremely effective in convincing members of Congress to support his positions.

Eastland knew that the old strategies of parliamentary sniping and delay were no longer viable. The Civil Rights Act of 1964 was sure to pass later that year. The Senate leadership was removing the Judiciary Committee's jurisdiction over it, effectively eliminating much of Eastland's influence. Furthermore, a major voting rights bill was already in progress and was likely to be voted on within the next year. That, too, could not be stopped, especially if, as Eastland expected, Lyndon Johnson received a landslide of support in the November elections and carried on his coattails many liberal Democrats from the North and the West. Eastland realized that legislation written and legislation enforced are two very different things. He knew he could not stop the enactment of the laws; but he could affect how they would be interpreted and enforced in the South, particularly in Mississippi. While liberals were buoyant over the prospective passage of civil rights legislation, Eastland, undetected by most, turned his attention to the Fifth Circuit Court of Appeals, which would occupy a crucial position in the application of the new civil rights legislation and in the continuing enforcement of the Supreme Court's *Brown* decision.

Eastland was infuriated by the liberal decisions of the Fifth Circuit, especially as they applied to his home state.[13] Moreover, the Cameron-instigated wrangle between Eastland and the judges over the panel-stacking charges occurred only three weeks before Chief Justice Warren's decision to honor

---

12. Charles Whalen and Barbara Whalen, *The Longest Debate* (Washington, D.C.: Seven Locks Press, 1985), p. 4.

13. Interview with Judge James C. Hill, Atlanta, Georgia, September 27, 1983.

Tuttle's request that a special conference committee be appointed to study the problems of the Fifth Circuit.

Eastland observed the activities of the Biggs Committee with interest.[14] The need for additional positions on the Fifth Circuit and the prevailing "Rule of Nine" theory among federal judges played right into his hands. No increase in judgeships could be obtained and no circuit division enacted without the approval of the Senate Judiciary Committee. And that committee was largely controlled by James O. Eastland, who would have a strong hand in shaping any proposals to resolve the circuit's caseload problems. Splitting the court and adding judges offered Eastland the potential of placing Mississippi under a court more favorable to the state's prevailing interests. But the division would have to be constructed in just the right fashion. If drawn without care, the boundaries could place Mississippi in an even more liberal circuit than was currently the case with the full six-state jurisdiction. Eastland realized that he had little control over civil rights in the rest of the nation, but he deeply desired to do what he could to preserve the racial status quo in his home state.

If a division were to occur, the senator concluded that only two options were viable, a 3–3 or a 4–2 split. Clearly, Texas and Louisiana would be placed in a western division and Florida, Alabama, and Georgia in an eastern circuit. Mississippi was the pivotal state. Its relatively small caseload meant that Mississippi could easily be placed either to the west or east with little administrative disturbance. Placement, however, made a big political difference to Eastland. He knew that a 3–3 split (Mississippi, Texas, and Louisiana forming a three-state circuit to the west, and Florida, Alabama, and Georgia a three-state circuit to the east) would endanger his policy objectives by putting the Mississippi district courts under the purview of certain liberal Texas and Louisiana circuit judges. Consequently, he made it known that he would support an increase in authorized judges for the region only in return for a 4–2 division, making Mississippi part of a four-state eastern circuit. Eastland's scenario for the Fifth Circuit can be appreciated only by a careful appraisal of what a 4–2 split would mean relative to the other alternatives.

It was of utmost importance to Eastland's objectives that the four-judge activist coalition be broken. Tuttle, Rives, Wisdom, and Brown had formed a cohesive subgroup that had imposed liberal civil rights rulings on Mississippi, and Eastland did not want them to continue their domination of the Fifth Circuit, especially with the interpretation and enforcement of the pending Civil Rights Act and Voting Rights Act still to come. A split of the Fifth Circuit

14. Eastland may have done more than simply observe what the Biggs Committee was doing. His communication to Tuttle, via Warren Jones, demonstrates that he was not completely passive at this time. Although there is no documentation to support it, there is a distinct possibility that Eastland may have been in communication with others associated with the Biggs Committee. It may well be more than a coincidence that the final report of the committee was exactly the alternative preferred by the senator.

using any of the suggested boundaries would accomplish his goal. Tuttle and Rives would be placed in the eastern circuit and Wisdom and Brown in the western circuit. With a Democratic president in the White House, Eastland would have substantial influence as a southern senator and as head of the Judiciary Committee over the nominees for the newly created judgeships. This influence could be used to block the appointment of any individual who might join the liberal judges. Eastland knew, moreover, that predicting the behavior of prospective judges was not an exact science, and he did not want to rely exclusively on the political vagaries of the nomination process to protect Mississippi's interests.

Placing Mississippi in a circuit to the west along with Texas and Louisiana was unacceptable to Eastland, in large part because of the individuals involved. His special dislike for the liberals from the western portion of the circuit was much more intense than his feelings about Tuttle and Rives to the east. One factor in the senator's opinions of Wisdom and Brown was the fact that they had been particularly vigilant in demanding civil rights enforcement in his home state. Eastland thought the Texas and Louisiana judges "were a bunch of wild men,"[15] much more dangerous to Mississippi's interests than the judges to the east. In fact, the senator was purported to have said, "If it is the last thing I do, I'm going to get those goddamn judges from Texas and Louisiana off the necks of the schools of Mississippi."[16] Peter Fay, who was to join the Fifth Circuit in 1976, explained, "Senator Eastland made no bones about how he felt...he made it very clear that as long as he was in the United States Senate, if there was any circuit division Mississippi would never be in the states where Judges Wisdom and Brown were."[17] The same point was made in personal interviews with Judges Wisdom, Brown, and Tuttle.[18]

15. Interview with Judge Thomas Gibbs Gee, Austin, Texas, March 18, 1983.

16. The Eastland statement, to our knowledge, is not documented in the public record. It was, however, widely reported in our interview sessions. The exact wording varied from session to session, as did the expletive modifying judges, but the central theme was always the same. Whether or not Eastland actually made the statement may be lost to history. Enough crucial people, however, believed that the statement was made, and this in itself substantially colored the politics of the issue.

17. Interview with Judge Peter Fay, Atlanta, Georgia, May 23, 1983.

18. The following direct quotations from personal interviews with Judges Wisdom, Brown, and Tuttle substantiate this point: "Dick Rives felt very keenly that it was a ploy by Eastland to break up the influence that he, Tuttle, Brown, and I had on a small court. The ploy was by dividing the circuit and increasing the number of judges for each new circuit and have Tuttle and Rives in one circuit and Brown and Wisdom in the other, and then have additional judges. Thereby our influence would be undermined." (Interview with John Minor Wisdom, New Orleans, Louisiana, May 28, 1985.); "The desire to split was stimulated by everybody's knowledge of what Senator Eastland thought. He didn't like John Wisdom, he didn't like John Brown.... He just thought that we were the leaders of an attitude and a philosophy that he was opposed to for Mississippi." (Interview with Judge John R. Brown, Houston, Texas, August 10 and 11, 1983.); "It was generally said about Senator Eastland that the reason he didn't like the Fifth Circuit as it then stood was that it was too liberal in

In addition to their ideological positions, Brown and Wisdom were a greater threat to Eastland's objectives because of their ages. Wisdom was fifty-nine and Brown only fifty-four, so both were in a position to continue in active status for a good number of years. Although Rives and Tuttle held equally strong liberal views on the race question, they were both nearing retirement age.

Eastland may have had personal reasons for having a particular dislike for John Wisdom and wanting to prevent him from having any influence over Mississippi affairs. Of great significance was Eastland's reaction to the confrontations between Wisdom and the Mississippi district judges, especially Harold Cox. Cox was Eastland's first choice for the slot ultimately given to Ben Cameron, but his nomination was vetoed by the Justice Department because of the degree of segregationist sentiment avowed by Cox. Cox had been Eastland's classmate at the University of Mississippi and subsequently became a close political ally.[19] Many of the voting rights cases pitted Wisdom directly against Cox, with Wisdom writing strongly worded opinions that reversed Cox's decisions. The outcome was no doubt perceived by Eastland as an insult to his friend. Similar ill will was likely to have arisen over the acerbic opinions of Judge Wisdom that overturned Mississippi District Judge Sidney Mize's decisions during the Meredith episode. Wisdom's actions were an affront not only to Eastland but to virtually every public official in the State of Mississippi.[20]

Eastland also had special reasons for trying to keep Mississippi out of the clutches of John Brown. Not only was Brown a liberal activist with formidable legal talent, but he was also the central figure in the panel-stacking charges leveled by Ben Cameron just prior to the Houston Conference. As the as-

its racial cases. John R. Brown was chief judge of our Court by this time (1968) and he got the idea which he has expressed to me occasionally that the reason Senator Eastland wanted to split the circuit was to get Mississippi out from under a court of which he was the chief judge." (Tuttle interview, October 20, 1982.)

19. The senator's loyalties to Cox were solidified in 1942 while Eastland was soliciting support for one of his early political campaigns. Cox reportedly told Eastland: "Jim, here's my wallet. I need $27.00 to pay my rent; everything above that is yours." Later Judge Cox and some of his decisions became an embarrassment even to Eastland and the senator informally (and unsuccessfully) urged Cox to retire. Eastland allegedly did not like the common reference to Cox as "Eastland's Frankenstein." See Carol Caldwell, "Harold Cox: Still Racist After All These Years," The American Lawyer 1 (July 1979): 1, 27–29, at p. 29.

20. An additional factor prompting the antagonism might have been at work. Read and McGough describe a widely rumored but otherwise unverified story revolving around Wisdom's confirmation. When Wisdom's appointment became jeopardized by senatorial objections to his liberal leanings, he allegedly satisfied Eastland by indicating that, if confirmed, he would support civil rights no more than would Judge Cameron. Once on the bench, however, Wisdom immediately assumed an activist civil rights position, explaining that he had simply changed his mind. Frank T. Read and Lucy McGough, Let Them Be Judged: The Judicial Integration of the Deep South (Metuchen, N.J.: The Scarecrow Press, 1978), pp. 55–56.

signing judge, Brown was largely responsible for matching the Mississippi civil rights cases with the judges who would decide them.

The threat Brown posed to Eastland's home state was clearly demonstrated in the voting rights case of *United States v. Mississippi*.[21] As an immediate and direct result of the Houston Conference panel-stacking charges, Judge Wisdom gave up his assignment on the three-judge district court panel assigned to hear the case so that Judge Cameron could participate in the decision affecting Mississippi. The panel was finally composed of Appeals Judges Cameron and Brown and District Judge Cox. Cameron and Cox constituted a majority upholding Mississippi's use of understanding tests in voter registration. Cameron published the majority opinion without Judge Brown's knowledge.[22] Brown responded by working for months on his dissent, skillfully crafting a history of voting discrimination in Mississippi extending back to the 1890 changes in the state's constitution designed to void the guarantees of the Fifteenth Amendment. It contained an analysis of voting statistics, as well as a comprehensive discussion of how the inferior educational system for blacks perpetuated voting discrimination. Brown's dissent was later adopted as the Supreme Court's rationale when it reversed the majority's decision the following year.[23] Obviously, for Brown to gain control over Mississippi cases would be unacceptable to Eastland and the state's entrenched white power structure.

What made Brown particularly dangerous to Eastland was the order of succession to the chief judgeship. To Eastland, it was bad enough for Mississippi and the other southern states to have judges like Brown on the circuit bench, but to have him as chief judge would mean the continuation of the same kind of activist leadership that Elbert Tuttle had exercised. Yet that was exactly what was scheduled to occur. If there were no split of the Fifth Circuit, John Brown would assume the chief judgeship in 1967 and by law could hold that post until the end of 1979.[24] The thirteen years during which Brown would serve as chief would be critical ones for interpreting the Constitution and the statutes controlling civil rights. Eastland could not look with optimism on a court led by John Brown during this crucial period.

If a 3–3 split were imposed, with Mississippi placed to the west with Texas and Louisiana, the situation would be even worse for Eastland. In that case, his home state would be placed in a circuit over which John Brown would

21. 229 F.Supp. 925 (1964).

22. Jack Bass, *Unlikely Heroes* (New York: Simon and Schuster, 1981), p. 273.

23. *United States v. Mississippi*, 380 U.S. 128 (1965). According to Read and McGough, Senator Eastland apparently "could think of no greater gift to Mississippi" than to break up the liberal coalition on the Fifth Circuit that was producing such decisions. *Let Them Be Judged*, p. 277.

24. Ben Cameron and Warren Jones were superior to Brown in seniority, but by the time Tuttle would step down as chief judge both would be over seventy and therefore ineligible to assume the chief judgeship.

immediately take control as chief judge. That leadership, combined with the scholarly power of the liberal John Wisdom, would be devastating. Their influence would be doubly felt because they would be serving a smaller circuit and could dominate it more easily than if the entire Fifth remained intact. Above all else, Eastland had to avoid the prospect of a 3–3 split.

Dividing the circuit at the river and placing Mississippi in a circuit with her three sister states to the east, however, would produce results much more acceptable to Eastland. His strategy, then, was to maneuver for acceptance of a circuit realignment that would impose a 4–2 split. In effect, such a division would gerrymander the liberal judges of Texas and Louisiana into a circuit of their own and remove the Mississippi district judges from the reaches of Judges Wisdom and Brown. It would create a four-state Deep South circuit firmly under the control of more conservative judges who could dominate the interpretation and application of civil rights law in Mississippi for the next twenty years.

Two factors were crucial to Eastland's accomplishing his goals. First, he needed to capitalize on the current problems facing the circuit and use them to achieve the solution he favored. He could parlay the feelings of desperation over workload to quick acceptance of a 4–2 division. A precipitous conference recommendation in favor of a 4–2 division would create the possibility that legislation would be enacted before the liberal forces realized the implications of realignment. Eastland also had to block any move toward 3–3 division. From his perspective, the placement of Mississippi to the west would be worse than no split at all. Consequently, he made it known that the Fifth Circuit would receive the desired increment of judges only if a division of the circuit at the Mississippi River took place. Second, Eastland knew that he had to keep a low political profile. In 1964, the nation was concerned with other matters. The Kennedy assassination and related affairs, as well as the upcoming presidential elections, dominated the news. As long as the Mississippi senator could pursue his goals quietly and away from the scrutiny of the press, his odds of victory were high. It was imperative for Eastland that the issue of realignment be presented as an administrative matter; if it exploded into a civil rights issue, other forces would enter the fray and Eastland would lose his advantage. No one understood this final point better than Richard Rives and John Minor Wisdom, who were poised to mount an offensive to outflank Eastland's maneuver.

RIVES AND WISDOM: THE CASE AGAINST DIVISION

After the conclusion of the Biggs Committee deliberations, Elbert Tuttle secured the permission of Chief Justice Warren to inform the members of his court about the committee's recommendations. (Such consent was necessary because committee actions are normally kept confidential until the Judicial Conference receives the committee report.) On January 13, 1964,

Chief Judge Tuttle wrote to the members of his court outlining the actions taken by the Biggs panel. He ended his communication on a note of sadness and inevitability: "This comes as a difficult problem for all of us, I know, but I am sure that we will have some considerable time yet together before we are separated by law."[25]

Tuttle was not alone in the remorse he felt over the projected demise of the Fifth Circuit. In spite of the conflicts that had erupted within the court, there was a true feeling of collegiality among the judges. Personal relationships were strong, even among those who differed greatly on interpretations of law. Ben Cameron and John Minor Wisdom, for example, remained relatively friendly, although their judicial positions could not have been more disparate. The judges prided themselves on being able to argue vigorously and disagree strongly in deciding appeals and still leave the conference room as friends. The civil rights controversy was creating a rift among them but it was also contributing to a special sense of identity for the court as a whole. All the judges felt great loyalty to the court and the circuit. None of them liked to see the circuit divided, but for the majority realignment was perceived as the only way to solve the caseload problems plaguing them.

The feeling of inevitability was also justified. Normally, once a proposal has received the support of the circuit council and of the relevant conference committee it has taken a long step toward enactment. It would be unusual for the Judicial Conference to reject the committee's recommendation. This was especially the case with regard to the Biggs Committee, some of whose members had great political influence within the conference. Furthermore, the Judiciary Committee of the Senate, under Eastland's direction, favored circuit division. It seemed only a matter of time before the legislative mechanism would work its way and realignment would become a reality. The circuit needed more judges. The Rule of Nine advocates were in control and were not about to budge from their position. Division appeared to most judges to be the only solution.

But Richard Rives and John Minor Wisdom did not share this sense of inevitability. Their opposition to circuit division was unequivocal, and they realized that there was still time remaining before realignment would be imposed. First, the conference had to meet to consider the Biggs recommendations. That meeting was scheduled for two months later, in March. If the conference adopted the recommendation in principle, it would then need time to consult with staff members of the congressional committees in order to draft the specific legislation necessary to enact the realignment measure. The conference would have to approve the specific bill, and that probably would not occur until September. Finally, it would take time for Congress to act. Consequently, Rives and Wisdom had at least nine months to work within

25. Letter from Chief Judge Elbert P. Tuttle to all members of the Fifth Circuit Court of Appeals, January 13, 1964.

the administrative apparatus of the judiciary itself, followed by additional time if the measure became seriously considered by Congress. They were willing to do whatever was necessary to block the plan.

For Richard Rives the central issue in the controversy over circuit realignment was civil rights. He was in direct opposition to Senator Eastland. Rives well understood that the senator was correct in his predictions of what the division of the circuit would mean to the implementation of civil rights policy in the South, and he was committed to insuring that these predictions did not come to pass. He also realized that the proposed 4–2 split would be the most dangerous of all to civil rights interests. Rives was particularly concerned with the condition of civil rights in the states of Mississippi and Alabama, which contained the most intense opposition to extending constitutional guarantees to blacks and housed the most virulent strains of recalcitrance. If any progress was to be made in Alabama and Mississippi, the supervising court of appeals would have to be a sturdy defender of equal protection of the laws. The Biggs Committee recommendation would not produce this result.

In other words, Rives saw through Eastland's plan. He knew that a 4–2 split was nothing more than a "second line attack" on civil rights.[26] He did not hesitate to argue that the judges of his court varied in their commitment to implement the principles enunciated in *Brown v. Board of Education*. Rives believed it would be tragic to eliminate the jurisdiction of the Texas and Louisiana judges over the Deep South states, particularly Mississippi and Alabama. Judges Wisdom and Brown had unflinchingly insisted on immediate civil rights progress. Placing the two in a western circuit of their own would leave the Fifth Circuit in substantially weakened form. The Supreme Court could not serve as an adequate replacement for a strong circuit bench: it had too many other demands and was too remote to provide the necessary constant supervision of the desegregation process. The end result would be a delay of many more years of the long overdue extension of constitutional rights to black citizens.

Rives, of course, had other objections to the division of the circuit. He thought realignment would be uneconomical, unnecessary, and unwise. It would require additional staff, building construction, and an entirely new clerk's office. Other alternatives, he claimed, should be tried before resorting to this rather radical alternative. Aside from these other arguments, however, Rives's overriding reason for opposing the split was its potentially negative impact on civil rights policy. Although he was to be criticized for advancing the argument, he accepted the role of the opposition's point man in voicing the civil rights objections to realignment.

To Richard Rives, then, Eastland's support of a 4–2 split was just another attempt to defeat the efforts of federal judges to bring equal rights to minorities in the South. What supporters of segregation could not accomplish

26. Letter from Richard T. Rives to Attorney General Robert F. Kennedy, May 19, 1964.

through legal maneuvering or personal threats, they were now trying to gain by altering the organization of federal judicial power. Rives was not about to let the forces of the old order define the issue as a simple administrative reform. He was not the type of individual to shy away from controversy or to abandon a cause when his principles were involved, even when the odds of success were minimal. According to one account, once Rives arrived at a position on an issue, "no earthly power could shake him."[27]

John Minor Wisdom also realized that the question of race relations was inextricably tied to the circuit division controversy. In a letter to Chief Judge Tuttle, he acknowledged: "Strive as we may to be objective and to apply what Wechsler calls 'neutral principles,' in civil rights cases the personality of the judge is an ineradicable element in the judicial process."[28] Dividing the circuit according to the plan approved by the Biggs Committee would distribute those personalities in such a way that civil rights would suffer. To Wisdom, however, the civil rights issue was only a symptom, albeit the most devastating one, of the real weakness in the circuit division plan. He explained: "I think that the civil rights issue was the predominant issue, but I think the whole question is bigger than that. . . . The big question is whether judges on a national court should be drawn from a base broad enough so that they will be a more representative group."[29] What could be said about civil rights in 1964 might also apply in the future to other areas—economic and employment discrimination, labor, taxation, oil and gas, criminal rights, or administrative regulation. Circuits with small geographical jurisdictions exhibit a provincialism on the court that can affect judicial decision making on a wide variety of issues.

For Judge Wisdom, the realignment proposal struck at the very heart of the proper role of the courts of appeals. Circuit splitting would challenge the ability of these tribunals to perform their vital role in the federal court system, the federalizing function. He maintained that to "adjust the body politic to stresses and strains" of national policy is the essence of this function and the institutional basis for the existence of the intermediate federal appellate courts.[30] Wisdom's position was based largely on arguments advanced by James Madison in the early years of the nation's development. The extent of national power over state autonomy had been a central issue since the genesis of the historical debates over federalism. The courts of appeals were one of the eventual by-products of those debates. These tribunals were designed to increase federal presence in the states, and also to alleviate some of the Su-

27. See Tinsley E. Yarbrough, *Judge Frank Johnson and Human Rights in Alabama* (University, Ala.: University of Alabama Press, 1981), p. 54.

28. Letter from Judge John Minor Wisdom to Chief Judge Elbert P. Tuttle, March 16, 1964.

29. Wisdom interview, May 28, 1985.

30. John Minor Wisdom, "The Frictionmaking, Exacerbating Political Role of Federal Courts," *Southwestern Law Journal* 21 (1967): 411–28, at 411.

preme Court's caseload burden by diverting routine appeals to the intermediate court level.

When Congress, at the urging of Chief Justice Taft, passed the 1925 Judges Bill expanding Supreme Court discretionary review over its docket, the courts of appeals gained increased national status. All but a fraction of the federal appeals were heard by the courts of appeals. As caseloads increased, these courts became the primary federal appellate tribunals in volume and, as a matter of practicality, the final arbiters in many areas of federal legal policy. While the Supreme Court developed national legal policy, the courts of appeals were responsible for applying that policy to a substantial portion of federal cases. Aligning local and state policies with national standards (the federalizing function) was a paramount judicial responsibility that fell to the courts of appeals.

In Wisdom's view the adequate execution of this function hinged upon a court staffed by judges with a wide diversity of background experiences. The federal appeals jurist should be familiar with regional and local thinking but also be free of the prejudices of region and community. Wisdom argued very strongly that a diversity of viewpoints emanates in large part from geographical diversity. In effect, a geographically large circuit provides the president with a wide variety of potential nominees from which to choose, increases the number of senators active in the appointment process, and generally broadens the set of political influences governing the recruitment of judges. Over time, this breeds a court with a variety of judicial and political viewpoints. In addition, Wisdom argued, a large circuit enjoys the advantages of a diverse caseload and greater immunity from public pressures generated at the local level.

One of the primary aspects of the federalizing function is the supervision of federal district courts to insure that they do not bow to local pressures when national standards should apply. The appellate bench of a small circuit would have attitudes and backgrounds so similar to those of the district court judges that proper supervision would not occur. From Wisdom's perspective, the 4–2 realignment would create just such a danger with respect to civil rights cases. It would remove the recalcitrant district judges, especially those in Mississippi, from the reach of Wisdom's usually poignant legal pen. The recent memory of the civil rights battle between the Fifth Circuit's liberal bloc and the Mississippi district judges provided Wisdom with a classic example of how lower courts had to be brought into line with national policy. The Biggs report, in Wisdom's opinion, proposed to do more than separate "the Four" by carving up the Fifth Circuit: the recommendation threatened the actual foundation and existence of the Fifth Circuit's place in the political/judicial system.

Furthermore, Wisdom feared that the division of the Fifth Circuit would be only the beginning of circuit proliferation. As other circuits increased in caseload to the point where nine judges could no longer handle the demands, they too would be divided. The Ninth and the Second circuits were already approaching this point. If the Fifth Circuit was divided in 1964, it would not be unreasonable to predict that twenty years later it might need to be split again. With each such division the capability of the courts to execute the federalizing function would decrease. If Congress split the Fifth Circuit without a proper examination of the issues, it might establish the precedent that circuit division is the proper way to cope with increased caseload burdens.

Thus, both Wisdom and Rives were committed to stopping the march toward realignment. At the very least, the decisionmakers needed to think through the significant issues involved in the circuit-splitting question. The axiomatic conclusion that division was the only logical answer to a large court's problems had to be challenged.

DISSENTING WITHIN THE SYSTEM

Following the announcement of the Biggs Committee, Rives and Wisdom had several discussions about possible ways to defeat the realignment proposals.[31] They decided that at least for the present they would continue to register their dissent within the confines of the judicial system. They had been outvoted by their fellow judges on the Fifth Circuit Council and had received unfavorable news from the Biggs Committee. The next step in the policy-making process of the judiciary would once again occur within the Judicial Conference of the United States. The conference was scheduled to meet in March to take action on the Biggs Committee recommendations. If Wisdom and Rives could somehow convince it to defeat the realignment proposal, the move toward circuit division would be killed, at least temporarily. In spite of Senator Eastland's firm support for a circuit split, the view in Congress was that the Judicial Conference should take the lead in proposing legislation dealing with the courts.[32] Without an endorsement from the conference, members of Congress were not likely to be receptive to the realignment plan.

The problem facing Wisdom and Rives was one of gaining access to the conference. Neither was a member; consequently, they needed to enlist the help of a conference delegate to argue the case in opposition to the Biggs report. Their first hope was to convince Chief Judge Tuttle to join their cause. Tuttle would have a great deal of influence among conference members on this issue. If he would announce his opposition to realignment and argue the case against it, the conference would likely defeat the recommendation. Given Tuttle's prestige and the norm among conference members to defer to the circuit on matters confined to a single court, the chief judge could carry the issue. Wisdom and Rives also knew that Tuttle's support for realignment was reluctant. As a member of the liberal "Four," he might be persuaded to join with Rives and Wisdom, as he had on so many judicial issues. Wisdom and

31. Wisdom interview, May 28, 1985.
32. Interview with Senator Roman Hruska, Omaha, Nebraska, July 29, 1983.

Rives had an abiding faith that when the chips were down, Tuttle would be with them.

Much to their disappointment, however, Tuttle would not change his position. He explained to Wisdom and Rives that as chief judge his duty was to follow the council's mandate to obtain additional judges however that could be accomplished, and he had reached the conclusion that a division of the circuit was the only means by which these additional judgeships would be authorized. Tuttle explained that when the Biggs Committee made clear its overwhelming opposition to increasing the court beyond nine judges, he had to support its recommendation to divide the circuit. He told Wisdom and Rives that because none of the controlling factors had changed, he intended to maintain his position at the March meeting of the conference.

Although Tuttle was firm in his stance, he remained sympathetic to the Wisdom/Rives efforts and suggested "that if they wished to be heard on their opposition they should get another member of the Conference to present their views."[33] The most effective advocate, in Tuttle's estimation, would be Judge Charles Fahy of the District of Columbia Court of Appeals, who had been a member of the Biggs Committee and was well informed about the facts surrounding the realignment issue. The chief judge urged his friends to contact Fahy, who was representing the District of Columbia Circuit in place of Chief Judge David Bazelon, and secure his services in representing their viewpoint.

In the seventy-one-year-old Charles Fahy, Wisdom and Rives had an able representative. He had done his undergraduate work at Notre Dame and received his law degree from Georgetown. After nineteen years in private practice, he began a long and distinguished career of service to the federal government. He used his legal expertise on behalf of the Department of the Interior, the Petroleum Administration Board, and then the National Labor Relations Board. As general counsel to the NLRB, Fahy had received considerable acclaim from the legal community for his role as one of the leading government attorneys in the landmark 1937 Supreme Court decision of *NLRB v. Jones and Laughlin Steel Corporation*, a major turning point in the Court's acceptance of Roosevelt's New Deal philosophy for the nation's economic ills.[34] After the Second World War, he was the government's legal adviser on the postwar occupation of Germany and then became solicitor general of the United States. Finally, in 1949, President Truman appointed Fahy to the Court of Appeals for the District of Columbia.[35]

Fahy agreed with Rives and Wisdom on realignment. Since his appointment

33. Tuttle interview, October 20, 1982.
34. 301 U.S. 1 (1937).
35. For a discussion of Fahy's career, see Peter H. Irons, *The New Deal Lawyers* (Princeton, N.J.: Princeton University Press, 1982). See also Peter H. Irons, *Justice at War* (New York: Oxford University Press, 1983).

to the bench he had been a member of the liberal minority on the District of Columbia Court of Appeals and had become a well-known advocate of desegregation. Having been born and raised in Rome, Georgia, he could furthermore speak with some authority on conditions in the Fifth Circuit region.

Wisdom and Rives were also in contact with another member of the conference, Chief Judge Simon Sobeloff of the Fourth Circuit. Sobeloff, noted for his knowledgeable approach to judicial administration and intricate governmental relationships, also agreed to work for the defeat of the Biggs Committee recommendations. Throughout the crucial months of 1964, Sobeloff was one of the strongest and most effective judges allied with the Wisdom/Rives efforts. He, too, was an individual of considerable reputation and substance. After having served in various legal capacities for the city of Baltimore during his early career, Sobeloff held positions as United States attorney, chief judge of the Maryland Supreme Court, and solicitor general of the United States. Like Wisdom, Sobeloff had been active in Republican party affairs and was appointed to the circuit court by President Eisenhower.

Sobeloff also shared Wisdom's views on the civil rights issue. His liberal racial attitudes had sparked strong opposition from southern senators during his 1956 confirmation hearings. At one point Senator Eastland had exclaimed, "The kindest thing that can be said about the nominee is that he is on the borderline of Red philosophy."[36] Senators from Virginia, North Carolina, and South Carolina also objected to his appointment because South Carolina was next in line to have a seat on the Fourth Circuit and Eisenhower had ignored that consideration in nominating the Maryland native. Because Eisenhower was a Republican, however, the opposition of southern Democratic senators did not merit the norms of senatorial courtesy. Nevertheless, Eastland showed his great displeasure with the Sobeloff nomination by bottling up confirmation inside the Judiciary Committee for one year before a vote was taken. Needless to say, Eastland's support for a division of the Fifth Circuit provided an additional incentive for Sobeloff to join the Wisdom/Rives opposition.

On March 16 and 17, the Judicial Conference of the United States convened its regular spring session. With Fahy and Sobeloff leading the opposition, Rives and Wisdom felt confident that their views would be made known. They had not given up hope, however, of convincing Elbert Tuttle to join them. Rives telephoned Tuttle immediately before the opening of the conference and reiterated his plea that Tuttle oppose circuit division, arguing that the 7–2 vote of the Fifth Circuit Council did not accurately reflect the views of the judges.[37] Although he was not authorized to speak for them, Rives claimed

36. J. W. Peltason, *Fifty-eight Lonely Men: Southern Federal Judges and School Desegregation* (New York: Harcourt, Brace and World, 1961), p. 24. See also *Congressional Record*, vol. 102, July 6, 1956, p. 12855.

37. This telephone conversation is referred to in a letter from Chief Judge Elbert P.

that he was sure Judges Hutcheson and Brown were sympathetic to the idea of keeping the circuit intact.

Wisdom wrote Tuttle a lengthy letter, delivered to him at the conference meeting, which contained a litany of objections to the realignment proposal.[38] He particularly protested that the issue was being voted on without adequate study of the problem. The Biggs Committee had considered caseload growth but had not paid any attention to alternative ways of handling increasing demands. Wisdom felt confident that the Fifth Circuit could easily cope with a court of more than nine judges. He cited the fact that the United States Tax Court and the courts of several European nations functioned quite effectively with more. Projecting into the future, Wisdom contended that the productivity of the court would undoubtedly improve as new and younger judges replaced those about to retire. Clearly, Judge Hutcheson at eighty-five and Judge Cameron at seventy-five, both in poor health and unable to carry full caseloads, would leave the court before too long. Judges Rives and Jones, according to Wisdom, had expressed their intentions to retire in 1965 but continue to hear cases in senior status.

Other methods to improve court output could also be instituted, including increased panel sittings, staff law clerks, and additional law clerks assigned to individual judges. Wisdom's argument was clear: alternative methods of handling caseload problems should be tried before resorting to carving up the circuit. In addition, he maintained that splitting the circuit would cause an enormous lowering of its prestige and that this would have an adverse effect on the ability of the court to supervise properly the decisions of district court judges whose rulings might run contrary to national law. In this regard, Wisdom informed Tuttle that Judge Frank Johnson of Alabama, who was gaining considerable national stature for his courageous and unpopular civil rights rulings, was now expressing strong disapproval of the Biggs recommendation. Wisdom's final plea urged "the conference to make an adequate study of alternatives to choosing a solution that will have the irreversible adverse effects of splitting the circuit."[39]

Although Tuttle once again indicated that he was attracted to the arguments made by Wisdom and Rives, he remained firm. He would go to the conference meetings and describe the conditions facing the circuit. He would even sympathetically express the opposing views, but he would remain committed to the Biggs Committee report.[40] Unless members of the court officially informed him of a change in position, Tuttle felt bound to carry out the

Tuttle to Judges Joseph C. Hutcheson, Jr., Richard T. Rives, John R. Brown, and John Minor Wisdom, March 25, 1964.

38. Letter from Judge John Minor Wisdom to Chief Judge Elbert P. Tuttle, March 16, 1964.

39. Ibid.

40. Letter from Chief Judge Elbert P. Tuttle to Judges Joseph C. Hutcheson, Jr., Richard T. Rives, John R. Brown, and John Minor Wisdom, March 25, 1964.

mandate voted by the council. He would continue to give informal encouragement to Wisdom and Rives, as he had by suggesting Judge Fahy as an appropriate advocate, but he would officially remain bound to the will of the court's majority.

As scheduled, the Judicial Conference took up the Biggs report when it convened on March 16. Chief Judge Biggs presented the case of his committee. First, the Ninth Circuit should be left intact. Second, the conditions facing the Fifth Circuit were so severe that an additional six judges would be required to cope with the cases being filed. Because this additional increment would boost the court above reasonable size limitations, the Fifth Circuit should be divided at the Mississippi River with Texas, Louisiana, and the Canal Zone becoming a new Eleventh Circuit and the states of Florida, Georgia, Alabama, and Mississippi forming a new Fifth Circuit. Third, Judge Biggs reported his committee's recommendation that no court of appeals be larger than nine judges. Tuttle discussed the committee's recommendations as they pertained to the Fifth Circuit. He explained to the conference members that, although there was a division in his council, the majority of the court's members had voted in favor of the proposal to divide the court if that was necessary to obtain adequate staffing. Tuttle explained that as chief judge he felt bound by his council's vote and would support the recommendation.

Judges Fahy and Sobeloff led the opposition. They cogently advanced the case developed by Wisdom and Rives. Also arguing against the division of the circuit was Chief Justice Earl Warren. Like Wisdom, the chief justice was concerned that the entire subject had received too little study. Not only had other alternatives not been considered, but Warren was not convinced that the particular geographic boundaries recommended by the committee were the best possible ones if a split were to take place. But most of all, Warren was not persuaded by the argument that no court should have more than nine judges. He later recalled the arguments he made to the conference on this point:

> I believe there is no particular virtue in fixing the limit for courts of appeals at nine judges. Historically, there is no reason for it; the only reason we haven't had more in any one circuit is because, in the wisdom of Congress, we have not had need for any more. The argument is raised that it makes hearings en banc unmanageable, but if we had fewer of them it would be a small price to pay for a sufficient number of judges to handle the work of the circuit.[41]

Despite the arguments made against division, the conference voted 11 to 8 to adopt the Biggs Committee recommendation to split the Fifth Circuit east and west along the Mississippi River.[42] The supporters of the Rule of

41. Letter from Chief Justice Earl Warren to Judge John Minor Wisdom, June 29, 1964.
42. *Report of the Proceedings of the Judicial Conference of the United States*, March 16–17, 1964. The votes of the conference are normally not made public. The 11–8 voting outcome

Nine were in control of the issue. In addition to the powerful Judge Biggs, Alfred Murrah of the Tenth Circuit, Harvey Johnsen of the Eighth, and Edward Lumbard of the Second argued in favor of division. The conference instructed Biggs, in cooperation with congressional staff, to begin drafting legislation to implement the adopted recommendations. The drafts would be considered later, quite probably at the September 1964 meeting of the conference.

Wisdom and Rives were thus unsuccessful at the conference, although by a narrow margin. Ironically, the final vote may have reflected less the substantive arguments on both sides of the issue than the internal norms of the conference. In this case, the Judicial Conference appears to have followed its formal policy of deferring to the wishes of a particular circuit on matters affecting that circuit alone. Support for this conclusion is provided by Earl Warren, who wrote to Judge Wisdom that "most of those who voted for the proposal believed that they were acting in accordance with the desires of your circuit council."[43]

RIVES AND WISDOM REGROUP

Richard Rives and John Wisdom were disappointed but not disconsolate over the action taken by the Judicial Conference. Far from accepting defeat, they redoubled their efforts to prevent the split of the circuit. They flatly rejected the notion that conference endorsement of realignment meant it was inevitable. To this point they had registered their views through the established channels of the judicial system itself. They had used the conventional methods of debate within the Circuit Council and insured that their arguments were represented in the Judicial Conference, albeit with unsatisfactory results. They were unable to halt the momentum of the judicial consensus-building process, which culminated in the conference vote.

Peter Fish prefaced his seminal study of the politics of judicial administration by noting that "Judges as administrators become deeply involved in politics. Yet they play politics in a system largely screened from public gaze."[44] Wisdom and Rives realized that if they were to succeed the arena of political battle would have to be expanded and the techniques of influence broadened beyond the normal bounds of judicial politics. The issue needed to be taken outside the protected confines of the Judicial Conference. To do this would radically alter the course of the controversy. As E. E. Schattschneider argued, when the scope of conflict broadens, the cast of characters changes, the sub-

here was revealed in a letter from Chief Justice Earl Warren to Judge John Minor Wisdom, June 29, 1964.

43. Letter from Chief Justice Earl Warren to Judge John Minor Wisdom, June 29, 1964.

44. Peter G. Fish, *The Politics of Federal Judicial Administration* (Princeton, N.J.: Princeton University Press, 1973), p. xii.

stance of the issues can be redefined, and the terms of the conflict are altered.[45] Such was the situation when Wisdom and Rives launched a major campaign in 1964 to halt the division of the Fifth Circuit. They realized that there were three crucial decision-making points in the process—the Circuit Council, the Judicial Conference, and the Congress. Their overarching plan was to proceed on all fronts as opportunities might arise.

Although the Fifth Circuit Council had already endorsed the split, that endorsement had been a costly one. Wisdom and Rives knew that the conference vote had been lost by a narrow margin in large measure because of the delegates' deference to the Circuit Council's majority resolution. It was reasonable to assume that if the Fifth Circuit Council were to alter its position, support for realignment within the Judicial Conference would decline. Both Wisdom and Rives believed that it was possible to convince the court to take a different stance. They knew that Tuttle, Hutcheson, and Brown had offered only weak support for division—Tuttle because of his concept of the role of chief judge and Hutcheson and Brown for the pragmatic reason that additional staffing was desperately needed. None of the three would support division under any other circumstances. Rives wrote Tuttle, Hutcheson, Brown, and Wisdom one week after the Judicial Conference had acted, suggesting that if the five of them stood together, acted "judiciously," and kept this activity among themselves, their position would prevail and maybe even receive support from the other judges.[46] Rives closed his letter on a note of seriousness to his colleagues: "This threatened destruction of the Fifth Circuit certainly deserves the best thoughts and efforts of each one of us."[47]

The voting balance on the council changed less than two weeks later. On April 3, 1964, Ben Cameron, the court's most reactionary member and a firm supporter of realignment, died. He had served slightly more than nine years. During the last of those years, his position had driven a wedge in the court and threatened the strong collegiality that marked its membership. After his demise, the court officially lined up with six judges for division and two against. Wisdom and Rives knew that an active effort to convert their colleagues held promise.

The Judicial Conference of the United States would be the second crucial decision-making body. Wisdom and Rives had already suffered a damaging defeat in the March conference meeting, but the battle for the Judicial Conference was not over. The closeness of the first vote (11–8) encouraged Rives and Wisdom to work for a reversal of that outcome. One strategy was simply to convince at least two conference members to change their positions. Because several had supported division out of deference to the resolution of the Fifth

---

45. E. E. Schattschneider, *The Semisovereign People* (Hinsdale, Ill.: Dryden Press, 1960).
46. Letter from Judge Richard T. Rives to Chief Judge Elbert P. Tuttle and Judges Joseph C. Hutcheson, Jr., John R. Brown, and John Minor Wisdom, March 23, 1964.
47. Ibid.

Circuit Council, Rives and Wisdom knew that changing the voting margin among their own circuit judges would have a powerful influence on the conference.

To insure that Rives and Wisdom would maintain the support and services of their friends in the conference, Rives contacted Fahy and Sobeloff, thanking them for their efforts and asking them to continue their opposition to a division of the circuit.[48] Both renewed their commitments. Judge Fahy responded, "I hope we have not heard the end of this matter and that as time goes on it will take a better turn."[49] The opponents also hoped for the continued cooperation of Earl Warren. They realized, however, that the chief justice was fully engaged in chairing the commission to investigate the assassination of President Kennedy, as well as his normal duties of running the Supreme Court. Consequently, Warren's activity in the Fifth Circuit controversy would understandably be limited.

Congress was to be the final battlefield. No split could be enacted without legislative approval. James O. Eastland dearly savored the prospect of dividing the Fifth Circuit. As head of the Senate Judiciary Committee, he would undoubtedly do what he could to expedite passage. He also had an edge on this issue because the Fifth Circuit states were considered part of his sphere of influence as a senator from Mississippi, and it was not likely that he would be seriously challenged on an issue of importance to that region alone. The House of Representatives provided a much better opportunity for the opponents of the split to make their influence felt. Judge Sobeloff explained the congressional situation in a letter to Judge Rives in March of 1964:

> When I expressed my disappointment to Judge Tuttle over the action of the Conference and the fear that the leadership of the Senate Judiciary Committee would use the Conference action as ground for ramming through the proposal to divide the Fifth Circuit, Judge Tuttle sagely observed, "There are two houses of Congress." So whatever your beliefs as to the efficacy of prayer, pray for (and to) the House of Representatives and the Chairman of *its* Judiciary Committee.[50]

Seventy-six-year-old Representative Emanuel Celler of New York chaired the House Judiciary Committee. The Brooklyn Democrat had been a member of the House since 1922. He was committed to liberal causes and received a great deal of support from labor and civil rights groups. The Columbia University–educated representative's devotion to the civil rights cause was unquestioned. He was an active supporter of the civil rights bills pending in

---

48. Ibid.
49. Letter from Judge Charles Fahy to Judge Richard T. Rives, March 20, 1964.
50. Letter from Chief Judge Simon Sobeloff to Judge Richard T. Rives, March 19, 1964.

Congress, arguing, "We must tear into the drum of discrimination and silence the clang of segregation."[51]

Given that the House and Senate Judiciary committees retained final power of approval over conference recommendations, the conference had always placed a high premium on maintaining an amicable relationship with the leadership of both panels. Wisdom and Rives perceived Celler as a formidable counterweight to Eastland, especially because the two often clashed on matters falling within their respective committees' shared jurisdiction. The only qualifying factor with regard to Celler's support was his long-standing insistence that nationwide circuit realignment should be studied. He considered the existing circuit boundaries as having no rational basis. Since 1956 he had urged the Judicial Conference to reevaluate the entire system and also threatened to have his own committee staff initiate such action if the conference did not. However, if Celler could be made to see the adverse impact that circuit division would have on civil rights interests, he might well take an active stand in opposition to Eastland. For the time being, all that Wisdom and Rives needed from him was a commitment to table any proposal until they could pursue the other elements in their long-term strategy. They also knew that any evidence of Celler's support for their cause could be used as ammunition in their council strategy.

Rives and Wisdom remained hopeful that the move toward realignment could be arrested. But a major campaign had to be launched immediately. Tuttle, in fact, had warned them that their active opposition might have begun too late to be effective.[52] The campaign would have to be pushed to include every segment of the political and legal communities that might be able to exert influence on behalf of their cause. It was no time to hesitate.

---

51. Celler press release of October 6, 1963. Emanuel Celler Papers, Library of Congress, Container 468.

52. Letter from Chief Judge Elbert P. Tuttle to Judges Joseph C. Hutcheson, Jr., Richard T. Rives, John R. Brown, and John Minor Wisdom, March 25, 1964.

4

The Campaign

The proposal to divide the Fifth Circuit had cleared the necessary regional and central decision points in the federal judiciary, receiving the preliminary approval of the Judicial Conference. The Biggs Committee and the Administrative Office staff had already begun to work with the staff of the Senate Judiciary Committee on drafting the specifics of the legislation. The odds against reversing the process and killing a conference-endorsed policy now were low; but it might be done if the realignment issue were politicized.

Spring and summer of 1964 were months of feverish activity for Richard Rives and John Wisdom, during which they initiated a far-reaching campaign to mobilize an elaborate interbranch communication network to prevent what they viewed as the destruction of the Fifth Circuit. Their plan was carefully constructed to use whatever influence they could muster with members of the Fifth Circuit Judicial Council, the Judicial Conference of the United States, and the Congress.

THE STRATEGY

In order to press their case and make it felt within these three key decision-making bodies, Rives and Wisdom mapped out a nine-point plan of attack:

First, directly to contact their colleagues on the Fifth Circuit Council and formally request the adoption of a resolution reversing the council's earlier endorsement of realignment. Such a reversal of council policy would be crucial in convincing the other decision-making bodies to question their own support of circuit division.

Second, to create public awareness of the consequences of dividing the Fifth Circuit. Those supporters of division, such as Senator Eastland, who had less than altruistic reasons for wanting realignment, were at an advantage if the issue remained outside the public eye and was played down as a simple administrative reform. The real consequences of realignment could be made known by encouraging the media to direct their attention to the problems facing the circuit.

Third, to develop well-constructed policy statements explicating the major objections to circuit division. Wisdom would do this by advancing his federalizing function position and Rives, by articulating the civil rights arguments. They would use these policy statements selectively to convince key individuals to join their opposition effort.

Fourth, to mobilize the academic community. Legal scholars and law professors can have a good deal of general influence on matters pertaining to the courts. Not only are they recognized for their expertise and have access to important law journals where they can articulate their views; some are also politically well connected. Furthermore, the academic community would undoubtedly be receptive to the kinds of arguments Wisdom and Rives were advancing.

Fifth, to encourage the executive branch to oppose division. The Justice Department, still run by Kennedy liberals, had a high degree of respect for the work of the liberal members of the Fifth Circuit in the civil rights controversy and would not like to see it succumb to Eastland's plans. President Johnson was fully committed to civil rights and might also be persuaded to become active, although, given his own agenda, the Fifth Circuit would not be a priority item in the turbulent months of an election year.

Sixth, to gain the support of respected legal organizations. Bar associations are particularly influential, especially with Congress, and to obtain their active participation against realignment would be most helpful.

Seventh, to gain the support of other members of the judiciary. The more judges who declared objections to the split, the more credible the Rives and Wisdom campaign would become. The two hoped to elicit support from all levels of the federal courts, but the stigma against getting involved in matters of a circuit other than one's own would be a major obstacle. It was crucial, however, for the campaign to be perceived as having widespread support among judges. Rives and Wisdom did not want to be seen as isolated dissenters.

Eighth, to approach members of the Judicial Conference and try to convince them to oppose circuit division. The 11 to 8 vote in favor of realignment at the March conference meeting meant that only a small number of conversions would be necessary to have the conference reverse itself.

Ninth, to cultivate support in Congress for their cause. Prospects in the Senate, with Eastland's looming presence, were not at all encouraging; but the House was a much different matter. Rives and Wisdom targeted Emanuel Celler as the key to their congressional strategy.

In executing these plans Wisdom and Rives coordinated their individual efforts and used an extensive network of personal and professional contacts to exercise influence where they could not do so directly. After long years in private practice and public service, the two veteran federal judges knew a wide array of individuals they could call upon to give assistance to their efforts.

Wisdom was well connected in Washington political circles, and particularly among the Republican "eastern establishment." Through his efforts to organize a viable Republican party in the South, he had earned a reputation among many Republicans in Congress and had easy access to them. V. O. Key, Jr., sent Wisdom a personal letter along with a copy of his classic work, *Southern Politics*,[1] in which he thanked Wisdom for his major contribution to making a two-party South a possible topic on which to write.[2] His years of service as Louisiana's Republican national committeeman gave him further entree to the party's top leaders. But Wisdom also had political connections to Democratic party officials. His decisions in the field of civil rights earned him high respect, particularly among Kennedy Democrats. Furthermore, the friendships he had cultivated during his service with the Office of Legal Procurement for the Army in World War II would pay dividends. Many of these individuals had become prestigious law professors, practitioners, judges, or government officials. They added to Wisdom's elaborate network of political contacts.

Rives had also formed extensive political and social connections throughout government circles and the legal profession. Considered a silent but forceful power in Alabama Democratic politics, he had successfully managed several political campaigns. In addition, he maintained a close relationship with Alabama Senator Lister Hill, who chaired the Committee on Labor and Public Welfare.

Underlying this network of friends and political allies was an informal communications system comprised of loyal former law clerks. Both Rives and Wisdom, like many other federal judges, were able to recruit clerks from among the top ranks of law schools, many of whom were able to move from these clerkships to various levels of government service and positions within the legal profession.

For the most part, the networks that Wisdom and Rives had developed over the years did not overlap. When combined, they formed a large and complex group of individuals active in almost every capacity that would be important to their campaign. At one point, Wisdom had a mailing list of well over a hundred well-placed individuals with whom he was in contact over the realignment issue. Throughout the spring and summer of 1964, the two judges mobilized these extensive political networks in an attempt to change the direction of the political and administrative momentum to divide the circuit. The ultimate goal was to kill the proposal outright. A more feasible

1. V. O. Key, Jr., *Southern Politics in State and Nation* (New York: Alfred A. Knopf, 1949).

2. Interview with Judge John Minor Wisdom, New Orleans, Louisiana, March 23, 1983.

prospect, however, was to gain a delay in implementing realignment until the entire scope of the problem could be studied in the context of revising the boundaries of the whole appellate court system rather than only one circuit.

THE CIRCUIT COUNCIL

The first opportunity for Rives and Wisdom to take concrete action toward executing their strategy came when the court convened for its regular meeting of the Circuit Council in Fort Worth on May 11. There were several items of business on the agenda for that meeting, and two concerned the proposal to realign the Fifth Circuit. First, the Biggs Committee, in conjunction with congressional staff, had drafted two bills to divide the circuit, to which the council was being asked to react. Second, Judge Wisdom had prepared a lengthy resolution calling for the council to rescind its earlier endorsement of the split.

Prior to the meeting Tuttle had circulated the proposed bills to the members of the court for their study and comment. He attempted to curtail bitter debate on the proposed legislation by urging his court not to argue about the merits of the general recommendation but only to comment on the "draftsmanship" and the "technical matters contained in the Bill." He also asked that the judges send him their comments quickly because the Biggs Committee was "anxious" to move ahead with its business.[3]

For the most part, the judges heeded Tuttle's request, but it was clear that tension was mounting over even the technical provisions of the proposed legislation. Rives, evidently concerned over the development of civil rights law, wrote back to Tuttle, arguing, "without implying agreement with the Bill in any form," that the legislation must include a provision making the precedents of the old Fifth Circuit binding upon both circuits resulting from the split.[4] Judge Gewin requested that Jackson, Mississippi, be added as a city in which the court would be authorized to sit, contending that Senator Eastland would not "feel kindly toward a bill which did not include Jackson."[5] Judges Gewin, Jones, and Bell also spoke to certain confusing aspects of the proposed legislation, later clarified, that might permit certain of the judges to select, by choice or by moving residences, which of the two post-split circuits they would serve. The calm that Tuttle had hoped would govern the council debate over the bills was to prove a chimera.

Two weeks earlier, on April 17, a front-page headline story had appeared in the *Alabama Journal*, Montgomery's daily newspaper, which began: "A proposed division of the Fifth U.S. Circuit Court of Appeals—disclosed in Wash-

3. Letter from Chief Judge Elbert P. Tuttle to All Circuit Judges of the Fifth Circuit, May 1, 1964.
4. Letter from Judge Richard T. Rives to Chief Judge Elbert P. Tuttle, May 4, 1964.
5. Letter from Judge Walter P. Gewin to Chief Judge Elbert P. Tuttle, May 4, 1964.

ington today—could have a substantial effect on civil rights litigation in Alabama and other Southern states for many years to come."[6] The story went on to note, "If adopted, the split would in effect remove the court from the control of judges who favor a vigorous approach to desegregation and place it in the hands of those who favor a go-slow approach." The author of the piece, Managing Editor Ray Jenkins, indicated that details of the proposed legislation had been disclosed by Hubert Finzel, chief counsel of the Senate subcommittee on Improvements in Judicial Machinery, chaired by Olin D. Johnston of South Carolina. The article claimed that the recommendation to split "reportedly coincides with the wishes of Senator James O. Eastland (D-Miss), who would like to see Judge John Minor Wisdom of Louisiana and John R. Brown of Texas—two of the strong civil rights judges—out of the Fifth Circuit." Following this claim were a categorization of who were the "liberal" and "conservative" judges on civil rights matters and a speculative assessment of voting blocs.

In addition, the article described Judge Gewin as perhaps the most conservative member of the court and explained that he would become chief judge of the four eastern states if realignment occurred. Without division, Jenkins continued, John Brown, a strong civil rights proponent, was scheduled to become chief judge of the entire six-state circuit in three years when Chief Judge Tuttle reached his seventieth birthday. The article argued that the line-of-succession issue was critical because of the power the chief judge holds to assign cases to particular panels. As a final point, Jenkins indicated that a confrontation between Celler and Eastland was likely, which would mean that the court would not receive the additional judges needed to handle the caseload.

Because the *Alabama Journal*'s circulation was primarily local, the article had little immediate impact; in fact, its existence was unknown to most members of the court. But Jenkins went on to publish the same piece three days later in the *Christian Science Monitor*, a newspaper with nationwide circulation and considerable prestige.[7] The article as printed in the *Monitor* was brought to the attention of Judge Warren Jones in Jacksonville, who was enraged by it.

Jones fired off a letter to each of the judges on the Fifth Circuit, enclosing a copy of the Jenkins article.[8] He openly questioned if Jenkins could possibly have relied exclusively on congressional staffer Finzel and said it was clear that he must have gotten information from someone who had firsthand knowledge of the court and its operations. His sarcastically worded communication

6. Ray Jenkins, "Split of 5th U.S. Circuit Court Proposed," *Alabama Journal*, April 17, 1964, p. 1.

7. Ray Jenkins, "Dixie Court Reforms Seen," *Christian Science Monitor*, April 20, 1964, p. 7.

8. Letter from Judge Warren L. Jones to All Fifth Circuit Judges, May 6, 1964.

contained cryptic references to Jenkins's informants, whom he called "Mr. Source and Judge Eager." Jones was disturbed that Jenkins had pinned liberal and conservative labels on members of the court and angry that he had pitted the judges against one another by doing so. He was also "distressed to learn from this article, what I had feared before, and what most of us had hoped could be avoided, that the question of dividing the Circuit is to be a civil rights issue; Eastland v. Celler." Alluding again to Mr. Source and Judge Eager, Jones chided Jenkins and his informant for reporting inaccurately that the panel and case assignment authority resided with the chief judge. He thought this point had been laid to rest at the Houston Conference in August 1963.

The next day, Judge Rives responded to Jones's accusations and probing curiosity in a letter, a copy of which was sent to the other members of the court.[9] Very incisively, Rives pointed out to Jones that he simply did not have the habit of concealing his views under a pseudonym of Mr. Source or Judge Eager. Rives acknowledged that Jenkins was managing editor of the *Alabama Journal*, that he had frequent discussions with him,[10] and that some parts of the article came from those conversations—although Jenkins had formed his own conclusions as to who was liberal and who was conservative. Rives was not the least bit apologetic about the civil rights arguments raised in the article.

> As to the question of civil rights being involved in the proposed division of our Circuit, I have no doubt that it is, and did not hesitate to so express myself to Mr. Jenkins, and shall not hesitate to so express myself to any other person who may discuss the matter with me. . . . I may say that it seems almost inconceivable to me that any Judge on the Court should fail to realize the effect of the proposed division of the Circuit on the future enforcement of civil rights.

Rives's use of his contact with Ray Jenkins to produce the *Journal* and *Monitor* stories was only a first step toward attracting public attention to the realignment issue through the media. Rives knew that if he continued these activities he would increasingly be the object of criticism, but he willingly accepted this role because of his firm commitment to bringing full civil rights to racial minorities in the South. He also understood that the importance of the issue and of the times demanded extraordinary actions. Years later, reflecting on his activities in 1964, Rives reportedly said: "The others were thinking about workload. I was in the gutter with Eastland."[11]

The Jones-Rives exchange immediately prior to the May 11 Circuit Council

9. Letter from Judge Richard T. Rives to Judge Warren L. Jones, May 7, 1964.

10. The Rives-Jenkins relationship had existed for quite some time. Three years earlier Jenkins had written a series of three articles on Judge Rives that appeared on the front page of the *Alabama Journal*. The series was highly favorable in its analysis of the judge's background and record on the court. See Ray Jenkins, "Decade on Bench Has Brought Rives Wide Recognition," *Alabama Journal*, May 8, 1961, p. 1; Jenkins, "McCord Insisted on Naming Rives When He Retired," *Alabama Journal*, May 9, 1961, p. 1; and Jenkins, "Rives Turns Up on Both Sides," *Alabama Journal*, May 10, 1961, p. 1.

11. Confidential Interview.

meeting caused the positions of the opposing sides to rigidify rather than flow together. Because the Cameron vacancy had not yet been filled and the ailing Judge Hutcheson was unable to travel, only seven judges were present in Fort Worth. Wisdom presented his resolution, asking for a delay in any implementation of circuit division until a full study of the problem could be conducted by the Administrative Office of the United States Courts and the Judicial Conference. After a full discussion, Rives and Wisdom voted for its adoption; Tuttle, Jones, Brown, Gewin, and Bell voted against.[12]

The disappointing outcome of the council meeting was only a temporary, and probably expected, setback for Wisdom and Rives. Over the long term, the council strategy would prove to be more successful. Although Brown and Tuttle voted with the majority, Wisdom and Rives were convinced that they would ultimately persuade their two close brethren to join them in opposing the division. The message that Jones had conveyed from Eastland, "no split, no judges," still dominated the council's thinking. Brown explained to Wisdom and Rives that his vote against their resolution was purely pragmatic, since he believed that the authorization of additional judges was contingent on a split of the circuit.[13] Tuttle's position was somewhat similar to Brown's, but he also believed that his duty as chief judge placed him in a more difficult situation.

Rives and Wisdom also remained confident that they would eventually be able to convince Hutcheson to join their side and communicate his opposition to the split. Rives and Wisdom left the May council meeting declaring themselves "free agents" and reserving the right to voice opposition to the split publicly.[14] Failure to convert the council to their point of view meant they were compelled to adopt the rather unusual tactic of challenging the recommendation of the Judicial Conference directly by making an end run around its decision. This meant broadening the cast of characters, as well as the scope of the conflict.

JUDICIAL, EXECUTIVE, AND OUTSIDE SUPPORT

Undaunted by Warren Jones's criticism, Rives continued to speak with members of the press. Precisely because the *Monitor* article had sparked attention, Wisdom and Rives used the media more frequently. Less than a week

12. Minutes of the meeting of the Judicial Council of the United States Court of Appeals, Fort Worth, Texas, May 11, 1964.

13. Letter from Judge John R. Brown to Judge John Minor Wisdom, June 9, 1964.

14. Read and McGough report that "at one conference tempers flared to such a point that Judges Rives and Wisdom left by a door different from that used by the rest of the members of the Court, to indicate their profound disagreement with their brethren." Frank T. Read and Lucy S. McGough, *Let Them Be Judged: The Judicial Integration of the Deep South* (Metuchen, N.J.: The Scarecrow Press, 1978), p. 277. Although Read and McGough do not indicate the date of this incident, it very probably occurred at the May 1964 meeting of the circuit council.

after the council meeting, Rives, again through his contact with Ray Jenkins,[15] was able to arrange for an article to appear in the *New York Times* reporting essentially the same information carried in the *Alabama Journal* and *Christian Science Monitor*.[16]

While attending an American Law Institute meeting in Washington in mid-May, Wisdom, a council member of this judicial research center, joined Rives in his media tactics in the hope that Washington influentials would be alerted to the Fifth Circuit issue. In a meeting with reporter Jim Clayton and with Russell Wiggins (a personal acquaintance and editor of the *Washington Post*), Wisdom was able to obtain an endorsement for his position from the *Post*. Based on this meeting, an editorial appeared on May 29 presenting what the paper considered to be strong arguments against splitting existing circuits, particularly the Fifth.[17] The implications of the proposed division for civil rights issues in the South were mentioned only briefly. Instead, the tone of this article, compared to the April account, was more in line with Wisdom's general objections to circuit realignment as a solution for meeting caseload demands and making room for additional judges.

In May Wisdom and Rives also completed work on policy statements explaining their individual objections to dividing the circuit. Rives's statement once again focused on the civil rights issue. His words were strong and hard-hitting. The statement was first released in a four-page letter to Attorney General Robert Kennedy in mid-May.[18] Rives asked Kennedy if they could discuss the proposed division of the circuit when the judge visited Washington in mid-June. He emphasized the importance of the issue by claiming that circuit division, if implemented, would probably delay "for many more weary years the dream of our Negro citizens for equality before the law." While acknowledging that Kennedy and President Johnson were preoccupied with securing passage of the Civil Rights Act, Rives thought the attorney general should be aware of this possible "second-line" attack on civil rights enforcement.

The message contained in Rives's letter to Kennedy became the basic civil rights policy statement of the division opponents. Its contents were used whenever a strong civil rights plea was needed. But the statement did not please other judges on the court because of the implication that, without Brown and Wisdom, the judges of the eastern part of the circuit would not vigorously enforce civil rights. Brown later acknowledged that Rives came very close to suggesting he did not trust his colleagues to carry out their duties properly.[19] Nonetheless, Rives remained committed to his position.

15. Letter from Judge Richard T. Rives to Judge John Minor Wisdom, June 9, 1964.

16. John Hebers, "Split Plan Vexes U.S. Judges," *New York Times*, May 16, 1964, p. 9.

17. Editorial, "New Eleventh Circuit," *Washington Post*, May 29, 1964, p. A18.

18. Letter from Judge Richard T. Rives to Attorney General Robert F. Kennedy, May 19, 1964.

19. Interview with Judge John R. Brown, Houston, Texas, August 10, 1983.

A week later, Rives's correspondence with the attorney general was followed by a similar communication from District Judge Frank Johnson, Jr. Any apparent impropriety, Johnson told Kennedy, in the involvement of district judges in such opposition was offset by the fact that they had "been required to take the brunt of the community reaction" to civil rights decisions.[20] Johnson maintained that this simply was not the proper time to divide the Fifth Circuit. Sympathetic as he was to the difficult political situation this request presented for Kennedy, Johnson expressed his understanding that Kennedy might not be able to become actively involved in the dispute. However, he did ask him to exert what influence he could in the matter.

Both Rives and Johnson realized that Kennedy and President Johnson were involved in strained and politically sensitive negotiations with Eastland in their efforts to secure passage of the Civil Rights Act and related legislation. To inject another element of tension into the political controversy in Washington would be unwise and possibly fatal for the pending bills. With political attention in Washington focused so intently on the civil rights legislation, it was not surprising that Rives received a rather noncommittal reply from Kennedy. The attorney general's personal circumstances also hampered his ability to join Rives and Wisdom actively. In the late spring of 1964, Robert Kennedy was still mourning the loss of his brother.[21] Family matters were particularly pressing for him in the aftermath of the assassination. Also, he was pondering his own political career and was on the verge of leaving the administration to run for the United States Senate.

However, Kennedy's response to Rives's plea did not deter Wisdom from trying to communicate similar views to the attorney general and his staff a month later.[22] Wisdom was no stranger to the internal operations of the Justice Department. He was a close friend of Herbert Brownell, who had served as attorney general under Eisenhower and had considerable contact with several Kennedy Justice Department attorneys working on civil rights issues. He especially had a great deal of respect for Burke Marshall and John Doar. Wisdom's strategy, then, was to keep the issue continuously before the attorney general throughout the summer. He realized that various members of the Justice Department would be sympathetic to his position and that this might result in the department's taking a stand against the proposed division.

The Administration's Civil Rights Bill had passed the House in February but was delayed in the Senate. The attention of the Justice Department was fixed on convincing the Senate to approve the bill. Finally, after the conservative coalition's filibuster was broken in June and the Senate approved the

20. Letter from Judge Frank M. Johnson, Jr., to Attorney General Robert F. Kennedy, May 27, 1964.

21. Telephone interview with Burke Marshall, April 26, 1985.

22. Letter from Judge John Minor Wisdom to Attorney General Robert F. Kennedy, June 17, 1964.

bill on July 2, the Justice Department could turn its attention to other issues, such as the proposed division of the Fifth Circuit. By September, Wisdom's efforts finally bore fruit. Although the Justice Department did not take an official, public position against realignment, Assistant Attorney General Burke Marshall reported that Wisdom's persistence had "completely persuaded" the department.[23]

Nicholas deB. Katzenbach had assumed duties as acting attorney general upon Robert Kennedy's resignation to run for the Senate. This shift in momentum at the Justice Department was not a result of any lack of support under Kennedy's guidance. Quite to the contrary, Kennedy met with Wisdom in Washington to discuss the judge's opposition views at a time when the pending civil rights legislation required almost daily monitoring by Kennedy and his staff. But although Kennedy had demonstrated a sympathetic view toward the Wisdom/Rives campaign, Katzenbach was a bit more active on its behalf. Under him, the Justice Department privately monitored the situation, an action Katzenbach thought sufficient because the department was certain that the split would not pass in Congress. The opinion in Justice was that Celler would never allow realignment of the Fifth Circuit to be approved by his committee, and there were also doubts about Eastland's capability of ever getting the circuit split bill to the Senate floor.[24] But should the supporters of realignment gain enough power to threaten passage, Katzenbach was prepared to take a more active role in the controversy. So Wisdom realized that he was receiving valuable undercover support from the Justice Department and was satisfied.[25]

Outside of the Justice Department, executive branch involvement was limited. Rives contacted Nicholas Johnson, one of Judge Brown's former law clerks, who clerked for Justice Hugo Black and then became the chief administrator for the Maritime Division of the Department of Commerce. Johnson provided additional help by bringing the issue to President Johnson's attention.[26] There was, however, no indication that the latter ever took a position on the issue.

Like Rives, Wisdom drafted a statement explaining his opposition to the division of the circuit. Wisdom spelled out his objections to realignment in a carefully drafted, five-page letter to Chief Justice Earl Warren which argued against the "Rule of Nine" theory and explained why division would jeopardize the federalizing function of the court.[27] He also stressed the fact that an

23. Letter from Assistant Attorney General Burke Marshall to Judge John Minor Wisdom, September 16, 1964.

24. Telephone interview with Nicholas deB. Katzenbach, May 8, 1985.

25. Wisdom interview, May 28, 1985.

26. Letter from Maritime Administrator Nicholas Johnson to Judge Richard T. Rives, May 27, 1964.

27. Letter from Judge John Minor Wisdom to Chief Justice Earl Warren, May 29, 1964.

insufficient amount of study had been directed to the whole subject of circuit division. Wisdom urged the Judicial Conference to take a "hard second look" at the decision to recommend Fifth Circuit division, taking into consideration the fact that a majority of the Fifth Circuit Council was in fact opposed to it. He claimed that this majority was not reflected in the council vote because some members—particularly Brown and Tuttle—had based their vote on the assumption that the Senate Judiciary Committee would not authorize additional judges without a split. He went on to argue that the irreversible action to split the circuit should not be taken on such a "shaky principle." Wisdom's communication to Warren was well timed. The chief justice had given an address to the American Law Institute on May 20 that was being interpreted as sympathetic to the Biggs Committee recommendation.[28] As Warren's assistance was essential to Wisdom and Rives, the reinforcement provided by Wisdom's letter was important in keeping him on the side of the opponents to division. In fact, Wisdom's letter to Warren became one of the most important documents in the 1964 realignment debate. Its basic message was widely distributed to influential judges, lawyers, members of Congress, and administration officials.

During the early part of the summer, Rives and Wisdom also targeted other Supreme Court justices for support, particularly Hugo Black. Rives presented his views to him in essentially the same form as he had his appeal to Attorney General Kennedy,[29] while Wisdom sent Black a copy of his correspondence with Chief Justice Warren. Both of them received supportive responses from the two justices. Black wrote to Wisdom saying he had "talked to the Chief Justice about this several times and am glad that your letter was written. I do hope something can be done to frustrate the plan."[30] Warren also contacted Wisdom and agreed that the entire subject of realignment needed more study before its implementation could be seriously entertained.[31] Black and Warren also encouraged Wisdom and Rives to meet with them on their upcoming visits to Washington,[32] which they did on two separate occasions, to discuss their opposition views and strategies.[33] Although the talks gained for them the support and cooperation of the justices, both Warren and Black preferred that Wisdom and Rives take the initiative. All agreed that the latter would keep Warren and Black informed of their efforts and would also be responsible for writing to every member of the conference,

28. See Lewis R. Morgan, "The Fifth Circuit: Expand or Divide?" *Mercer Law Review* 29 (Summer 1978): 885–97.

29. Letter from Justice Hugo L. Black to Judge Richard T. Rives, June 1, 1964.

30. Letter from Justice Hugo L. Black to Judge John Minor Wisdom, June 5, 1964.

31. Letter from Chief Justice Earl Warren to Judge John Minor Wisdom, June 29, 1964.

32. Letter from Justice Hugo L. Black to Judge Richard T. Rives, June 1, 1964.

33. Letter from Judge John Minor Wisdom to Professor Charles Alan Wright, June 24, 1964.

expressing their views, before the regular September meeting.[34] At that meeting, Rives and Wisdom hoped the conference would vote to repeal its earlier recommendation and prevent the legislation drafted by the Biggs Committee from being transmitted to Congress with conference approval.

CONGRESSIONAL SUPPORT

Elated by their success with Chief Justice Warren and Justice Black, Rives and Wisdom now turned to their political networks to expand the campaign. Their target was Congress.

Given Eastland's position, Wisdom and Rives knew their prospects in the Senate were not good, but this did not deter them from making contact with members who might be supportive of their cause. As early as May, the split opponents had received valuable help from Walter Gellhorn, a professor of law at Columbia University. Gellhorn had three important contacts in the Senate whom he approached with the Rives/Wisdom arguments against circuit division. All three were northern senators with strong civil rights credentials— Clifford Case and Harrison Williams, both of New Jersey, and Philip Hart of Michigan. Gellhorn warned that the proposed division would impede the progress of civil rights in the South and that Chief Judge Tuttle was "trapped" in a position of support. He also expressed concern over the role of the Justice Department, which he claimed "was playing along with the idea for reasons I do not fathom."[35]

Senator Hart, a Democratic member of the judiciary subcommittee with jurisdiction over the matter, informed Gellhorn that the Senate was responding to the conference recommendation but that he should not be alarmed, because the bill would receive no more than an initial hearing that year.[36] Gellhorn received similar assurances from Senator Williams, who said that "no bill has officially been introduced, and my best guess is that there will be no Congressional action on this matter until next year."[37] Williams went on to clarify for Gellhorn the position of the Justice Department. After some firsthand examination of the problem, Williams said there was "considerable disappointment within the Justice Department concerning the proposed geographical boundaries of the division." As a matter of preference, the department would have placed Mississippi with Texas, Louisiana, and the Canal Zone, constituting a 3–3 division of the circuit. Williams agreed that the Justice

---

34. Letter from Judge Richard T. Rives to Judge John Minor Wisdom, June 29, 1964.

35. Letters from Professor Walter Gellhorn to Senators Clifford P. Case, Philip A. Hart, and Harrison A. Williams, Jr., May 14, 1964. Gellhorn was also instrumental in contacting other influentials such as lawyer Abe Fortas and Alfred Friendly of the *Washington Post*.

36. Letter from Senator Philip A. Hart to Professor Walter Gellhorn, May 18, 1964.

37. Letter from Senator Harrison A. Williams, Jr., to Professor Walter Gellhorn, May 26, 1964.

Department's alignment suggestion would "certainly improve the prospects for uniform civil rights decisions in both circuits."

Judge Wisdom was also in contact with Senator Hugh Scott of Pennsylvania who, like Wisdom, was a Republican with strong civil rights attitudes. Wisdom asked Scott, who served on the Judiciary Committee, to "nose around a bit" and find out how determined Eastland was in his quest to split the Fifth Circuit.[38] Wisdom had also met with the senator and had given him a copy of his letter to Chief Justice Warren outlining his objections to the division of the circuit. Scott assured Wisdom that he would try to discuss the matter with Eastland but would have to wait until Eastland's mind was "less on the current subject."[39]

On the House side of Congress, prospects seemed brighter. In that chamber Emanuel Celler was the key. Wisdom wrote directly to him registering the objections he and Rives had to division.[40] He also included a copy of his policy-statement letter originally sent to Chief Justice Warren. (The inclusion of the Warren letter had become standard practice for Wisdom when making new contacts about the realignment issue.)

Wisdom and Rives received encouraging news about Celler's attitudes on division. Judge Sobeloff, still working hard against the split, informed Wisdom that in a dinner conversation Celler had authorized Sobeloff to inform Wisdom and Rives of "his assurance that the question of dividing the Fifth Circuit would not be decided in isolation, but in relation to all pertinent factors, including proposed revision of circuit boundaries throughout the nation."[41]

The opponents to a split were further encouraged by a speech Celler gave on June 26 to the Conference of New York State Trial Judges. In that address, he strongly criticized the federal circuit boundaries, calling them "geographically absurd, demographically ridiculous, and in the volume of caseload unrealistic." He argued strongly for realignment of the entire system. On the heels of this attack, Celler had even sharper words for the civil rights situation in the South. "There are a few maverick judges in the South," he said, "who refused to recognize the principles of integration. As a result, civil rights cases, simple cases at that, have been held up for over a year. This is a diabolical scheme. It treats a Negro merely as a sack of potatoes."[42] Celler was making his position abundantly clear. Realignment should be approached only as a

38. Letter from Judge John Minor Wisdom to Senator Hugh Scott, June 8, 1964.

39. Letter from Senator Hugh Scott to Judge John Minor Wisdom, June 11, 1964.

40. Letter from Judge John Minor Wisdom to Representative Emanuel Celler, June 8, 1964.

41. Letter from Chief Judge Simon Sobeloff to Judge John Minor Wisdom, June 3, 1964.

42. Emanuel Celler, "The Legislature and the Courts," address to the Conference of New York State Trial Judges, June 26, 1964. Emanuel Celler Papers, Library of Congress, Container 539.

national problem, not one of concern to the Fifth Circuit alone, and whatever boundary adjustments were made must not adversely affect the civil rights of black Americans.

NEW ALLIES

In June of 1964, Wisdom and Rives enlisted three important allies in their campaign against circuit division, all of whom were to have an enormous impact on the future of the controversy.

The first of these was Judge J. Skelly Wright of the District of Columbia Circuit Court of Appeals.[43] Wright was a native of Louisiana and had served as a federal district judge in that state from 1949 through 1962. His years on the bench in Louisiana were turbulent ones. Wright vigorously enforced civil rights, demanding desegregation and strict application of the principles of the *Brown* decision. Along with Judge Frank Johnson of Alabama, he became known as one of the most courageous members of the southern trial bench.

The Kennedy administration had wanted to promote Wright to the Fifth Circuit Court of Appeals in 1961, but the plan had to be dropped when opposition from Eastland and other southern segregationists made it clear that his nomination would never be confirmed. Only months later, however, a vacancy occurred on the District of Columbia Circuit, and President Kennedy nominated the Louisiana district judge for the position. The decision was applauded by southern senators, who were anxious for Wright to leave the South.[44]

Judge Wright joined the opposition to the split for a number of reasons. First, as a strong defender of civil rights, he did not want to see the South turn its back on the progress that had been made thus far. Second, he had no love for Senator Eastland. The Mississippi senator had cost Wright a promotion to the Fifth Circuit. Furthermore, Eastland had called Wright "a no-good son of a bitch,"[45] which certainly did not endear him to the judge. Third, Skelly Wright felt deeply loyal to Tuttle and Rives. He explained: "As chief judges of the circuit Judges Rives and Tuttle were a tower of strength to those of us at the District Court level who had to face the problems, not only in the courtroom, but generally in our districts as well. I do not think that either of these judges has been sufficiently recognized for the support they gave to the

43. For a review of Judge Wright's life and judicial philosophy, see Arthur Selwyn Miller, *A "Capacity for Outrage": The Judicial Odyssey of J. Skelly Wright* (Westport, Conn.: Greenwood Press, 1984).

44. Jack Bass, *Unlikely Heroes* (New York: Simon and Schuster, 1981).

45. Ibid., p. 133. Wright had similar feelings about Eastland. In an interview, the judge said about the senator: "He wanted to control Mississippi absolutely. That's how I saw the man. I didn't know him actually, but I followed him like I followed other people in the press. He just wanted to be the king of Mississippi, and as far as I was concerned, he could be the queen, too." Interview with Judge J. Skelly Wright, Washington, D.C., May 22, 1985.

district judges throughout the circuit during this troubled time."[46] Given these feelings of admiration, it is not surprising that Wright responded favorably to Rives's plea for assistance. Wright also knew that Tuttle's sympathies were for keeping the circuit whole and he would therefore not be upset if Wright joined the opposition. Finally, Wright was a colleague and close friend of Judge Charles Fahy, an active ally of the Rives/Wisdom forces.

Judge Wright recalls his efforts against the split as having been limited to "keeping everybody advised of what was going on,"[47] but his activity was actually much more extensive than maintaining a simple channel of communication. In fact, Wright proved to be one of the most important allies in the Rives/Wisdom campaign. In early June, he was in contact with the staff of the House Judiciary Committee and reported back to Rives that "any proposed legislation to split the Fifth at this time will never even receive Committee consideration in the House."[48] He was also in touch with Judge Biggs[49] and actively tried to thwart the realignment plan by delaying its consideration by the Judicial Conference.

In early June, there was yet another positive sign that the campaign was becoming effective. John Brown wrote to Rives inquiring about the possibility of getting copies of newspaper accounts about the split that he and Wisdom might have saved.[50] Brown also told Rives that he did not intend to communicate this information to their opposition. After receiving the information from Wisdom, including the Warren letter, Brown explained that his opposition to Wisdom's resolution had been based on the pragmatic need for judges. He congratulated Wisdom on the publicity he had generated through the campaign—publicity that Brown believed would result in a national study and thus delay any action to split the Fifth Circuit.[51]

As a final signal that he was actively joining the campaign, Brown volunteered to discuss the opposition views with chief judge of the Second Circuit Edward Lumbard.[52] Brown believed he could be somewhat influential in persuading Lumbard to change his pro-division opinion, and because of Lumbard's influence within the conference, this conversion could be a major factor in persuading other members to vote against division. Brown also encouraged Wisdom to send a copy of the Warren letter to Judges Biggs and Maris, both of whom he believed could be convinced to vote for Wisdom's position. But because Chief Judges Harvey Johnsen and Alfred P. Murrah were such strong

46. Letter from Judge J. Skelly Wright to authors, May 23, 1985.
47. Skelly Wright interview.
48. Letter from Judge J. Skelly Wright to Judge Richard T. Rives, June 2, 1964.
49. Ibid.
50. Letter from Judge Richard T. Rives to Judge John Minor Wisdom, June 8, 1964.
51. Letter from Judge John R. Brown to Judge John Minor Wisdom, June 9, 1964.
52. Ibid., letter from Judge John R. Brown to Judge J. Edward Lumbard, July 14, 1964.

advocates of the "nine-judge maximum" principle, Brown told Wisdom that these two jurists would be "lost causes."

Clearly, Brown had done his homework on the subject and become an asset to the campaign. Moreover, his newly articulated position meant that the Fifth Circuit Council's majority vote had shifted from 6–2 to 5–3. At this point, Wisdom was sure he could convince Hutcheson and Tuttle to join the minority side of the issue, thereby presenting a 5–3 council vote against division to the conference at its September meeting.

By mid-June the Wisdom and Rives network was active in a variety of interinstitutional relationships concerning division. Professional and personal connections and communications had been established with Congress, the Supreme Court, the Justice Department, major newspapers, and an intricately woven group of federal judges who had either direct or indirect ties with the conference. Momentum for the campaign seemed to be increasing primarily as a result of Wisdom's articulate and persuasive argument that circuit division would ultimately undermine the federalizing function of circuit courts as judicial forums. Many participants who joined the campaign did so because they were more inclined to support and accept an anti-division viewpoint based on this broad institutional argument rather than on the narrower issue of civil rights.

Charles Alan Wright, noted expert on federal courts at the University of Texas School of Law, became a third addition to the campaign in June, valuable largely because of his scholarly credentials and compelling writing style. He agreed with Wisdom's federalizing argument and contended that the destruction of regional diversity in the intermediate federal appellate courts was a valid enough reason to oppose division. Although he believed the proposed division's effect on civil rights cases was obvious, it was difficult to use this as a basis for opposition because of the personal implications it carried for some Fifth Circuit judges. In effect, Wright believed that more compelling arguments could be presented than that of civil rights, which involved current personalities and underestimated the judges in the eastern division.[53]

On June 20, Wright wrote a long letter to Wisdom outlining his position.[54] It corresponded closely with Wisdom's own views, which the judge had shared with Wright in a letter three days earlier.[55] Wright closed with a pledge of support and active participation: "If you wish to show this to Judge Rives— or anyone else for that matter—feel free to do so. I am about to write a letter to the *New York Times*, and perhaps something for the *Texas Law Review*, on

53. Interview with Professor Charles Alan Wright, Austin, Texas, March 21, 1983.

54. Letter from Professor Charles Alan Wright to Judge John Minor Wisdom, June 20, 1964.

55. Letter from Judge John Minor Wisdom to Professor Charles Alan Wright, June 17, 1964.

the subject. I had hesitated to speak out publicly against the proposal, since the Chief Justice seemed to endorse it at the ALI, but he has told me I am free to launch a campaign against it, and that this will not embarrass him." Wright carried through. His letter opposing the split was published in the *New York Times* on July 10,[56] and his article in the *Texas Law Review*, which appeared in late summer, proved to be one of the opponents' most effective weapons in their attempts to block or delay the realignment of the circuit.

LEGAL ORGANIZATIONS

From mid-June until the September meeting of the conference, Wisdom and Rives, assisted by their new allies, pursued a course of action designed to convince decisionmakers that the problems division was supposed to address were national in scope. Because heavy workload pressures were not restricted to the South, a nationwide study of the problems and possible administrative alternatives was needed to assess the viability of various solutions. Wisdom, in particular, believed that, as the problem was not circuit-specific, a viable solution including realignment should be applicable to other circuits as well. In essence, he was revitalizing Representative Celler's call for a national boundary study.

Wisdom believed that this tactic would not only delay Fifth Circuit division but also would force the conference and Congress to adopt a comprehensive view of administrative problems, solutions, and especially consequences. In his views, the undesirable effects of realignment for the federal court system could be avoided if administrative alternatives were found for all circuits with heavy caseloads and large numbers of judges. Quite simply, Wisdom thought that realignment would ultimately lead to the destruction of federal appellate courts. It was this philosophy he would vociferously promote.

To make his call for a comprehensive study compelling, Wisdom needed to show that a project of this magnitude was feasible. Thus, he sought to enlist the support of outside organizations that would have to be involved in such an undertaking. He was convinced that if he could obtain appropriate commitments from research organizations, decisionmakers would be willing to postpone immediate action on the Fifth Circuit until a nationwide study was completed. Endorsements from two key organizations were soon forthcoming.

First, Wisdom succeeded in gaining the cooperation of the prestigious Institute of Judicial Administration, affiliated with the New York University School of Law. Through a personal contact, Fannie Klein, assistant director of the institute, Wisdom's views were expressed to its director, Delmar Karlen. Wisdom had made an appeal based on a brief but effective statement concerning the English court system's use of appellate tribunals with more than

56. Charles Alan Wright, "Split Court Areas Opposed," *New York Times*, July 10, 1964.

nine judges.[57] This argument "struck a very responsive chord" with Professor Karlen, who had just written a highly regarded book on English and American appellate courts.[58] Karlen offered the services of the institute to conduct a feasibility study of courts consisting of more than nine members.[59]

While Wisdom was enlisting the institute's support, Rives turned his efforts toward the American Bar Association. He met with his two longtime acquaintances, Judge Skelly Wright and Burke Marshall, during a mid-June visit to Washington.[60] At that meeting Wright told Rives that he thought Bernard G. Segal, an influential member of the Bar, could be convinced to propose a nationwide study of circuit realignment. So Wright contacted Segal, who chaired the ABA's Committee on the Federal Judiciary and also the Committee on Judicial Selection, Tenure, and Compensation, as well as being a council member on the Section of Judicial Administration.[61] Wright also contacted Judge William J. Jameson, who chaired the Association's Section of Judicial Administration.[62] Bernard Segal also received similar correspondence from Professor Charles Alan Wright who, fortuitously, had been appointed to serve on the same Judicial Conference committee as Segal.[63] In addition to Judge Wright's and Professor Wright's presentations, Wisdom personally expressed his views to both Jameson and Segal.[64]

Realizing that congressional and conference acceptance of the study alternative was probably contingent upon a nonpartisan approach, Wisdom suggested to Segal and Jameson that the Bar Association, possibly in conjunction with the American Judicature Society, support such a research endeavor by the Institute for Judicial Administration. Conducting the study in this manner would not only demonstrate a broad base of organizational support from outside the judiciary; the study would also appear to be removed from any political maneuvering. Wisdom's confidence both in Segal and in the impact the study might have was reflected in his concluding remark that, if Segal could recommend the study, "a large part of the war will be won." Within a week Wisdom, primarily due to Judge Wright's efforts, was assured that the section's council would place the study on the agenda for its early August meeting and Segal present the idea for consideration. Also, Jameson's response concerning the likelihood of supporting the study was very optimistic.[65]

57. Letter from Judge John Minor Wisdom to Fannie J. Klein, June 8, 1964.

58. Letter from Fannie J. Klein to Judge John Minor Wisdom, June 18, 1964.

59. Letter from Professor Delmar Karlen to Judge John Minor Wisdom, June 17, 1964.

60. Letter from Judge Richard T. Rives to Chief Judge Simon Sobeloff, July 2, 1964.

61. Letter from Judge J. Skelly Wright to Bernard G. Segal, June 22, 1964.

62. Letter from Judge J. Skelly Wright to Judge William J. Jameson, June 22, 1964.

63. Letter from Professor Charles Alan Wright to Bernard G. Segal, June 30, 1964.

64. Letter from Judge John Minor Wisdom to Bernard G. Segal, June 24, 1964. Letter from Judge John Minor Wisdom to Judge William J. Jameson, June 24, 1964.

65. Letter from Judge William J. Jameson to Judge J. Skelly Wright, June 24, 1964. Letter from Judge William J. Jameson to Judge John Minor Wisdom, June 29, 1964.

Delighted by the progress they had made by the end of June, Rives expressed his gratitude for the "statesmanlike" approach Wisdom had taken in presenting their opposition to division.[66] In fact, at one point Rives, in his usual humble manner, admitted to Chief Judge Sobeloff that Wisdom's approach was much more effective than his own narrow civil rights position.[67] He also reminded Wisdom of the promise Rives had made to Warren and Black that every conference member would receive a written communiqué explaining their opposition views prior to the September conference session.[68] Rives and Wisdom agreed that, as their position would be strengthened by the American Bar Association's explicit support for a nationwide study, they would delay formal communication with each conference member until after the Section of Judicial Administration's August council meeting.[69]

THE TURNING POINT

As the month of July began, Rives and Wisdom could survey the progress of their campaign with a great deal of satisfaction. They had made excellent strides toward carrying out each of the strategies they had planned after the March meeting of the Judicial Conference. But the big showdown was not scheduled until September, when the conference would consider final approval of the Biggs Committee's recommended legislation. The issue was far from settled. Rives and Wisdom knew that they could not sit idly by as the days of July passed. They needed to keep applying pressure. Consequently, they spent much of the month busily laying the groundwork for a convergence of their strategies by September. Once again, they devoted their efforts to the three decision-making groups that would have a determinative impact on the resolution of the controversy—the Fifth Circuit Council, the Judicial Conference, and the Congress.

Never losing sight of their overall objective to have the conference reverse its position on the Fifth Circuit issue, Wisdom and Rives poured their energies into direct and indirect maneuvers. They once again enlisted the support of faithful allies Simon Sobeloff, Skelly Wright, and Frank Johnson, Jr., in order to persuade two key conference members to change their positions. Although Wisdom and Rives agreed that it was too early to contact all conference members, they believed there was a slight possibility that Chief Judges Lumbard and Biggs might change their positions. If this chance existed, as Judge Brown had indicated when he joined their ranks in June, then these two votes would have the power to reverse or table the issue.

Upon Frank Johnson's suggestion, Rives asked Sobeloff to present Wis-

66. Letter from Judge Richard T. Rives to Judge John Minor Wisdom, June 29, 1964.
67. Letter from Judge Richard T. Rives to Chief Judge Simon Sobeloff, July 2, 1964.
68. Letter from Judge Richard T. Rives to Judge John Minor Wisdom, June 29, 1964.
69. Letter from Judge John Minor Wisdom to Judge John R. Brown, July 17, 1964.

dom's arguments and correspondence to Chief Judge Lumbard.[70] Since the days when Sobeloff had been solicitor general and Chief Judge Lumbard a U.S. attorney, Lumbard had held Sobeloff in high esteem. Sobeloff promptly spoke to Lumbard, who expressed the opinion that the Fifth Circuit would have to be split eventually. However, he was not opposed to the Fifth Circuit's using visiting judges until a nationwide study could be completed, which he and Celler preferred to a piecemeal approach to redrawing boundary lines.[71] Judge Brown, a personal acquaintance of Lumbard's, also contacted him, informing him that Wisdom would be attending the Appellate Judges' Sessions at New York University in late July and asking Lumbard to listen to his views.[72] Lumbard was very receptive to the idea of a meeting with Wisdom but never wavered on his stand that nine judges was the maximum size for a collegial court.[73]

Wisdom and Rives also tried to persuade Judge Biggs to leave the Fifth Circuit intact and experiment with more than nine judges on the court. On a regular basis, Wisdom communicated both his and Rives's positions on the matter and the progress their campaign was making.[74] Each time, Biggs would promptly acknowledge receipt without indicating that he had or would change his opinion.[75] Once again Judge Frank Johnson intervened by contacting his personal acquaintance Chief Judge Thomas M. Madden of the New Jersey District Court. As chief judge of one of the Third Circuit's districts and that circuit's district judge representative to the conference, Madden regularly conferred with Biggs on administrative matters. Though Johnson explained to Madden his candid objection based on the civil rights issue, like Rives, he recognized that Wisdom's broader approach was the better of the two opposition views. He asked Madden to discuss these views personally with Biggs.[76]

After visiting Biggs, Madden relayed a less than optimistic message to Johnson. A reversal of the conference's position was problematic, he said, primarily because that action would place it in an "unsatisfactory position, particularly, with the legislative branch when they are interested in a matter

70. Letter from Judge Richard T. Rives to Chief Judge Simon Sobeloff, July 2, 1964.

71. Letter from Chief Judge Simon Sobeloff to Judge Richard T. Rives, July 6, 1964.

72. Letter from Judge John R. Brown to Chief Judge J. Edward Lumbard, July 14, 1964.

73. Letter from Judge J. Edward Lumbard to Judge John Minor Wisdom, July 16, 1964.

74. For example, letter from Judge John Minor Wisdom to Chief Judge John Biggs, Jr., July 11, 1964.

75. For example, Judge Biggs responded to Judge Wisdom's materials by simply noting in reply: "I am in receipt of your letter of July 11 with its enclosures. Be assured that I will read them carefully and they will receive most serious consideration." Letter from Chief Judge John Biggs, Jr., to Judge John Minor Wisdom, July 14, 1964.

76. Letter from Judge Frank M. Johnson, Jr., to Judge Thomas M. Madden, July 13, 1964.

as they are in this." Madden concluded that the opponents of division had very likely "waited too long and are now moving too late."[77]

Although disappointed by this news, Wisdom and Rives seemed to view it merely as a temporary defeat that strengthened their resolve. As Wisdom said to Biggs at one point, they were simply girding their loins in preparation for September.[78] Both judges seemed much more concerned about the fact that Chief Judge Tuttle had not yet joined their active efforts than about their unsuccessful personal lobbying of key conference members.

In a rather long, homey letter to Justice William Brennan, Jr., in mid-July, Wisdom discussed the latest events concerning the campaign and expressed some candid thoughts on the subject:

> All in all, Dick and I are optimistic about the chances of the Judicial Conference reversing itself when it meets in September. But we are running scared. As we see it, the key to the solution is Judge Tuttle. We are both very close to him and are usually on the same side in civil rights decisions. We realize therefore that his agreement last May with the proposal to split the circuit was predicated solely on his belief that he had no alternative if we wished more judges. We hope to convince him that now the political facts and more considered thinking on the subject seem to indicate that the slow way to go about getting judges is to tie them in with splitting the circuit. Brown has already said that he is willing to go along with our views. If Tuttle too can be persuaded, Judge Hutcheson would probably follow and we would be able to go to the Conference with a favorable recommendation from the majority of our Judicial Council. This is a longer letter than I started out to write. My opinions always turn out that way too. I can't understand it.[79]

Less than a week after this letter all Fifth Circuit judges received notice from Chief Judge Tuttle that the Biggs Committee would meet in New York City on August 23 to decide whether to approve the draft of legislation pertaining to the split. Tuttle followed this information with the somewhat startling announcement that he would not attend the meeting. He explained that he intended to take off the entire month of August and planned to be in the vicinity of California or Montana on the date of the Biggs Committee meeting, and he noted that Judge Biggs had been informed of these plans prior to scheduling the date. Tuttle then invited each judge to submit his views to the Biggs Committee and appointed Judge Jones to transmit the Fifth Circuit Council's reaction to the technical aspects of the draft legislation.[80]

77. Letter from Judge Thomas M. Madden to Judge Frank M. Johnson, Jr., July 24, 1964.

78. Letter from Judge John Minor Wisdom to Chief Judge John Biggs, Jr., July 11, 1964.

79. Letter from Judge John Minor Wisdom to Justice William J. Brennan, Jr., July 16, 1964.

80. Letter from Chief Judge Elbert P. Tuttle to All Circuit Judges of the Fifth Circuit, July 20, 1964.

Any disappointment that Wisdom and Rives may have felt at Tuttle's announcement was offset when two weeks later Wisdom received a copy of a lengthy letter written along the lines of his own objections to the split. Addressed to Judge Biggs and signed by Judge John Brown, the letter had a note attached informing Wisdom that Judge Hutcheson had also written a similar letter to Biggs.[81] The official notice that Brown and Hutcheson had been converted to oppose the split meant that the Fifth Circuit Council was now deadlocked: Tuttle, Jones, Gewin, and Bell in favor of the split; Rives, Wisdom, Brown, and Hutcheson against. There was no longer a majority council position.

The month of July also saw Wisdom and Rives continuing to work on gaining the support of Emanuel Celler. There was every indication that Celler would be on the side of the foes of realignment, but to get a public statement from him committing himself to a firm position until a nationwide study could be conducted was becoming imperative. The urgency was prompted by reports that Senator Eastland's position was firmly anchored. Again in correspondence with Justice Brennan, Wisdom explained: "Senator Eastland is our stumbling block in the political arena. He originated the notion of a split and, supposedly, stands firm. He has told Jones of our Court, "No split—no judges." I believe that we do not have to pay that kind of a price. If the civil rights issue could be brought out in the open, my guess is that we would have a majority on the Senate Judiciary Committee and in Congress."[82]

As some support for division was predicated on filling the need for judicial help, Celler's statement was essential. His commitment could possibly change some Fifth Circuit judges' views, particularly Tuttle's, a change in whose vote would have a substantial influence on convincing the conference to reverse its position. Even those conference members who could not be swayed by Tuttle's vote very likely would be by Celler's support.

In early July, the *New York Times* published an encouraging article about Celler's position. It reported that Celler had heard that some southern judges whose views were out of line with federal court orders prohibiting racial discrimination favored redrawing circuit lines in such a way that their influence would be strengthened. Celler was quoted as responding, "They won't have their way so long as I am chairman of the House Committee on the Judiciary."[83]

Although such statements were helpful, they fell short of providing the circuit division opponents with the explicit stand against Eastland's plans for

81. Letter from Judge John R. Brown to Chief Judge John Biggs, Jr., July 31, 1964. Memorandum from Judge John R. Brown to Chief Judge Elbert P. Tuttle and Judges Richard T. Rives and John Minor Wisdom, July 31, 1964.

82. Letter from Judge John Minor Wisdom to Justice William J. Brennan, Jr., July 16, 1964.

83. Paul Crowell, "Change in Areas of Courts Urged," *New York Times*, July 5, 1964, p. 42.

which they had hoped. Celler responded to the packet of "campaign materials" Wisdom had sent him with a brief note saying that he was "aware" of the issues surrounding the realignment proposal.[84] Wisdom was probably hoping for a much stronger response. Yet he had also received assurances on several occasions from Simon Sobeloff, Skelly Wright, Burke Marshall, and Charles Alan Wright that Celler would indeed fight against realignment when the time came.

An important turn of events occurred, however, when Rives received an offer of assistance from Dean Joseph O'Meara of Notre Dame Law School.[85] O'Meara informed Rives that he had a close friend (who would remain anonymous) who knew Celler very well and had agreed to confer with him on the Fifth Circuit issue. Delighted, Rives explained to O'Meara that Celler's public opposition to a split could be the key to persuading Chief Judge Tuttle to change his official position.[86] Rives predicted that if Celler would openly commit to a firm stance against division, Tuttle might not be so swayed by Eastland's "no split, no judges" threat. He asked O'Meara to request that his anonymous friend try to obtain an agreement from Celler authorizing Wisdom and Rives to communicate Celler's views to their Fifth Circuit brethren. If O'Meara's friend were successful, Rives believed that the objectives of the opponents to division would be "boosted substantially." A month later, the O'Meara connection paid handsome dividends.

July 1964 ended on a positive note for Wisdom and Rives. Although attempts to convince key members of the Judicial Conference to change positions were largely unsuccessful, progress was clearly being made. Emanuel Celler appeared to be on the verge of expressing his opposition, and the conversions of Judges Brown and Hutcheson neutralized the previous realignment endorsement by the Fifth Circuit Council. The Wisdom/Rives campaign had turned the corner.

THE CONVERGENCE OF STRATEGIES

On August 9, the fortunes of the realignment opponents were substantially enhanced when the ABA's Council of the Section of Judicial Administration adopted a proposal for a nationwide study of the problems facing the courts of appeals. Primary responsibility for shepherding the proposal through the council had been assumed by Bernard Segal. The incoming head of the section, David W. Peck, then appointed a committee consisting of Justice Brennan, Judge Jameson, and Mr. Segal to draft recommendations regarding the

---

84. Letter from Representative Emanuel Celler to Judge John Minor Wisdom, July 7, 1964.
85. Letter from Dean Joseph O'Meara to Judge Richard T. Rives, July 9, 1964.
86. Letter from Judge Richard T. Rives to Dean Joseph O'Meara, July 13, 1964.

scope of the study and how it would be conducted and financed.[87] Five days after this action, Jameson, Wisdom, and Segal met to discuss the matter and agreed that Segal would draft the recommendations for committee approval. The national study proposal was given greater prominence when Lewis F. Powell, Jr., the newly installed president of the American Bar Association, endorsed the plan as the proper approach to the problem.[88] The Wisdom/Rives strategy to delay any division of the Fifth Circuit until completion of a comprehensive national study was beginning to succeed.

Following on the heels of this event came the highlight of Wisdom and Rives's month. Through Dean O'Meara's efforts, Celler had taken a firm stand against splitting the Fifth Circuit before a complete study of all circuits could be made and openly acknowledged that he would support expansion of the court beyond nine judges, at least on an experimental basis. Celler explained:

> I also understand that it has been suggested that unless the circuit is divided the Congress will not authorize additional judges for the existing circuit. In view of these representations, I think you and the other judges should be aware of my position. I am against division of the Fifth Circuit, or any other circuit, at this time until an overall study of the advisability of further division of the circuits has been completed. . . . I am confident that my Committee would want to know where we are headed with divisions of the circuits generally before it would favorably consider the division of the Fifth Circuit.[89]

Beginning with "forgetting our past differences," Rives transmitted Celler's message to all the Fifth Circuit judges. After informing them that both Chief Justice Warren and Justice Black agreed with Celler's view, Rives concluded, "is it not now obvious that the presently proposed split of our Circuit is in dramatic opposition to our getting additional Judges in the foreseeable future?"[90]

Immediately upon receiving Celler's statement and Rives's commentary, Judges Jones and Gewin were provoked into an exchange similar to that which had occurred over the April newspaper account. In a brief communication, Jones very curtly told Rives that he should explain his inferences regarding the procurement of additional judgeships and wondered whether by "forgetting past differences" Rives simply meant that the "majority should join the the minority."[91]

Gewin's comments were more critical and specific. While attending the American Bar Association's meeting at which the national realignment study

---

87. The actions of the council are outlined in a letter from Judge John Minor Wisdom to Professor Herbert Wechsler, September 1, 1964.

88. Letter from Lewis F. Powell, Jr., to Judge John Minor Wisdom, September 9, 1964.

89. Quoted in a letter from Judge Richard T. Rives to All Judges of the Fifth Circuit, August 20, 1964.

90. Ibid.

91. Letter from Judge Warren L. Jones to All Circuit Judges of the Fifth Circuit, August 21, 1964.

was authorized, Gewin told the court that he had learned of an extensive campaign being waged against the court's own council. Offended primarily by outside interference, Gewin thought it "regrettable" that individuals, Congress excepted, who did not reside in or have responsibility to the circuit had become involved in the issue. He seemed just as disturbed that the minority had abandoned the council decision and made a "national issue out of the matter."[92] In the event, Gewin warned, that both sides waged a campaign, it was entirely likely that nothing would be done to aid the court, which would collapse under its excessive workload.

A week later Wisdom circulated his response to the sharply worded criticisms of Jones and Gewin.[93] In a five-page letter, he reminded the members of the court that in May he and Rives, without any objections being registered by the others, had declared themselves free agents from the council's resolution. The letter continued by outlining the reasons for mounting this campaign over the summer months, and how it had rallied support around their position. A number of key figures had now expressed their opposition to dividing the circuit, including Representative Celler, Chief Justice Warren, and Judges Hutcheson and Brown. Importantly, the action by the American Bar Association to commission a study of the problems facing federal appellate courts nationwide made it prudent to postpone any action to realign the Fifth Circuit. These changed circumstances, Wisdom argued, warranted reconsideration of the council's May resolution. Consequently, he asked the judges to support his statement calling for: (1) a postponement of any action to divide the circuit until completion of the ABA study; and (2) the immediate authorization of additional judges for the court. Finally, Wisdom warned that if the majority could not support his resolution, he would appeal to the Judicial Conference of the United States.

In order to apprise his supporters of this internal exchange, Wisdom selectively distributed his letter, which was accompanied by a file of supportive materials. Part of this information packet was a copy of Charles Alan Wright's article published in the University of *Texas Law Review*.[94] Wright's piece was not only a persuasive explication of the issues facing the Fifth Circuit but became a leading article in the field of federal judicial administration. Reprints of the article became a standard part of the campaign material Wisdom and Rives continued to distribute to those who might have influence over this issue.[95] Rives was so impressed by Wisdom's materials that he urged him to

92. Letter from Judge Walter P. Gewin to All Fifth Circuit Judges, August 21, 1964.

93. Letter from Judge John Minor Wisdom to All Circuit Judges of the Fifth Circuit, August 27, 1964.

94. Charles Alan Wright, "The Overloaded Fifth Circuit: A Crisis in Judicial Administration," *Texas Law Review* 42 (October 1964): 949–82.

95. The Wright article was widely distributed by the opponents of circuit division. By his own accounting, Professor Wright sent reprints to 125 individuals. Rives distributed

distribute the documents to as many sympathetic people as possible. Rives and Wisdom had planned to send every conference member statements of their views immediately prior to the September meeting. Now, with the meeting just three weeks away, Rives felt time was of the essence.[96]

In the interim, the Biggs Committee met in New York on August 23 to consider the fate of the proposed legislation to divide the circuit. Despite Fahy's continued opposition and dissenting vote, the ad hoc committee approved the draft, with Chief Judges Murrah and Lumbard strongly opposed to a circuit court of more than nine judges. Fahy believed that Wisdom's views were not reaching the conference, and he encouraged Wisdom to contact each member individually.[97]

However, many participants who had received Wisdom's letter were very optimistic about its impact. In fact, Justice Black told Wisdom that after speaking with many judges he had "reason to believe" that the Wisdom, Rives, and Brown campaign was "being felt."[98] Black's response was bolstered by similar reactions from many individuals, including Justice Brennan[99] and Dean Erwin Griswold of the Harvard Law School.[100]

On September 10, Wisdom initiated his last-gasp effort to convince the conference to defeat the realignment proposal. He sent his materials to every member of the Judicial Conference. Then followed similar mailings to each Supreme Court justice, every Fifth Circuit district judge, and a host of other influentials, including key judges, law professors, and legal practitioners. The opponents hoped that this well-timed, final assault would exert sufficient pressure to defeat or delay final conference endorsement of division.

Although many of Wisdom and Rives's strategies were beginning to show signs of success, one important effort had not yet been rewarded. In a communication with Chief Justice Warren, Wisdom openly admitted how concerned he was that Chief Judge Tuttle had not yet publicly committed himself to the campaign. Particularly confusing to Wisdom was Tuttle's encouragement throughout the summer of Wisdom's anti-division activities when he would not rescind his council vote. He sought to explain to Warren: "Stout Presbyterian that he is and conscientious Chief Judge that he is he feels some sort of moral compulsion not to go back on a proposal he initiated. I have

---

twenty-five copies and Wisdom mailed two hundred. Letter from Professor Charles Alan Wright to Justice Tom C. Clark, October 13, 1964.

96. Letter from Judge Richard T. Rives to Judge John Minor Wisdom, August 31, 1964.

97. Letter from Judge Charles Fahy to Judge John Minor Wisdom, September 2, 1964.

98. Letter from Justice Hugo L. Black to Judge John Minor Wisdom, September 9, 1964.

99. Letter from Justice William L. Brennan, Jr., to Judge John Minor Wisdom, September 4, 1964.

100. Letter from Dean Erwin Griswold to Judge John Minor Wisdom, September 8, 1964.

not given up, however. As late as this morning he said that he had not reached a final conclusion."[101]

Wisdom and Rives had considered making a personal appearance at the meeting of the Judicial Conference, but after considerable reflection they decided that such an action would be unwise, especially if Tuttle did not reverse his position. Because they had such a close relationship with him, they wished to avoid any appearance of "pitting themselves against Tuttle," Wisdom told the chief justice. Instead, he asked Warren if Professor Wright might be permitted to attend the conference to present their views. When Wright was informed of Wisdom's suggestion he responded: "I could not help but think of the boxing manager who said to his fighter just before the round began, 'Go on in there and hit, they can't hurt us.' Seriously, if the Chief Justice does want me to go into the lines then I will make my will, increase my insurance, and do so."[102]

A while passed before Wisdom received a response from Warren, who had been busy working on President Johnson's Commission on the Assassination of President Kennedy. Warren, however, told Wisdom that anything short of an invitation from Tuttle to Wright would probably not be received well by the conference, especially since Wright was advocating the chief justice's position.[103]

TEMPORARY JUDGESHIPS: A COMPROMISE

Obviously, without Tuttle's explicit support Wisdom and Rives were not highly optimistic about gaining the official support of the Circuit Council. Yet they remained hopeful. After all, they had managed to bring Brown and Hutcheson into their fold, and it remained possible that another might be persuaded to join them.

Their hopes were partially rewarded in mid-September when Griffin Bell, hitherto a firm supporter of division, announced a modification in his position. Bell was now willing to accept any conference action as long as the court received the additional judges. Always anxious to find solutions to political deadlocks, Bell offered a viable compromise. Because he believed that an impasse had been reached in both the Congress and the council, he suggested that the legislature create a temporary judgeship for each member of the court who was eligible to retire but had not yet elected to take senior status. At a subsequent date, when the eligible judge did take senior status, his position would not be filled. Relief, therefore, would be on an interim basis,

101. Letter from Judge John Minor Wisdom to Chief Justice Earl Warren, September 9, 1964.

102. Letter from Professor Charles Alan Wright to Judge John Minor Wisdom, September 11, 1964.

103. Letter from Chief Justice Earl Warren to Judge John Minor Wisdom, September 18, 1964.

giving the court additional judge power while the question of a more permanent solution was being debated. Bell's proposal was a compromise between Wisdom's preference to experiment with a larger court and the Rule of Nine advocates who were adamantly opposed to exceeding the traditional size. Bell asked each member to transmit his vote on the resolution to Chief Judge Tuttle.[104]

The chief judge seized upon Bell's suggestion as a viable way out of the court's predicament and wrote to the members of his court urging them to support the resolution. Tuttle remained convinced that Eastland's threat, as relayed by Judge Jones, was a "fact of political life of unquestioned importance." It had caused both the Biggs Committee and Tuttle to support division. Tuttle believed it was virtually certain that the senator would kill any permanent expansion in the number of judgeships unless the circuit was divided. He hoped, however, that Bell's suggestion "might be approved by the Conference and might not run counter to Senator Eastland's announced position."[105]

For Tuttle the compromise carried an additional bonus. Though personally opposed to dividing the circuit, as leader of the court he felt bound by the council's determination that realignment offered the only avenue for obtaining new judges. If adopted, Bell's proposal would provide the court with its necessary staff and, as a consequence, would release Tuttle from his obligation to support the council's recommendation to split the circuit.

By a unanimous vote the council authorized Tuttle to offer Bell's proposal at the conference meeting. Although Jones endorsed the compromise, he indicated that this proposal would most likely be futile.[106] As Jones had been the primary means through which Eastland's views had been transmitted, he seemed to be convinced that the senator would not yield on the issue; Wisdom, to the contrary, told Judge Brown that he was unsure just how strongly Eastland held his view because Jones had been the only person communicating it.[107]

Eventually, Wisdom accepted the possibility that Eastland's stance was firm, or at least influential among some conference members, and consequently voted for Bell's suggestion. Wisdom was also convinced that some of the key conference members were against his position because they did not want the Fifth Circuit to have more judges than their own circuits. Also, some opposition in the conference was generated, Wisdom told Brown, because of the feeling that Wisdom, Rives, and Brown did not "come into court with clean

104. Letter from Judge Griffin B. Bell to All Fifth Circuit Judges, September 14, 1964.

105. Letter from Chief Judge Elbert P. Tuttle to All Circuit Judges of the Fifth Circuit, September 16, 1964.

106. Letter from Judge Warren L. Jones to All Fifth Circuit Judges, September 16, 1964.

107. Letter from Judge John Minor Wisdom to Judge John R. Brown, September 15, 1964.

hands because of Judge Hutcheson."[108] In effect, Wisdom thought some judges looked unfavorably upon their pursuing Hutcheson while he was not in good health. To remove any confusion about where they stood, Wisdom sent another letter to every conference member only a few days before their meeting, reaffirming his and Rives's undiminished opposition to division. That they had voted for Bell's proposal, Wisdom said, in no way meant that they were less opposed.[109]

THE CONFERENCE FINALE

Throughout September much of Wisdom's correspondence indicated that support for his viewpoint was building. Communications were especially optimistic during the week before the conference meeting. Seven members of the Supreme Court responded favorably to the Wisdom/Rives campaign materials. Judge Skelly Wright sent a note to Wisdom and Rives the day before the conference, stating that Celler would appear before the meeting to restate his opposition to splitting the circuit and to urge the adoption of a nationwide study on realignment.[110]

Representative Celler did appear before the conference when it convened on September 23. He delivered a five-page address that left no doubt about his position on the issues facing the Fifth Circuit. The speech was an extremely forceful one, more supportive of the case against division than Wisdom and Rives could ever have hoped. First, he argued that the problems facing the Fifth Circuit were not unique to it. The question of circuit boundaries was a national one and the issue should not be dealt with on a piecemeal basis. A study of the entire problem was long overdue. Second, Celler saw no great reason to limit courts to nine judges, especially those, like the courts of appeals, that operate in three-judge panels. He personally was quite willing to consider adding judges above the number nine if they were truly needed in any given court. Third, he suggested several ways to improve the capacity of the courts of appeals to handle their caseloads and urged the conference to take them under consideration.

Celler, however, did not confine his remarks simply to these administrative matters pertaining to realignment. He also launched into a discussion of the civil rights implications of the proposed division. He minced no words:

> This is certain, that judges appointed from Texas and Louisiana who would no longer be included in the Fifth Circuit are likely to be vigorous in their support of civil rights, but judges appointed from Alabama, Florida, Georgia

108. Ibid.
109. Letter from Judge John Minor Wisdom to the Members of the Judicial Conference of the United States, September 17, 1964.
110. Letter from Judge J. Skelly Wright to Judges Richard T. Rives and John Minor Wisdom, September 22, 1964.

and Mississippi, States which would make up the new Fifth Circuit, might not
be so sanguine in their strict adherence to recent Supreme Court rulings. These
are practical political considerations. They cannot be disregarded. As a pragmatic politician, I do not disregard them.[111]

The implications of Celler's words were not lost on the delegates. It was
abundantly clear that the House would not be amenable to any legislation
dividing the Fifth Circuit until a comprehensive study of the entire system
was completed. Celler's position was anchored in his deep feelings concerning
civil rights and his obvious anger that the conference had ignored his previous
warnings to conduct a systematic study of circuit boundaries. Under these
circumstances, the conference was reluctant to act favorably on the Biggs
Committee's recommendation.

In the meantime, Chief Judge Tuttle was carefully campaigning for Judge
Bell's temporary judgeship compromise. Armed with data on the overwhelming need for additional judges and supported by the unanimous endorsement
of the Fifth Circuit Council, Tuttle promoted the compromise proposal as
the only viable option left to the conference. This action would give the circuit
the immediate help it needed while avoiding the thicket of disagreement over
realignment.

Even before the conference meeting ended, the communication lines were
filled with news of encouragement for Wisdom and Rives. Justice William O.
Douglas sent a note to Wisdom on the first day of the meeting expressing his
view that dividing the Fifth Circuit would be unwise.[112] Then, on the second
day of the session, Justice William Brennan wrote to Wisdom: "From what I
hear around this building your enclosures have done the trick at the Conference. My sincerest congratulations!"[113]

These optimistic communications proved to be well deserved, as it was soon
learned that the conference had tabled the proposal to divide the Fifth Circuit.
The opponents of division had successfully blocked final approval of the Biggs
Committee recommendation. Following a rather bland description of Celler's
address,[114] the conference report recommended to Congress, with respect to
the Fifth, "that there be created immediately four additional judgeships for
that court on a temporary basis."[115]

---

111. Representative Emanuel Celler's comments to the Judicial Conference of the United
States, September 23, 1964. Emanuel Celler Papers, Library of Congress, Container 539.

112. Letter from Justice William O. Douglas to Judge John Minor Wisdom, September
23, 1964.

113. Letter from Justice William J. Brennan, Jr., to Judge John Minor Wisdom, September 24, 1964.

114. *Report of the Proceedings of the Judicial Conference of the United States*, September 23–
24, 1964, p. 49.

115. Ibid., p. 63.

CELEBRATION AND WORDS OF CAUTION

Congratulatory greetings flew among the campaign supporters like a whirlwind. Much of the credit for convincing the conference to table the proposal was given to Wisdom.[116] Among the many who acknowledged the persuasiveness of his communications and complimented him on his style were such prominent jurists as Justice Black, Judges Wright and Fahy, and noted law professors Paul Freund (Harvard) and Paul Mishkin (Pennsylvania). Justice Tom Clark also sent a hand-scribbled note to Wisdom, which began, "in your usual effective way you have 'demolished' those favoring the split."[117] Judge Fahy wrote that Wisdom's arguments had "played perhaps a decisive role at the last testing of the matter at the Conference."[118]

Judge Rives seemed to be equally, if not more, delighted with the conference's decision. Even before formal release of the conference action, Rives, excluding no participant, began disseminating expressions of his gratitude to those who had helped the campaign. He congratulated every ally for the great public service to which he had contributed. Wisdom, among the first, received the following personal note: "Most of all, I cannot begin to express my thanks to you and my admiration for the skill and intelligence with which you have conducted this 'campaign.' "[119] Reminding Judge Sobeloff of his recommendation that they all pray for and to the chair of the House Judiciary Committee, Rives noted that the advice had been "sound and prophetic."[120]

The day after the conference concluded, Rives sent an especially warm note to his three Fifth Circuit colleagues (Hutcheson, Brown, and Wisdom) who had voted with and actively supported the opposition strategy. In this correspondence he stated: "Those of us who have opposed the division of our Circuit are indebted to Chairman Celler. We owe a major debt of gratitude to John Wisdom's intelligence and untiring efforts, to Professor Charles Alan Wright for his article, to Judge Skelly Wright for brilliantly field marshalling our forces, to Judges Fahy and Sobeloff for bearing the brunt of the fight in the Conference, and to many others."[121]

Amidst the backslapping that occurred throughout the autumn months, a few participants uttered words of caution. Judge Rives constantly reminded

116. Wisdom was famous for writing eloquent opinions. Many participants would compliment Wisdom on his current decisions, referring to many of them as masterpieces, during a communication concerning the division.

117. Letter from Justice Tom Clark to Judge John Minor Wisdom, October 5, 1964.

118. Letter from Judge Charles Fahy to Judge John Minor Wisdom, October 21, 1964.

119. Letter from Judge Richard T. Rives to Judge John Minor Wisdom, September 25, 1964.

120. Letter from Judge Richard T. Rives to Chief Judge Simon Sobeloff, September 25, 1964.

121. Letter from Judge Richard T. Rives to Judges Joseph C. Hutcheson, Jr., John R. Brown, and John Minor Wisdom, September 25, 1964.

realignment opponents of the need to cooperate with the nationwide study. In a somewhat tentative response, Fahy warned that although the situation was better in the sense that "an effort [would] be made to obtain additional judges without the necessity of a division, the latter possibility [remained]."[122] After all, the temporary judgeships required legislative authorization, and there was no reason to believe that Eastland had changed his position on realignment.

Some of the opponents of division had already shifted their attention to Congress. For example, when Justice Clark expressed his admiration for Charles Alan Wright's *Texas Law Review* article, the professor did not hesitate to point out in response that the battle had yet to be won in Congress and consequently asked Clark to distribute reprints of the article to his friends there.[123] Judge Rives, in a similar vein, distributed reprints of the Wright analysis along with a Houston newspaper article to Alabama senators Lister Hill and John Sparkman.[124]

For the most part, supporters of the Wisdom/Rives campaign agreed to resume their efforts as the focus moved to Congress. For example, Nicholas deB. Katzenbach, who had become acting attorney general, renewed his commitment.[125] Rives and Wisdom, however, received news from one ally that was particularly disappointing. Simon Sobeloff, whose efforts had been invaluable in the conference debates, said that he would soon be required, because of age, to step down as chief judge of the Fourth Circuit. As he would consequently lose his membership in the Judicial Conference, he would no longer be strategically placed to carry on the fight within that body. He was reasonably confident, however, that his successor, Judge Clement F. Haynsworth, Jr., would be predisposed to support the national study, even though his and Sobeloff's approaches to certain issues were not similar.[126] Implicit in Sobeloff's comment were labor and civil rights, as Haynsworth had a conservative record on both of those issues.

By the end of 1964, Wisdom and Rives had battled Goliaths and won—at least temporarily. They had encountered a majority opinion completely at odds with their views and had convinced the policy-making arm of the federal judiciary to suspend its judgment. Even the original council vote had been transformed into a tie. By executing deliberate strategies and organizing a well-developed lobbying campaign, the two had succeeded in turning a re-

---

122. Letter from Judge Charles Fahy to Judge Richard T. Rives, October 5, 1964.

123. Letter from Professor Charles Alan Wright to Justice Tom C. Clark, October 13, 1964.

124. Letter from Judge Richard T. Rives to Senators Lister Hill and John Sparkman, December 5, 1964.

125. Letter from Acting Attorney General Nicholas deB. Katzenbach to Judge John Minor Wisdom, October 27, 1964.

126. Letter from Chief Judge Simon Sobeloff to Judge John Minor Wisdom, October 21, 1964.

gional administrative matter into an issue of national concern. The official conference policy failed because Rives and Wisdom had been able to politicize it. But the politics of the issue did not die here.

Moving the issue into the congressional arena, however, necessarily changed the nature of the conflict. Rives and Wisdom were no longer operating on their own political turf. Legislative politics, dominated by considerations of constituencies, the effects on reelection, and the demands of competing policy areas, was played very differently. Here they were confronting essentially new political actors and, because of the separation of powers doctrine, were treading on a precarious ground of political relationships. Yet Wisdom and Rives had demonstrated by their successful strategy to mobilize Emanuel Celler's support that they would not hesitate to plunge into congressional politics.

At the beginning of 1964, the realignment issue had little relevance to anyone other than the Fifth Circuit judges and the members of the Judicial Conference. By the end of the year, however, the politics of judicial reform had attracted a much larger audience, both inside and outside government. The Fifth Circuit controversy became the subject of major pieces appearing in the *Houston Chronicle*, the *Washington Post*, and the *New York Times*.[127] Not only had the issue taken on national significance, but the "Four," as Judge Cameron had labeled them, had almost become national figures in their own right. The December 4 issue of *Time* magazine carried a two-page article on Tuttle, Rives, Wisdom, and Brown, focusing on their trailblazing civil rights decisions and the less-than-straightforward administrative proposal to carve up their circuit, thereby threatening to lessen their impact in that area.[128] Civil rights concerns were now inextricably tied to the realignment proposal. In many respects, the personal and political relationships established in 1964 set the tone for discussions on the issue for the next sixteen years.

---

127. Editorial, "U.S. Fifth Circuit Court of Appeals Must Be Enlarged," *Houston Chronicle*, November 19, 1964; editorial, "Overburdened Courts," *Washington Post*, October 5, 1964; Anthony Lewis, "Court Logjam," *New York Times*, November 1, 1964.

128. "The Fascinating and Frenetic Fifth," *Time*, December 4, 1964, pp. 46–47.

5

A Simmering
Issue

Compared to 1963 and 1964, the politics surrounding the division of the Fifth Circuit ebbed to a much slower pace from 1965 until 1970. The Wisdom/Rives campaign had injected enough controversy into the process of judicial reform to induce Congress, the United States Judicial Conference, and the Fifth Circuit to put the the issue on the back burner. None of these key decision-makers wanted to resurrect the acrimonious debates of 1964, which had left many reluctant to proceed as long as dissension existed among federal judges.

The flare sent up by the Wisdom/Rives campaign was a clear warning that civil rights progress in the South was seriously threatened by the move to split the Deep South circuit; and because realignment was thus politicized by the civil rights issue, all reform measures would arouse suspicion. Also, until the Fifth Circuit judges presented a united front on an alternative, no reform could be sanctioned. The court's internal struggle over civil rights, dating back to the Freedom-Rider cases, made unanimity virtually impossible. As a result, any court reform that would alter the balance of power on the southern federal bench was to be a dead letter for the next six years.

After the Judicial Conference's rejection of circuit division, the court faced two related problems that demanded immediate attention—collegiality and caseload. One was easier to resolve than the other. The innuendos, allegations, and attacks that the Fifth Circuit had undergone, both internally and exter-nally, had fractured the court's collegiality, a central element in its ability to perform the monumental tasks that lay ahead. The judges realized that the court would not be well served by continuing polemics and thus called a "truce" on the subject. That opponents of division had in fact turned the tide of opinion in their favor was perhaps equally important in rendering the issue dormant. The judges began to close rifts in relationships and, as a first step, removed circuit splitting from the court's agenda. But, as one member re-called, "no judge serving on the court could not be conscious of the overlay of the problem."[1] Because no solution had yet been found, the court's swelling docket, additional judges, and internal administrative reforms would ultimately bring circuit splitting back into the political forum for discussion.

THE SWELLING DOCKET

The court's caseload crisis could not be ignored. During the 1960s the Fifth Circuit became the nation's busiest appellate court: appeals increased twofold from 1960 to 1964 and doubled again from 1965 to 1970. Its docket was almost twice that of the median in the U.S. Courts of Appeals from 1965 to 1970, exceeding even circuits with the next heaviest dockets by 17 to 27 percentage points. Overall case filings during the decade jumped 249 percent in the Fifth Circuit compared to 190 percent nationwide.

Sheer volume of cases, however, was only part of the litigation picture. Commensurate with the rise in caseload was the increasing complexity of issues brought before the court. Federal litigation spawned in the Fifth Circuit involved some of the nation's most perplexing and explosive issues. Many of the Fifth's decisions were on the cutting edge of national policy. Resolving these socially sensitive and politically volatile issues required judicial attention and time far beyond that indicated by caseload figures alone. Sizable increases occurred in all categories of the court's docket, but none as significant as civil rights. The Fifth Circuit's caseload included the most divisive issues—school desegregation, voting rights, jury and employment discrimination.

Enactment of the 1964 Civil Rights Act and the 1965 Voting Rights Act formalized the nation's commitment to equality under the law. These landmark statutes entailed the broadest societal ramifications for the Deep South to that point. They were double-edged swords for the Fifth Circuit. While the judges could render decisions supported by strong federal law, these new causes of action greatly accelerated the pace of litigation in the toilworn Fifth Circuit.

By the mid-1960s, many members of the Fifth Circuit realized that operating under the "with all deliberate speed" doctrine was substantially hampering progress toward public school desegregation. Resigned to the fact that the lower federal courts were losing ground in the struggle to supervise school desegregation, John Wisdom, speaking for a majority of Fifth Circuit judges in two landmark Mississippi school cases, *Singleton v. Jackson Municipal Separate School District* (1965)[2] and *Singleton II* (1966),[3] required school systems to develop affirmative desegregation plans. These pronouncements were followed by *United States v. Jefferson County Board of Education* (1966)[4] and the en banc

1. Interview with Judge Irving Goldberg, Dallas, Texas, December 14, 1983.
2. 348 F.2d 729 (5th Cir. 1965).
3. 355 F.2d 865 (5th Cir. 1966).
4. 372 F.2d 836 (5th Cir. 1966).

hearing *Jefferson II* (1967).[5] Judge Wisdom's majority opinion in *Jefferson I* has been referred to as "one of the four most important school desegregation cases yet decided."[6] *Jefferson I* and *II* went beyond the idea that the Fourteenth Amendment merely prohibits state laws from establishing racial barriers and held that states had an affirmative duty to adopt plans to effectuate racial integration forthwith.

Major school desegregation cases became routine for the Fifth Circuit during this period (1965–70). The court issued more than twice as many school desegregation decisions (164) as it had in the previous decade of implementing *Brown v. Board of Education of Topeka* (1954)[7] and *Brown II* (1955).[8] The Justice Department entered sixty-six school desegregation cases during 1966, double the number filed in 1965. In just one year (1969), "the Fifth Circuit handed down 166 opinion orders involving eighty-nine separate school districts."[9] Two of these school desegregation cases involved thirty-three segregated counties in Mississippi and precipitated fifty-seven opinions.[10]

These cases were only the tip of the iceberg. By the mid-sixties a virtual Pandora's box of civil rights issues had been opened on the doorstep of the New Orleans courthouse. The scope of conflict over desegregation broadened to include incidents at amusement parks, public swimming pools, and other nongovernmental establishments.[11] The judges plowed through a landslide of discrimination claims of all varieties. The court chose the en banc hearing as a central means for creating powerful precedents in novel and controversial civil rights litigation. In an effort to establish uniform standards for state and federal juror selection, the judges scheduled six major jury discrimination cases for their en banc calendar in 1966 alone. In one, *Rabinowitz v. United States* (1966),[12] the court, through Judge Rives, deemed the key-man system, used to identify qualified federal jurors, an inadequate reflection of cross-sectional representation of the community. Congress "virtually codified"[13] the *Rabinowitz* decision in the 1968 Jury Selection and Service Act.

The mid-1960s also brought the Fifth Circuit to the forefront of its activist stance on voting rights. Wisdom's majority opinion in *United States v. Louisiana*

5. 380 F.2.d 385 (5th Cir. 1967).

6. Frank T. Read and Lucy S. McGough, *Let Them Be Judged: The Judicial Integration of the Deep South* (Metuchen, N.J.: The Scarecrow Press, 1978), p. 436.

7. 347 U.S. 483 (1954).

8. 349 U.S. 294 (1955).

9. Read and McGough, *Let Them Be Judged*, p. 469.

10. Ibid., p. 453; Harvey C. Couch, *A History of the Fifth Circuit 1891–1981* (Washington, D.C.: Government Printing Office, under the auspices of the Bicentennial Committee of the Judicial Conference of the United States, 1984), p. 148; Lester A. Sobel, *Civil Rights 1960–1966* (New York: Facts on File, 1967), p. 413.

11. Couch, *A History*, pp. 142–43.

12. 366 F.2d 34 (5th Cir. 1966).

13. Read and McGough, *Let Them Be Judged*, p. 344.

$(1963)^{14}$ and Brown's dissent in *United States v. Mississippi* $(1964)^{15}$ were treatises on the discriminatory effects of those states' use of "understanding tests" to bar black voter registration. These tests had been used in several states in addition to "literacy tests." Based on the 1964 Civil Rights Act and the opinions of Judges Brown and Wisdom, the Supreme Court unanimously struck down state laws containing understanding tests in 1965. The Voting Rights Act of 1965 suspended the literacy requirement in state election laws.

While the court was facing the final showdown in these long-standing conflicts over civil rights, it was also blazing paths on the periphery of individual rights and the due process revolution. As a consequence, unconventional civil rights issues appeared across the court's docket. For example, the Vietnam War gave rise to ninety-five conscientious objector cases from 1964 to 1968, of which the most noted was Muhammed Ali's appeal. Only fourteen draft cases had been docketed from 1946 to 1958.[16] In 1969, the court, through Judge Wisdom, took up yet another civil rights challenge and cleared new ground from the thicket of employment discrimination. By taking the stance that bona fide seniority systems perpetuating past discriminatory hiring and promotion practices were unconstitutional, Wisdom developed the supporting legal rationale for what almost twenty years later became one of the more controversial issues before the Supreme Court: affirmative action.[17]

Civil rights litigation took its toll on the Fifth Circuit, not only because the issues were explosive by nature, but also because they demanded time and procedures beyond other types of cases. During this period the circuit tailored administrative procedures to enforce its decisions in local school cases. These controversial, expedited rules included a mandatory priority schedule that provided civil rights litigants with immediate access to the circuit on appeal from the district court ruling. The court also stabilized the judicial environment for these litigants by using an assignment system similar to an individual calendar system. Once assigned to a case, the panel would monitor its ruling and retain jurisdiction over subsequent controversies flowing from it.[18] Often, en banc hearings were required to resolve these conflicts. Although en bancs were a tremendous drain on judicial resources, requiring most judges to travel hundreds of miles to attend, they marshaled institutional support and uniformity for civil rights law. From 1965 to 1970, between one-quarter and one-half of all en banc hearings in the eleven U.S. Courts of Appeals were held in the Fifth Circuit.

The energies of the court were further taxed when the judges were regularly siphoned out of their courtrooms to sit on the three-judge district court

14. 225 F.Supp. 353 (E.D. La. 1963), aff'd 380 U.S. 145 (1965).
15. 229 F.Supp. 925 (S.D. Miss. 1964), rev'd 380 U.S. 128 (1965).
16. Couch, *A History*, p. 144.
17. *Local 189, United Papermakers and Paperworkers v. United States*, 416 F.2d 980 (5th Cir. 1969), cert. denied, 397 U.S. 919 (1970).
18. Read and McGough, *Let Them Be Judged*, p. 469.

cases at a rather high rate relative to other circuits. For example, in 1965, 39 percent of all three-judge district courts in the eleven circuits were convened in the Fifth. One-half of these cases involved civil rights issues. The Fifth Circuit's proportion of three-judge cases never dropped below 39 percent and increased to a high of 49 percent in 1970.

Civil rights litigation in the U.S. district courts within the Fifth Circuit also contributed to the speed of this pace. It fell within the authority, indeed within the responsibility, of the circuit judges to perform their supervisory function over all circuit and district court business. Ninety-one percent of civil rights cases commenced nationwide in 1965 were handled by the district courts within the Fifth Circuit. Slightly more than 91 percent of the Fifth Circuit's cases, or 83 percent of civil rights cases nationwide, were filed in Mississippi alone.[19] Thus, recalcitrant district court attitudes were just one side of the coin; the concentration of cases in one region was equally important.

Although civil rights cases were perhaps the most burdensome, time-consuming, and certainly the most controversial cases brought before the judges, ironically enough, they never comprised more than 2 or 3 percent of the Fifth Circuit's docket.[20] Criminal filings, in contrast, constituted from 17 to as much as 25 percent of the court's caseload from 1965 to 1970. The Fifth Circuit got the full brunt of the due process revolution of the sixties. Such landmark Supreme Court decisions as *Gideon v. Wainwright*[21] and *Miranda v. Arizona*[22] had a profound impact on the court responsible for transforming the South's often obstinate attitude toward change. The judges added to the fast pace of their criminal appeals by expanding the newly granted rights of defendants which emerged as doctrines from the Supreme Court in the sixties. The court further escalated criminal appeals when Chief Judge Tuttle issued a novel precedent permitting civil rights demonstrators to move their appeals for criminal trespassing and breach of peace to federal court under the authority of the 1964 Civil Rights Act.[23] During these five years, the rate of increase for the Fifth Circuit was almost three times the national rate of increase in criminal filings (133 percent to 47 percent). Rounding out the court's workload were diversity cases, for which the Fifth Circuit led the nation in appeals; and in the mid-sixties the court issued several noted libel decisions.[24]

This doctrinal profile was the product of the busiest federal judges and perhaps the most controversial tribunal in the nation's history. The Fifth Circuit accepted its institutional role and willingly performed the pivotal task of ushering a troubled South from a dying status quo to a new era of history.

19. *Annual Report of the Director of the Administrative Office of the U.S. Courts* (Washington, D.C.: Administrative Office of the United States Courts, 1965).
20. Couch, *A History*, p. 98.
21. 372 U.S. 335 (1963).
22. 384 U.S. 436 (1966).
23. *Georgia v. Rachel*, 342 F.2d 336 (5th Cir. 1965), aff'd 384 U.S. 780 (1966).
24. Couch, *A History*, pp. 129–30.

While many were aware of the court's outstanding accomplishments with respect to litigation, little was ever known of the political battles fought over realignment. In the midst of this tremendous caseload crisis, the judges were mindful that they had to stay attuned to the halls of Congress. The proposal to divide had been stayed, but the fate of additional judgeships lay in the hands of the Senate Judiciary Committee and Senator Eastland. While the civil rights revolution loomed in the background, the press of circuit business demanded its own degree of attention.

GAINING ACCESS TO THE LION

With Lyndon Johnson in the White House, the wheels of the Democrat-controlled Congress began to turn, albeit slowly. In February 1965, five months after the conference had tabled the notion of division and accepted the compromise, Representative Celler introduced a bill to provide four temporary judges for the Fifth Circuit (H.R. 5279). After it was referred to the House Judiciary Committee, no subsequent action was taken nor hearings held on the bill. Among the Fifth Circuit judges a concern filled the air that something was amiss in Congress. All signs indicated that the proffered compromise of additional judgeships as an alternative to circuit splitting was in jeopardy. By now the conference showdown was eight months old, and the court's needs carried less exigency for most decisionmakers. For three months Celler's proposed bill had been in limbo. The Judicial Conference approved the temporary appointments proposal in March, as part of the omnibus judgeship package sent to Congress requesting an additional forty-nine judgeships nationwide. Yet the positions remained unauthorized, with little apparent progress having been made other than when Senator Olin D. Johnston (D-SC), at the request of the Judicial Conference, introduced the recommended judgeship package in April. More importantly, two years had lapsed since the Fifth Circuit Council had agreed with Chief Judge Tuttle that the plea for additional judicial help was indeed an urgent one.

Delays in the legislative process were only part of the problem. More worrisome was the political environment in which the Fifth Circuit, an institution in less than favorable stead with Senator Eastland, had requested the additional judges. Mississippi was under severe scrutiny. After holding five days of voting rights hearings in Jackson in February 1965, the Civil Rights Commission issued a stinging report in mid-May declaring that Mississippi had the worst voting rights record of any state in the South. From January through May, the Justice Department vied with the commission for priority to investigate civil rights incursions in Mississippi. Attorney General Katzenbach was in Mississippi pursuing indictments against a lynch mob that had killed three civil rights workers in the summer of 1964.[25] The Mississippi Board of Ed-

25. Foster Rhea Dulles, *The Civil Rights Commission: 1957–1965* (East Lansing: Michigan State University Press, 1968), pp. 232–41.

ucation was facing a total loss of federal funding because of lack of compliance with Fifth Circuit school desegregation orders. Finally, in the larger political arena, the Senate started formal debate on the proposed 1965 Voting Rights Act in April. After the nation had witnessed the violence suffered by voting rights demonstrators in the planned march from Selma to Montgomery known as Bloody Sunday, President Johnson urged Congress to act on voting rights legislation. As long as Senator Eastland, in concert with other powerful members of the conservative coalition, was filibustering the proposed Voting Rights Act, he had little interest in responding to a request for more federal judges.

Ever more impatient and desperate for additional judges, Chief Judge Tuttle decided to take action, albeit indirect, to obtain the temporary judicial positions. He contacted Sobeloff's successor, Chief Judge Clement F. Haynsworth, Jr., of Greenville, South Carolina. Although Sobeloff had been a loyal opponent of division, he could probably not have provided the effective assistance that Chief Judge Haynsworth ultimately gave to the judgeship request. Because Eastland and the southern Democratic senators from the states comprising the Fourth Circuit had held up Sobeloff's nomination for a year, Sobeloff was on less than cordial terms with the powerful conservative coalition members. Haynsworth, on the other hand, not only had a favorable relationship with Senator Strom Thurmond (R-SC), but also had access to Senator Olin Johnston (D-SC), chairman of the Subcommittee on Improvements in Judicial Machinery, which had jurisdiction over the judgeships. Johnston and Eastland were close political allies. The two senators had a combined forty-four years of seniority in the Senate, were the second- and fourth-ranking Democrats on the Agriculture and Forestry Committee, the top-ranking Democrats on Judiciary, and served together on three subcommittees with Eastland as chair and Johnston the second-ranking Democrat. The two also had scrutinized and temporarily delayed Judge Wisdom's appointment to the bench in 1957.

Chief Judge Tuttle, realizing that his good friend Haynsworth had access to the southern Democrats and a working arrangement with Eastland that he himself did not, called him and explained the previous clash between Eastland and Celler, with which Haynsworth was already somewhat familiar. Tuttle's request was straightforward: "If you could, explain to Senator Eastland that his good friends who are lawyers in Jackson, Mississippi, handling ordinary civil/federal cases will never get their cases argued in our court unless we get some additional help."[26]

As a supplement to this message, Tuttle suggested that Haynsworth offer the four temporary judgeships as a means to break the impasse between Celler and Eastland. At first Haynsworth intended to contact Eastland indirectly through Senator Johnston, but because of Johnston's unexpected illness and

26. Interview with Chief Judge Elbert P. Tuttle, Atlanta, Georgia, October 20, 1982.

death, he turned his attention to another source, indicating to Tuttle that he might have "indirect access to the lion himself."[27]

One of the vice presidents of J. P. Stevens and Company, Gordon McCabe, had long been the principal liaison between the textile industry and Congress for agricultural legislation. McCabe was in charge of raw materials acquisitions and paid special attention to legislation affecting cotton. As the senior senator from Mississippi and owner of a sizable family cotton plantation, Eastland had a strong interest in agricultural matters. Former Attorney General Katzenbach, who often negotiated with Eastland, recalled that the senator held agriculture in higher political regard than civil rights.[28] Consequently, Eastland played an important role as the fourth-ranking Democrat on the Agriculture Committee, as head of the Subcommittee on Soil Conservation, and as second-ranking member on the Agricultural Research and General Legislation Subcommittee. Over the years, McCabe had developed an "extremely close" friendship with Senator Eastland.[29] Chief Judge Haynsworth, himself no stranger to the textile industry or to J. P. Stevens and Company, believed McCabe to be a "thoroughly honorable fellow," and one who might be able to persuade Eastland to support the temporary judgeships.[30]

Ultimately Haynsworth succeeded in having Tuttle's message relayed through McCabe. He talked at length with Eastland, urging him to support the much needed judgeships regardless of the designs he might have concerning organization of the circuit. Eastland returned a favorable response, expressing the view that he would support the bill for the temporary judgeships. Meanwhile, Judge Griffin Bell informed all the Fifth Circuit judges that Senator Talmadge (D-GA), another formidable member of the conservative coalition who served on the Agriculture Committee with Eastland, had arranged a conference between Bell and Eastland. Bell told his brethren, "Eastland stated that he favors the relief to the court which will be afforded through the temporary judgeships."[31] About a week later, Senator Hill relayed a similar interpretation of Eastland's view to Judge Rives.[32]

Although delighted by the news that the temporary positions were likely to be approved, the judges were apprehensive about what appeared to be yet

27. Letter from Chief Judge Clement F. Haynsworth, Jr., to Chief Judge Elbert P. Tuttle, May 10, 1965.

28. Telephone interview with Nicholas deB. Katzenbach, May 8, 1985.

29. Letter from Chief Judge Clement F. Haynsworth, Jr., to Chief Judge Elbert P. Tuttle, May 10, 1965.

30. Haynsworth letter; Haynsworth's stock holdings in J. P. Stevens and Company would later become a source of controversy during his confirmation hearings as an unsuccessful nominee to the Supreme Court. For a more extended account, see *Congressional Quarterly Almanac 1969* (Washington, D.C.: Congressional Quarterly Service, 1970), pp. 337–49.

31. Letter from Judge Griffin B. Bell to All Active Judges of the Court, May 21, 1965.

32. Letter from Judge Richard T. Rives to Senators Lister Hill and John Sparkman, May 20, 1965; letter from Judge Richard T. Rives to Judge John Minor Wisdom, May 21, 1965.

another of Senator Eastland's maneuvers against the court. This time the bone of contention was the wording of Section C of the proposed Omnibus Judgeship Bill, which defined the temporary status of the judgeships. The sentence in question read, "The first four vacancies occurring in the office of circuit judges in said circuit shall not be filled."[33] Ordinarily, the temporal condition was attached to the position itself rather than to the court. In effect, this meant that any of the Fifth Circuit judges approaching the nonmandatory retirement age of seventy in the immediate future would have to step down before the president signed the bill in order to ensure the court the benefits of four additional judges.

Yet the caseload crisis dictated the need for a full complement of the court's current positions *plus* the additional judicial help. Specifically, for the Fifth Circuit the clause meant that Judges Rives and Jones, both of whom had turned seventy, would have to retire before the judgeship bill became law or their vacancies would go unfilled. This provision also meant that Chief Judge Tuttle, who was two years from retirement privileges, would have to step down from active to senior status to ensure the court that it would not lose his position. Aside from doubts as to the propriety of the action, loss of the authorized judgeships also concerned the court. Notwithstanding Tuttle's possible retirement, the potentially adverse effects of the clause led Judge Brown to warn the court that, with nine authorized judgeships, it would be temporarily administered by a circuit council of only five active judges, since the vacancies caused by Cameron's death and Hutcheson's retirement had not yet been filled. Important decisions decided en banc, as well as administrative ones, therefore might possibly be decided by a majority of three, which Brown pointed out was merely the size of their regular panels. He went on to explain that in the event that Tuttle, Rives, and Jones succumbed to the pressure to retire before the bill's enactment, the Fifth Circuit within two years would lose the strength of three of the four temporary positions.[34]

As Tuttle, Jones, and Rives retired and the caseload increased, especially the number of complex school desegregation cases, the Fifth Circuit's judge power would dwindle from a thirteen- to a ten-judge court, a net gain of one judicial position for the decade of the sixties. Underlying these workload considerations, however, lay the deep political rift between Senator Eastland and the liberal members. This time it appeared that Senator Eastland was wryly giving with one hand and taking away with the other. More importantly, the clause was perceived to be an attack on two members of "the Four" (Rives and Tuttle). Rives, especially disturbed by the clause, asserted that he was "constitutionally opposed" to retiring under such unnecessary pressure.[35]

Rives was disturbed by the coercive implications rather than the idea of

33. Letter from Judge John R. Brown to All Members of Fifth Circuit, June 9, 1965.
34. Ibid.
35. Letter from Judge Richard T. Rives to Senators Lister Hill and John Sparkman, May 20, 1965.

retirement per se. He actually had been somewhat busy communicating with Alabama senators John Sparkman and Lister Hill since January concerning his retirement plans. When Rives turned seventy in January, he sent word to the senators through his former law partner, John C. Godbold of Montgomery, that he intended to retire. As soon as he received the nod from the senators, Rives wished to take senior status, but not to relinquish the majority of his workload. He simply wanted to secure his "Alabama seat" on the court for Godbold. He told the senators that having his friend Godbold "step into his shoes" was "a hope close to my heart since the day I came on this Court."[36]

Although anxious to have the provision stricken, Rives asked Senators Hill and Sparkman not to jeopardize or delay passage of the entire bill because of his concern about Section C, unless Senator Eastland was very agreeable to omitting the provision. He made it clear to everyone that he believed the fate of the judgeship bill lay in the hands of Senator Eastland.[37] Brown came to Rives's aid on the matter when he approached him about the possibility that Griffin Bell would be "a good advocate with Senator Eastland."[38] After considerable discussion, Judges Bell and Brown agreed that Brown would draft a statement that Bell, after obtaining the court's approval, would then submit to Senator Eastland. The ten-page document stated all the court's concerns about the possible adverse effects of Section C.[39] Chief Judge Tuttle then assigned Bell the official task of persuading Eastland to alter the provision's language. But Bell was unable to change Eastland's mind on the subject; the bill passed the Senate on June 30, 1965, with Section C unaltered. Still, as Chief Judge Tuttle had observed in 1964, there are two houses of Congress.

A MORE URGENT PLEA FOR JUDGESHIPS

Not so ironically, then, passage of the Omnibus Judgeship Bill was dependent upon a somewhat slow legislative pace in the House. Celler introduced another judgeship bill in mid-June of 1965, but did not begin hearings until September. In the interim, his response to Professor Wright for quick enactment was "quite noncommittal."[40] In mid-August, Celler told Wright that he did not know when the subcommittee would schedule hearings on the legislation.

At the same time, Wright also wrote to President Johnson stressing the urgency of providing the additional judges. He encouraged the president to

36. Letter from Judge Richard T. Rives to Senators Lister Hill and John Sparkman, January 29, 1965.

37. Letter from Judge Richard T. Rives to Senators Lister Hill and John Sparkman, May 20, 1965.

38. Letter from Judge John R. Brown to Chief Judge Elbert P. Tuttle, June 9, 1965.

39. Letter from Judge John R. Brown to All Members of Fifth Circuit, June 9, 1965.

40. Letter from Charles Alan Wright to Judge John R. Brown, September 3, 1965.

lend his support because he believed the situation in the Fifth Circuit was critical.[41] Two weeks later President Johnson responded that he had indeed "urged the Judiciary Committee of the House to review the matter and report the bill, if at all possible, during the current session."[42] On September 1, 1965, the day Wright received the president's message, Celler opened his subcommittee's first day of hearings on the proposal. In keeping with standard practice, Chief Judge Biggs (head of Court Administration) and Chief Judge Harvey Johnsen (head of Statistics) traveled to Washington to present the Judicial Conference report on the evaluative needs for federal judicial positions. Almost as soon as they began to report the statistics supporting the conference requests, Celler launched into a lecture. Reminding Biggs that "2 or 3 years ago" he had requested a nationwide study on obsolete court boundaries, he emphasized that he still did not know what progress had been made: "Unless the Judicial Conference acts with great expedition on this matter, I am going to appoint a subcommittee of this committee to go into this very matter. I do not wish to take jurisdiction away from the Judicial Conference, but I have to sound this warning. These lines must be changed."[43]

Referring to the 1964 battle over Fifth Circuit division, Judge Biggs essentially told Celler that when his committee's recommendation met with no one's approval, he realized that the problem was too large for the staff of the Administrative Office of the United States Courts. Quite frankly, he stated, a subcommittee would probably be the best approach, as it was simply not feasible for federal judges to conduct such a study. At this point Judge Johnsen, apparently miffed about the issue, chimed into the conversation. Not only were the temporary judges no solution to the Fifth Circuit's problems, Johnsen said, but also the number of proposed judges had not been based on a realistic evaluation of its needs. If it had been, he continued, then the Fifth Circuit would be a court of fifteen, and that number was too large. Johnsen also complained that his committee had no authority even to make a recommendation to Congress about the situation because of the bargain that had been struck concerning the temporary nature of the Fifth Circuit's judgeships. Instead of evaluating need, the conference had merely endorsed what the Fifth Circuit judges wanted, Johnson curtly told Celler.[44] Implicit in Johnsen's exchange with Celler was the accusation that the Fifth Circuit judges were asking for fewer judges than the caseload demanded in order to avoid division.

A week later, Bernard Segal testified before Celler's subcommittee on the status of the nationwide study as well as on support for the Judicial Conference

41. Letter from Charles Alan Wright to President Lyndon B. Johnson, August 16, 1965.

42. Quoted in Letter from Charles Alan Wright to Judge John R. Brown, September 3, 1965.

43. U.S. Congress, House, Subcommittee No. 5 of the Committee on the Judiciary, *Federal Courts and Judges*, 89th Cong., 1st sess., 1965, p. 29.

44. U.S. House, *Federal Courts*, pp. 29, 30, 33, 138, 143.

request for additional judges. Segal had worked diligently since January 1965 to secure a commitment from the ABA to conduct the study. Wisdom, who was following the ABA activities closely, learned in February that the Section of Judicial Administration had approved the study proposed by Segal's sub-committee. In May, the Bar Association's board of governors adopted the endeavor and agreed to examine nationwide the "underlying causes for the current conditions" and "all possible remedial measures," but resolved against circuit splitting.[45] Furthermore, Segal assured Wisdom that the Association would be able to secure funding for the project.[46] Segal testified to these commitments before Celler's subcommittee, and also urged Celler to consider that the uncertainty over solutions indicated a need for temporary judges. He assured Celler that the American Bar Foundation had undertaken the national realignment study for the ABA. Celler indicated that he nonetheless planned to appoint a subcommittee for this purpose; but again the issue was left essentially unsettled. The ABA did follow through with its commitment, and issued its report three years later. After eight days of hearings, Representative Celler and ranking minority member McCulloch (R-OH) expressed "doubts about the need for more judges"[47] and held the bill over to the next session of Congress.

At the close of 1965, the Fifth Circuit was still shy the additional judgeships. In July, President Johnson appointed two judges to fill the vacancies left by Judge Cameron's death and Judge Hutcheson's ill health and retirement. To fill the Hutcheson vacancy, Johnson chose his longtime friend Homer Thornberry, a populist U.S. Representative from 1949 to 1963. In 1963 President Johnson appointed him to the United States District Court for the Western District of Texas in Austin. Elevated after serving only two years as a district judge, Judge Thornberry became highly respected for his personal integrity and judicial temperament. His swearing-in ceremony that summer took place on the LBJ ranch. Three years later Johnson nominated him to the Supreme Court contingent upon the successful promotion of Abe Fortas to chief justice. The president's hopes were dashed, however, when the Fortas nomination was withdrawn.[48]

To fill Judge Cameron's seat, President Johnson appointed James P. Coleman, whose political career included many prominent positions, not least of which was governor of Mississippi from 1956 to 1960. Even as counsel for some of the University of Mississippi's trustees during the Meredith/Barnett

45. American Bar Association draft resolution accompanied by letter from Bernard G. Segal to Judge John Minor Wisdom, February 12, 1965.

46. Letter from Judge John Minor Wisdom to Judges Richard T. Rives and John R. Brown, February 18, 1965.

47. *Congressional Quarterly Almanac 1965* (Washington, D.C.: Congressional Quarterly Service, 1966), p. 646.

48. Telegram from Judge Homer Thornberry to The President accompanied by letter from Judge Thornberry to All Fifth Circuit Judges, October 3, 1968.

episode, Coleman was a voice of moderation in state politics. In fact, he lost his bid for governor in 1963 because he had supported President Kennedy in 1960.[49] Political moderation notwithstanding, civil rights groups, members of Congress, and law professors expressed "great shock" and stern opposition to Coleman's appointment.[50] His political record and campaign rhetoric were dredged up to demonstrate that his career as a politician had been based on a segregationist theme. Among those who opposed Coleman was Clarence Mitchell, director of the Washington bureau of the NAACP, who presented that organization's resolution referring to Coleman as one of the "architects of racial discrimination." Representative John Conyers (D-MI), a member of the Judiciary Committee, labeled Coleman a "dedicated and effective segregationist,"[51] "the thinking man's segregationist."[52] Similar sentiments emerged from various other groups, including the Student Non-Violent Coordinating Committee, the Leadership Conference on Civil Rights, Americans for Democratic Action, law professors from Columbia and Georgetown, and noted constitutional scholar Thomas I. Emerson of Yale Law School.[53]

In his own defense, Coleman testified that, although some of his actions were dictated by the wishes of the state legislature and the people of Mississippi, other decisions had been "mistakes,"[54] and that he would "abide by the decisions of the Supreme Court."[55] In spite of the record, however, Coleman's honesty and advocacy against violence during the Freedom Rides and the Meredith ordeal had impressed officials in the Kennedy Justice department, especially Nicholas deB. Katzenbach who, as attorney general, came to Coleman's defense. Throughout the controversial nomination, Katzenbach insisted that Coleman was a fair man of personal integrity who had not taken the politically expedient route when many times it would have been the easiest course. He urged the Senate not to consider Coleman's record in a "vacuum."[56]

Steadfast support from the attorney general and the president and the norm of senatorial courtesy (which meant that Senator Eastland had planted his support firmly behind Coleman, who was Senator Stennis's personal choice) ultimately led to Coleman's confirmation on July 26 by a vote of 76 to 8.[57] Thornberry's nomination had been approved by voice vote three weeks earlier.[58] Although Thornberry's and Coleman's styles differed, they shared

49. "The Judiciary," *Time*, July 23, 1965, p. 18.

50. "Mississippi Delegation Challenge," *Congressional Quarterly Weekly Report*, June 25, 1965, p. 1243.

51. "Federal Judgeships," *Congressional Quarterly Weekly Report*, July 9, 1965, p. 1326.

52. "The Judiciary," *Time*, p. 18.

53. "Coleman Nomination," *Congressional Quarterly Weekly Report*, July 16, 1965, p. 1379.

54. "The Judiciary," *Time*, July 23, 1965, p. 18.

55. "Coleman Nomination," p. 1379.

56. Ibid.

57. "Coleman Confirmed," *Congressional Quarterly Weekly Report*, July 30, 1965, p. 1490.

58. "Federal Judgeships," p. 1326.

a warm personal manner that proved to have a long-lasting positive influence on the court.

From his appointment until the eventual circuit division in 1981, Judge Coleman remained steadfast in his view that the workload of individual judges dictated the need for two smaller courts, as opposed to one large, unwieldy bench. Judge Thornberry aligned himself with the opponents of division and remained in their camp until 1977. Even then, his support for a split was predicated on a belief that it was the inevitable price to pay for additional judges.

THE REPRIEVE

The House Judiciary Committee eventually reported favorably on the Omnibus Judgeship Bill in early February 1966, the full chamber released the bill the following month, and President Johnson signed it in mid-March. Now authorized, the president began appointing the judges with dispatch.

In addition to listening to Senator Eastland rage about the "summer freedom rides" in Mississippi, which he referred to as "Martin Luther King, Jr. and his travelling circus,"[59] the Senate Judiciary Committee was occupied with Fifth Circuit confirmations throughout the summer of 1966. Because the so-called retirement clause was never stricken from the legislation, Judges Rives and Jones retired in February 1966. After a brief consultation about the possibility of retiring, Jones indicated to Rives that they had "kind of balanced each other off" during their tenure, and they subsequently announced their retirement on the same day.[60] This left the Fifth Circuit with six new positions to be filled.

Including the two prior appointments of Judges Coleman and Thornberry, eight members of the Fifth Circuit's thirteen-judge bench were now new political actors in the court's ongoing controversy over division. With this influx of new individuals, the collective personality of the institution naturally began to change. Of course, all the new jurists were either already familiar with the debate over splitting the circuit or were quickly assimilated into the discussion. The Fifth Circuit's "old guard" held such strong views on the topic of realignment and were so divided in their opinions on the matter that it was inconceivable that any newcomer to the bench could not take sides. Perhaps that is why the court's fate, regardless of personalities, seemed to be inextricably bound to the prospect of circuit division rather than any other type of reform.

The new members of the court, however, began to shift the focus of the discussion in a very subtle but significant way. Almost immediately they began

59. U.S. Congress, Senate, 89th Cong., 2d sess., 16 June 1966 *Congressional Record*, p. 13557.

60. Jack Bass, *Unlikely Heroes* (New York: Simon and Schuster, 1981), p. 303.

to express concern about the worsening caseload conditions facing the circuit and how to find expedient measures to handle the situation. For the first time since the caseload crisis had begun, the discussion shifted away from civil rights and toward more procedural concerns of judicial administration. Overall, these newcomers were powerful, articulate individuals who could be formidable participants in the debate over the circuit's future. By mid-fall 1966, five of the new Johnson appointees had taken their seats, and the sixth appointment was filled the following year.

Just as Rives had hoped, John C. Godbold assumed the Alabama seat on the court. Godbold had completed one year of law school at Harvard when World War II interrupted his studies. After the war he returned to Harvard and received his Juris Doctor degree in 1948. Upon his return to Alabama, he first practiced law in Montgomery with Rives for about a year, after which he opened his own practice with two partners. He continued practicing in Montgomery until President Johnson selected him for the Fifth Circuit bench in July 1966. An extremely capable jurist of high integrity and with a firm, statesmanlike manner, Judge Godbold was to become one of the court's most respected leaders. Later he also became the only federal judge in history to hold the position of chief judge in two U.S. courts of appeals.[61] He was such a powerful advocate of circuit division that a majority of the judges later appointed him to represent them on the subject. Godbold's primary concern was the damage a large court was doing to the en banc function.

Judge Jones's vacancy was filled by chief judge of the Southern District of Florida, David W. Dyer. Although a native of Columbus, Ohio, and an undergraduate at Ohio State University, Dyer received his law degree from Stetson College of Law and practiced in Miami for twenty-eight years. Like many other Fifth Circuit judges, his concentration on the law was interrupted for three years during World War II while he served in the Judge Advocate General's department. After the war he entered into partnership with George Smathers, who later became a U.S. senator. Dyer was a distinguished member of the Florida legal community, serving as president of the Dade County (Miami) Bar Association, member of the Executive Committee of the Board of Governors of the Florida Bar, and head of the Florida Bar's Committee on Admiralty Law. Dyer's expertise in two highly specialized areas of law, admiralty and aviation, won him national and international recognition. Long after Judge Dyer took senior status, he continued to respond to the court's request to fashion opinions on tedious, complex admiralty cases. Some were so complicated that he had to invest a year or more of his expertise into

61. See Read and McGough, *Let Them Be Judged*; Bass, *Unlikely Heroes*; Couch, *A History*; John R. Brown, "Revision by Division? 1975 Fifth Circuit Symposium," *Texas Tech Law Review* 7:319. Each of these works contains a rich source of information on the backgrounds of the judges during this period and provided relevant material for the analysis presented here.

resolving the issues of a single case.[62] One year after President Kennedy appointed him to the district court bench, Dyer became chief judge of the district. Four years later, Johnson appointed him to serve on the Fifth Circuit.

Dyer was perhaps best known for his stance against the de jure/de facto distinction in school desegregation cases, which was more advanced than the Supreme Court's doctrine. Writing for a unanimous en banc court on this point in 1972, he maintained that regardless of de jure/de facto or intent to segregate, federal courts should look only at the results of school board plans. If the results of a school board policy (action or inaction) had the effect of racially segregating the public schools, the plan must be considered state action and thereby not out of the remedial reach of federal courts.[63] As one of the judges who stood amid the court's divided factions on school cases, Dyer became adept at building and holding together coalitions, and at negotiating among members of the court and between the court and school boards. He captured the essence of the personal anxiety and tedious judicial processes associated with these decisions:

> I am proud to have been a member of the old Fifth when we had those challenges; and they were *great* challenges. . . . School cases were a great burden . . . because they were *so* difficult. Every locale is different. . . . We had the *Austin* School case and the panel I was serving with went to Austin and sat down with twenty members of the school board just to hear what *their* problems were. We spent a day with them and . . . when we got . . . through we simply said we understand your point of view, . . . your difficulties but they're not sufficient to overcome the necessity of realigning the school system. It got down to almost a personal basis instead of a judicial "off-hand-way-up-high" sort of thing you're faced with. . . . It was a *very* difficult period and I think we met it exceedingly well.[64]

Dyer's very polite and low-key manner added a well-reasoned, experienced voice to the court's opinions.

Florida received a second seat on the court in the fall of 1966 with the appointment of Bryan Simpson, who had served as a federal district court judge since 1950. Simpson had an impressive family and judicial background. He earned his law degree from the University of Florida in 1926, the law school that his uncle, Nathan Bryan, had helped to establish. Bryan, for whom Simpson was named, represented Florida as a United States senator and thereafter served for fifteen years (1920–35) with distinction as a Fifth Circuit judge. Judge Simpson had an equally impressive record. He brought eleven years of state trial and appellate judicial experience to the federal district court bench for the Southern District of Florida. After serving another eleven

62. Interview with Judge David W. Dyer, Highlands, North Carolina, June 14, 1983.
63. See *Cisneros v. Corpus Christi Independent School District*, 467 F.2d 142 (5th Cir. 1972).
64. Dyer interview.

years on the district court for the Southern District of Florida, Simpson became chief judge. The following year (1962) he was chief judge of the Middle District of Florida, until President Johnson appointed him to the Fifth Circuit bench in 1966. So Simpson brought a combined twenty-seven years of judicial experience, mostly from the federal trial courts, to the Fifth Circuit. It has been said of him that "Whenever one of his brethren on the Fifth Circuit [wanted] the viewpoint of a trial judge, he [sought] the advice of Bryan Simpson."[65]

This experience, however, had been costly. Simpson served as a federal trial judge during some of Florida's more turbulent civil rights years, particularly when he was chief judge of the Middle District. Some of the more recalcitrant pockets of white supremacy in the South, certainly in Florida, fell under Simpson's jurisdiction. In 1964, Chief Judge Simpson took charge of an incendiary situation in Saint Augustine by tracking down its source. When he discovered that the ongoing racial violence and inhumane conditions in the county jail were the result of the sheriff department's recruiting and deputizing members of the Ku Klux Klan and allied organizations, Simpson enjoined a list of those involved from further activity. He cited two central figures for contempt, one of whom was a deputy sheriff, and dismissed the latter from his position. During this ordeal the FBI investigated threats made on Simpson's life and warned him to sit with his back against the wall. Security was also placed on his car to watch for possible explosives. Simpson's decision in the Saint Augustine case prompted Senator Strom Thurmond to warn that this was the beginning of a "judicial dictatorship."[66]

While such decisions earned Judge Simpson respect from some colleagues, who referred to him as "courageous," they also led to his being ostracized by his community and friends. Dyer recalled that Simpson on occasion experienced difficulty in finding a place to stay, or even someone to play a round of golf with him, all because "he upheld the constitutional rights of people."[67] But, undaunted by this abuse, Simpson was the "first federal district judge to order an end to faculty segregation."[68]

In the annals of civil rights martyrdom, Simpson's name has often been included with those of federal judges Frank Johnson, Skelly Wright, Richard Rives, John Wisdom, Elbert Tuttle, and John Brown—all of whom received boxes of hate mail. Yet Simpson was linked with these judges in another important way. As the elected district court representative from the Fifth Circuit, he held official membership in the Judicial Conference from 1962 to 1965. There he had conferred sympathetically with Wisdom during the 1964

65. Read and McGough, *Let Them Be Judged*, p. 418.
66. Ibid., p. 422.
67. Dyer interview.
68. Read and McGough, *Let Them Be Judged*, p. 424.

campaign and, acknowledging that Wisdom had made a good case, stated that, "in theory," he too was opposed to a split of the circuit.[69] Like Chief Judge Tuttle, however, Simpson believed that the only way additional judges would be forthcoming from the Senate was on condition the circuit was divided. Simpson, whose vote Wisdom was trying to secure in 1964, agreed to try to find some hint that judgeships would be provided without a split, in which case he would support Wisdom's campaign in the conference. Although a new member, Simpson was no novice concerning the circuit's internal and congressional squabbles over circuit realignment.

The Fifth Circuit gained the services of another native Texan that summer. Irving L. Goldberg of Dallas filled one of the temporary positions and joined the court on the same day as Judge Godbold. Like Godbold, Goldberg was a graduate of Harvard Law School, earning his degree in 1929. He was a prominent lawyer and longtime partner in one of Dallas's most prestigious law firms, which included Robert Strauss, who was influential in Democratic national politics.[70] Goldberg was also the first Jewish judge to sit on the Fifth Circuit bench. He was highly respected by members of the court for his legal scholarship, compassion, and lively wit.

Goldberg devoted great amounts of time and energy to the social betterment of the Dallas community through membership in many civic and Jewish welfare organizations. In 1968 he was honored with the Brotherhood Citation of the National Conference of Christians and Jews. A self-labeled "liberal" who describes his judicial philosophy in one word, "C-H-A-N-G-E," he aligned himself with the well-known liberal voting bloc on the court.[71] In fact, Goldberg, who was influenced by Chief Judge Tuttle's innovative judicial activism, became the court's most reliable liberal activist.[72] The results of one study of the Fifth Circuit's decisions in race relations cases from 1965–77 showed that Goldberg's support for civil rights claims was the highest and most consistent on the Fifth Circuit.[73] Given this view of his judicial role, it is not surprising that Goldberg, in a per curiam opinion for a three-judge district court, authored perhaps the most far-reaching decision on public education. Although his contention was rejected by the Supreme Court, Goldberg held that the Texas educational system, financed as it was by local taxable property, was so economically varied that this disparity resulted in discriminatory school dis-

---

69. Letter from Chief Judge Bryan Simpson to Judge John Minor Wisdom, September 14, 1964.

70. Bass, *Unlikely Heroes*, p. 305.

71. Goldberg interview.

72. Bass, *Unlikely Heroes*, p. 327.

73. Elkin Terry Jack, "Racial Policy and Judge J. P. Coleman: A Study in Political Judicial Linkage," presented at the annual meeting of the Southern Political Science Association, Memphis, Tennessee, November 5–7, 1981.

tricts, and consequently was unconstitutional.[74] Goldberg was also an ardent supporter of Judge Wisdom's federalizing function argument leveled against splitting the circuit. He strongly believed that diversity in judges prevented parochialism in the federal appellate court system.

Louisiana's temporary judgeship was filled by U.S. District Judge Robert A. Ainsworth, Jr., of the Eastern District in New Orleans. He was given the official nod the same day as Goldberg and Godbold, and was proud to be the first Catholic appointed to the circuit. Ainsworth received the Weiss Award of the National Conference of Christians and Jews in 1966, for his tireless community and civic efforts. He grew up in the same lower-middle-class neighborhood and attended the same university (Loyola of New Orleans) as Judge Skelly Wright. After receiving his law degree in 1932, he entered private practice with his brother and, upon his election to the state senate in 1950, began a successful political career. He remained in the legislature for eleven years and was twice elected to the office of president pro tempore of the senate.

Throughout his state political career Ainsworth's was a voice of moderation—sometimes one of only a handful trying to calm both sides of the integration crisis that hit New Orleans after the *Brown* decision. Perhaps his political toleration on civil rights issues was responsible for his being Senator Ellender's (D-LA) last choice when President Kennedy appointed him to the district bench in 1961. Ainsworth's reluctance to accept a federal trial court position elicited a visit from Burke Marshall, sent by Kennedy to coax him into taking the post. It proved to be an appointment ill suited for Ainsworth. Unhappy with the rigid docket, he preferred to contemplate and study issues more encompassing in scope, and to write significant opinions. Five years later, when President Johnson elevated him to the Fifth Circuit bench, Ainsworth was pleased to have the opportunity to expand his legal talents.[75]

Ainsworth quickly became one of the more highly regarded judges of the Fifth Circuit and the epitome of a moderate judicial philosophy. His close friend on the court, Judge Thomas Gee, who was appointed in 1973, described him as a "wonderful man" who had a "rare combination of political ability and integrity."[76] These traits were not only appreciated at the Fifth Circuit, as shown in the committee assignments given him, but were also recognized by Chief Justice Burger, who appointed Ainsworth chair of the powerful Court Administration Committee of the Judicial Conference. Ainsworth's political finesse and balance were evident in his middle position on splitting the circuit, where he expressed his desire to hold the circuit together but rec-

74. *San Antonio Independent School District et al. v. Rodriguez et al.*, 337 F.Supp. 280 (W.D. Tex. 1971); Bass, *Unlikely Heroes*, p. 325.

75. Confidential interview; Read and McGough, *Let Them Be Judged*, p. 179.

76. Interview with Judge Thomas G. Gee, Austin, Texas, March 18, 1983.

ognized that a division was probably inevitable, as the caseload was over-whelming the court.[77]

The last of the temporary judicial appointments was not made until fall 1967. Mississippi's new position went to Northern Mississippi District Judge Claude F. Clayton. As one of the conservative district judges with whom the Fifth Circuit had battled on previous civil rights cases, Judge Clayton was possibly the most conservative of the temporary appointments. He served only eighteen months on the court before his death.

The vacancy left by Clayton's demise was ultimately filled by Nixon appointee Charles Clark in October 1969. After receiving his degree from the University of Mississippi in 1948, Clark practiced law in Jackson for twenty-nine years. During this time he built a highly respected legal career based on his sharp talents, hard work, and oratorical ability as a trial attorney. Clark served as the special assistant to the attorney general of the State of Mississippi from 1961 to 1966. It was to be a dubious honor for him, as his defense of the board of trustees of "Ole Miss" and pleas to Fifth Circuit Judge Cameron in setting aside orders to enroll James Meredith in the university dogged his political career henceforth.[78] Clark did, however, earn respect from the Fifth for the integrity and honesty he displayed during various appearances before the circuit in the Meredith/Barnett litigation. Ultimately, Clark relinquished his support for former Governor Barnett and became more interested in preventing violence, keeping the university open, and preventing the Fifth Circuit from jailing the members of the board of trustees.

Nonetheless, Clark's conservative viewpoint was undeniable. His political philosophy, combined with his alliance with Senator Eastland, made him a candidate appealing to Nixon in his search for strict constructionists but an equally certain target for civil rights advocates. Rather than have Clark's nomination languish in the Judiciary Committee, as had so many controversial liberal appointments, Eastland protected Clark from the politics of liberal vengeance by delaying consideration of his candidacy until the "liberal" senators on the Judiciary Committee were out of town for Moratorium Day, in protest of the Vietnam War. Eastland then shrewdly brought it up first before the committee and then the full Senate; the nominee at both points was confirmed with dispatch.[79]

Soon after Clark joined the Fifth Circuit he began to challenge the "liberal stalwarts" on the court with sharply worded conservative dissents. He proved to be a formidable opponent of the liberal members in litigation as well as on administrative matters. He was stern and persuasive in advocating division of the circuit. His arguments were always based on caseload/workload conditions,

77. Robert A. Ainsworth, "Fifth Circuit Court of Appeals Reorganization Act of 1980," *Brigham Young University Law Review*, 1981, p. 533.

78. Read and McGough, *Let Them Be Judged*, p. 228.

79. Bass, *Unlikely Heroes*, p. 312.

and as the court continued to grow in numbers of judges, caseloads, and administrative problems, he effectively advanced his administrative rationale for division. Overall, however, Clark rose above his controversial reputation, and in spite of his consistent, conservative opinions, became one of the more respected leaders before and during his tenure as chief judge of the Fifth Circuit. Members of the court across the political spectrum, including some of the more liberal members such as Goldberg, Brown, and Wisdom, have praised Clark for his administrative talents, statesmanlike manner, and fairness.[80]

All these judges served either as a direct or indirect result of the 1966 Omnibus Judgeship Act. The Fifth Circuit was an institution undergoing considerable change through regeneration. With only a few more additions, it was this group that shepherded the court through some of its worst caseload, litigation, and administrative conditions.

GOING BACK TO THE WELL

Before the ink was barely dry on the temporary judges' commissions, and even before Clayton's appointment, the Fifth Circuit again went to Congress for help. Brown had since assumed the chief judgeship of the circuit. Chief Judge Tuttle stepped down from the position on July 17, 1967, his seventieth birthday, but gave the court his assurance that he would not take senior status until the problem of the temporary judgeship language was resolved. In January, Tuttle had conveyed a message to the conference that the litigants in the Fifth Circuit did not deserve a reduction in the number of judges on the court when the caseload was so great. This was bound to take place, Tuttle warned, anticipating his own retirement, unless the language authorizing the temporary judges was changed. This was no time to debate circuit splitting, according to Tuttle; judicial help was imperative.[81]

Once he relinquished the chief judgeship, Tuttle began to express his opposition to circuit division openly and actively. His vocal opposition to splitting the circuit from this point forward seemed to reaffirm what many participants in 1964 had believed, that he had been trapped into an official position of supporting the proposed realignment though personally opposed to the idea.

Chief Judge Brown traveled to Washington in late August 1967 to make an official appearance before the Judicial Conference to discuss the needs of his circuit. While there, he called upon individual members of the House and Senate Judiciary committees and senators from the states covered by the Fifth

80. Interviews with Judges Goldberg, Brown, and Wisdom.
81. William Shafroth, *Survey of the United States Courts of Appeals: A Report*, Report to the U.S. Judicial Conference Committee on Statistics (Washington, D.C.: Administrative Office of the United States Courts, 1967).

Circuit to ascertain the extent of support for making the temporary judges permanent and adding two new positions. He was able to confer with all the senators except two who were unavailable, and he also met with Representatives Celler and Jack Brooks (D-TX). Although the mood among the senators was one of general enthusiasm for addressing the caseload problem along the lines suggested by the circuit, the two influential House members indicated that they would not act favorably upon additional judgeships but would consider converting the temporary positions to permanent ones. Brown reported to all the Fifth Circuit judges that Eastland was especially enthusiastic about the court's proposal; he had even called Senator Joseph Tydings (D-MD), who chaired the subcommittee previously headed by Olin Johnston, and arranged for a bill to be introduced and hearings held on the bill—all within two weeks. Events were happening so fast in Washington that Brown was testifying before Tydings's subcommittee before the Fifth Circuit judges could receive Brown's memorandum.[82] Ironically, once the initial dam of wisdom against having appellate benches larger than nine finally broke, the floodgates opened for more requests and increases in the federal bench, particularly in the South, and became a political pattern that continued unabated for federal courts of appeals nationwide.

Exhilarated by his positive meeting with Eastland, Brown prepared to use his most persuasive arguments in his testimony before Congress. In early September, Brown asked Senator Tydings to proceed with the proposals to help the Fifth Circuit.[83] Not only was Tydings the new subcommittee leader; he was also the committee and subcommittee's second most junior member. Leadership of the subcommittee had changed hands three times from 1965 to 1967. Not surprisingly, then, Tydings seemed unfamiliar with the situation and naively asked Brown why the conference had not made the judgeships permanent at the time they were created. Without too much detail, Brown recounted the compromise that had emerged between opposing views on division in 1964, describing the temporary appointments as a "sort of palliative measure."[84]

Chief Judge Biggs, also in attendance, asked to speak more "frankly" on the subject and proceeded to tell Senator Tydings of how the "storm broke loose" when his committee recommended splitting the circuit.[85] He warned that at some point the Fifth Circuit would have to take action other than

82. Letter from Chief Judge John R. Brown to All Judges of the Fifth Circuit, September 6, 1967; Minutes of the Meeting of the Judicial Council of the United States Court of Appeals for the Fifth Circuit, New Orleans, October 24 and 25, 1967.

83. U.S. Congress, Senate, Subcommittee on Improvements in Judicial Machinery of the Committee on the Judiciary, *1967 Omnibus Judgeship Bill*, 90th Cong., 1st sess., 1967.

84. U.S. Senate, *Judgeship Bill*, p. 12.

85. Ibid.

asking for additional judgeships. Agreeing that Biggs had touched upon an important point, Brown defended his request by pointing to the caseload figures and the fact that the court was operating efficiently with more than nine judges—in fact, beyond an authorized bench of thirteen. Because of the large number of visiting judges employed by the Fifth Circuit, the court's judicial capacity of fifteen judges had actually been violating the sanctity of a bench of nine since 1963.[86]

Brown's arguments were successful in the Senate. The Judiciary Committee reported out the bill on November 15, 1967, about ten weeks after it was introduced. The House, on the other hand, did not act on it until the following June. Once again Congress gave the Fifth Circuit the judges it requested and made the temporary judgeships permanent. These new positions brought the official size of the court up to fifteen, making it the largest federal appellate bench in history and at the same time avoiding the realignment issue.

On June 1, 1968, about two weeks before President Johnson signed the 1968 Omnibus Judgeship Bill, Judge Tuttle took senior status. The former chief's decision left three vacancies, including those under the new act. Tuttle's position was filled within two months by Chief Judge of the Northern District of Georgia Lewis R. Morgan. After receiving his law degree from the University of Georgia and admission to the bar in 1935, Morgan had practiced in his hometown of La Grange, Georgia, for twenty-nine years. He served in the Georgia House of Representatives for one term before entering World War II. After he returned, he served as the city attorney for La Grange and later as the attorney for Troup County. In 1961, President Kennedy appointed him to the federal trial court bench after the Justice Department insisted that Georgia's senators present them with a list of candidates who were not segregationists. Wary of appointing another Judge Cox to the district bench, the Kennedy Justice department gladly accepted Morgan's candidacy.[87]

On the district bench, Morgan, though not a trailblazer on civil rights issues, stood firm on many of what he called the "bellwether" cases, particularly apportionment and public accommodations.[88] He participated on the three-judge district court assembled to hear the first constitutional challenge to Title II of the 1964 Civil Rights Act. Two hours after President Johnson signed the landmark legislation, the head of Heart of Atlanta Motel filed suit challenging Congress's authority to pass Title II (barring racial discrimination in public accommodations). A simultaneous challenge for enforcement came from the black individuals chased away at gun point by avowed racial segrega-

---

86. Ibid., p. 13.
87. Bass, *Unlikely Heroes*, p. 168.
88. Interview with Lewis R. Morgan, Newnan, Georgia, May 3, 1983.

tionist Lester Maddox from his restaurant, the Pickrick. Morgan, Chief Judge
Tuttle, and federal District Judge Frank Hooper resoundingly rejected the
attack on the constitutionality of the statute,[89] a ruling later upheld in a
landmark decision of the Supreme Court.[90] Once on the Fifth Circuit,
Morgan immediately sided with the court's contingent who favored circuit
realignment, as he believed that a court of fourteen or fifteen judges was
unwieldy.[91]

Although they were authorized in June 1968, a year elapsed before the
recently elected Nixon administration filled the Fifth Circuit's two new judicial
positions. Nixon turned to one of Eisenhower's district court appointees, Joe
McDonald Ingraham of Texas, to fill one of the newly created positions. After
receiving his law degree in 1927 from National Law School (later a part of
George Washington University) Ingraham practiced in his native Oklahoma
before moving to Fort Worth and later Houston. His Houston practice was
interrupted during World War II when he served as a lieutenant colonel in
the army, during which time he met another young man in Officers' Training
School, John Minor Wisdom. Ingraham served on the district bench for fifteen
years before his elevation to the Fifth Circuit. At age sixty-six he was the oldest
appointee, serving only three and one-half years before taking senior status.
In the few en banc race relations cases in which he participated, Ingraham
ranked with the moderates.[92] He recalled having discussed circuit realignment
with Wisdom on several occasions. Ingraham supported division for caseload
reasons, and his stance on both judicial philosophy and the central issue of
realignment prompted him to muse about his relationship with Wisdom,
"We've always been on opposite sides."[93]

The final circuit vacancy was filled in June 1969 by President Nixon's
unfortunate selection of G. Harrold Carswell. Carswell had had a meteoric
political ascent. He received his undergraduate degree from Duke University
in 1941. Afterward he entered the University of Georgia Law School, but his
education there was interrupted by service in World War II. He transferred
to Mercer Law School when he returned. Upon earning his law degree in
1948, he went back to his small hometown of Irwinton, Georgia, to practice
law and serve as editor of the weekly newspaper. After losing a bid for Congress, he left Georgia to live in his wife's hometown of Tallahassee, where he
immediately entered practice with Governor Leroy Collins's law firm in 1949,
formed his own firm in 1951, and then gained an appointment as U.S. attorney
in 1953 as reward for his support of Eisenhower. Five years later he

89. "High Court to Get Rights Cases," *The Capitol Times*, July 23, 1964, pp. 1, 4.

90. *Heart of Atlanta Motel v. United States*, 379 U.S. 241 (1964).

91. Morgan interview; Lewis R. Morgan, "The Fifth Circuit: Expand or Divide?" *Mercer Law Review* 29 (Summer 1978): 885–97.

92. Jack, "Racial Policy."

93. Interview with Judge Joe McDonald Ingraham, Houston, Texas, March 16, 1983.

was appointed to serve as U.S. District Judge of the Northern District of Florida. For ten years Carswell was the only federal district judge in northern Florida. In May 1969, Nixon elevated him to the Fifth Circuit over strenuous objections voiced by the NAACP concerning his "hostile" and "obstructive" civil rights record.[94]

Seven months later, in January 1970, Nixon nominated Carswell to be associate justice of the Supreme Court. Just two months before Carswell's nomination the Senate had handed Nixon a political defeat by rejecting Chief Judge Haynsworth for alleged conflict of interest while on the bench. This time the Senate was expected to confirm Nixon's second attempt to put a southern strict constructionist on the Supreme Court. Although opposition existed from the outset, it grew in intensity over the next three months. Group representatives lined up to level charges against the nominee. Various civil rights lawyers and labor witnesses discussed the harsh way they were treated in Carswell's court. Prominent law professors and deans from universities across the nation—including Duke, Rutgers, New York University, and Yale—spoke harshly about the candidate. Two professors issued a statement saying that Carswell did not have the "legal or mental qualifications" for the position, and another said that he was "the most hostile Federal district court judge I have ever appeared before."[95] The list of opponents included the Republican Ripon Society, more than five hundred civil service employees who challenged his legal qualifications, an attorney from the Justice Department, twenty-seven U.S. Representatives, and retired Supreme Court Justice Arthur Goldberg. The nomination turned into chaos and created serious problems among the Fifth Circuit judges.

Excited by the prospect of one from their ranks being elevated, many of the judges submitted letters of support to the Judiciary Committee. In fact, Dyer proposed a joint statement for members of the court. Wisdom adamantly refused to sign such a general statement of support and threatened instead to denounce it publicly. Chief Judge Brown decided not to carry through with the statement unless the court was unanimous. Instead, individual judges, including Chief Judge Tuttle, wrote letters of support to the Senate Judiciary Committee. But upon learning more about Carswell's activities, particularly his involvement in having a municipal golf course transferred to private ownership to avoid desegregation, Tuttle discreetly withdrew his support. Despite his discretion, the media in general and the *Atlanta Constitution* in particular discovered that Carswell's colleagues were less than unanimously behind his candidacy and that Tuttle had actually withdrawn his support.[96]

94. *Congressional Quarterly Almanac 1970* (Washington, D.C.: Congressional Quarterly Service, 1971), pp. 156, 158.
    95. *Almanac 1970*, p. 156.
    96. Ibid., pp. 7667–75.

A furor arose in the Senate debates between Senator Eastland, who supported Carswell, and Senator Tydings, who led the opposition, over Tuttle's changed position. Tydings was disturbed that Tuttle's letter was put in the record after he had withdrawn his support, and that Carswell had not notified any senators to that effect. Tuttle, through telegrams to Tydings, expressed his belief that the unfortunate incident had been an error in timing. In a heated exchange with Tydings, Eastland insisted that Carswell had acted on what he believed to be support from Tuttle. While trying to read Tuttle's handwritten endorsement, Eastland, whose patience was wearing thin and who wanted to discredit him, grew more irate, stopped reading, and said, "I cannot read his writing, he is getting so old."[97] He went on to say that if these events surrounding the withdrawal of support cast a "bad light" on anyone, "it would be Judge Tuttle."[98]

The negative publicity over the Carswell affair dealt yet another blow to the court's collegiality. Carswell resigned from the Fifth Circuit less than two weeks after the Senate vote rejecting his nomination. He subsequently lost the Florida Republican primary to become a senatorial candidate and was later arrested on vice charges.[99]

When Nixon chose Carswell's replacement it was as if the pendulum on qualifications had swung in the opposite direction. Six months after Carswell left the court, Paul H. Roney, a prominent attorney from St. Petersburg, joined the Fifth Circuit. Roney had an outstanding educational background, beginning with an undergraduate degree in economics from the University of Pennsylvania in 1942. After World War II Roney entered Harvard and received his law degree in 1948, the same year as John Godbold. Ironically, each would subsequently serve as chief judge of the circuit eventually carved from the former Fifth Circuit, Roney succeeding Godbold as the new circuit's second chief judge. Roney's legal experience was also impressive. Immediately upon graduation, he went to practice with a prestigious Wall Street law firm. After two years, however, he moved to St. Petersburg, where he had once attended junior college, and practiced law there for the next twenty years. Judge Roney, noted for his sharp intellect, keeps a low profile on and off the bench. He was a consistent supporter of circuit realignment yet always acted independently, going to great pains to disassociate himself on this matter from the core group of division advocates.

The appointments of Judges Ingraham and Roney represented the court's last expansion for the next ten years. New judges joined the court only through attrition.

97. U.S. Congress, Senate, 92d Cong., 1st sess., 17 March 1970, *Congressional Record*, p. 7672.

98. U.S. Congress, Senate, 92d Cong., 1st sess., 17 March 1970, *Congressional Record*, p. 7670.

99. Read and McGough, *Let Them Be Judged*, p. 464; Bass, *Unlikely Heroes*, pp. 318–23; Couch, *A History*, p. 151.

A NEED FOR ADMINISTRATIVE INNOVATION

Halting the expansion of the bench was a unanimous decision on the part of the Fifth Circuit judges. Even those opposed to a split, like Wisdom, agreed that routine functions were becoming arduous. Collegiality was difficult to maintain with the large influx of new judges. The sheer size of the court made monitoring each other's decisions a burden. These factors, coupled with the knowledge that further expansion would give new impetus to the circuit division issue, resulted in a complete lack of enthusiasm for any growth beyond the fifteen judgeships already authorized. The hiatus in the creation of judgeships was a national political phenomenon that lasted for the next decade, largely as the result of a Republican-controlled White House and a Democratic majority in both houses of Congress.

As early as 1968, Chief Judge Brown realized that the problems caused by a constant increase in cases could not be solved solely by adding more judges. He decided it was time the court used its authority, granted under the Federal Rule of Appellate Procedure 47, to adopt new internal rules for caseload disposition. He subsequently appointed a special committee comprised of Bell, who chaired the committee, Ainsworth, and Dyer. Its mission was to develop innovative means of handling the court's overcrowded docket and reduce delay in the appellate process, "without a proliferation of courts and judgeships."[100] As Brown later explained before Congress, it was a "germ of an idea" originally suggested by retired Justice Tom Clark.[101] Clark, who in 1968 was appointed the first director of the Federal Judicial Center (created in 1967), suggested at that organization's first meeting that the chief judges might want to try screening procedures such as those experimented with in the Sixth and Tenth circuits.[102] Bell also chaired the court's committee on development of the Federal Judicial Center, and was quickly becoming recognized for his progressive ideas on improvements in judicial administration, a reputation that would later aid his elevation and mark his tenure as the U.S. attorney general.

Under Bell's guidance the committee developed a docket classification scheme known as the summary calendar and the screening system patterned after the Sixth and Tenth circuits. Under this system, a case was assigned to an appropriate calendar depending on whether or not it merited full oral argument, limited oral argument, or no oral argument. After considerable study and debate, the Fifth Circuit Council adopted by majority vote the new classification docket, with only Wisdom and Coleman dissenting.[103] The streamlined system was embodied in Local Rules 17 and 18.

100. Griffin B. Bell, "Toward a More Efficient Federal Appeals System," *Judicature* 54 (January 1971): 237.

101. U.S. Congress, House, Subcommittee No. 5 of the Committee on the Judiciary, *Commission on Revision of Judicial Circuits*, 92d Cong., 1st sess., 1971, p. 120.

102. Bell, "Federal Appeals System," p. 239.

103. Interviews with Judges Coleman, Wisdom, and Brown.

There were two main parts to the new system: screening and the summary calendar. The court implemented the screening process by first organizing itself into five standing panels of three judges each. When cases were fully briefed, or ready to be placed on the docket, they were assigned by random rotation to one of the judges on a standing panel, who then classified the case. Class I cases were frivolous suits that could be dismissed or affirmed without further treatment. A Class II case was deemed unworthy of oral argument but meritorious enough to receive an opinion on the briefs or record. Disposition of a Class III case required limited oral argument, fifteen minutes per side. Finally, those cases requiring full oral argument, thirty minutes per side, were placed in Class IV. At this point the second aspect of the new system would be used. If the "screening" judge categorized a case in either Class III or IV, the case was returned to the court's clerk for the regular oral argument docket. The Class I and II cases were transferred to the other two judges on the standing panel. Should those judges be in unanimous agreement, the case would be placed on the summary calendar, the litigants notified, and an opinion drafted by the screening judge. Again, if the panel unanimously agreed with the screening judge's decision on the issues, then his opinion was entered as judgment on the case. If one judge dissented, then the case was automatically returned to the regular oral argument docket.

In addition to the screening and summary procedures, the court adopted an innovative but controversial reform known as Rule 21. This procedure, adopted at the suggestion of Judge Bell, accorded the court the discretion to affirm or enforce lower court opinions without providing written opinions. Such actions could be taken if the court determined that a written opinion would have no precedential value and one or more of the following circumstances existed: (1) a judgment of the district court was based on findings of fact that were not clearly erroneous; (2) the evidence in support of a jury verdict was not insufficient; (3) the order of an administrative agency was supported by substantial evidence on the record as a whole; (4) no error of law appeared.[104]

The combined impact of the new procedures on the court's ability to handle its caseload was immediate and substantial. In just six months, delay in assignment of cases to panels had been reduced by 300 percent. More importantly, case disposition time, the period from filing to final decision, was cut in half.[105] The median disposition time dropped from a high of 12.5 months in 1968 to 6.5 in 1971.[106] This was well below the national average of 8.3 months, and much of the drop was due to screening rather than additional

    104. Bell, "Federal Appeals System," pp. 243–44.
    105. *Huth v. Southern Pacific Company*, 417 F.2d 526, 529 (5th Cir. 1969).
    106. See *Isbell Enterprises, Inc. v. Citizens Casualty Co. of N.Y.*, 431 F.2d 411 (5th Cir. 1970); Charles R. Haworth, "Screening and Summary Procedures in the United States Courts of Appeals," *Washington University Law Quarterly* (Spring 1973), pp. 282–83.

judicial help.[107] Equally impressive, over the four-year period, panel sittings were reduced from nine to seven weeks, while productivity (output per judge) increased by the equivalent of twelve weeks of panel sittings.[108] By 1972, output almost doubled compared to the period prior to adoption of the new rules. Commensurate with the increase in productivity and reduction in delay was a dramatic decrease in the use of visiting judges. For example, after a year under the new system, the number of visiting judges dropped from forty-one to one outside jurist.[109]

In the first year of Rule 21, affirmances without opinion jumped from 2.6 percent to 12.6 percent of the court's caseload disposition. The following year, 1971 to 1972, Rule 21 decisions increased to 26.8 percent of the opinions.[110] Six years later, in 1977, 35 percent of the court's decisions were rendered pursuant to Rule 21.[111]

The new rules' effects went beyond changes in case processing. During the first six months of screening and summary procedures, the court denied oral argument to almost 33 percent of its litigants. Only two cases were considered frivolous, thereby falling into Class I. At the end of the first year, 34.7 percent of the cases were placed on the summary docket; 80 percent of the summary cases were affirmances. In 70 percent of its summary cases the court disposed of the matter with a per curiam opinion, the remainder being decided by signed opinion.[112]

In the span of four years (1969 to 1972), those cases receiving full oral argument declined from 27.6 percent to 9.6 percent, while cases without oral argument rose sharply from 32.7 percent to 59.1 percent.[113] Of the Class II cases, civil suits comprised by far the largest category, fluctuating between 39.8 percent and 52.7 percent. The types of civil cases that had large proportions (49 percent or above) placed on the Class II calendar included bankruptcy, National Labor Relations Board appeals, and admiralty (which increased to the highest level in civil cases at 66 percent in 1972). Fewer civil rights cases were placed on the summary calendar than any other type of civil action. During this same four-year period, direct criminal appeals comprised between 26 and 29 percent of Class II cases and habeas corpus and Section 2255 constituted between 26 percent and 35.5 percent of the summary category. The proportion of criminal appeals assigned to the Class II docket almost doubled from 32.7 percent in 1969 to 64.8 percent in 1972. The remainder of criminal cases (habeas and Section 2255) were also placed on the summary calendar in disproportion to other cases. For example, in 1972,

107. *Isbell*, 431 F.2d at 413.
108. Bell, "Federal Appeals System," p. 242.
109. Haworth, "Screening," p. 283.
110. Ibid., p. 288.
111. Couch, *A History*, p. 152.
112. Bell, "Federal Appeals System," p. 242.
113. Haworth, "Screening," p. 278.

81.7 percent of habeas petitions and 93.6 percent of Section 2255 were denied oral argument, i.e., handled through the summary procedure.

Rule 21 operated in the opposite direction. In 1972, for instance, 20.9 percent of the direct criminal appeals were decided without an opinion, while 64.8 percent were disposed of summarily. In contrast, 35.9 percent of diversity cases and 44.4 percent of admiralty cases were decided without an opinion. In sum, a large proportion of criminal cases received opinions but no oral argument, while a large proportion of civil cases received neither. Civil cases in general constituted almost one-half of all Rule 21 decisions. The latter two case types (diversity and admiralty) comprised a large portion of the summary calendar and of the court's total docket. Through the use of these streamlining procedures, the court was able to dispose of large segments of its docket with reduced time and effort.

During this period of innovation, Chief Judge Brown chose four opinions through which he conveyed to the legal community exactly how the Fifth Circuit was reforming its judicial process.[114] In addition, Judge Bell wrote an article that appeared in *Judicature*, explaining the new rules and their use.[115] Moreover, the Supreme Court upheld their validity on two occasions.[116] This, however, was not enough to appease everyone. Although the procedures in one form or another were being used nationwide, the extent to which the Fifth Circuit employed them drew criticism from a variety of sources. In fact, reactions were so strong that an actual dialogue through law reviews began among eminent jurists, lawyers, law professors, and politicians.[117] As many opinions on the use of these procedures and alternative reforms were offered as there were authors. Eventually even Congress began to question the advisability of such truncated modes of decisionmaking.

Two members of the circuit were not convinced that the administrative reform measures were the answer to the caseload problem. Both Wisdom and Coleman, "men who did not always agree on what the Constitution of the United States meant," as Coleman later recalled, thought the solutions lay elsewhere.[118] Wisdom advocated more staff and a reduction in federal juris-

---

114. See *Isbell*, 431 F.2d at 411. *Huth*, 417 F.2d at 526; *Murphy v. Houma Well Service*, 409 F.2d 804 (5th Cir. 1969); *NLRB v. Amalgamated Clothing Workers*, 430 F.2d 966 (5th Cir. 1970).

115. Bell, "Federal Appeals System," pp. 237–44.

116. *Isbell*, 431 F.2d at 413.

117. In addition to the Bell and Haworth articles, the following were among the more visible works spawned by the debate: Edward Lumbard, "Current Problems of the Federal Courts of Appeals," *Cornell Law Review* 54 (1968): 29–44; American Bar Foundation, *Accommodating the Workload of the U.S. Courts of Appeals* (Chicago: American Bar Foundation, 1968); Paul D. Carrington, "Crowded Dockets and the Courts of Appeals: The Threat to the Function of Review and the National Law," *Harvard Law Review* 82 (January 1969): 542–617; Quentin Burdick, "Federal Courts of Appeals: Radical Surgery or Conservative Care," *Kentucky Law Journal* 60 (1971): 807–15.

118. Interview with Judge James P. Coleman, Jackson, Mississippi, January 26, 1983.

diction, in particular, the elimination of diversity cases. Coleman, in contrast, believed that by adopting the summary calendar the court was trying to handle its problems by "temporizing" and "saw it as a maneuver to defer the split of the circuit."[119] But the fact remained that these reforms managed to keep the nation's largest and busiest federal appellate tribunal afloat for the next several years.

In 1969, Chief Judge Brown did return to Congress for more judicial help; but this time he requested twenty additional district judges for the Fifth Circuit, an extraordinarily large number by any measure, especially as each new district judge could be expected to generate approximately forty appeals per annum. Like a broken record, Celler again asked Brown about the status of action pertaining to the boundary lines. This time Celler referred to the request he had made "several years ago," instead of two or three years ago.[120] Brown, however, managed to sidestep the issue by insisting that the national study was not forgotten, and that the Fifth Circuit was functioning smoothly with fifteen judges.[121]

The realignment question, though not forgotten, certainly did not command center stage as it had before 1965. The judges focused on building collegiality, assimilating new judges, and trying frantically to keep pace with the swelling docket. There was little opportunity or desire to rekindle the realignment battles of 1964. Yet, as Wisdom later recalled, "the issue was simmering all the time, it did not boil over ... [but] each time Congress increased the number of judges, the issue boiled again."[122] Eventually, however, the judges agreed on two important points: that they were overworked to the breaking point and had reached a size at which they could not accommodate any more judges. Caught between the realities of politics and the pressures of caseload, they turned to internal administrative reforms. In so doing, the court changed the entire nature of judicial process in the Fifth Circuit.

By 1970 even the increase in district judges that Brown had requested prompted a stir among participants, indicating that circuit division might be revitalized. Coleman's concern in the following communication showed that the issue was far from settled. He wrote to a colleague:

> We have just recently acquired a number of new District Judges to generate appeals, so the mercury in the thermometer is bound to rise even more rapidly in the future. ... I think what we have to face up to is that the Fifth Circuit is simply going to have to be divided ... before the structure, through sheer weight, comes tumbling down upon our heads ... and before some of our

119. Coleman interview.

120. U.S. Congress, House, Subcommittee No. 5 of the Committee on the Judiciary, *Federal Courts and Judges*, 91st Cong., 1st sess., 1969, p. 185.

121. U.S. House, *Federal Courts*. pp. 185–186.

122. Wisdom interview, March 23, 1983.

judges damage their health trying to keep up with an impossible load, we ought to get realistic about this situation and go to the Congress and get a remedy. It strikes me as being rather odd that we who *decide* so many controversies for hundreds of others do not take decisive action as to our own problems.[123]

123. Letter from Judge James P. Coleman to Judge Griffin B. Bell, November 14, 1970.

The Eleven Federal Judicial Circuits

See 28 U.S.C.A. § 41

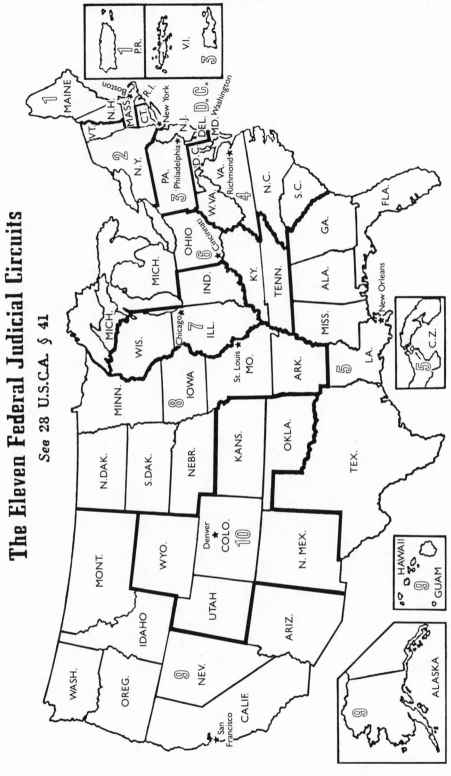

Map of U.S. Courts of Appeals prior to realignment of the Fifth Circuit. Reprinted with permission of West Publishing Co.

Members of the Fifth Circuit, May 9, 1959. *Top Row*, left to right: Warren L. Jones, Benjamin F. Cameron, John R. Brown, John Minor Wisdom. *Bottom Row*: Richard T. Rives, Joseph C. Hutcheson, Elbert P. Tuttle. Courtesy of the Fifth Circuit.

United States Court of Appeals of the Fifth Circuit

Elbert P. Tuttle

Joseph C. Hutcheson, Jr.

Richard T. Rives

Ben F. Cameron

Warren L. Jones

John R. Brown

John Minor Wisdom

Walter P. Gewin

Griffin B. Bell

1963

Members of the Fifth Circuit, 1963. Courtesy of the Fifth Circuit.

Emanuel Celler. Chaired the House
Judiciary Committee, 1949–52,
1955–72. Reprinted with permission of the *New York Post*.

Barbara Jordan. Member of the
House Judiciary Committee, 1973–
78. Courtesy of Barbara Jordan.

Peter W. Rodino. Chaired the House
Judiciary Committee, 1973–1988.
Courtesy of Peter Rodino.

Edward M. Kennedy. Chaired the
Senate Judiciary Committee, 1979–
80. Courtesy of Edward Kennedy.

Members of the Fifth Circuit, 1965. *Top Row*, left to right: Homer Thornberry, Walter P. Gewin, John Minor Wisdom, Griffin B. Bell, James P. Coleman. *Bottom Row*: John R. Brown, Richard T. Rives, Elbert P. Tuttle, Warren L. Jones. Courtesy of the Fifth Circuit.

James O. Eastland. Chaired the Senate Judiciary Committee, 1956–78. The Eastland Collection, University of Mississippi School of Law.

JOHN R. BROWN, CHIEF JUDGE
UNITED STATES COURT OF APPEALS
FIFTH CIRCUIT
HOUSTON, TEXAS 77002

* SENIOR,
that is

Federal Times

" ... We interrupt this program to bring you the following
news bulletin: ... Half of the 5th Cir.   has broken off
and is drifting out to sea ... to all those west of the Mississippi ... Bon voyage ... "

Cartoon distributed by Chief Judge John Brown to members of the Fifth Circuit
during congressional debates over realignment in 1975, copyright Harbaugh-
Rothco. Reprinted with permission of Rothco Cartoons, Inc., and Judge John
R. Brown.

THE NEW FIFTH CIRCUIT EN BANC COURTROOM

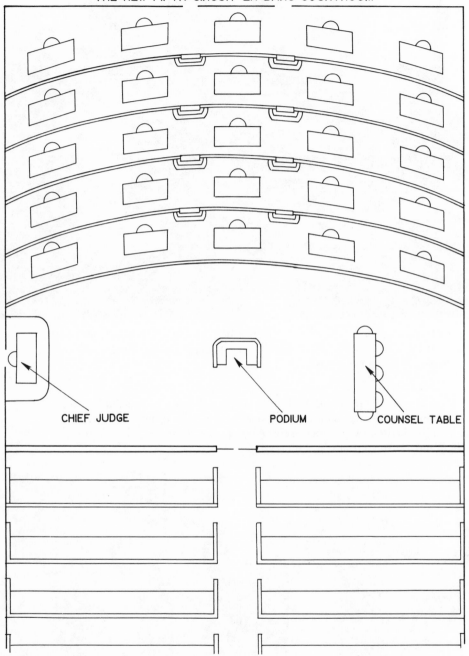

CHIEF JUDGE   PODIUM   COUNSEL TABLE

Anonymously drawn cartoon depicting a twenty-six judge en banc court, circulated among Senate staff members during conference committee deadlock in 1978.

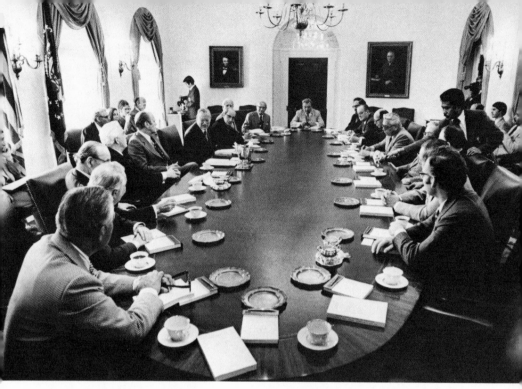

President Gerald R. Ford and Chief Justice Warren Burger meeting with members of the Commission on Revision of the Federal Court Appellate System. Courtesy of Roman L. Hruska.

President Jimmy Carter and Attorney General Griffin B. Bell meeting with the Committee for the Appointment of Blacks to the Federal Judiciary in the Fifth Circuit in the Roosevelt Room of the White House, June 29, 1977. Courtesy of the Jimmy Carter Presidential Library.

Active and senior members of the Fifth Circuit, December 1979. *Top Row*, left to right: Thomas A. Clark, Albert Tate, Jr., R. Lanier Anderson III, Henry A. Politz, Albert J. Henderson, Frank M. Johnson, Jr., Phyllis A. Kravitch, Reynaldo G. Garza, Thomas M. Reavley, Joseph W. Hatchett, Carolyn Dineen Randall, Sam D. Johnson. *Middle Row*: Alvin B. Rubin, James C. Hill, Thomas Gibbs Gee, Joe M. Ingraham, Lewis R. Morgan, David W. Dyer, John C. Godbold, Bryan Simpson, Charles Clark, Paul H. Roney, Gerald B. Tjoflat, Peter T. Fay, Robert S. Vance. *Bottom Row*: Robert A. Ainsworth, Jr., James P. Coleman, Walter P. Gewin, Warren L. Jones, Richard T. Rives, John R. Brown, Elbert P. Tuttle, John Minor Wisdom, Homer Thornberry, Irving L. Goldberg. Courtesy of the Fifth Circuit.

PETITION TO THE CONGRESS

The undersigned judges in regular active service of the United States Court of Appeals for the Fifth Circuit respectfully petition the Congress of the United States to enact legislation dividing the presently existing Fifth Circuit into two completely autonomous circuits, one to be composed of the states of Louisiana, Mississippi and Texas with headquarters in New Orleans, Louisiana, to be known as the Fifth Circuit, and the other to be composed of the states of Alabama, Florida and Georgia with headquarters in Atlanta, Georgia, to be known as the Eleventh Circuit;

By separate documents we will, at an appropriate time provide to the Congress a summary of the problems that occasion this petition and of the justification for the proposed legislation.

This 5th day of May, 1980.

Respectfully submitted,

Jas. P. Coleman
Chief Judge

Robert A. Ainsworth

Charles Clark

John Godbold

Paul H. Roney

Thomas Gee Jr.

Reynaldo Garza

James C. Hill

Gerald Tjoflat

James Randall

Thomas A. Clark

Henry A. Politz

Frank M. Johnson Jr.

Albert J. Henderson

Sam D. Johnson

Peter Fay

Robert S. Vance

Phyllis Kravitch

Jerre Williams

Joseph W. Hatchett

Thomas M. Reavley

R. Lanier Anderson

Alvin Rubin

EXH. C

Unanimous petition to Congress to divide the Fifth Circuit with all twenty-four signatures affixed, May 5, 1980. Courtesy of the Fifth Circuit.

6

Commission
Politics

During the next phase (1971–76) of the Fifth Circuit controversy, an effort was made to separate the issue from politics. A blue ribbon commission, chaired by Senator Roman L. Hruska (R-NB), was created to recommend viable solutions to the problems facing the federal appellate courts. This was an attempt to allow experts in the field of judicial administration to study the judiciary's mounting problems insulated from political pressures. At the end of the the six-year period, however, the Fifth Circuit remained unaltered, caseload excepted. Case filings rose from 2,316 in 1971 to 3,600 in 1976. This 55 percent increase was especially burdensome for the court, as it followed on the heels of a decade (1960–70) that had spawned a 249 percent increase in appeals.

The Fifth Circuit realignment debate continued to be fraught with political controversy and delay, leaving a seemingly straightforward administrative situation unresolved. In 1974, with his commission's task only partially completed, Senator Hruska wrote: "One reason for decade-long intervals between the perceived need for reform and implementation is the serious concern of the law for the process of change, no less than the substance of the change itself. Lawyers, judges, and legislators are concerned not only with the ultimate product, but with rulemaking powers and procedures and with the relationship of courts and legislatures."[1]

This caveat was certainly appropriate for the Fifth Circuit issue during its commission phase. Two years were spent solely debating the scope of the commission's authority and the subsequent task it was to perform. In the following year the commission held its own slate of hearings, during which supporters and opponents of division continued to disagree over the conse-

1. Roman L. Hruska, "The Commission on Revision of the Federal Court Appellate System: A Legislative History," *Arizona State Law Review*, 1974, p. 604.

quences of realignment. When the issue returned to Congress, the commission's primary recommendation was ignored, and interbranch communication settled once again into a familiar pattern of political rhetoric. Recommendations notwithstanding, the commission was unable to save the issue from the political controversy that had enveloped it from its inception.

THE CALL FOR A COMMISSION

By 1971, the Judicial Conference had grown impatient with the Fifth Circuit issue, primarily because its requests for judgeships were constantly intertwined with and delayed by the controversy surrounding circuit division. The prospect of a reconciliation seemed bleaker than before, given the unsuccessful attempt that had been made three years earlier by the American Bar Association. When the American Bar Foundation study[2] failed to receive favorable attention, conference calls for the creation of an independent, congressionally created commission became louder and more specific.

Under the direction of Professor Paul D. Carrington (University of Michigan Law School) and the Project Advisory Committee, chaired by Bernard G. Segal, the ABF study reported its recommendations in 1968. Its conclusions concerning the courts of appeals' workload problems and possible solutions were controversial even among the prestigious members of the advisory committee, which included Leon Jaworski, Thurgood Marshall, and Paul J. Mishkin.

In the study's preface, Carrington candidly stated his disagreement with the advisory committee's priority of recommendations and noted his intention to publish his remarks separately, which he subsequently did, in the *Harvard Law Review*.[3] In particular he disagreed with the committee's recommendation that courts of appeals sit in panels of two judges. The study group, however, did agree that adding judges to existing circuits was more desirable than creating more circuits.[4]

Carrington emphasized that, in his opinion, although a court of fifteen judges was an acceptable size, at some point beyond nine and before fifteen, courts should be subdivided into sections specializing in particular areas of the law. Cases would then be assigned to a division according to the subject matter of the appeal. Five to seven judges selected on a rotational basis would staff each division and have final authority over the circuit's law in that area. Divisions would streamline the process and help avoid realignment up to a point. The study group, however, added to its conclusion that if caseload

2. American Bar Foundation, *Accommodating the Workload of the U.S. Courts of Appeals, Report of Recommendations* (Chicago: American Bar Foundation, 1968).

3. Paul D. Carrington, "Crowded Dockets and the Courts of Appeals: The Threat to the Function of Review and the National Law," *Harvard Law Review* 82 (January 1969): 542–617.

4. American Bar Foundation, *Workload*.

continued to increase, particularly in the Fifth and Ninth circuits, even fifteen judges would not be able to "stay abreast of their work for very long."[5] In subsequent Senate testimony, Carrington indicated that although the study group agreed that realignment was not the answer, it also agreed that in the event it became necessary, then splitting the Fifth Circuit between Mississippi and Alabama "would not be all bad."[6]

Carrington continued to emphasize that the decision entailed value judgments which had to be made by Congress. Members of the study group did not make a final decision among these judgments, he said, because "we were also in general agreement...that as of 1968 the country was not really ready politically, the profession wasn't ready, the judiciary wasn't ready, to resolve this matter...."[7]

Judge J. Skelly Wright, speaking on behalf of the Judicial Conference, agreed with Carrington. Wright told congressional members that "since the failure of the American Bar Foundation's study to come up with the answers, we in the judiciary have felt that this is a problem for Congress and that only Congress is able to solve it."[8] Wright attributed the ABF study's failure to the group's having underestimated the magnitude of the problem they had undertaken. Not only was it beyond the judiciary's resources, Wright maintained, but it was a "political as well as a judicial question and consequently that is the reason why the conference has recommended that the Congress undertake a study of the problem."[9] The Wright and Carrington remarks before Congress were indicative of the perception by the majority of the participants of the need for change in 1971, as the commission stage of Fifth Circuit division began.

Immediately before the conference's meeting in March 1971, its prestigious Court Administration Committee reissued a recommendation concerning nationwide realignment. By this time Fifth Circuit Judge Robert A. Ainsworth had replaced Chief Judge Biggs as head of that committee. Because of his evenhanded manner, Ainsworth excelled in administrative matters. Chief Justice Burger's selection of him to chair the committee was a clear sign of the Louisiana judge's growing stature within the judiciary. When Ainsworth subsequently asked the conference to adopt his committee's recommendation that Congress create an independent commission to study a nationwide realignment, it did so with relative calm. In fact, for those conference members who remembered the 1964 fracas it was a welcome suggestion.

As a member of the Fifth Circuit, Ainsworth could speak to Congress with

5. Ibid.
6. U.S. Congress, Senate, Subcommittee on Improvements in Judicial Machinery of the Committee on the Judiciary, *Revision of Appellate Courts*, 92d Cong., 2d sess., 1972, p. 140.
7. U.S. Senate, *Revision*, p. 139.
8. Ibid., p. 20.
9. Ibid., p. 19.

special authority on the realignment issue. He had joined the unanimous recommendation of the Fifth Circuit Council that the court should not be expanded beyond fifteen judges. Yet, as he explained to both the Judicial Conference and to Congress, the preference of all circuits to have relatively small courts was becoming impractical because caseloads were increasing nationwide. According to the conference's own quadrennial study of judgeship needs, the Fifth and Ninth circuit's current caseloads would require twenty-two- and eighteen-judge courts, respectively, to handle their dockets. Other circuits, too, would be forced to turn down statistically justified judgeships in order to maintain a nine-member court. Ainsworth admitted that the needs produced by rapidly climbing caseload, combined with a prevailing opinion of circuit courts not to increase their sizes, produced a confusing situation. Ainsworth concluded that a comprehensive study by an independent commission was the only measure that might produce meaningful solutions.[10]

The conference decision in March 1971 to endorse the creation of a special study commission brought with it one significant change in the politics of the realignment issue. By recommending that an independent, nonpartisan panel assume responsibility for the circuit division question, the Judicial Conference formally withdrew from the scene. Undoubtedly stung by the politics of earlier battles and frustrated by the lack of progress made on the issue, the conference gave notice that it would no longer comment on any legislative proposal recommending realignment. In all future instances, it would defer to the opinions of the judges sitting on the affected courts.[11] This action removed a significant participant from the policy-making process.

CONGRESSIONAL REACTION

Two weeks after Ainsworth's conference-endorsed recommendation was received by Congress, Emanuel Celler introduced H.R. 7378, legislation providing for the creation of a commission on revision of the judicial circuits. Of course, Celler was anxious to move forward with this idea, as he had been calling for such a study for fourteen years. His intervention to stop the proposed Fifth Circuit division in 1964 was based on his suspicion of the motivations for the isolated incident and on his opposition to a piecemeal approach to circuit boundary revision. Even with substantial agreement on the need for a commission, more than a year passed between the time the bill was introduced and its respective passage in each chamber. And then the differences

10. U.S. Congress, House, Subcommittee No. 5 of the Committee on the Judiciary, *Commission on Revision of Judicial Circuits*, 92d Cong., lst sess., 1971, pp. 19–29.

11. The action by the Judicial Conference is reviewed in the August 22, 1980, statement of James E. Macklin, Jr., Executive Assistant Director of the Administrative Office of the United States Courts. U.S. Congress, House, Subcommittee on Courts, Civil Liberties, and the Administration of Justice of the Committee on the Judiciary, *Federal Court Organization and Fifth Circuit Division*, 96th Cong., 2d. sess., 1980.

between the House and Senate versions were so great that six months elapsed
before a conference committee could reconcile them.

From mid-June through mid-July of 1971, Representative Celler held five
days of hearings before Subcommittee Number 5, which he chaired. Prior to
the hearings Celler solicited the views of each circuit's chief judge. There was
an overwhelming consensus favoring national realignment, accompanied by
an equally strong view on the part of each chief judge that *his* current circuit
boundary lines were ideal. Regardless of region, all circuit boundary lines
seemed to evoke political attachments.

During Celler's hearings an overwhelming majority of experts testified that
realignment was simply too political to allow either branch, legislative or judicial, to study or recommend specific alignments. Retired Justice Tom C.
Clark, who as the director of the Federal Judicial Center had to contend with
the possibility of conducting the study, prophetically testified that the political
pressures which had prevented the center from undertaking a review of circuit
boundaries would also circumvent congressional action. Justice Clark candidly
told Representative Celler:

> [T]he only answer to the problem is to have a distinguished commission, created
> by the Congress, organized by the appointive authorities and staffed by experts
> and scholars who would research this matter in depth.... In addition, I submit
> that there are tremendous pressures involved.... Judges have personal attach-
> ments to their circuit, somewhat like a wife.... I have talked with judges and
> the chief judges in particular, and they say, "Change the geographical limits
> of my circuit? Well, that is like changing the name of Arkansas. It just won't
> go."... So you could not, in my opinion, reach the right answer through them.
> Now the same is true with Congress... you, too, have too many pressures along
> with so much work that a first-class job could not be done. Political pressures
> would prevent it.[12]

Chief Judge Henry Friendly of the Second Circuit and Professor Carrington opposed the commission concept. Friendly characterized a twelve-member
commission with a two-year period for study and more than a half-million
dollar budget as using a "steamroller to crack a nut."[13] Both Friendly and
Carrington claimed that realignment was limited as a solution for caseload
problems; nor was it politically feasible on a national basis. The real issue was
to realign the Fifth and Ninth circuits, and divisions limited to these two
regions would not require a commission.

Celler strongly disagreed. He explained that although he was not "wedded
to" the idea of a commission, there would be tremendous pressures on Congress if a nationwide realignment bill went to the floor. He feared that every

12. U.S. House, *Commission*, p. 18.
13. Ibid., p. 63.

congressional member would have a "finger in the pie,"[14] adding that political pressure already was mounting at the mere mention of a commission.

Testimony supporting a broader scope for the commission was echoed by many witnesses, including Justice Clark, former Chief Judge Lumbard (Second Circuit), Chief Judge Brown, and Thomas E. Kauper, deputy assistant attorney general under President Nixon. Realignment views notwithstanding, most of the participants wanted the commission to undertake a major federal court reform study, including clarifying the Judicial Code and streamlining federal court jurisdiction. For congressional members, however, more than the substance of the mission was at issue.

Throughout the hearings Representative Richard H. Poff (VA), the second-ranking Republican on the House Judiciary Committee and Subcommittee Number 5, warned members that the bill drafted by the Judicial Conference bordered on being unconstitutional.[15] In the conference-approved proposal, the commission's recommendations would become law unless either house negated them within ninety days. By eliminating the necessity for Congress to consider and vote on such recommendations, the legislators avoided the intense political pressures that would otherwise inevitably arise. This so-called rules enabling mechanism became a source of considerable controversy in the House.

Other Republicans, as well as Kauper from the Justice Department, argued intently against the legislative veto provision. Kauper claimed that the customary practice of using the legislative veto to change court rules was quite different from using it to reorganize court structure where questions of jurisdiction were involved. He also argued that the president should not be asked to waive his role in the legislative process.[16]

Celler and Poff seemed to agree with Kauper. Both lectured witnesses that their current apprehension about using a legislative veto was magnified by requests made to broaden the scope of the commission's task. The hearings ended on this note, leaving unanswered for almost a year the fate of the commission bill in the House.

When the issue was finally debated on the House floor in mid-May of 1972, the legislative veto clause had been deleted. A month earlier, the subcommittee had unanimously reported a bill substantially revised from the proposal of the Judicial Conference. Celler explained that its purpose was to create a short-term commission whose sole objective was to study and recommend changes in the geographical boundaries of circuit courts. The commission's report would not be self-executing, Celler stated, because Congress should

14. Ibid., p. 71.
15. Ibid.
16. U.S. House, *Commission*, p. 48.

determine where the boundary lines were to be drawn, and the president's veto power should not be eliminated.[17]

A drastic reduction was made in the proposed longevity and budget of the commission. Instead of a two-year study for $600,000, the committee settled on a six-month term for $50,000. Part of the difference in financing was made possible by its decision to have the commission use the services of the Administrative Office and the Federal Judicial Center instead of having independent staff and executive director.

A change in membership representation from the Judicial Conference version was particularly irritating to Chief Justice Burger. Rather than a commission comprised of four appointees from each branch of government, as the conference had recommended, the House Judiciary Committee increased the total size to fifteen members, giving four appointments to the president, four each to the House and Senate, and reducing the number of the chief justice's appointments by one, leaving him three. Burger reportedly stated that "he would decline to exercise the power of appointment unless there were absolute equality between the Legislature, Executive and the Judiciary."[18] Despite the chief justice's disappointment, however, this version passed the House by 319 to 25, on May 15, 1972.[19]

When the Senate devised a considerably different approach from that taken by the House, the Judicial Conference enthusiastically endorsed the Senate version (S. J. Res. 122). Before Celler could conclude his subcommittee's final hearing in July 1971, Senator Quentin N. Burdick (D-ND), who chaired the Subcommittee on Improvements in Judicial Machinery, introduced a hybrid version of the House and conference bills. In regard to the length of the commission's life and the size of its budget, Burdick's bill was closer to the conference proposal. He suggested a two-year study for a price of $370,000, with an independent director and staff. But where the Senate bill differed most from the House and conference proposals was in the scope of the study.

When Burdick introduced the Senate bill he stressed the facts that realignment would provide only temporary relief for federal appellate courts and that additional judges were only a temporary solution to caseload problems.[20] According to him, what was needed was a comprehensive study on how to restructure the entire federal appellate court system, including an in-depth examination of all related problems and appellate court procedures. Even the

17. U.S. Congress, House, 92d Cong., 2d sess., 15 May 1972, *Congressional Record*, pp. 17274–81.

18. Letter from Chief Judge John R. Brown to All Active Fifth Circuit Judges, July 28, 1972.

19. U.S. House, 92d Cong., 2d sess., 15 May 1972, *Congressional Record*, p. 17281.

20. U.S. Congress, Senate, 92d Cong., 1st sess., 29 June 1971, *Congressional Record*, p. 22746.

Supreme Court's caseload problems were to be examined under the Senate resolution.

Although the conference was pleased that the legislative veto procedure had not been eliminated in Burdick's proposal, the chief justice's insistence on interbranch equality was not honored; in fact, appointees of the chief justice were further reduced to two. Half of the appointments to the twelve-member commission would be presidential, according to the Senate bill.

Senator Burdick did not hold hearings on the Senate version of the commission until May 1972. During three days of testimony the subcommittee received overwhelming support for the Senate's broader mandate. Although the Senate version was somewhat different than the narrow task approved by the Judicial Conference, Judge Ainsworth transmitted the conference's enthusiastic support for it.[21]

In late June the Senate passed without debate the Burdick subcommittee draft defining the commission. Obviously the differences between the House and Senate interpretations were substantial. A month later a conference committee chaired by Celler was established to reconcile the disparities. Composed of four Democrats and three senior Republicans, House conferees finally reached agreement with Senators Eastland, Burdick, and Hruska in late September. Unlike the reconciliation process associated with many conferences, it appeared that very little negotiation and compromise took place during the discussions. Instead, the conference report essentially merged the two approaches.[22]

In line with the House version, the commission was given a short term (180 days) to report on the necessity of realigning any circuits. In addition, it was to issue a more extensive report on structural and procedural changes within fifteen months, closer to the two-year period in the Senate and conference drafts. An explicit limitation prohibiting the commission from studying jurisdictional problems was imposed. The final appropriation ($270,000) was more in line with the Senate request ($370,000). All of the separate staff positions requested by the Senate were authorized. Not surprisingly, the final conference draft omitted the legislative veto provision. Objections from the chief justice were met, however, by increasing the size of the commission to sixteen. This allowed four appointments each for the chief justice and the president but failed to achieve interbranch equality, since half the members were to be chosen by Congress, four by each chamber.

Considering the extent to which all participants were accommodated in the final draft, immediate passage in both the House and Senate was as ex-

21. U.S. Senate, *Revision*; U.S. Congress, Senate, Committee on the Judiciary, *Commission on Revision of Appellate Court System*, S. Rept. 92–930, 92d Cong., 2d sess., 1972, p. 11.

22. U.S. Congress, House, Committee on the Judiciary, *Commission on Revision of Appellate Court Structure*, H. Rept. 92–1457, 92d Cong., 2d sess., 1972; U.S. Congress, House, 92d Cong., 2d sess., 28 September 1972, *Congressional Record*, pp. 32755–56; U.S. Congress, House, 92d Cong., 2d sess., 4 October 1972, *Congressional Record*, pp. 33728–29.

pected. President Nixon signed into law the Commission on Revision of the Federal Court Appellate System on October 13, 1972. But, unbeknownst to the members at the time, it would be eight years to the month before their statutory purpose met with political acceptability.

THE COMMISSION RIDES THE CIRCUIT

Almost a full year passed before the commission had its membership constituted and commenced the initial hearing process. Once assembled, however, it was an impressive group of experts on the federal court system, who represented a wide array of points of expertise. Congressional appointees, among whom there was partisan equality, included Senators Roman L. Hruska (R-NB), who chaired the panel, Quentin N. Burdick (D-ND), Edward J. Gurney (R-FL), and John L. McClellan (D-AR), and Representatives Jack Brooks (D-TX), who had also served on the conference committee that created the commission, Walter Flowers (D-AL), Edward Hutchinson (R-MI), and Charles E. Wiggins (R-CA). The congressional appointments were drawn from the House and Senate Judiciary committees. Emanuel Celler, who had lost his seat in 1972, was appointed by the president, in addition to Dean Roger C. Cramton (Cornell Law School), Francis R. Kirkham (San Francisco Bar Association), and Judge Alfred J. Sulmonetti (Oregon State Circuit Court).

Names familiar to the past controversy surrounding Fifth Circuit realignment also emerged among the chief justice's appointees. These were Judge J. Edward Lumbard (Second Circuit), who had been an active member of the conference in 1964; Judge Roger Robb (District of Columbia); Bernard G. Segal (Philadelphia Bar Association), who had played an instrumental role in preventing Fifth Circuit division in 1964; and Professor Herbert Wechsler (Columbia University Law School), who also opposed Fifth Circuit division in 1964 as director of the American Law Institute. To this distinguished membership list was added another important participant, Professor A. Leo Levin of the University of Pennsylvania Law School. Enlisted by Bernard Segal to serve as the commission's executive director, Levin was credited with having kept the entire commission working effectively.[23]

In general, the commission approached the responsibility of separating realignment from politics with good intentions. The task would prove troublesome, however, since more than half of the members had been involved to some degree in the past politics of the realignment proposal. Also, any recommendation would eventually return to a political forum— Congress— for final disposition. Although authorized to study national realignment, Hruska noted that the Fifth and Ninth circuits were the only ones with "real

23. Interview with Senator Roman L. Hruska, Omaha, Nebraska, July 29, 1983; interview with A. Leo Levin, Washington, D.C., October 27, 1983.

problems that splitting might help."[24] Consequently, of the ten cities in which hearings were held, four were located in the Fifth Circuit.

A few months before the commission's first hearing, Judge Robb contacted Chief Judge Brown and informed him that the commission was contemplating hearings across the nation, as funds permitted. At that stage Robb asked Brown to solicit the other judges' views on how the commission might proceed with its task but to avoid any substantive suggestions on realignment.

Notifying the Fifth Circuit judges, both active and senior, of Robb's request, Brown assured his colleagues that he would not "undertake to distill a consensus" based on the individual responses. He asked all judges to indicate whether the Circuit Council should seek a consensus. In a slightly reluctant tone, the chief judge indicated that such council action would require a meeting likely to produce "many different views."[25] Perhaps in an attempt to avoid factional splits, the correspondence ended by encouraging the judges to circulate their views among all members of the court.

Although Brown could see that conditions were not the same as in 1964, remnants of past political battles lingered. First, responses from the judges were overwhelmingly supportive of two points. Everyone, including Rives and Tuttle, argued that the court was in great need of some relief.[26] All but four (Rives, Tuttle, Goldberg, and Wisdom) explicitly called for a split; and most indicated, rather emphatically, the desire to have a court of nine members. Ironically, Rives even suggested the possibility of two courts operating within the circuit, each deriving the benefit of the six-state diversity and less than full en banc sittings. (This nascent idea later became an important legislative provision in the 1978 Omnibus Judgeship Act.) One of the members even quipped that just because the court was operating with fifteen judges did not mean that it was operating at maximum efficiency, in individual or institutional terms.[27]

Second, none of the judges requested a meeting of the Circuit Council; in fact, nine of them quite candidly stated that a council meeting would most likely be very unproductive. As one explained, the council should not sit as a "junior commission" and discuss "legislative concerns that are most certainly fraught with political and personal considerations."[28] When all the views were assembled, Judge Coleman's perspective seemed to reflect the majority opinion: "I know that our present fifteen judges can never agree as to how this will be done, any more than you can get a state legislature to agree on how it should be reapportioned . . . I think this is going to be the real function of the Circuit Realignment Commission. They are going to do for us what we

24. Hruska interview.

25. Letter from Chief Judge John R. Brown to All Fifth Circuit Judges, May 24, 1973.

26. Various letters from all Fifth Circuit Judges to Chief Judge Brown, May 26, 1973, through June 15, 1973.

27. Letter from Judge John C. Godbold to Chief Judge John R. Brown, June 1, 1973.

28. Letter from Judge Paul H. Roney to Chief Judge John R. Brown, June 15, 1973.

do for litigants, simply decide that which is best for the federal court system and then it will be up to us to comply, grumble though we may."[29] Subsequently Brown informed Judges Robb and Lumbard that no council resolution would be forthcoming.[30]

Throughout August and September of 1973, the commission managed to hold hearings specific to the Fifth Circuit in Washington, Houston, New Orleans, Jackson, and Jacksonville. As soon as the first hearing began in Washington, a major issue in the realignment debate surfaced. Clearly, no other complaint about the Fifth Circuit was lodged by as many sources as that over the extended use of summary procedures that limited oral argument. The bar association representatives were especially concerned about the lack of oral argument in well over 50 percent of the Fifth Circuit's appeals. In fact, one of the first witnesses called was Orison S. Marden, a representative from the American College of Trial Lawyers, who chaired a special committee on Preservation of the Right to Oral Argument. Another witness, former Solicitor General Erwin Griswold, who stated how impressed he was by the Fifth Circuit's innovative procedures and their ability to hold down scandalous backlogs, admitted that the procedures had resulted in too much reduction of oral argument. Judge Skelly Wright also testified that he was concerned about the overuse of screening procedures.[31] In contrast, complaints about the Ninth Circuit centered on the extent of unresolved intracircuit conflicts, which witnesses claimed stemmed from overuse of visiting judges and avoidance of en bancs. Fifth Circuit lawyers apparently placed more value on being heard— i.e., oral argument—than who was listening—i.e., visiting judges. As the tone of this first hearing indicated, the context of the realignment debate, if not the central issues, had been slightly restructured.

When the hearings moved to Texas later in August, commission members once again faced criticisms from the bar associations concerning the Fifth Circuit's denial of oral argument in a large number of cases. At one point a Dallas attorney, disgruntled about the lack of oral argument, quizzed Representative Jack Brooks (D-TX) about the possibility of the commission's simply splitting the circuit according to one of the hypothesized maps that the Federal Judicial Center had drawn based only on caseload statistics. Brooks replied that there were political considerations in getting the legislation passed; for instance, "there may be some feeling on the part of the Mississippi people that they would rather be with the Old South, and some of the Mississippi Senators, some of them are Chairman of the Judiciary Committee."[32]

On August 22, the commission opened hearings in New Orleans, where

29. Letter from Judge James P. Coleman to Chief Judge John R. Brown, May 26, 1973.
30. Commission on Revision of the Federal Court Appellate System, *Hearings First Phase* (Washington, D.C.: Government Printing Office, 1973), p. 506.
31. Ibid., pp. 10–32, 102.
32. Ibid., p. 304.

conflict within the court emerged for the first time during the hearing process. Again the commission members were repeatedly told by bar members that a majority of their attorneys believed the court's limitation on oral argument had gone so far as to "prejudice due process."[33] This time, however, the witnesses offered a variety of solutions as alternatives to splitting the circuit. Obviously influenced to some degree by Wisdom's viewpoint, the Louisiana attorneys adamantly stressed that splitting the Fifth Circuit was not necessary or desirable and would be a deplorable move.[34]

Although a formal resolution from the Louisiana Bar was not issued until three months later, it was the only bar association from the six states to oppose the split, a position it maintained until 1980. The Louisiana witnesses also indicated why the state was not enthusiastic about entering into a two-state circuit with Texas. This position was best articulated by Judge Ainsworth, who very candidly told the commission that diversity from six states created a national court. He explained that, although he "loved" his Texas colleagues, if Louisiana were placed alone with Texas, the Louisiana judges would be outnumbered by "two-to-one."[35] The judges from Texas had "their point of view" and Louisiana judges had another, which could make a difference in oil and gas, taxation, and community property cases.[36] Regarding the prospect of being alone with Texas, he said the Louisiana judges would "feel somewhat put on by a two-to-one majority against us all the time."[37] When Ainsworth was asked about the impact of a 3–3 state alignment, he responded that "it would not have the regional character the six states have," but at least the two Louisiana judges could be joined by two Mississippi ones, producing a "four-to-four" situation between the Texas and Louisiana/Mississippi judges.[38]

In addition to Ainsworth, Wisdom and Godbold were called to testify at the New Orleans hearings. Unlike him, they were categorical in expressing their positions on realignment. Wisdom launched directly into the controversial issues, addressing them one by one. Complaints about the lack of oral argument, he claimed, were confusing the issue of circuit splitting. Anyone who thought oral argument could be granted in every case should forget about division and favor redesigning the entire "creaking" federal court system.[39] There was also, according to Wisdom, no reason to have every member sit en banc. He believed equally as strongly that federal jurisdiction had to be curtailed to provide relief for federal courts from their heavy caseloads. Before he was finished he had chided both the commission and some members of the court. He told the commissioners that: "Indeed, without this authority

33. Ibid., p. 330.
34. Ibid., p. 332.
35. Ibid., p. 348.
36. Ibid.
37. Ibid.
38. Ibid., p. 352.
39. Ibid., p. 358.

[to consider jurisdiction] . . . the Commission's task is limited to little more than rationalizing the prior determination of Congress to split the Fifth and Ninth Circuits."[40] Then, upon learning of a signed statement from the "eastern" judges that was to be presented the following day in Jackson, Wisdom continued: "In a statement . . . signed or approved by all of the judges on the court from Alabama, Florida, Georgia, and Mississippi, my brothers scaled new heights of unreality. They say: 'It should be emphasized that any circuit realignment should result in a Federal Appellate System which will suffice without further realignment for a period in excess of 25 years.' This ignores all past statistics. . . . "[41] In effect, Wisdom thought that there was absolutely no rational argument to justify the damage circuit splitting would do to the federal court system and, more importantly, that it was not a long-term solution to excessive caseload.

On the other side of the debate, Godbold offered his position in similarly unequivocal terms. "The matter that I particularly wish to emphasize . . . is the imperative necessity that there be a realignment *now*," he told the commission.[42] Noting that a substantial majority of the judges were "committed to the view that realignment . . . must not be postponed," he warned the commission that unanimity among the court's members would be a "miracle" and that it was "unrealistic" to expect that they would ever be closer to a unanimous agreement.[43] His concluding remarks were a persuasive appeal, which was echoed for many more years:

> I share the view that the Court of Appeal must avoid parochialism and must be diverse in the character of their membership. . . . yet this diversity is essentially unrelated to state lines. . . . performance of the federalizing function . . . depends largely upon the hearts and the minds of the men who sit on the bench and upon the selection process which puts them there, and only secondarily upon the number of states from which each court draws its members.[44]

In essence, Godbold thought that the size of the court was creating some serious administrative problems affecting its judicial decision-making processes. For instance, he told the commission that an en banc of fifteen judges was so cumbersome that judges would "shrink from invoking the en banc machinery."[45] Moreover, even when the court did call for an en banc, especially in multiple-issue cases, a "silencing effect" occurred: its large size made judges reluctant to express their views when there were so many other viewpoints to be discussed; and even if a judge did express his opinion, it might be "lost or obscured in the shuffle."[46]

40. Ibid., pp. 357–58.
41. Ibid., p. 43.
42. Ibid., p. 375.
43. Ibid., p. 376.
44. Ibid., p. 377.
45. Ibid.
46. Ibid.

By this time it was clear that proponents of division had been busily preparing a persuasive argument for splitting the Fifth Circuit. Wisdom's opponents would prove to be much more effective than the group he and Rives had defeated in 1964. If Wisdom was not frustrated by the conclusion of the New Orleans hearing, he must have been thoroughly irritated by the time the Jackson, Mississippi, hearing ended. Ten years afterward, Wisdom recalled that Griffin Bell had been his most formidable rival during the very early years of the Fifth Circuit realignment debate. Without flinching and with a sharp glance, he added that there was no question that Charles Clark was his most formidable opponent during the latter stages.[47] The events and testimony of the commission hearings in Jackson undoubtedly contributed to Wisdom's assessment of Judge Clark as a most worthy opponent.

In some ways those hearings in Jackson were a turning point in the realignment debate. Two events made the commission's short visit a significant one. First, Walter Gewin's presentation of a statement that Griffin Bell, Lewis Morgan, and he had prepared was particularly persuasive. Later referred to as the "Manifesto from the East" by Judge Brown, the document was signed by all the judges of the four eastern states, with one exception. Those who signed expressed the view that fifteen judges were six too many. Judge Roney from St. Petersburg, who did not sign the document, later submitted a separate statement at the Jacksonville hearing, calling for the same congressional action.[48]

Gewin, who was given a warm introduction by his former law partner, Walter Flowers, told the commission that intracircuit conflicts were a growing concern which could not be remedied by circulating all the court's opinions, because of the large number of judges. Nor could conflicts be resolved by en bancs, because of the administrative difficulties of having so many judges deciding a case. As an example he pointed out that fifteen en banc cases required "37 1/2 hours of conference time."[49]

The so-called Eastern Manifesto rejected "out of hand" any fear that division would lead to parochialism. To support this point its adherents had devised a retirement chart demonstrating the large turnover that would occur over the following three to five years. "Elusive concepts of 'liberal' or 'conservative' "[50] as labels on judicial philosophy were strongly rejected by the eastern judges, who also pointed out that the six southern states in question were "far more integrated on all levels than any other six states in the nation."[51] Emphasizing that one circuit could not accommodate such rapidly growing states as Texas and Florida, the judges made one statement that had a lasting

47. Interview with Judge John Minor Wisdom, New Orleans, March 23, 1983.
48. Commission, *Hearings*, pp. 398, 487.
49. Ibid., p. 392.
50. Ibid., p. 393.
51. Ibid.

impact and was even cited in the commission's report: "Jumboism has no place in the Federal Court Appellate System."[52] By taking a unified position independent of their Texas and Louisiana counterparts, these judges of the four eastern states created a lasting impression. From this point on, the court already seemed to be "divided" along a 4–2 alignment.

After the dramatic presentation of the Eastern Manifesto, the commission witnessed a second impressive display. When the time came for Judge Charles Clark's testimony, he began by asking if he might visually demonstrate to the commission his point concerning the court's workload and its resulting administrative problems. In a classic trial court maneuver, he produced three stacks of printed-slip opinions—measuring over four feet tall—to illustrate the volume of Fifth Circuit output for the year. He then showed the commission another stack of opinions over one foot tall—the decisions in which he had directly participated (authored, concurred with, or dissented from).[53]

Clark further testified that not only should the commission recommend division, it should split the circuit along the Mississippi River. Adding Mississippi to the eastern division should not be a concern, because the Mississippi judges were actually surplus help, as they disposed of many more appeals than their state contributed to the court's caseload. J. P. Coleman also pleaded for a split that would place Mississippi with the eastern states in the Fifth Circuit. In his humorous way, Coleman added: "Mississippi standing alone might be called provincial, but I don't think we're going to be allowed to stand alone.... that's not a problem.... We're going to be put somewhere."[54] All of the Mississippi lawyers who testified were supportive of the Mississippi judges' position. However, one law professor from the University of Mississippi, George Cochran, who had clerked for Chief Justice Earl Warren in 1964–65, said, "the cure [of realignment] may also be worse than the disease."[55]

When the commission resumed hearings the first week in September 1973, it heard more conflicting views. In Jacksonville, Judges Bell and Roney again stressed the immediacy of the administrative crisis in the circuit and prescribed realignment as the solution, whereas Chief Judge Brown offered a strong plea not to split the circuit. He weakened his position, however, by discussing projected caseloads and stating that, much as he wanted to postpone it, he recognized that the court needed help. He eventually admitted to the commission that the night before Bell had asked him, " 'When are you finally going to give up?,' to which Brown responded, 'Along about 3:30 tomorrow afternoon.' "[56]

Although he tempered his opposition to realignment, Brown continued to

52. Ibid.
53. Ibid., pp. 403–15.
54. Ibid., p. 410.
55. Ibid., p. 418.
56. Ibid., p. 636.

insist that Wisdom's concern over parochialism was valid. He continued, "Judge Godbold made a very beguiling argument—and I think beguiling is the thing the snake did, too, at one stage—argumentation about how state lines were irrelevant to parochialism."[57] Brown praised the degree of diversity presently existing within the borders of the Fifth Circuit. He explained how unique to Louisiana was the "Cajun, so-called, in the evangeline country of Louisiana," and that a similarly unique people lived in east Texas and in the "hill country" of west Texas and Georgia.[58] He concluded that the boundaries had a political nature with which the commission would have to reckon. At the end of the hearings Representative Flowers told Brown, "There's more a fear of a lack of cross-pollination on the part of you judges than I would have myself as just a layman or a former practicing attorney."[59]

Wisdom, apparently disgruntled with the tone of the commission hearings, especially the suggestion in the Eastern Manifesto that he was eligible to retire, issued a supplemental statement to "rebut the circuit-dividers." In a style reminiscent of the 1964 campaign, he sent this and his previous statement to various prominent officials in Washington, federal jurists (including his Fifth Circuit brethren), and former law clerks. One of his former clerks recalled that at the time Wisdom had his "own troops," referring to former law clerks, "working" for him in Washington.[60]

Three such congressional aides received a letter from Wisdom after the hearings. Realizing that his views were receiving less than a favorable hearing and that his campaign was quickly becoming a solo performance, Wisdom began to rally his "forces" in Washington. He wrote:

> In my opinion, this is an Eastland-engineered maneuver: the political decision has already been made that the Fifth and Ninth Circuits should be divided promptly. The hearings were designed as window-dressing.... I am about the only judge on our Court who is still actively fighting against splitting the Fifth. Ainsworth would settle for any division of the circuit that would not allow Louisiana to be overwhelmed by Texas. And, of course, he has the pragmatic approach of an experienced politician. "Buster" has been all wind, no fury, and collapsed like a pricked balloon at the Commission's last hearing...where our friend...Judge Mushmouth worked on him the night before.[61]

57. Ibid., p. 646.

58. Ibid.

59. Ibid., p. 650.

60. Interview with Thomas Susman, Washington, D.C., April 26, 1983. The enlisting by federal judges of former law clerks, who either served on congressional staffs or were strategically placed in Washington legal circles, as a means for communication or to influence public policy was frequently cited in documents and interviews consulted in this research.

61. Letter from Judge John Minor Wisdom to Robert Barnett, Jack Weiss, and John Buckley, September 20, 1973.

Obviously discouraged by the political reality that he was becoming the sole opponent of the split, Wisdom was unaware that he was about to gain an effective and enthusiastic ally.

In July 1973, after the retirement of Ingraham, the court gained the services of Thomas Gibbs Gee of Austin, Texas. A West Point and University of Texas Law School graduate with a young-looking face and boyish grin, Judge Gee, by his own admission, is probably one of the most conservative members of the court.[62] Yet soon after taking his place on the bench he joined Wisdom as an opponent to division. Although he did not formally testify in 1973, a few months after his appointment he wrote to Leo Levin, stating that "to dismember a proud and effective institution such as the Fifth Circuit as a preliminary measure and in pursuit of benefits which can only be short-haul, ... would be unwise."[63] Even years later, after Wisdom had taken senior status and could no longer actively fight the split, Gee continued to carry the opposition banner.

Thirteen of the sixteen commission members assembled on December 11, 1973, for discussion of the testimony it had heard. The desires of Senator Eastland dominated the discussion. In a letter to Senator Hruska urging a 4–2 division of the circuit, Eastland had written that the interests of the people of Mississippi were more compatible with the southern states that lay east of the Mississippi River than those to the west. Commission members were not unaware that Eastland opposed joining Mississippi to Texas and Louisiana because of the activist roles played by Brown and Wisdom in civil rights. One member, Roger Cramton, who had served as an assistant attorney general for the Office of Legal Counsel from 1972 to 1973, noted that most of the "national experts" and lawyers from Texas and Louisiana from whom the commission had heard supported the 3–3 alignment. The commission, he went on, had to contend "only with a question of political opposition in Mississippi against what seems to be a more sensible plan."[64] Jack Brooks was quoted as having stated during the meeting, "There is no question... (placing Mississippi in the west) is the best plan, but it is my impression that a powerful old curmudgeon of the Senate doesn't want it."[65]

On December 18, 1973, a week after their debate and just a few days shy of their six-month deadline, the commission issued its report. It recommended by an 8–5 vote that the Fifth Circuit be divided, with Mississippi, Louisiana, and Texas comprising a new Eleventh Circuit and Alabama, Georgia, and

62. Interview with Judge Thomas G. Gee, Austin, Texas, March 18, 1983.

63. Letter from Judge Thomas G. Gee to Professor A. Leo Levin, December 20, 1973, quoted in letter from Judge John Minor Wisdom to Professor A. Leo Levin, January 8, 1974.

64. Richard E. Cohen, "Justice Report/Commission proposes boundary changes, seeks to ease workload of appeals court," *National Journal*, December 29, 1973, p. 1948.

65. Ibid., p. 1948.

Florida (and the Canal Zone) constituting the new Fifth. All but one of the congressional members present at the commission meeting voted for a 4–2 alignment, according to the wishes of Senator Eastland. Brooks, Hruska, Burdick, and McClellan, joined by Judge Robb, formed the five dissenting votes.[66]

The recommendation was based on five criteria:

1. There should be at least three states in a circuit;
2. No more than nine judges should be initially authorized for a new circuit;
3. Circuits should have diversity of population, and of legal, business, and socioeconomic interests;
4. Excessive interference should not be had for marginal benefits;
5. No circuits should contain noncontiguous states.[67]

If the primary (3–3) alignment was not possible, then the commission offered Plan A, a 4–3 alignment adding Arkansas to Texas and Louisiana, or Plan B, a 4–2 alignment dividing the Fifth Circuit along the Mississippi River. Professor Levin later noted that the commission presented several plans that would accomplish the objective of a split, and "hoped that at least one of the plans would fly politically."[68]

According to Senator Hruska, the commission was "strongly committed" to its marginal interference criterion, the purpose of which was to avoid moving states from one circuit to another, thus disturbing settled circuit law. As a result, national realignment was not recommended, and splitting a circuit, only for clear and compelling reasons. The Fifth and Ninth circuits met the necessity, according to the report.[69]

Relief through realignment for the Ninth Circuit was achieved by splitting the State of California between circuits, as it generated over 60 percent of the Ninth's caseload. Southern and central California would be placed with Arizona and Nevada, creating a new Twelfth Circuit; northern California would join the northwestern states as the Ninth Circuit. In conclusion, the commission reaffirmed its commitment to realign the two circuits but acknowledged that it was not of one mind on all the issues.

Just before the December report the commission had issued a preliminary one that was widely circulated among participants and interested parties. Wisdom had made a final attempt to try to convince Levin that the commission should change its recommendation. Charging that Fifth Circuit division was pointless and misleading, Wisdom urged the commission to study how liti-

66. Ibid., p. 1949.

67. Commission on Revision of the Federal Court Appellate System, *The Geographical Boundaries of the Several Judicial Circuits: Recommendations for Change* (Washington, D.C.: Government Printing Office, 1973).

68. Levin interview.

69. Commission, *Recommendations*.

gation input could be reduced. In a last failing attempt before the report was transmitted to Congress, Wisdom wrote to Levin: "If the persuasive language of the report and the distinguished membership of the Commission lead Congress to the conclusion that division of the Fifth Circuit offers any substantial relief, the Commission will have seriously retarded effective revision of the Federal Court Appellate System.... In short, the division ... does not, as you say, 'provide a firm base on which to build more enduring reforms.' It is quicksand."[70] Exactly two months later three bills, each embodying one of the commission's recommended plans, were introduced in the Senate.

REMEDIAL LEGISLATION

Over the next three years the realignment issue moved into the congressional forum with continued debate, more hearings, and unaltered viewpoints. Two more slates of hearings were held in the Senate, resulting in three separate bills, only one of which was reported out of the full Judiciary Committee. Even then, no floor action was ever taken on the bill. As the political controversy heated and federal judges argued, Congress proved that it does not resolve policy disputes well under such conditions.

Although Senator Burdick introduced the commission's recommendation in February, hearings were not scheduled until late September and early October of 1974. In the interim the House and Senate Judiciary committees considered a commission request for an extension to complete its work on appellate procedures, and an additional appropriation of $730,000, some of which was later returned. During the spring, subcommittees in both houses were busy holding hearings on the extension, and in the Senate, Burdick's subcommittee considered a conference-drafted omnibus judgeship request for all circuits except the Fifth and Ninth. Eventually, in September when opportunity permitted, hearings were announced and all the Fifth Circuit judges notified.[71]

Arrangements had been made to have Brown, Wisdom, and Gewin express the two major viewpoints on the subject. Burdick, however, did extend an invitation to testify to all the other Fifth Circuit judges. Only Coleman and Clark accepted. The active judges from the four eastern states deferred to Gewin, who would be presenting the statement they had prepared as a group. In the "western" states, Gee authorized Wisdom to speak for him. Ainsworth,

70. Letter from Judge John Minor Wisdom to Professor A. Leo Levin, December 6, 1973.

71. U.S. Congress, House, Subcommittee on Courts, Civil Liberties, and the Administration of Justice of the Committee on the Judiciary, *Relating to Commission on Revision of Federal Court Appellate System*, 93d Cong., 2d sess., 1974; U.S. Congress, Senate, Subcommittee on Improvements in Judicial Machinery of the Committee on the Judiciary, *Circuit Realignment, Part 1*, 93d Cong., 2d sess., 1974; U.S. Congress, Senate, 93d Cong., 2d sess., 7 February 1974, *Congressional Record*, pp. 2586, 2609–12.

Goldberg, and Thornberry expressed their dissatisfaction with the unequal caseload that a 4–2 split would place on the Texas and Louisiana judges. Joe Ingraham was the only judge from the so-called western portion of the circuit to support division emphatically, noting he had heard "that Senator Eastland has said that the Fifth Circuit is not a Court but a convention."[72] Differences of opinion were being expressed even before the hearing started. Senators Burdick and Hruska, however, were familiar enough with the problem at that point to acknowledge openly at the introductory hearing that they were prepared for a much less-than-harmonious presentation.

One of the commission's alternatives was eliminated from consideration almost immediately: the suggestion to place Arkansas with Louisiana and Texas aroused such opposition from the Arkansas Bar Association and Senator John McClellan (D-AR) that it faded from the congressional scene without debate. No Fifth Circuit judge was present to promote actively the commission's primary recommendation, a 3–3 alignment. As a result, once the realignment debate was under way in Congress, the political actors were either advocating a 4–2 split of the circuit or none at all.

At the outset of the hearing, Chief Judge Brown explained that because opinion on the court was so "sharply divided" he could not "represent the full court as [he] would ordinarily as chief judge in congressional matters."[73] He then told the subcommittee that his views ran "parallel" to Wisdom's. They differed only in that Brown, unlike Wisdom, did not support a less than full en banc procedure. Brown was very critical of the commission. Marginal interference was just another way of the other circuits saying "Leave us alone," he claimed.[74] Moreover, the commission had only studied two courts, whereas the congressional mandate was to study all the circuits. He was just as irritated about Levin's reference to the Fifth Circuit's "truncated procedures."[75] Insisting that the summary procedures had not resulted in a denial of justice, Brown maintained that the need to have oral argument in every case is a "myth."[76]

Wisdom expressed equivalent dissatisfaction to the subcommittee concerning the commission's report. Also obviously offended by the retirement eligibility chart, which was presented again, he told the subcommittee more than once during his testimony that he had no intention of taking senior status. Another object of reprimand was the commission's applying the name "Fifth Circuit" to the eastern states in the circuit regardless of alignment. Wisdom maintained, as did Brown, that New Orleans had been the headquarters for the circuit since 1866; even the words "Fifth Circuit" were chiseled into the stately marble courthouse.

72. Letter from Judge Joe M. Ingraham to Senator Quentin Burdick, September 8, 1974, quoted in U.S., Senate, *Realignment, Part 1.*
73. U.S. Senate, *Realignment, Part 1,* p. 78.
74. Ibid., p. 79.
75. Ibid., p. 86.
76. Ibid.

Disagreeing with both Wisdom and Brown, Gewin again presented the statement of the active judges from the four eastern states. He also pointed out the substantial benefit that would derive from having to keep up with the output of eight other judges rather than fourteen. Frustrated by the prospect of additional judges without a split, Gewin quipped to the subcommittee: "If you need eleven judges in each circuit after a split, then it means without a split we would have a court of twenty-two judges. I don't know how to say good morning to twenty-two judges over the phone and do anything else."[77]

On the second day of the hearings, Coleman and Clark, along with the president of the Mississippi Bar Association, made their oral presentations to the subcommittee. Confining their comments to the placement of Mississippi in the possible division, both judges based their remarks on the historical arguments. A 4–2 alignment that placed Mississippi east of the river was more than justified in their opinion because Mississippi's legal antecedents, and in fact the state itself, had all been part of Georgia at one point. They also claimed that Mississippi would actually enhance diversity in the eastern portion of the circuit by adding its unique "river admiralty" cases, as well as oil and gas litigation. Clark noted that under a 4–2 alignment the western part could be conceived as a circuit of more than two states because Texas was more than one state in a geographical, political, and judicial sense. Coleman added that the Mississippi River was the dividing line for all the other circuits contiguous to it. Both stressed that a 4–2 alignment would leave nine judges in the eastern division, a sufficient number without additional appointments.[78]

At one point in his testimony Coleman made the plea that the four states in the eastern division should be separated from Texas and Louisiana because those two states had such unique law, and operated "distinctly ... from civil law beginnings," that they required specialized legal training.[79] Although Coleman was very explicit in explaining that his position in no way indicated a "lack of love or respect or affection"[80] for the two states, Gee and Wisdom were greatly offended. Wisdom was incensed that Coleman had placed Louisiana's very proud legal heritage in the same category as that of Texas. He called the statement an egregious error and tried to correct it many times at various stages of the hearings; but it seemed to recur in reports, each time infuriating him. Gee later remarked that the Mississippi judges' positions made him think that "the judges from Texas and Louisiana must have done something bad, to be sent to hold hands and stand in the corner in such a manner."[81]

If Senator Burdick believed that the September hearings on the Fifth

77. Ibid., p. 126.
78. Ibid., pp. 128–38.
79. Ibid., p. 129.
80. Ibid., p. 128.
81. U.S. Congress, House, Subcommittee on Monopolies and Commercial Law of the Committee on the Judiciary, *A Proposal to Divide the Fifth Circuit*, 95th Cong., 1st sess., 1977, p. 35.

Circuit posed problems for the subcommittee, he surely was presented with a dilemma when he opened hearings on splitting the Ninth Circuit in October 1974. Complaints against the circuit ranged from a two-year backlog and reluctance to call en bancs to extensive use of visiting judges meaning that most panels contained at least one district judge. Nevertheless, opposition to the split came primarily, but not exclusively, from the California participants, including then Governor Ronald Reagan. That opposition was so overwhelming that the final Senate report on both circuits was altered to accommodate their views. Two aspects of the commission's recommendations aroused the most controversy. First, everyone associated with the Ninth Circuit was opposed to splitting California between circuits. There was considerably less agreement on the second objection, which involved Californians traveling to the Supreme Court to resolve possible federal conflicts within their state.

After considerable debate for the next two months on how to accommodate the Ninth Circuit's objections, the subcommittee issued a clean bill in the form of a committee print on December 2, 1974. Of the three bills originally introduced, only S. 2290, the 4–2 division of the Fifth Circuit, survived—albeit in substantially revised form. The revised version formally introduced the concept of administrative "divisions," a hybrid proposal designed to provide the necessary administrative relief for the Fifth and Ninth circuits yet avoid the disadvantages of creating separate circuits.[82] The committee recommended that both circuits be divided into two separate compartments or divisions, with each remaining under one circuit roof. At the suggestion of Deputy Attorney General Robert Bork, Senator Tunney (D-CA) proposed an amendment that would give the Ninth Circuit special authorization to call for a joint en banc to resolve any interdivisional conflict, as California would be split between the two Ninth Circuit divisions.[83] The Southern and Central U.S. Judicial Districts of California would be placed with Arizona and Nevada in the Ninth Circuit's Southern Division, and California's Northern and Eastern Districts would be attached to the Northern Division, which included the states of Alaska, Idaho, Montana, Washington, Oregon, Hawaii, and the territory of Guam. However, because of the objections of the California Bar Association, represented, ironically, until 1974 by the retired Chief Justice Earl Warren, the Senate Judiciary Committee reported that it did not have "sufficient time to solve . . . the problems in the Ninth Circuit,"[84] explaining that although it favored administrative divisions there, it would not further

82. U.S. Congress, Senate, Subcommittee on Improvements in Judicial Machinery of the Committee on the Judiciary, *Circuit Realignment, Part 2*, 94th Cong., 1st sess., 1975, p. 2; U.S. Congress, Senate, Committee on the Judiciary, *Reorganization of Fifth Judicial Circuit*, S. Rept. 94-513, 94th Cong., 1st sess., 1975, pp. 1–4; U.S. Congress, Senate, Committee on the Judiciary, *Omnibus Judgeship bill*, S. Rept. 95–117, 95th Cong., 1st sess., 1977, pp. 38–42.

83. Cohen, "Justice," p. 1949.

84. U.S. Senate, *Reorganization*, p. 5; Cohen, "Justice," p. 1949.

delay action on the Fifth Circuit pending the remaining political obstacles in the Ninth. A year had passed since the commission's report, and although the Senate produced a clean bill from the process, more hearings were scheduled.[85]

Chief Judge Brown hesitated to comment on the bill when first apprised of its contents.[86] However, Gewin, on behalf of the judges in the entire eastern division, communicated to Brown and Burdick his support for the proposed legislation.[87] A resolution of overwhelming support had been passed at a meeting of the active judges of the proposed eastern division on December 13, 1974, in New Orleans. Along with the resolution, Gewin sent a message of deep affection from the eastern division judges to their brethren in the western division.[88]

In an almost retaliatory manner, Chief Judge Brown held a conference of the western division's active judges on January 7, 1975, in Houston. At this meeting they decided to appoint a committee of the three most senior members of their division to meet with a committee from the eastern division. During a joint session, representatives from both sides of the circuit would try to reconcile any administrative problems which the proposed legislation might generate. William P. Westphal, chief counsel to Burdick's subcommittee, was advised to withhold further action on the bill until the two committees issued a joint resolution.[89]

At Houston, the western judges resolved that any additional judges should be in place before division and, although some objected to any division, surprisingly they agreed that if there had to be one, it should be in the form of a clean split. Afterward Brown called Gewin, who according to seniority would have been the designated chief judge of the eastern division, and arranged for a joint meeting on January 15. Both judges agreed that it would be beneficial to have Westphal attend, as he was so familiar with the situation.[90]

On the agreed date, Brown, Wisdom, and Thornberry, representing the western division, met with Gewin, Bell, and Coleman, speaking for the proposed eastern one. Logistical issues like cross-assignment of judges between divisions without approval from the chief justice and separate conferences with discretion to call for a joint conference were ironed out in an agreeable

85. U.S. Senate, *Realignment, Part 2*; U.S. Congress, Senate, 94th Cong., 1st sess., 18 February 1975, *Congressional Record*, pp. 3257, 3283–87.

86. Letter from Chief Judge John R. Brown to Senator Quentin Burdick, December 10, 1974.

87. Letter from Judge Walter P. Gewin to Chief Judge John R. Brown, December 16, 1974.

88. Ibid.

89. Letter from Judge Thomas G. Gee to Judges John R. Brown, John Minor Wisdom, Homer Thornberry, Irving L. Goldberg, Robert A. Ainsworth, Jr., January 8, 1975.

90.Interview with William P. Westphal, Minneapolis, Minnesota, May 12, 1983; U.S. Senate, *Realignment, Part 2*, p. 29; Letter from Judge Walter P. Gewin to Judge John Minor Wisdom, January 9, 1975.

manner. One point on which the western judges insisted was that any proposed additional judges must be on the bench prior to the effective date of the split, because the division would leave them with a glaringly inadequate number of judges to handle the caseload.[91]

Noting that a "great deal had been accomplished without any substantial disagreement," Gewin and Brown acknowledged the reserved right of the western judges to state their individual objections at any time. On the letterhead of the memorandum, Judge Gewin's name had been affixed after Chief Judge Brown's name and title, and both judges attached their signatures.[92] On the surface it seemed that all of the judges were resigned to the inevitability of division, though obviously some were reluctant.

The clean bill was introduced in the Ninety-fourth Congress a month later as S.729, and yet more hearings were slated for March and May 1975. During the latter, a majority of Ninth Circuit judges and bar associations from the Pacific Northwest opted for the "division" concept; but the California, Los Angeles, and San Francisco bar associations still vigorously opposed splitting California. An obvious tension between the Pacific Northwest and California lawyers, and to some extent the judges, became more apparent and even explicit when the Washington State Bar Association noted that it would oppose any division that placed it with California. In addition to the political problems posed by the Fifth Circuit division, Burdick's subcommittee was quickly reaching an impasse with the Ninth Circuit on the possibility of a realignment.[93]

Testimony from the Fifth Circuit was given by the previously designated judges of the western and eastern divisions, with the exception of Gee, who replaced Thornberry. Perhaps voicing the thoughts of many by that time, Chief Judge Brown began: "I can not help but remark what Judge Goldberg has said, there has been more said on splitting the [F]ifth than on splitting the atom, and we are adding to that today."[94]

Once again the subcommitee heard two conflicting viewpoints because none of the positions had changed. The western judges seemed to take small pleasure in the fact that both divisions would be the Fifth Circuit. Much of the discussion focused on the mechanics of the legislation—specifically, if and how the Fifth Circuit could conduct limited en banc sessions. Three of the senior-status judges responded to an invitation of their views with letters to the subcommittee. Their viewpoints remained adamant. Tuttle and Rives expressed opposition while Jones strongly favored a split.[95]

91. U.S. Senate, *Realignment, Part 2*; Letter from Chief Judge John R. Brown and Judge Walter P. Gewin to All Active Fifth Circuit Judges, January 16, 1975.

92. Letter from Chief Judge John R. Brown and Judge Walter P. Gewin to All Active Fifth Circuit Judges, January 16, 1975.

93. U.S. Senate, *Reorganization*; U.S. Senate, *Judgeship Bill*; U.S. Congress, Senate, 94th Cong., 1st sess., 18 February 1975, *Congressional Record*, pp. 3257–87.

94. U.S. Senate, *Realignment, Part 2*, p. 38.

95. U.S. Senate, *Realignment, Part 2*; Letter from Judge Richard T. Rives to William J.

In his statement, Rives said that the victory over racial discrimination was far from complete, pointing to the fact that there had never been a black appointed to either a circuit or a district judgeship in the Fifth Circuit. For a while the effect of the split on civil rights cases was an issue that had lain dormant. During this particular hearing, however, it was beginning to reappear, at least to the extent that congressional members would need an answer. A former law clerk to Judge Goldberg informed him that some lawyers in his firm would be sending a very strongly worded statement to the subcommittee concerning civil rights. He was referring to Terrence Roche Murphy and Neal P. Rutledge, who together submitted a statement on behalf of the Lawyers Committee for Civil Rights under Law.[96]

Organized in 1963 at the request of President Kennedy, the Lawyers Committee had been a major force throughout the South in defending black litigants whose black attorneys were prohibited in many instances from providing counsel. Their statement relied heavily upon Judge Wisdom's contention that division would promote provincialism in the federal courts. Although their written testimony had been submitted in part to assist Wisdom, the committee was also convinced that a 4–2 division was a deliberate attempt to alter the outcome of civil rights cases in the Deep South for the next twenty years.[97]

Commending the Lawyers Committee for their efforts, Wisdom explained that although the current division proposal was more sophisticated and statistically justified, it, like the attempt eleven years earlier, would still undermine the civil rights movement in the Deep South. He continued that the court was sitting for only half as many weeks as when he had joined it, and that with two extra weeks of bench time the circuit could stay abreast of its caseload. Wisdom then made a cordial request that the group solicit the aid of other "interested organizations to oppose division of the Fifth Circuit."[98] At that time the Lawyers Committee's testimony was enough to evoke concern among members of Congress interested in civil rights issues.

Before the Senate Judiciary Committee could issue its report, Wisdom made a final attempt to persuade certain committee members at least to delay the circuit's division. This prompted one last exchange between the two factions on the court. Having nothing to lose at this point, Wisdom wrote directly to Senator Eastland.[99] Realizing that the argument against the unwieldy fif-

---

Weller (Deputy Counsel, Subcommittee on Improvements in Judicial Machinery), May 6, 1975.

96. Letter from Judge Irving L. Goldberg to Judge John Minor Wisdom, August 7, 1975.

97. Interview with Frank R. Parker, Washington, D.C., April 8, 1983.

98. Letter from Judge John Minor Wisdom to Terrence Roche Murphy, August 19, 1975.

99. Letter from Judge John Minor Wisdom to Senator James O. Eastland, October 15, 1975.

teen-member en banc procedure was becoming a pivotal issue in the congressional debate, Wisdom tried to minimize the impact of en bancs on the court's overall adjudicatory process. To demonstrate its infrequent use, he pointed out that, of the 3,197 appeals terminated in 1974–75, fourteen had been en banc cases, and only nine of those were orally argued. He then referred to the Hruska Commission's suggestion of a nine-member en banc as a simple solution for the few cases that were orally argued before the full court. In addition, he asked Senator Eastland to delay a decision until the circumstances of the newly organized central staff for the court were known.

Finally, Wisdom respectfully called attention to the error that had been made about Texas's legal antecedents deriving from civil law background. He mentioned this point because he did not want other members to rely on a common background argument in order to place Texas and Louisiana together. In fact, he told Eastland, disparate judicial backgrounds were actually the strength of the federal court system. His appeal ended: "We are not ambassadors from our respective states to the federal system. Texas and Louisiana share a common interest in oil and gas. Many of the judges in these states, at both levels, have common views. I submit that the federalizing function of the Court, as distinguished from its dispute-settling function, will be seriously diluted by the division proposed in S.729."[100]

When Senator Eastland received Wisdom's letter, he immediately sent a copy to Judge Coleman for a response. Acknowledging that Wisdom had already informed him of the letter, Coleman indeed answered the Senator with a lengthy presentation of the other side of the issue. Though pointing out that he and Wisdom had always been on the "most cordial terms," Coleman told Eastland he regretted that Wisdom "so strongly differs with us about the stern necessity for dividing the Circuit." He warned that in less than a year, given the court's caseload, the judges would be able to "hear oral argument only on criminal appeals and prisoner cases," because these appeals had precedence over other types, including civil rights appeals.[101]

In reference to Wisdom's remarks concerning en bancs, Coleman countered that the reason there were not many more en banc cases was due to the judges' reluctance to ask for them because of the "logistical and practical difficulties" involved. As far as Texas and Louisiana were concerned, Coleman believed the differences between the two states were greater than their common interests. Outweighing that issue in his view was the fact that the Fifth Circuit was the only one required to "straddle the Mississippi River, with its left wing resting on El Paso and its right wing on Savannah and Key West." Finally, Coleman cautioned Eastland: "It is very apparent right now, however, that if something is not done the Fifth Circuit judicial house will inexorably

100. Ibid.
101. Letter from Judge James P. Coleman to Senator James O. Eastland, October 27, 1975.

fall in of its own weight. The fall is imminent."[102] The influence of Coleman and the other judges from the eastern states was more than obvious when the Senate's report was made public. So, too, was Wisdom's impact.

On December 2, 1975, two years after the Hruska Commission had submitted its recommendation, the Senate Judiciary Committee issued its most significant report to date. A majority of the Judiciary Committee favorably reported a new bill (S. 2752) excluding the Ninth Circuit. The report was an important turning point. For the first time since the origin of the debate, the issue of dividing the Ninth Circuit was separated from that of splitting the Fifth. The report explained that although six of the nine bar associations in the Ninth Circuit had supported division, the California Bar Association, among others, was still strongly opposed to "divisions." Consequently, the committee concluded that "rather than hold up remedial legislation on the Fifth Circuit" until the problems associated with the Ninth could be resolved, legislative action to divide the Fifth should proceed.[103]

Relying heavily on the testimony of judges from the eastern states, the committee recommended creating two independent divisions of the circuit organized in a 4–2 alignment. The first alternative from the Hruska Commission's report had been disregarded because Arkansas would be disturbed by being placed with "two states which have a Civil Law background springing from the Napoleonic Code,"[104] thereby violating the "marginal interference" criterion. The commission's primary recommendation that the Fifth Circuit be divided on 3–3 state alignment was discounted because of "Mississippi's interest in remaining with the states with which it has been historically aligned."[105] A 3–3 alignment would have created a 79-case difference, whereas the 4–2 alignment would result in more than double (187) the caseload differential of the former configuration. According to the committee report, this "slight" increase in caseload deviation would not seem to outweigh Mississippi's concern.[106] Obvious deference had been given to Senator Eastland's views, as his state's interests were at stake.

Another significant aspect of the report was the extent to which, as well as the manner in which, Judge Wisdom had influenced the Judiciary Committee. As a result of his backstage political tactics, for the first time various senators made public who was disagreeing with whom and why. Senators Eastland, McClellan, Burdick, and Robert Byrd had joined the Republicans to comprise the committee's majority position. Five of the nine Democratic majority members of the Senate Judiciary Committee filed a minority viewpoint entitled

102. Ibid.
103. U.S. Senate, *Reorganization*, pp. 1–4; U.S. Congress, Senate, 94th Cong., 1st sess., 5 December 1975, *Congressional Record*, p. 38820.
104. U.S. Senate, *Reorganization*, p. 8.
105. Ibid., p. 10.
106. Ibid.

"Separate Views."[107] As leader of the Senate opposition, Senator Kennedy was joined by Senators Hart, Bayh, Tunney, and Abourezk to sign the minority report.

Quoting extensively from Wisdom's statements and Charles Alan Wright's 1964 article, the minority report was obviously written in deference to Wisdom's viewpoint. Kennedy joined Wisdom's position largely due to the efforts of Thomas M. Susman, the senator's long-time aide and chief counsel to the Subcommittee on Administrative Practice and Procedure, which was chaired by Kennedy. Susman had been one of Wisdom's closest law clerks and Professor Wright's research assistant after Wright published the 1964 law review article. He now took the initiative to rally support among liberal senators on the Judiciary Committee for Wisdom's position.

Prior to the report, however, Senator Kennedy had expressed his reluctance to become embroiled in an issue which did not even involve his region of the country, much less his own state, and would require "bucking" the head of the Judiciary Committee on a matter which very much concerned Eastland's home state. Because Susman believed that Wisdom would be better able to persuade Kennedy if he could personally present his case, he urged the senator at least to listen to Wisdom's position. It was after Wisdom and Kennedy's discussion that the senator signed and circulated the draft of the minority view. Susman, who had written the draft and shared it with Wisdom for his comments, contacted two other former Wisdom law clerk protegés (Nora M. Manella and Ricki R. Tigert) who were serving on the staffs of Senators Bayh and Tunney. They were encouraged to have their "bosses" sign the minority view report, as were other members of the staffs of Senators Mathias, Scott, Abourezk, and Hart.[108]

In the "separate views" statement, the Senate was urged to reject "the Judiciary Committee's bill (S. 2752) because the irretrievable dismantling of the Fifth Circuit, and little more—[was] not compelled by the evidence."[109] The statement expressed "deep concern" about the potential effect that splitting would have on civil rights litigation in the region and also anticipated the possibility of a "deleterious effect in cases involving energy-related industries."[110]

Two days after the recommendations were issued, the bill was reported favorably to the Senate floor, but no action was taken. Susman explained that the leadership in the Senate was not willing to engage in a floor battle, when Peter Rodino, who chaired the House Judiciary Committee with a solid liberal majority behind him, would not budge in his opposition to a split. Thus, the

107. Ibid., pp. 27–32.
108. Susman interview; letter from Thomas Susman to Judge John Minor Wisdom, December 11, 1975; Draft of Proposed Minority Views from Thomas Susman to Certain Staff Members, November 25, 1975, copy to Judge Wisdom.
109. U.S. Senate, *Reorganization*, p. 31.
110. Ibid.

lengthy legislative endeavor and the commission's efforts had stalled temporarily, as had the efforts of the Judicial Conference in 1964.[111]

For Wisdom, the year had been a productive one in which the circuit had narrowly escaped division once again. Opposing the division was an issue that seemed to pervade Wisdom's life, sometimes in even humorous ways. When his law clerks gathered for a reunion at the New Orleans's posh French restaurant Antoine's, Wisdom's favorite "spot," they honored the judge in a unique way. A cake was brought to the head table, shaped like a map of the Fifth Circuit, with Texas and Louisiana separated from the four eastern states, and topped by a tiny figure resembling a judge who straddled the Mississippi River, holding the two sides together.[112]

THE POLITICAL CLIMATE IN TRANSITION

Although the bill was reported out of committee again in the fall of 1976, proponents of the split never recouped enough of the support lost in the 1975 battle to overcome a skeptical Senate.[113] A partial explanation is that the Senate Judiciary Committee was going through a major period of transition. The three top-ranking minority members, Senators Hruska (NE), Fong (HI), and Scott (PA), and the third-ranking Democrat, Hart (MI), were all retiring, and there was the possibility that McClellan and Eastland would also retire. Tension among these senators had been responsible for the committee's having one of the less productive legislative records during the previous twenty years, despite the fact that it had one of the larger staffs. Hart and Scott had consistently supported civil rights legislation, while Eastland and McClellan regularly opposed and delayed such bills. Furthermore, it was widely rumored that Senator Eastland was "starting to lose voting control of the committee as well as interest in its activities."[114] Through yet another of Wisdom's former law clerks serving on the staff of Senator Mondale, information was relayed to the judge that the Senate Judiciary Committee would increasingly be dominated by Senator Kennedy.[115]

Aside from the politics of the issue and the changing dynamics in the Senate Judiciary Committee, members of the House and Senate Judiciary committees

111. Susman interview; U.S. Senate, *Judgeship Bill*; U.S. Congress, Senate, 94th Cong., 1st sess., 5 December 1975, *Congressional Record*, p. 38820; U.S. Congress, Senate, 95th Cong., 1st sess., 23 May 1977, *Congressional Record*, p. 16087.

112. Susman interview.

113. U.S. Senate, *Judgeship Bill*, p. 35; U.S. Congress, House, Subcommittee on Monopolies and Commercial Law of the Committee on the Judiciary, *A Proposal to Divide the Fifth Circuit*, 95th Cong., 1st sess., 1977.

114. Richard E. Cohen, "A New Look for Judiciary," *National Journal*, March 6, 1976, p. 311.

115. Ibid.; memorandum from Robert B. Barnett to Judge John Minor Wisdom, ca. March 1976.

were heavily involved in the Watergate investigations throughout 1973 and 1974. This situation undoubtedly played an important role in delaying a resolution of the debate over realignment.

Also changing was the membership of the Fifth Circuit. During 1975 and 1976, Judges Gewin, Simpson, and Dyer took senior status, and Bell resigned. President Ford made appointments to fill three of these vacancies, but the Gewin seat remained unfilled until the fall of 1977. Judge Gerald B. Tjoflat of Jacksonville was elevated from a federal district court position in the Middle District of Florida to fill Judge Simpson's vacancy. A native of Pennsylvania, Tjoflat had received a prestigious southern education. He attended the University of Virginia and took his law degree from Duke in 1957 while serving as associate editor of *Duke Law Journal*.[116] Judge Tjoflat, with his firm manner, quickly became a prominent member of the court. His reputation as an expert in the area of criminal law has been enhanced by his work on the Judicial Conference Committee on the Administration of the Probation System, which he chaired, and the Advisory Corrections Council. He is known for his "sharp-edged" questioning of attorneys and unvarnished treatment of district court judges.[117]

Before Judge Dyer took senior status he expressed an interest in having District Judge Peter T. Fay of the Southern District of Florida replace him on the bench, because he had been so impressed by Fay's legal abilities.[118] Fay graduated first in his class and served on the law review at the University of Florida Law School. He had also proved himself in six years of service on the overburdened district court bench for the Southern District of Florida.[119] A young, energetic, and friendly person, Fay took Dyer's place on the Fifth Circuit in October 1976.

Judge Bell, who was growing weary of the caseload, especially the constant flow of criminal appeals, announced his resignation in order to return to private practice.[120] He did not know at the time that he would soon serve as attorney general in the Carter administration. Bell's resignation left open a major role to be filled. Ironically, he was replaced by a judge with a "down-home" wit and style of his own. Judge James C. Hill was elevated to the circuit after serving two years as a district judge for the Northern District of Georgia. Although a native of South Carolina, he received his law degree from Emory University in 1948 and settled in Atlanta to practice law.[121] Hill's dry wit,

116. Couch, *A History*, p. 168.

117. Ann Woolner, "Appeals Judge Criticizes Religious Case Rulings," *Atlanta Journal*, 6 August 1985, sec. B, p. 4.

118. Interview with Judge David W. Dyer, Highlands, North Carolina, June 14, 1983.

119. Couch, *A History*, p. 169.

120. Griffin B. Bell, *Taking Care of the Law* (New York: William Morrow and Company, 1982).

121. Couch, *A History*, p. 169.

flavored by a thick southern accent, significantly contributed to the court's collegiality.

Any prospect of wholesale federal court reform died in the commission stage. Congress seemed far more concerned about the form the commission would take and its powers than about helping the federal courts. It created a special commission to perform a narrow task: splitting the Fifth and Ninth circuits. Many of the participants believed that because Congress had purposely excluded the study of reduction in federal court jurisdiction, the commission's import had been stymied from its inception. The same participants also warned Congress that even realignment on a national level was not a feasible solution for caseload. At least, studying the causes of excessive caseload and the complex interrelationships between litigation and jurisdiction would be a necessary basis for a reform measure capable of relieving caseload problems in the long term. Congress acknowledged that the multiple and complex claims of entrenched interests outweighed any benefits conferred on the federal courts by some alternatives. With respect to the call for jurisdictional reform, the following statement from the Senate Judiciary Committee was indicative of the majority opinion:

> Many knowledgeable observers have suggested that the answer is to curtail the incoming caseload either by removing certain cases from the jurisdiction of federal courts or by convincing the Congress that it should not create additional jurisdiction for the federal courts. However, excluding certain cases from federal courts is akin to cutting a budget: there are usually good reasons for retaining either appropriations or jurisdiction. Furthermore, the benefits of curtailment in jurisdiction would not afford a full solution to the problem.[122]

On a positive note, the commission phase of the debate did make two long-term contributions toward resolving the specific controversy. First, the hearings revealed that most participants had caseload and its problems as their primary concern. Second, in some sense experiencing this period seems to have reconciled the judges to the inevitability of some form of division.

---

122. U.S. Senate, *Reorganization*, p. 6.

7

A Game
of Chicken

The presidential elections of 1976 were a new chapter in the nation's political history. By rejecting Gerald Ford's bid to return to the White House and replacing him with Jimmy Carter, the American people were exhibiting a desire for political change. Carter's campaign, which focused on the need to return honesty and decency to government, had touched a responsive chord in the electorate. The selection of a southern Democrat and a political outsider to lead the country demonstrated that the voters were ready to put the Watergate years behind them and refocus the attention of our political institutions on the process of governing.

Democratic successes at the ballot box in 1976 had a profound effect on the issue of realigning the Fifth Circuit. Carter had consistently pledged that if elected he would initiate significant changes in the federal judiciary. On the campaign trail he advocated increases in judgeships, appointments based on "merit" rather than "politics," and the infusion of women and minorities into the ranks of federal judges. With the presidency and both houses of Congress in the firm control of the Democrats, conditions were promising for the newly elected chief executive to accomplish his federal court objectives. Success, however, was not to be easily achieved. For the next two years, legislators engaged in political battle over Carter's proposals for improving the court system. Though sufficient majorities existed for the enactment of much of the president's legislative package, disagreement over the issue of Fifth Circuit realignment caused repeated deadlock and delay.

JAMES EASTLAND AND THE NINETY-FIFTH CONGRESS

As the Ninety-Fifth Congress convened in January of 1977, James O. Eastland remained a crucial player in the legislative process. Although membership changes had reduced his control over the Senate Judiciary Committee,

Eastland's approval remained a virtual necessity for the success of any legislative proposal dealing with the federal judiciary. For Jimmy Carter to fulfill his campaign pledges he had to enlist Eastland's support. The senator from Mississippi was disposed to cooperate with Carter. For reasons of both partisanship and regional pride, Eastland wanted Carter's presidency to be a successful one.[1] But the senator also had firm principles regarding the operation of the federal courts that he preferred not to compromise. And, of course, he had some unfinished business with respect to the Fifth Circuit.

Eastland found himself in an excellent position to help his party's president and accomplish his own goals at the same time. Nor did he wait until the convening of Congress to initiate his strategy. Shortly after the November elections, Eastland met privately with President-elect Carter in the Governor's Mansion in Atlanta to discuss a legislative agenda for the judiciary.[2] Four issues dominated the meeting.

First, there was the continuing pressing need to expand the size of the judiciary, a need that Congress had failed to meet. During the previous eight years, the Judicial Conference of the United States had regularly sent messages to Capitol Hill requesting new judgeships. But because of the immediate demands of other issues such as the Watergate crisis, and also for partisan political reasons, Congress failed to respond. The Democratic majorities in the House and Senate were unwilling to create new judicial positions that would be filled by Nixon or Ford appointees. Now, with the executive and legislative branches securely in the hands of the Democrats, the conditions were ripe to provide the needed relief. Carter and Eastland were of one mind on this issue.

Second, the president-elect pushed for merit selection of federal judges. Carter proposed the creation of blue ribbon commissions to suggest nominees for each judicial vacancy. To the traditionalist Eastland, such an idea was out of the question. The senator jealously guarded the political prerogatives of the upper house, and especially the norm of senatorial courtesy. Since the earliest years of the Republic, senators of the same political party as the president had held virtual appointment authority over federal officers serving in their home states. The creation of merit selection panels was seen by Eastland as stripping senators of key patronage powers. Although he opposed the entire concept, there were grounds for compromise. Eastland was willing to withhold active opposition to merit selection panels for courts of appeals appointments if the use of nominating commissions at the district court level was a matter of voluntary choice by individual senators.

Third, Carter discussed with Eastland his plans for an active effort to appoint women, blacks, and Hispanics to federal judgeships. Given Eastland's established record on civil rights questions, it is not surprising that his reaction

1. Interview with Griffin B. Bell, Atlanta, Georgia, October 18, 1982.
2. Interview with President Jimmy Carter, Atlanta, Georgia, April 13, 1983.

to this proposal was less than enthusiastic. Yet the senator understood political prerogatives. The ultimate power to appoint rested with the president, and Eastland was content to defer, especially if individual senators retained their influence over district court nominations in their home states. Further, as Carter's plan to employ affirmative action standards for judicial appointments did not require legislative approval, Eastland had little choice in the matter.[3]

Finally, Senator Eastland broached the subject of the realignment of the Fifth Circuit. He explained to the president-elect the heavy caseload conditions affecting the circuit and the problems that would result from expanding the number of circuit judgeships to a level sufficient to deal with its docket. Eastland offered his circuit division proposal as the most appropriate remedy for the Fifth Circuit's troubles. Importantly, Eastland's plan had not changed since he had first suggested it in 1963. He remained committed to dividing the circuit at the Mississippi River, resulting in his home state's being placed to the east, with Alabama, Georgia, and Florida. Eastland presented his case for division fully but did not press the president to support his position.[4]

By the end of the Atlanta meeting, Carter and Eastland had an appreciation of each other's positions. They agreed on what needed to be accomplished in the upcoming congressional session, and they understood which issues they would be able to cooperate on and which they would not. More than a decade earlier James Eastland had reportedly pledged that he would get the liberal Texas and Louisiana judges out of Mississippi affairs if it was the last thing he did. Already well into his seventies and considering retirement at the conclusion of the Ninety-fifth Congress, he now realized that this might be his final chance to make good on his resolution.[5]

Eastland knew that he occupied a strategically sound position in the Senate for two reasons. First, as head of the Senate Judiciary Committee and the

3. According to former attorney general Griffin Bell, Eastland cooperated with the Carter administration in working toward the goal of getting blacks appointed to the southern district courts. Bell interview, October 18, 1982.

4. Carter was not satisfied with the views only of Senator Eastland on the matter of realignment but also requested a meeting with Judge Frank Johnson, whom he hoped to convince to become director of the FBI. Johnson, of course, had spotless civil rights credentials and had been active in the Wisdom/Rives campaign to defeat circuit division in 1964. Carter and Johnson met in Atlanta on December 13, 1976. Tinsley E. Yarbrough, *Judge Frank Johnson and Human Rights in Alabama* (University, Ala.: The University of Alabama Press, 1981), p. 219.

5. Mississippi judges Clark and Coleman, the two members of the court in the 1970s who knew Eastland best, both denied that he had ulterior motives for supporting circuit division during that period. In their contacts with the senator, they claimed that his expressed interest was only with caseloads and what effects various circuit configurations might have on them. They also said that Eastland was interested in supporting whichever plan the Mississippi judges wanted. The idea that his advocacy of realignment was an attempt to gerrymander grew from the bitter battles of 1963–64. Interviews with Judges J. P. Coleman and Charles Clark, Jackson, Mississippi, January 26, 1983.

senator from a state affected by the proposed legislation, he could expect other members of the Senate to defer to his wishes. This strength was threatened only by the possibility that the civil rights issue might arise again, elevating the circuit split proposal from a matter of essentially regional concern to one of national importance. Second, Democratic members of the Senate would be interested primarily in legislation to increase the number of federal judgeships. It was projected that an omnibus judgeship bill would be introduced, calling for the largest expansion of the federal bench in United States history. Each senator would want his share of this pork barrel legislation. Additional judgeships, of course, would not only allow the federal courts in each of the states to operate more efficiently, but would also provide the senators with a large number of political patronage plums to allocate. Eastland understood the political motivations of his colleagues. Most would be willing to concede to his desire to split the Fifth Circuit if a rider to that effect was appended to the judgeship bill. Eastland had played a southern "no split, no judges" strategy to a nearly successful conclusion in the early 1960s. Now it was time to play the same political game once more—only this time the entire federal judiciary would be involved.

Eastland was less than sanguine about his chances in the House of Representatives. Additional judgeships did not mean political patronage to members of the lower house who have little influence on judicial appointments. Furthermore, the House Judiciary Committee loomed as a major obstacle. Having gained enormous prestige for its handling of the Watergate controversy, the House committee was riding a crest of political power. Its membership contained some very liberal advocates of civil rights interests, who would regard any proposal to split the Fifth Circuit with utmost suspicion. Peter Rodino, who chaired the House Committee on the Judiciary, represented a liberal New Jersey constituency and had a long history of promoting the positions taken by civil rights groups. Eastland knew that he was facing a replay of the battles he had fought earlier, when Emanuel Celler chaired the committee. With a Senate-House standoff probable, the issue would likely be determined by political compromises made in a congressional conference committee.

Because the new administration's positions on the federal judiciary would primarily be articulated through the Justice Department, Eastland had a particular interest in Carter's nominee for attorney general. When it turned out to be Griffin Bell, Eastland had ample reason to be pleased. Bell, of course, was a fellow southerner whose stances on many issues were in line with Eastland's and whose political style was one with which the senator could be comfortable. In fact, his views on certain social issues prompted civil rights advocates to attack Bell's nomination. Although this opposition delayed his taking office with the other members of the new cabinet, Bell ultimately survived the strenuous confirmation challenge, which he later likened to being hauled before Judge Roy Bean.[6] Of special pleasure to Eastland was Bell's long history of support for the senator's plan to divide the Fifth Circuit according to the 4–2 configuration. Unlike his early attempts to realign the circuit during the Kennedy and Johnson administrations, James Eastland now had an attorney general who would be on his side.

A final personnel matter that gave Eastland cause for optimism was the unexpected announcement from New Orleans that Judge John Minor Wisdom would take senior status effective on January 15, 1977. There was speculation that health considerations had prompted the seventy-one-year-old jurist to retire. Wisdom explained, however, that his primary reason for opting for senior status was to allow for the appointment of a new full-time judge.[7] Filling his vacancy would give the court additional judge power to cope with its caseload. As far as the judicial function, Wisdom retired in name only. He continued to carry a caseload nearly equivalent to that of a judge in active status.

Wisdom's retirement had much greater political repercussions. Although senior-status judges may continue to hear cases, they forfeit their membership on the circuit council. Consequently, his retirement meant that he would no longer be able to lead the fight against realignment within the circuit's formal decision-making body, a fact that later caused Wisdom to regret his decision to step down from active service,[8] as it left John Brown as the only realignment opponent on the Fifth Circuit Council who had experienced the political wars over the issue in the 1960s. Eastland realized that Wisdom's retirement did not mean that he would acquiesce to the senator's plans. In fact, Eastland fully expected the New Orleans jurist to be just as vigorous an opponent as he had been over the years. Wisdom's philosophical objections to a parochialized judiciary and the political bad blood between the two men ensured that their feud would continue. But Wisdom's loss of council membership meant that he would have a slightly diminished political base from which to operate.

As Congress convened in January of 1977, Eastland made preparations for his committee to handle the expected rush of judicial business. With Democrat Quentin Burdick and ranking Republican Roman Hruska no longer on the committee, Eastland was in a weakened position. Both had proven to be able and cooperative allies in the past. A new set of more liberal members, like Biden (D-DE), Culver (D-IA), Metzenbaum (D-OH), and DeConcini (D-AZ), along with the continuing presence of Edward Kennedy (D-MA) and Birch Bayh (D-IN), was a possible threat, but Eastland expected his record of fairness with the members of the committee to buffer him against a liberal

6. Griffin B. Bell, *Taking Care of the Law* (New York: William Morrow and Company, 1982), p. 65.
7. Interview with Judge John Minor Wisdom, New Orleans, Louisiana, May 28, 1985.
8. "If I were doing it over again, I would not take senior status." Wisdom interview, May 28, 1985.

revolt. An active public presence by Eastland in support of the split, however, would probably awaken the civil rights forces. Consequently, Eastland selected eighty-year-old John McClellan (D-AR) to take the lead on the issue. Mc-Clellan, the number-two Democrat on the committee, was a southerner with views similar to those of Eastland. He also had a great deal of experience on the issue of circuit realignment.

By the end of the first month of the congressional session, bills had already been introduced in the House and the Senate advocating expansion in circuit and district court judgeships. The stage was set for a major legislative confrontation.

THE SENATE ACTS

McClellan initiated work on the federal judiciary by introducing proposed legislation, known as S. 11, on January 10, 1977. The bill was cosponsored by eight members of the Senate Judiciary Committee representing a broad spectrum of ideological positions. McClellan's proposal authorized the creation of forty-five additional district court judgeships. As such, it was identical to S. 287, which had been passed by the Senate the previous year but died from lack of House action.

The introduction of S. 11 was only the starting point. It fell far short of the 107 new district court judgeships that the Judicial Conference of the United States was recommending. The bill was also silent on two key questions: the expansion of court of appeals positions and the realignment issue.

McClellan scheduled initial hearings on S. 11 before the full Judiciary Committee on February 21 and 22. From the very beginning, the need for additional court of appeals judgeships became a central question. It surfaced with respect to conditions existing in the Ninth Circuit. Testimony by Judge John D. Butzner, who chaired the Judicial Conference Subcommittee on Judicial Statistics, and Chief Judge James R. Browning of the Ninth Circuit built a strong case for the need of additional help to cope with the growing caseload in the Pacific Coast states. Browning argued for ten additional judgeships for his circuit's appeals court, increasing the total number of authorized positions to twenty-three. Questions were raised during these hearings regarding the ability of a court to operate efficiently with such a large number. Serious doubts were particularly expressed about how en banc hearings would be held. Predictably, this triggered a discussion on the need to split the circuit. Chief Judge Browning's response was direct: "We could deal with 23 judges sitting en banc, but we cannot deal with 13 judges trying to do the work that it requires 23 to do."[9] Reinforcing Browning's testimony, all eighteen senators of the nine states comprising the Ninth Circuit sent written communications

---

9. U.S. Congress, Senate, Committee on the Judiciary, *Omnibus Judgeship Bill*, 95th Cong., 1st sess., 1977, p. 241.

to McClellan arguing that the need for additional judges was too great to be delayed by resolution of the circuit realignment question. Though McClellan had grave doubts about the wisdom of a court of appeals of twenty-three judges, he also realized both the need for more judgeships in the Ninth Circuit and the almost insurmountable problems associated with trying to divide a geographically huge circuit in which one state, California, generated most of the case filings. Reluctantly, he agreed to support an experimental period in which the Ninth Circuit would remain intact and the number of judgeships be expanded to the requested twenty-three.

Chief Judge John Brown and Judge Robert Ainsworth were in Washington on Judicial Conference business when they heard of the Judiciary Committee's willingness to allow the Ninth Circuit to expand in size without demanding circuit division. Brown served on the conference's Executive Committee and Ainsworth chaired the important Court Administration Committee. On February 25, just three days after Browning's testimony, Brown and Ainsworth sent a mailgram to the other members of the Fifth Circuit informing them of the most recent developments. In light of the concessions apparently granted to the Ninth Circuit, the chief judge asked each active Fifth Circuit judge to telephone or teletype to Brown's Houston office his position on two issues. The first was a resolution asking Congress for twelve additional judges, and the second was to make the new judgeships contingent on a division of the circuit. The mailgram continued by informing the judges that Ainsworth supported the addition of new judges and circuit realignment. Brown, while favoring the request for new positions, reserved his opinion on the split issue.[10]

The judges reacted to the mailgram by requesting an emergency meeting of the Circuit Council. The matter was of such importance that it was thought appropriate to have a full discussion of the issue rather than rely on teletyped votes. Consequently, the court agreed to meet in New Orleans on March 4.

In the short time between the Brown/Ainsworth mailgram and the meeting of the council, John Wisdom made it quite clear that his having taken senior status six weeks earlier did not mean he was retiring from the circuit division battle. In a three-page letter to his colleagues, he vigorously attacked the notion of a circuit split. He called for the court to support changes in federal jurisdiction, in addition to the new judgeships, as the proper solution to the caseload crisis. He proposed that Congress eliminate diversity jurisdiction, use alternative forums for deciding certain welfare and regulatory cases, and modify remedies with respect to prisoner suits. He argued that dismemberment of the Fifth Circuit was an unacceptable substitute for the failure of Congress to face the jurisdictional problems of the court system. And finally, Wisdom wanted it plainly known to all concerned that "Senior Judge Wisdom,

10. Western Union Mailgram from Chief Judge John R. Brown to each member of the Fifth Circuit, February 25, 1977.

because of recent developments, is even more opposed than ever before to division of the Fifth Circuit."[11]

At the New Orleans meeting of the Circuit Council there were as many viewpoints as there were judges. The entire court was present, save Judge Hill, who was unavoidably absent and subsequently made his preferences known via telephone. There was overwhelming support for the addition of twelve new judges. The caseload problem had simply grown to proportions unmanageable by a court of fifteen. In 1976, case filings had reached 3,629, a 476 percent increase since 1961, when the notion of circuit division was on the verge of being seriously discussed for the first time. The members of the Fifth Circuit were continuing to carry more cases per judge than any other circuit. In spite of agreement on staff needs, however, the assembled judges still disagreed on the circuit division question. Serious reservations were expressed about the operation of a twenty-seven-judge court, primarily the concern that such an increment would alter its very nature. It was feared that the court's highly valued atmosphere of collegiality could not survive it. En bancs, it was predicted by some, would be unmanageable. One judge claimed that such a large court would be a "monstrosity." To these judges, circuit division seemed to be the only alternative.

Ultimately, the council voted on a series of five resolutions that represented the judges' views on two core issues. On the key question of dividing the circuit, the council voted 10–3 in favor. Judges in the majority were Thornberry, Coleman, Ainsworth, Godbold, Morgan, Clark, Roney, Tjoflat, Fay, and Hill. Opposing division were Chief Judge Brown and Judges Goldberg and Gee. On the important question of the relationship between circuit division and addition of new judgeships, the vote was much closer. However, a majority of seven (Coleman, Ainsworth, Godbold, Morgan, Clark, Tjoflat, and Hill) held the position that the court should not accept the twelve new judgeships if circuit realignment was not enacted.[12] In spite of the unbearable conditions facing the circuit, they viewed the prospect of a twenty-seven-judge court as even more dismal.

Two important aspects of the council meeting are worthy of note. First, the judges avoided taking any position on the geographical contours of any circuit division; their votes were on the principle of realignment rather than on any specific plan. Some considered the particulars of any circuit division as more properly a matter for congressional authority. Avoidance of geographic concerns also allowed the issue to be discussed more in administrative than in political terms. Two members of the council majority, for example,

11. Letter from Judge John Minor Wisdom to Judges of the Court of Appeals for the Fifth Circuit, March 2, 1977.

12. The voting distribution on all five resolutions can be found in the Senate Judiciary Committee records. U.S. Senate, Committee on the Judiciary, *Judgeship Bill*, p. 616.

although supporting realignment, were opposed to the prevailing notion of a circuit comprised only of Texas and Louisiana. Robert Ainsworth feared that Louisiana might be dominated by Texas, and Thornberry had reservations about a circuit comprised of two states dominated by oil and gas interests. Second, the voting patterns at the New Orleans meeting did not conform to the strict liberal/conservative dimensions present during the 1963–64 period. The three-judge coalition expressing firm opposition to any circuit split was comprised of two liberal judges (Brown and Goldberg) and Thomas Gibbs Gee, perhaps the most conservative member of the court. The supporters of circuit division represented a broader spread along the ideological continuum than had been the case in the 1960s. Though political questions were still important, it was clear that administrative concerns were now playing a more prominent role inside the court.

On the night before the New Orleans council meeting, Chief Judge Brown received notification from Senator McClellan that the Judiciary Committee would be holding hearings on March 14. The senator requested that Brown be present to testify about the needs of the Fifth Circuit. Consequently, the council agreed to send a resolution to Congress. This statement had a sense of urgency, describing the court as in a state of "crisis," in the unanimous view of the judges. It included the votes on the five resolutions, to demonstrate that there had been lack of complete agreement on the best solution to their problems. Chief Judge Brown was also instructed to inform the Senate committee of the needs of the circuit, the support for division, and the resolution that, without a split, new judges should not be added.[13]

By the time the Judiciary Committee met on March 14, it had become clear that the committee could not confine itself to the problem of district judgeships. Consequently, Senators Cranston (D-CA) and Metcalf (D-MT), who both represented Ninth Circuit constituencies, had introduced an amendment to S. 11, supported by the Judicial Conference of the United States, calling for the creation of twenty-five circuit court judgeships. The proposal included increases in authorized positions for every circuit (including ten for the Ninth) except the Fifth. The prevailing view was that the issue of circuit realignment had to be resolved before the Senate could act on judicial needs in the Deep South.

Chief Judge Brown found himself in a difficult spot when he appeared before the Senate Judiciary Committee. Though as leader of the Fifth Circuit it was his duty to represent accurately the views of the council, his personal position was quite different from that of the majority. His opening remarks reflected this conflict: "In my dual role as spokesman for the court and my personal views, where they differ," Brown explained, "I must be scrupulously accurate in reporting the actions taken and must avoid as Chief Judge putting my interpretations on the meaning or effect of the Resolutions" adopted by

13. Ibid., pp. 592–95.

the council. He dutifully presented their official position, including the votes of the individual judges on the five resolutions considered at the New Orleans meeting ten days before. He noted that "Nearly all of the judges of our court agree that we are at the end of our rope. We cannot, consistent with the quality of work demanded by our consciences, the public interest, the litigants, and the historical reputation of the Fifth Circuit, do more. We are unanimous that the present condition cannot continue." All members of the court, however, did not agree on the most appropriate solution. Ten of the thirteen sitting judges had concluded that "there is an imperative need to split," so Brown characterized support for circuit division as "substantial," but said the recommendation that no judges should be added unless there was a split had passed by a "thin margin." He also described at which points he departed from the council majority.[14]

The chief judge presented his personal views as being at one with the arguments advanced by Judge Wisdom over the past fifteen years. He particularly advised the Senate not to enact a 4–2 division because of the dangers of parochialism. Brown, admitting that he was speaking only for himself and not for his court, argued that administrative innovations could be developed to cope with a court of twenty-seven judges.[15] He urged the committee to allow the Fifth Circuit to experiment with a larger court, the same opportunity that was being given to the Ninth Circuit.

Also before the Judiciary Committee that day was Judge Robert Ainsworth, who testified in his capacity as head of the Judicial Conference Committee on Court Administration. His comments supported a nationwide increase in the number of court of appeals judges, but questions about conditions in the Ninth and Fifth circuits pulled him into the circuit realignment controversy. Ainsworth expressed support for the majority resolutions passed by the Fifth Circuit Council. When Senator McClellan, apparently growing wary of the debate, remarked to Ainsworth that "judges who are capable of resolving all other issues should be capable of working out this problem," Ainsworth retorted bluntly, "This is more political than judicial, Senator," to which McClellan replied, "You may have a very strong point there."[16]

At the end of the hearings, McClellan took the lead in preparing a bill for final committee approval and floor action. The pressure to divide the Fifth Circuit was mounting. Chief Justice Warren Burger had issued a statement, reinforced by a letter to Senator Eastland, arguing that no court could function properly with as many judges as were being proposed for the Fifth and Ninth circuits and therefore circuit division should be considered.[17] The American

14. Ibid., pp. 592–95, 618–19.
15. Ibid., p. 618.
16. Ibid., pp. 572–77.
17. Letter from Chief Justice Warren E. Burger to Senator James O. Eastland, March 11, 1977.

Bar Association had also recommended circuit division, and under Griffin Bell's direction the Justice Department had conducted a study to recommend proposals for realignment.[18] On March 30, John Wisdom wrote to McClellan asking to testify against division of the Fifth Circuit.[19] The senator responded by explaining that Judges Brown and Ainsworth had already relayed Wisdom's views to the committee at the March 14 session, that extensive hearings on the division proposal had been held by Senator Burdick the previous year, and that no additional hearings were needed.[20]

By the end of April, McClellan had succeeded in devising a favorable report on S. 11 (with no dissenting views). The bill called for the creation of 111 additional district court judgeships and 35 new court of appeals positions. In addition, it called for the creation of a new Eleventh Circuit, consisting of Texas and Louisiana, and a new Fifth Circuit comprised of Florida, Georgia, Alabama, and Mississippi. Under the S. 11 proposal, the Eleventh Circuit would be staffed by twelve judges and the Fifth by fourteen, a total of twenty-six judgeships for the region that had previously had fifteen authorized positions. In the Senate report, the geographic alignment was justified by a political rationale that had been advanced on many occasions. Simply stated, the Senate Judiciary Committee deferred to the desires of the Mississippi senators and judges to have their state located in a circuit east of the Mississippi River. The bill allowed the Ninth Circuit twenty-three judges on the condition that it comply with a one-year "report back provision," according to which the circuit would reevaluate its administrative procedures and recommend methods to improve its efficiency.[21]

Floor debate on S. 11 was held on May 23 and 24 and was marked by a complete lack of acrimony. Senator Eastland acted as floor manager for the committee and was supported in his views by Senators Thurmond and DeConcini. At the close of the second day of debate, the Senate passed S. 11 by voice vote. Division of the Fifth Circuit was never raised as a controversial issue on the floor. For the first time in the long history of the debate to split the Fifth, Senator Eastland had managed to get full Senate approval for division. He had correctly estimated his colleagues: attaching realignment provisions to a bill creating 148 political patronage plums had effectively disarmed his opposition. Even Senator Kennedy, generally acknowledged as the leader of the liberal forces on the Judiciary Committee, spoke on the floor in favor of the bill, but restricted his comments to the need for adequate

18. Letter from Assistant Attorney General Daniel J. Meador to Chief Judge John R. Brown, March 21, 1977.

19. Letter from Judge John Minor Wisdom to Senator John L. McClellan, March 30, 1977.

20. Letter from Senator John L. McClellan to Judge John Minor Wisdom, April 18, 1977.

21. U.S. Congress, Senate, Committee on the Judiciary, *Omnibus Judgeship Bill*, Report no. 95–117, 95th Cong., 1st sess., 1977.

judicial staffing in his home state of Massachusetts. Senator McClellan's efficient processing of the bill had ensured its passage without raising the issue of civil rights.

PREPARING FOR THE BATTLE IN THE HOUSE

It was clear from the outset that this rather hurried action that had taken place in the Senate would not be replayed in the House. Whereas McClellan had not seen the necessity of protracted hearings in the upper chamber, Representative Rodino and other House Judiciary Committee influentials were willing to open the deliberations to interests not granted a forum during Senate consideration of S. 11.

Indeed, even before Rodino introduced a companion bill, John Wisdom had written to express his objection to "the section of the bill, added at the last minute, that dismembers the Fifth Circuit." The judge asked to testify before the relevant subcommittee in order to protest, "this radical proposal to divide the Fifth Circuit [which is] an irreversible step toward the destruction of the federal courts system as an instrument for preserving American Federalism."[22] Wisdom's first communication was followed up just eleven days later by a second letter addressed to Rodino with copies to the chief justice, the director of the Federal Judicial Center, all members of the House Judiciary Committee, and members of the Louisiana congressional delegation. This five-page attack on the circuit division section of S. 11 was particularly critical of the 4–2 division as a plan that would ensure unacceptable parochialism.[23] Wisdom requested that, at the least, the Fifth Circuit should be permitted the same freedom of experimentation that was being allowed the Ninth. Rodino responded that the House would hold hearings and that Wisdom would be invited to present his views.[24]

The months between Senate passage of S. 11 in May and the House hearings in September gave interested parties time to prepare for a battle over circuit division. It was during this period that, according to one member of the Fifth Circuit, the "tiger" of "civil rights hysteria" was "unleashed."[25] The relative calm that had characterized action in the Senate was about to come to an abrupt end.

22. Letter from Judge John Minor Wisdom to Representative Peter W. Rodino, Jr., May 26, 1977.
23. Wisdom was particularly enraged that supporters of the 4–2 division occasionally argued that Mississippi should not be placed with Texas and Louisiana because these two states shared legal systems based on the civil law code. Wisdom, both a student of history and an expert on the Louisiana civil code, provided ample historical evidence that the Texas system was explicitly based on English common law origins. Letter from Judge John Minor Wisdom to Representative Peter W. Rodino, Jr., June 6, 1977.
24. Letter from Representative Peter W. Rodino, Jr., to Representative W. Henson Moore, June 16, 1977.
25. Interview with Judge Gerald B. Tjoflat, Atlanta, Georgia, May 23, 1983.

In the early summer of 1977, just after Senate passage of S. 11, Alabama state senator U. W. Clemon noticed an article on the Senate bill while reading a local newspaper. Clemon, who was also president of the new and loosely organized Alabama Black Lawyers Association, was quite familiar with the issue of circuit division. He later recalled that, "there had been talk ever since I have been practicing law of splitting the Circuit, but up to that point it had really never gotten off the ground." Because the article mentioned Senator Eastland as the bill's sponsor, Clemon said, "I thought I had better look into that."[26]

Clemon contacted Elaine Jones, an assistant counsel and the chief lobbyist for the NAACP Legal Defense Fund, who joined forces with Clarence Mitchell, director of the Washington Bureau of the NAACP and referred to by some as the 101st senator, to mount a campaign against the split. Other civil rights groups, such as the Lawyers Committee for Civil Rights Under Law, were also enlisted to join the fray. Clemon explained that, while the civil rights interests believed there was a "sinister motive on the part of Senator Eastland," they were "primarily opposed" to dividing the circuit along a 4–2 alignment.

Civil rights proponents were also concerned about the relative ease with which S. 11 had passed the Senate. Clemon acknowledged that Eastland had handled the matter very deftly by including it as part of the Omnibus Judgeship Bill. The civil rights implications had gone unnoticed, even by Senator Kennedy. For years Eastland had wanted to ally Mississippi with the states of what he considered the "good South," separating them from the liberal judges of Texas and Louisiana, and he was on the verge of attaining his goal. Individual senators, according to Clemon, were more interested in "looking at the number of judgeships they were or were not going to get in their states more so than anything else, and they pretty much left things alone in states other than their own."[27]

Clemon, Jones, Mitchell, and other civil rights activists were not about to let the same thing happen in the House. They began a concerted attempt to recast the circuit division issue from one of administrative necessity to an attack on civil rights. Their message was blunt. Oscar Adams, an official of the Alabama Black Lawyers Association, for example, wrote to House Judiciary Committee member Walter Flowers (D-AL), warning: "We do not believe it to be in the best interest of blacks to split the Fifth Circuit and, even worse, to create an Eleventh Circuit comprised of only Texas and Louisiana. We feel a vote on your part favoring either of these propositions would be a vote against Civil Rights."[28]

26. Interview with Judge U. W. Clemon, Birmingham, Alabama, November 4, 1983.
27. Ibid.
28. Letter from Oscar W. Adams, Jr., to Representative Walter Flowers, June 21, 1977. Flowers confronted this attempt to restructure the issue in the October 19, 1977, hearings before the House subcommittee: "It's been suggested—and I have heard from a few black lawyers in Alabama—that this is a paramount issue of civil rights, and that the manner in

On June 16, 1977, Rodino introduced H.R. 7843, the House version of
an Omnibus Judgeship Bill. From the very beginning it had been clear that
Rodino was not sympathetic to circuit division; the House bill dealt only with
authorization for the badly needed judgeships. To retain control, he assigned
the bill to the Subcommittee on Monopolies and Commercial Law—a very
significant assignment in the eyes of those who opposed circuit division. The
Subcommittee on Monopolies was chaired by Rodino and had as one of its
most influential members Representative Barbara Jordan (D-TX). Jordan, a
black member of Congress from Houston, had a lifelong history of civil rights
activity and was a close acquaintance of Chief Judge Brown. So this move, of
course, gave civil rights groups excellent representation in any House
deliberations.

Jordan was well aware of the gains blacks had achieved through the rulings
of the Fifth Circuit and could hardly be sympathetic to legislation that would
structurally change an institution which had responded so favorably to the
legal claims of minorities. She was concerned primarily about future civil rights
cases and how they might be affected by the creation of a Deep South circuit.
Furthermore, Jordan was shocked by the lack of activity displayed by liberal
Senate members: "What was the surprise to me was that friends of civil rights
who were members of the Senate let the split of the circuit get through without
any opposition being voiced, as far as I could tell. And once it got to us on
the House side, we were looking around, 'Well, where's Senator Kennedy?
Where's Senator Bayh? Where were those people?' "[29] Consequently, Jordan
accepted responsibility for leading liberal House forces against a division of
the circuit. Her close relationship with Rodino served her well in this role:
"What I had primarily working for me was the support of my chairman. Peter
Rodino said, 'Barbara, nothing's going to happen that you don't want to
happen on this.' So ... you are in a very strong position to begin with when
you've got your chairman working with you, because Rodino was both chairman of the subcommittee and chairman of the full committee."[30]

The rebirth of the civil rights issue and the initial actions of the House
Judiciary Committee encouraged the opponents of realignment. Conversely,
the majority of judges on the Fifth Circuit Court of Appeals did not like the
new turn of events. Their hope of confining the debate to administrative
issues was crumbling. With hearings in the House imminent, the judges
wanted to make sure the case for division was effectively presented. Since the
Senate hearings in March, there had been a growing belief that Chief Judge

---

which I vote on this will be judged a civil rights vote, and, quite frankly, gentlemen, I can't
accept it that way." U.S. Congress, House, Committee on the Judiciary, *A Proposal to Divide
the Fifth Circuit*, Hearings before the Subcommittee on Monopolies and Commercial Law,
95th Cong., 1st sess., 1977, p. 111.

29. Interview with Barbara Jordan, Austin Texas, March 22, 1983.

30. Ibid.

Brown, an opponent of division, could not adequately represent the views of the majority.

A meeting of the Circuit Council was called for July 5, in New Orleans. All members of the court were present except the ill Judge Thornberry, who was consulted by telephone. According to Judge Brown, he had no idea of the purpose of the gathering but soon realized that *he* was the subject.[31]

The judges were upset that Brown, in his testimony before the McClellan committee, had both represented the court and acted as an outspoken opponent of the action favored by the council majority. Their feeling was that the "Chief Judge was *required* to sound as effectively as he could the position of the majority on the issue." Brown recalled that the judges were particularly critical of his characterization of the council's "no split, no new judges" resolution as passing by a "thin margin," claiming that this description disparaged the court's majority vote.[32]

Brown countered that he had made the council's position clear to the Senate and had sharply distinguished his own views when they constituted a minority sentiment. But his explanation was not enough to satisfy the assembled judges. The majority of them no longer wanted to be represented by Chief Judge Brown, whose stance was at odds with that of the court.[33]

The council proceeded to take two major actions at the New Orleans meeting. First, it voted on a new resolution regarding the proposed division. Rather than cloud the issue with a series of five motions as it had done in its March meeting, the judges wanted to send a single, unambiguous message to Congress. The new resolution stated that circuit division was the only practical solution to the Fifth Circuit's caseload problems. Ten judges voted in favor: Thornberry, Coleman, Ainsworth, Godbold, Morgan, Clark, Roney, Tjoflat, Hill, and Fay. Three voted against: Brown, Goldberg, and Gee. This array of votes indicated that no changes in opinion had occurred since the last poll taken on the issue. To forestall any confusion, the council, with Gee not voting, also agreed to rescind the five resolutions adopted in March.

Second, the council voted on a motion to designate John Godbold and Gerald Tjoflat as its representatives on all matters relating to legislation concerning the future composition of the circuit. Brown recalled being instructed

31. Interview with Judge John R. Brown, Houston, Texas, August 10–11, 1983.
32. Ibid.
33. Whether valid or not, some members of the court privately held the view that Brown was being swayed by a desire to be chief judge of the largest court in the English-speaking world. If the division of the Fifth Circuit occurred, Brown would lose that distinction to Chief Judge Browning of the Ninth Circuit (confidential interviews). This speculation was fueled by some of Brown's own statements. For example, he argued, "if the Ninth Circuit can handle 23, [we] can handle 27" (Western Union Mailgram from Chief Judge John R. Brown to Fifth Circuit Judges, February 25, 1977). And in testimony before the Senate Judiciary Committee, Brown declared, "I am just vain enough to say that if Judge Browning can run 23, I can run 27" (U.S. Senate, Committee on the Judiciary, *Judgeship Bill*, p. 618).

that he was not even to communicate with anyone in Congress on the subject. He objected that such a prohibition would be an indignity to the office of chief judge and requested that he at least be permitted to transmit the resolution to Congress, a duty he carried out at the September House hearings. This highly unusual resolution was passed unanimously, with Judge Gee abstaining. Three days after the New Orleans gathering, Judges Godbold and Tjoflat notified both Judiciary Committees of the change in authority, and from that point onward, they spoke to Congress for the court on the issue of circuit division.[34]

Disturbed by what had happened and sympathetic to Brown's views, Judge Gee wrote to Rodino renewing an earlier request to testify. He explained: "Though a sizeable majority of the judges on the Court endorse the views which will be put forward by Judges Godbold and Tjoflat, there is a deep division of opinion among the judges and several of us hold a very different view from theirs. I hope that if a hearing is to be accorded . . . that, in fairness, both sides may be heard."[35]

Reflecting on this period, Brown said that, although he had been in the minority on the circuit division issue for so many years, "this was the only place where I thought it was a little unfair." He believed that he had always been very careful to distinguish his role as chief judge from his position as an individual member of the court. Noting that the New Orleans meeting had occurred just three days before the death of his wife, Brown said that he was so discouraged by the council action that he almost resigned as chief judge.[36]

Obviously Brown had found himself in a difficult situation, but not an unprecedented one. Chief Judge Tuttle had experienced the same conflict of roles during the 1963–65 circuit realignment battle. However, the two handled the situations differently. Tuttle, while giving tacit support to the Wisdom/Rives campaign, in public remained the representative of the council majority. This position caused him considerable personal discomfort, but he felt compelled to give the demands of his leadership role precedence over those of his personal beliefs. Brown, on the other hand, tried to carry out his official duties as council representative yet still articulate his own position.

THE POSITION OF THE HOUSE

When Congress returned to business after the summer recess, the members of the Judiciary Committee turned their attention to the federal judiciary. As ever, there was general agreement on the need to increase judgeships, but

34. Brown interview.
35. Letter from Judge Thomas Gibbs Gee to Representative Peter W. Rodino, Jr., July 13, 1977.
36. Brown interview.

the question of circuit division in the Deep South was proving to be a stumbling block. Rodino scheduled hearings on the proposal to add circuit realignment to H.R. 7843 to begin in late September.

By this time feelings of frustration and near panic were beginning to surface among the nation's judges. As summer turned into fall, the first session of the Ninety-fifth Congress was entering its last stages. The nation's overburdened circuit and district court judges had thought that congressional action to create the needed judgeships would be much more advanced by this time. Some were beginning to predict that unless a major change in the legislature occurred, the proposal for new judgeships would die with the end of the Ninety-fifth Congress.

These pessimistic feelings were fully vented at the fall meeting of the Judicial Conference of the United States, which was held in Washington on September 15–16. Attorney General Bell appeared before the group and informed them of what they already suspected, that there would be some delay in the authorization of the new judgeships.[37] Representatives of the other circuits believed that the new positions they so desperately needed were being held hostage by the Fifth Circuit realignment issue. Once again, Chief Judge Brown was the target of criticism.[38] The other judges knew that a unanimous vote by members of the Fifth Circuit Council in favor of realignment would probably break the legislative deadlock. The minority positions of Brown, Goldberg, and Gee were seen as unreasonably jeopardizing the best interests of the rest of the federal judicial system. Pressure mounted on Brown to do something to break the logjam and avert the death of the omnibus judgeship legislation.

The judges' fears had some basis in reality. There is evidence of a September meeting of House Speaker Thomas P. "Tip" O'Neill (D-MA), Representative Rodino, and Attorney General Bell, in which O'Neill told Rodino that unless committee hearings were concluded by October 8, 1977, there would be little chance that the judgeship bill could be brought up for floor action during the Ninety-fifth Congress.[39]

On September 21, the House subcommittee held its first day of hearings on the Fifth Circuit issue. The session was reserved for testimony from the circuit judges. Chief Judge Brown was the first to speak.[40] He presented for the record his "State of the Federal Judiciary in the Fifth Circuit" report, which outlined the caseload crisis facing the circuit and the administrative responses the court had made. He also introduced the most recent resolution passed by the council and noted that Judges Godbold and Tjoflat were present

37. U.S. Congress, House, Committee on the Judiciary, *A Proposal*, p. 83.
38. Tjoflat interview; interview with Judge Clement Haynsworth, Jr., Greenville, South Carolina, August 9, 1983.
39. Letter from Judge Thomas Gibbs Gee to Judge John Minor Wisdom, September 30, 1977.
40. U.S. House, Committee on the Judiciary, *A Proposal*, pp. 5–28, 38–39.

to represent the council majority. Toward the end of the day's hearings, Brown did offer his personal views, but in deference to the position taken by the Circuit Council in July, he was uncharacteristically brief in his remarks.

Brown was followed by circuit division opponents John Minor Wisdom and Thomas Gee, who reiterated that realignment as proposed in S. 11 was not an answer to the problems confronting the Fifth Circuit, problems that would soon confront the other circuits as well.[41] Division would do nothing to ease increasing caseloads. The root of the problem was jurisdiction, and Congress sooner or later would have to face up to its responsibility to consider jurisdictional reform. Without such reform, they argued, ever larger numbers of judges would be required, entailing more circuit splitting. The result would inevitably be circuit proliferation, parochialization of the bench, and destruction of the federalizing function of the judiciary. They saw S. 11, which would create the nation's first two-state circuit, as a major step toward this unacceptable situation. Combining Texas and Louisiana into a single unit would also open the door to creating a court parochialized by oil and gas interests.

Judge Gee, increasingly active since the council had reduced Chief Judge Brown's role, went even further than Wisdom, attacking the view that the court was overburdened. Upset because his fellow judges had voted against a proposal to use extra volunteer panels to reduce backlog, Gee boldly stated that the judges were not overworked: "I don't know anyone who has a taste for golf or for motor tours, vacations or what not, who has had to give them up because he's overworked."[42] Gee's claim was especially credible as he had written far more opinions during the previous year than any other member of the court.

In opposition, speaking for himself and Judge Tjoflat on behalf of the council majority, John Godbold presented an effective litany of arguments supporting circuit division.[43] Underlying Godbold's position was the metaphor of "the Titanic . . . sinking and we have run out of lifeboats." The increased workload was already taking its toll. The number of short, unsigned opinions had increased; the frequency of oral argument had decreased; creative administrative experimentation had been pushed to the limit. The workload had to be reduced by the creation of additional judgeships.

It was this expansion in judgeships, Godbold continued, that made circuit division necessary. He believed that a court with a proposed membership of twenty-six active judges would be simply unworkable. Because majority opinions written by each judge are binding on every other judge, all members of the court are required to read and know the opinions issued by other members. With a court of twenty-six (coupled with a cadre of eight senior judges who also regularly heard cases), Godbold argued, this process would be almost

41. Ibid., pp. 28–38, 39–51.
42. Ibid., p. 50.
43. Ibid., pp. 51–58.

impossible, and the "law of the circuit" would inevitably suffer. En banc cases with twenty-six judges would be an administrative monstrosity, and the members of the Fifth Circuit, as a matter of principle, were opposed to operating with en banc courts consisting of less than the full membership. Similar problems would arise in the Circuit Council meetings, which Godbold opined as being ineffective if held with more than fifteen judges; the loss of essential collegiality would naturally occur.

Following Judge Tjoflat's endorsement of Godbold's remarks, the committee heard the views of J. P. Coleman. Coleman had been hastily invited to participate when it was learned that his civil rights record would be the object of attack by liberal interest groups in subsequent sessions. The committee wanted the Mississippian's position on record. While acknowledging that drawing circuit boundaries was a legislative rather than a judicial matter, Coleman briefly restated why the Mississippi judges preferred to be coupled with the judges to the east.

Members of Congress attending the hearings were clearly not pleased about the division of opinion among the judges. With almost 150 federal judgeships hanging in the balance, they were eager to reach a compromise. If the Circuit Council had presented a united front, the issue could have been resolved quickly. But there was no evidence that a convergence of opinions was emerging. Representative William J. Hughes (D-NJ) at one point quipped, "What we have seen here today is pretty evidence that in your en banc deliberations, I would suspect, that once we get beyond one judge, we're in trouble," to which Godbold responded, "we're on our good behavior today." Brown, in response to the en banc issue, humorously noted that in conference, "Everybody is so filled with a case, so anxious to say his piece, the gavel is sometimes nearly worn out, and sometimes never heard." Rodino, referring to his experience running the Watergate hearings with a thirty-eight-member committee, expressed the view that administering a large court might be possible. Nonetheless, he had to admit that the wholly opposite points of view advanced by equally distinguished judges had left him "perplexed."[44]

In the following days, Chief Judge Brown found himself once again the object of criticism. This time he was in trouble for what he did *not* say at the congressional hearings. Anticipating some arguments, the supporters of division had placed a high priority on convincing the House subcommittee that the civil rights issue was not relevant in the context of 1977. Judge Godbold testified that the Fifth Circuit had decided thousands of civil rights cases and that in most of them the opinion had been unanimous. "No judge," he argued, "can, with accuracy, claim to have a monopoly of concern for individual rights." Even the opponents believed that the core issue was no longer the civil rights question. Toward the end of Judge Wisdom's remarks on the first day, Representative Charles E. Wiggins (R-CA), a former Hruska Commission

44. Ibid., pp. 71, 66, and 61.

member, bluntly asked the judge: "It has been quietly suggested that perhaps the contemplated division of the fifth circuit would, in some way, adversely affect the quality of decision in civil rights cases in the eastern segment of the fifth. Do you believe that argument has merit?" Wisdom responded: "I don't think that argument has any real merit today. I think it would have been a serious problem in the early days of the civil rights movement. . . . But I am sure—and I'm sure that each judge today would be intellectually honest in his actions—but I can't help feeling that in the civil rights field, as in oil or gas or even if you get down to a railroad crossing accident, there are built-in attitudes."[45]

In the course of the hearings, Judge Brown testified that as a member of the Judicial Conference he had the responsibility to insist that the nation needed additional judges. Furthermore, he stated that "I would not pay the price of there being no judgeships if it all hung on the decision of whether to split the fifth circuit."[46] This may have lessened any disharmony Brown had with his colleagues at the Judicial Conference, but it was not enough for the judges of the Fifth Circuit. Brown had earlier told them that if the civil rights issue were raised, he would voice his opinion that it was a false one. In the confusion and rush to adjourn for the day, he failed to speak up and endorse Wisdom's response to Wiggins's query. According to Brown, John Godbold was so disturbed by Brown's omission that he contacted the chief judge and asked if he could come to see him about the matter.[47] Brown admitted that he should have spoken up on the issue and on the same day prepared a statement rectifying the situation. On October 12, the chief judge sent an explanation to all members of the court, accompanied by a supplemental statement to the Judiciary Committee describing what had transpired and declaring: "Although I have long opposed the split of the Fifth Circuit, I do not for even a moment base my opposition in the slightest degree on any supposed apprehension on civil rights. I do not support directly or indirectly, expressly or implied, any such suggestions. . . . I completely reject and disavow it as an issue in the problem of Court division."[48]

The second day of subcommittee hearings took place on September 27. The entire session was devoted to a dialogue with division supporter Griffin Bell, who spoke as attorney general and as a former member of the Fifth Circuit.[49] He argued that the Fifth Circuit could not continue to operate at current levels of staffing. Already caseload was taking its toll. No oral argument was being held in half of the cases; no written opinions were being

45. Ibid., pp. 58, 71–72.
46. Ibid., p. 61.
47. Brown interview.
48. U.S. House, Committee on the Judiciary, *A Proposal to Divide the Fifth Circuit*, pp. 27–28; Letter from Chief Judge John R. Brown to All Active Fifth Circuit Judges, October 12, 1977.
49. U.S. House, Committee on the Judiciary, *A Proposal*, pp. 75–96.

issued in a quarter of decided disputes; and senior and visiting judges were being used to an excessive degree in order to handle the docket. According to the attorney general, the court was already having difficulty knowing what the law of the circuit was with fifteen judgeships. The time had run out for administrative adjustments and making better use of staff assistance. The only choice left was for increased judgeships and circuit division.

Bell emphasized that the problem had been studied for years and that it was now time to act. He urged the subcommittee to follow the lead of the Senate and attach a circuit splitting provision into the Omnibus Judgeship Bill. Representatives Rodino and Jordan explained to Bell that to consider circuit realignment as part of the judgeship authorization bill would seriously delay the creation of the needed positions. The House had no intention of recommending division until civil rights groups and other opponents had a chance to make their cases. There would be no rushed hearings like those in the Senate.

The attorney general scoffed at the idea that the Fifth Circuit could operate with as many as twenty-six judges. When Rodino mentioned that Judges Brown and Gee thought they could function with a twenty-six judge en banc, Bell replied, "I would like to have a picture of that at the time when they try it. They should sell tickets. . . . I know something about running an appellate court. . . . That would be an abomination," and went on to criticize Rodino for citing the views of only two of the judges, adding, "That's why they [the Court] elected a spokesman to come up here, Judge Godbold."[50]

Finally, Bell's testimony turned to what he considered the real issue in the debate: "where are we going to put Mississippi? . . . That's what it is all about. That's the fight." He stressed that there was no compelling administrative reason to place Mississippi to the east or to the west. In the absence of such, Bell expressed the view that the state should be placed where it wanted to be, with her three sisters states to the east. He assured the subcommittee that such a move would make "little, if any, difference from a philosophical or civil rights vindication standpoint" and that the president and he would diligently seek judicial appointments "to vouchsafe the rights of every American, wherever located."[51] Bell's pledge, on behalf of the administration, to nominate judges sensitive to civil rights later became a crucial factor in removing the reservations harbored by civil rights groups.[52]

---

50. Ibid., p. 84. Bell also explained that in his judgment the Ninth Circuit would not be able to function effectively with twenty-three judges, but explained that he was not pursuing circuit division for that court because the senators from the affected states had unanimously requested that the circuit not be split.

51. U.S. House, Committee on the Judiciary, *A Proposal*, pp. 78, 91.

52. The Administration had consistently made pledges to appoint minorities to the federal bench. In particular, President Carter desired to increase black presence in the Fifth Circuit states. On June 29, 1977, the president and the attorney general met in the Roosevelt Room of the White House with a delegation of civil rights leaders called the Committee for

Bell's appearance before the committee included a somewhat strained exchange with Representative Barbara Jordan.[53] Hoping that Bell's position was not "set in concrete," the Texas lawmaker expressed disappointment at his assertion that the Fifth Circuit issue would have to be settled before the judgeships could be approved. She challenged Bell's argument that in a large court the judges carry an unreasonable burden in having to keep up with the law of the circuit as expressed in panel decisions. Jordan argued: "I regret that the judges don't want to read all of the opinions that would ensue from this many judges being together in any one circuit. You say it is difficult for them to know the law of the circuit, but they would know the law if they can read. And I would assume that with all of the qualifications you are assigning to people appointed to the bench, that most of them could read. I would assume that." And finally Jordan, while explicitly avoiding any claim that the split might have an adverse impact on civil rights, stressed the historical importance of the Fifth Circuit as a bulwark of liberty. The status of that court, particularly among minorities, demanded that it not be altered in a precipitous or hasty manner.

October 19, the third and final day, was reserved for the arguments of the civil rights groups.[54] Representatives were present from the Legal Defense Fund, the NAACP, the Alabama Black Lawyers Association, and the Lawyers Committee for Civil Rights Under Law. The testimony of the witnesses indicated a degree of cooperation among the groups, and there is also some evidence that the civil rights activists had been in contact with members of the Fifth Circuit who opposed division.[55] The overriding theme was that the Eastland-inspired provisions in S. 11 would have a damaging effect on civil rights. For years, opponents of segregation and racial discrimination had looked to the Fifth Circuit as the only government institution before which

---

the Appointment of Blacks to the Federal Judiciary in the Fifth Circuit. The group included Martin Luther King, Sr., Coretta Scott King, Aaron Henry of Mississippi, Joe Reed of Alabama, and eight other prominent leaders from the region. Carter renewed his commitment to find qualified blacks for the Southern bench. To fulfill this pledge he needed the judicial positions authorized in the Omnibus Judgeship Bill, so he was eager to break any deadlock over the realignment controversy that might jeopardize passage of the judgeship legislation. Carter interview; records of the June 21 meeting can be found in the Carter Presidential Library, Atlanta, Georgia.

53. U.S. House, Committee on the Judiciary, *A Proposal*, pp. 87–89.

54. Ibid., pp. 97–136.

55. U. W. Clemon, for example, contacted John Brown requesting copies of the prepared remarks Brown had submitted to the House subcommittee (Letter from U. W. Clemon to Chief Judge John R. Brown, September 22, 1977). Brown, knowing that his activities were being closely watched by his colleagues on the bench, refused to cooperate with Clemon (Letter from Chief Judge John R. Brown to U. W. Clemon, October 4, 1977). Brown informed Judges Wisdom, Coleman, Godbold, Gee, and Tjoflat of the correspondence (Letter from Chief Judge John R. Brown to Judges Wisdom, Coleman, Godbold, Gee, and Tjoflat, October 5, 1977). In response, Judge Gee sent some materials and an encouraging letter to Clemon (Letter from Judge Thomas Gibbs Gee to U. W. Clemon, October 7, 1977).

they would receive a fair hearing. Any change in that court was regarded as an attack on the progress that had been made. In the words of the NAACP's Clarence Mitchell, placing Mississippi in a circuit with the eastern states was "an unconscionable attempt to try to turn back the clock to the old days... an effort to put the black man behind the eight ball."[56]

This conclusion was based on two arguments. First, the civil rights groups believed that placing Mississippi with Georgia, Alabama, and Florida would create a Deep South circuit consisting primarily of judges insensitive to the legal needs of blacks, the liberal judges being gerrymandered into the new Texas/Louisiana circuit. This argument was identical to that articulated by Judge Rives more than a decade earlier. As evidence for the legitimacy of this position, both Eric Schnaper of the Legal Defense Fund and Charles Bane of the Lawyers Committee for Civil Rights Under Law presented studies of voting patterns in Fifth Circuit en banc cases. Their conclusions were identical. Texas and Louisiana judges were far more liberal than those in the four eastern states, especially on questions of civil rights and criminal due process. They concluded that the outcomes of cases would have been significantly different if the 4–2 split plan had been in effect when these disputes were adjudicated.

The second argument focused on Judge J. P. Coleman. If a 4–2 split were enacted, Judge Brown would become chief judge of the new Texas and Louisiana circuit, and Coleman, next in line of seniority, would lead the eastern states circuit. This the civil rights groups found unacceptable. Mitchell expressed a "very real fear" of Coleman, and U. W. Clemon of the Alabama Black Lawyers Association charged that the Mississippian's "judicial philosophy and record is almost totally devoid of civil rights sensitivities." In short, the civil rights representatives found Coleman to be the least supportive of their cause of all of the judges in the circuit.

The attack on Coleman was not well received by his fellow judges. Charles Clark, Coleman's Mississippi colleague, called it "the most baseless charge that was ever made." John Godbold referred to the attack as a "great disservice" to Coleman; and Tjoflat acknowledged that Coleman was treated "pretty badly" at the subcommittee meeting. However, Coleman, who was next in line to be chief judge of the entire Fifth Circuit if it remained intact, did not seem particularly wounded by the attack. He said, "It really didn't bother me that much, because that particular limited group had been doing that for so long until it was par for the course for them."[57]

At the close of the hearings in the House, prospects for the resolution of

56. U.S. House, Committee on the Judiciary, *A Proposal*, pp. 122, 123.

57. Charles Clark interview; interview with Judge John C. Godbold, Atlanta, Georgia, December 3, 1982; Tjoflat interview; Coleman interview. Interestingly, when U. W. Clemon was later appointed to a U.S. District Court judgeship, he invited Judge Coleman to his swearing-in ceremony. Coleman, accompanied by Judge Clark, attended the event in part to demonstrate that there were no hard feelings over previous political battles.

the Fifth Circuit issue were bleak indeed. The Judiciary Committee proceeded with the legislation, and on November 30, 1977, the House version of an Omnibus Judgeship Bill was favorably reported by a 31 to 2 vote. The committee recommendation varied substantially from S. 11. It proposed three fewer district judgeships, required merit selection of district court judges, and had no provisions to split the Fifth Circuit. Unless modifications were made on the House floor, a major conference committee battle seemed certain.

Committee action on the bill was completed so late in the legislative year that floor action could not be scheduled until the second session of the Ninety-fifth Congress was convened in early 1978. In the interim, political pressures continued to mount. Judge Wisdom, repeating a strategy so effective in 1963–64, directed a constant stream of correspondence to his contacts around the country, urging them to oppose circuit division. The results were not as productive as his earlier efforts. Some of his old allies saw the battle as inevitably lost. For example, Professor Charles Alan Wright, whose support for the Wisdom/Rives campaign had been so meaningful, admitted, "I would like to think that the good efforts you and Tom [Gee] have made will kill this proposal, but I am not optimistic."[58] Wisdom found Louisiana interests to be the most responsive to his arguments. There was general concern among the lawyers of the state that Louisiana would be dominated by Texas if the proposed two-state circuit were to become a reality. Louisiana interests were also concerned about a rumor that had surfaced the previous year that the headquarters of the new circuit would be moved from New Orleans to Houston.[59]

Civil rights groups, led by Elaine Jones of the Legal Defense Fund, continued to lobby members of Congress, urging them to reject Senate demands for a divided circuit. In a January 26, 1978, meeting between Bell and civil rights leaders, the attorney general asked the groups to give up their fight to keep the Fifth Circuit whole. In an attempt to allay their fears, he repeated his promise to fill the newly created judgeships with individuals open to civil rights claims. The attorney general, in what one participant described as a "heavy-handed approach," boasted that supporters of division had the forces to win and that the civil rights groups had better drop their opposition or the train was going to roll over them.[60]

In addition to these political maneuverings, a number of changes took place in the cast of players involved in the Fifth Circuit controversy. On November 28, just days prior to House Judiciary Committee approval of H.R. 7843, Senator John McClellan died at his Little Rock home at the age of

58. Letter from Professor Charles Alan Wright to Judge John Minor Wisdom, October 3, 1977.

59. Chief Judge John Brown denied the validity of this rumor in a letter to the judges as well as in statements made to the press (Letter from Chief Judge John R. Brown to All Fifth Circuit Judges, April 21, 1977). "Judge Doesn't See Circuit Court Here," *The Houston Post*, April 20, 1977.

60. Clemon interview.

eighty-one. His death meant that Senator Eastland would be forced out of the background and would have to reassume public leadership of the Senate drive for circuit division.

Two crucially important congressional retirements were also announced. On December 10, 1977, Representative Barbara Jordan indicated that she had no intention of seeking a fourth term in the November 1978 elections. The forty-one-year-old Democrat offered no explanation for her decision. Of perhaps even greater importance was the March 22, 1978, announcement that seventy-three-year-old James O. Eastland would not seek an eighth Senate term. Publicly, Eastland claimed that the demands of his Senate duties precluded his devoting the necessary time and effort to a reelection campaign. Privately, though, he was increasingly uncomfortable with what he considered unreasonably restrictive ethical restraints imposed on members of Congress in the post–Watergate period.[61] Not coincidentally, perhaps, Eastland's announcement came just two days after former Democratic governor William Waller declared his candidacy for Eastland's senate seat and polls began to show that Eastland's advanced age was making him vulnerable at the ballot box.[62] Neither Eastland nor Jordan, however, were signaling their retirement from the Fifth Circuit issue. Both resolutely prepared for one last showdown over the controversy before bowing out of Congress.

The cast of characters was also changing on the Fifth Circuit. President Carter's first two appointments were confirmed by the Senate, bringing the court up to its fully authorized strength of fifteen judges. Judge Wisdom's vacancy was filled by Alvin B. Rubin, a United States district judge for the Eastern District of Louisiana since 1966. The intellectual Judge Rubin, the former editor of the Louisiana State University law review, was viewed as an excellent successor to the scholarly Wisdom. The opening created by the retirement of Judge Gewin was filled by Robert Smith Vance, who chaired the Alabama Democratic Committee. Although Vance had no previous judicial experience, he practiced law in Birmingham for more than twenty years. His political experience and personal attributes had formed his valuable abilities to find solutions and forge compromises to resolve disputes.

H.R. 7843 finally arrived on the House floor on February 7, 1978. The lack of a Fifth Circuit division section did not become an issue in the full House. Instead, the representatives were more interested in the merit selection provision and the number of judgeships authorized.

An amendment to impose selection procedures for district court judgeships had been proposed by John Seiberling (D-OH). Although it had been defeated in the House subcommittee, the full committee approved the provision. Seiberling, who called the merit selection requirement a "formal endorsement

61. Bell interview, October 18, 1982.
62. *Congressional Quarterly Weekly Report*, March 25, 1978, p. 757.

of Jimmy Carter's campaign promise,"[63] received strong support from Representative Robert McClory (R-IL), ranking Republican on the committee, who argued that merit selection was essential because H.R. 7843 created more new judgeships than any other piece of legislation in the nation's history. "To allow one President—no matter who he is—to reshape the Federal judiciary without such safeguards is an awesome prospect," McClory explained.[64] Merit selection grew in importance to House Republicans after President Carter "fired" U.S. Attorney David W. Marston of Philadelphia, a Ford appointee, who was investigating two Democratic congressmen. This dismissal was seen as a case of pure politics, causing some Republicans to argue for stronger merit selection provisions in the judgeship bill.[65] McClory, however, was able to convince his party members that the committee's amendment had reached the constitutional limit in restricting the president's authority over judicial appointments.

By endorsing merit selection of district judges, the House was running counter to the compromise agreement reached between Carter and Eastland in late 1976, which confined merit selection to circuit judgeships. The senator from Mississippi certainly would mount vigorous opposition to this provision, which he saw as an attack on the traditional prerogatives of the Senate and the constitutional powers of the president. A bitter conference committee fight appeared certain.

Rodino's subcommittee had originally pared down to 81 the Judicial Conference's recommendation of 107 new district court judgeships. When the bill emerged from the full committee, however, the number of district judgeships had grown to 110, three less than authorized by S. 11. Republicans, already agitated because judgeships had been withheld for the past two GOP administrations, thought the numbers too extravagant. Some Democrats, including the influential Jack Brooks of Texas, voiced similar objections. Even Barbara Jordan admitted that "We on the Subcommittee... deferred to politics and certain political realities," but that perhaps "we will not have to come to the 96th and 97th Congresses seeking additional judgeships because of the increasing load."[66]

These objections, however, were far short of the majority in either party. Most representatives were delighted that judicial pork barrel, in abundance, was being provided in an election year. As Representative Quayle (R-IN), who had a judgeship cut in subcommittee and then restored by a friend, Tom Railsback (R-IL), in the full committee, astoundingly proclaimed, "This is the

63. Alan Berlow, "House Votes to Create 145 New Judgeships," *Congressional Quarterly Weekly Report*, February 11, 1978, p. 369.

64. *Congressional Record*, February 7, 1978, p. 2445.

65. "New Judgeships: A Patronage Plum for Carter," *Congressional Quarterly Almanac 1978* (Washington, D.C.: Congressional Quarterly, 1979), pp. 173–77.

66. *Congressional Record*, February 7, 1978, p. 2449.

legislative process at its best."[67] Ironically, the number of circuit court judge-ships was never an issue in House or Senate, as both agreed with the Judicial Conference request for thirty-five new positions.

Anxious to pass the judgeship bill and move into a conference with the Senate, Rodino circumvented procedures, further heightening discontent among some House members. In an effort to avoid amendments pertaining either to additional judgeships or to a Fifth Circuit split, Rodino moved to have the bill considered under a suspension of the rules. During the twenty minutes of debate set aside for each party, the identity of the individuals speaking changed as quickly as a kaleidoscope. Republicans and opponents expressed resentment that a bill with such major provisions was being "rail-roaded." Protests notwithstanding, the suspension motion and the legislation passed the House on February 7, by a vote of 319 to 80.

THE CONFERENCE SHOWDOWN

The House and Senate versions of the Omnibus Judgeship Bill differed radically, and both sides were strongly committed to their respective positions. Undoubtedly, political hardball was about to be played in the House/Senate conference committee saddled with the duty of reaching an acceptable com-promise. Hanging in the balance were nearly 150 new judgeships. The new positions were desperately needed by the federal court system, and judges from coast to coast resented that their much needed help was being held for political ransom. Jimmy Carter was demanding that the authorization be en-acted. Chief Judge Warren Burger pleaded for passage. The days of the Ninety-fifth Congress were passing; and if the Congress ended before the judgeship bill passed, the measure and all the work that had gone into it would die. Merit selection and Fifth Circuit division were the stumbling blocks to passage. Senator Eastland and the liberal members of the House, led by Representative Jordan, faced off in one last battle. Eastland implicitly threat-ened to let the whole bill die rather than compromise his goals. It was truly, as one staff member described, "a game of chicken."[68]

Political maneuvering began immediately. On the same day the House passed H.R. 7843 Senator Eastland asked that S. 11 be inserted as an amend-ment to the House-passed version and that the Senate insist on its amendment. Eastland's motion, designed to initiate the conference committee process, was passed without objection.

Two days later Rodino asked the House to agree to a Senate-requested conference. Representative McClory took the floor and issued a strongly worded statement asking that the House managers be instructed to insist on

---

67. Ibid., p. 2448.

68. Alan Berlow, "Compromise on Fifth Circuit Issue Clears Way for Bill Creating 152 New Judgeships," *Congressional Quarterly Weekly Report*, September 23, 1978, p. 2579.

retaining the merit selection provision. As the bill had been brought to the floor under a suspension of the rules without a separate vote on merit selection, McClory suggested that members air their views and then vote specifically on his motion. This action, he claimed, would show the Senate that the overwhelming vote for passage of the bill was not solely on the judgeships but for the idea that merit should replace the Senate's "wheeling and dealing" on judicial nominations. Expressing support for Carter's campaign pledge, McClory leveled criticism at the Senate: "Can we trust so awesome a responsibility to cronies and political hacks ... lifetime appointments should deserve greater care than politics as usual ... if the House holds fast to this provision the only losers will be campaign managers and buddies of U.S. Senators who all too often have the inside track ... candidates of true merit who have no political pull will no longer be embarrassed into silence."[69]

Although many of his colleagues praised McClory's position, some House members, not to mention senators, took strong exception to his views of the selection process, as well as to the motion to instruct. Nevertheless, the House vote on the Rodino and McClory motions (321–19) indicated overwhelming support. Clearly, from the debates that had ensued, conferees from both chambers were facing many long hours of negotiation.

Delayed for two months by debate on the Panama Canal treaty, the first conference session was held on April 11, 1978. Representing the House were all ten members of the Subcommittee on Monopolies and Commercial Law: Rodino (D-NJ), Brooks (D-TX), Flowers (D-AL), Seiberling (D-OH), Jordan (D-TX), Mazzoli (D-KY), Hughes (D-NJ), McClory (R-IL), Wiggins (R-CA), and Cohen (R-ME). Three of the House managers had had previous experience with the Fifth Circuit issue as Hruska Commission members. Of the ten conferees, Rodino, Jordan, and Seiberling were committed to leaving the circuit whole. Hughes and McClory were willing to give the circuit an experimental administrative time period. Brooks, Wiggins, and Flowers were firmly in favor of division. Cohen and Mazzoli had not yet taken a public stand on the issue.

The Senate conferees were Eastland (D-MS), Kennedy (D-MA), Bayh (D-IN), Byrd (D-WV), DeConcini (D-AZ), Thurmond (R-SC), Scott (R-VA), and Hatch (R-UT). Because the committee's unanimous vote on S. 11 had been driven primarily by judicial pork barrel considerations, the Senate conferees could not be assumed to be committed to realignment of the Fifth Circuit. Though Eastland had long supported division, Kennedy and Bayh could safely be predicted to endorse the position of the civil rights groups. The position of the other Senate conferees was unknown. However, Eastland could expect some deference to his views because he was the only member representing a state affected by the division controversy and because of his position as head of the committee. Since McClellan's death, Eastland was directly in-

69. *Congressional Record*, February 9, 1978, p. 2961.

volved in managing the legislation. Consequently, any senator opposing division was now directly challenging Eastland rather than opposing a representative of his views. Eastland's announced decision to retire, however, undoubtedly reduced his influence.

Six sessions were held from April 11 to May 17. At the end of this five-week period, conferees had satisfactorily decided both the number of judges to be authorized, and when and how they were to be appointed. In typical logrolling style, the Senate accepted four House-proposed judgeships not included in S. 11, and the House approved nine Senate-proposed judgeships not part of H.R. 7843. The House lost two proposed judgeships, a permanent appointment in Wyoming and a temporary judgeship for Florida. The net result was a provision to create 117 district court judgeships. Jack Brooks described the committees' approach to the bargaining process, "To save a lot of talk and discussion of who shot John, it might be wise to accept all the House judges and all the Senate judges and everybody love everybody and just create judges abracadabra."[70]

At the insistence of the Senate conferees, the House relented on the merit selection provision. The senators, unwilling to relinquish their substantial influence over nominations, successfully argued that the House provision would amount to an unconstitutional limit on the president's nominating authority.[71] The result was a watered-down, nonbinding set of standards and guidelines for merit appointments that the president could waive at his discretion.

Also at the Senate's request, the conferees decided that the nomination process for the new judgeships would not go into effect before November 1, 1978. This assured senators running for reelection that they would not be forced to disclose their choices for the patronage positions in the middle of their campaigns.[72] The legislative liaison office of the Administrative Office of the United States Courts sent a memorandum to all federal judges explaining that, since no postelection session of Congress was planned, this provision effectively precluded any nomination confirmations until at least January or February of 1979.[73]

Though compromises were reached on other issues, the conferees still had to resolve the question of Fifth Circuit division. Eastland reportedly remained committed to his stand that he would try to kill the bill if the Fifth Circuit was not divided. Throughout the negotiations he publicly held this "all-or-

70. Alan Berlow, "Judgeships Bill Conferees Face Decision on Splitting South's Fifth Circuit," *Congressional Quarterly Weekly Report*, June 3, 1978, p. 1418.

71. Eastland, however, reportedly had in his possession a letter from Assistant Attorney General Patricia Wald expressing the position that the House language posed no constitutional problem. Berlow, "Judgeships Bill," p. 1418.

72. Ibid., p. 1416.

73. Memorandum from William James Weller to All Federal Judges and Circuit Executives, June 7, 1978.

nothing" posture. Opinions were divided over whether the senator was bluffing, or if he really would sabotage the new judgeships if he failed to get his way. In many respects Eastland's threat was credible. After all, he was retiring after thirty-six years in the Senate and had little to lose. Furthermore, the Omnibus Judgeship Bill contained no new judges for his home state of Mississippi, and therefore his constituents would not be hurt if the bill failed. The threat had to be considered real.

On May 17, the House conferees, by a 6–4 vote, agreed to take a formal stand against splitting the Fifth Circuit. One reporter observed that if Eastland was surprised, "he didn't let on. He just did what he always does, which is lean back and puff on his ever-present cigar."[74] Known for his confidence in the committee process and his ability to count votes, Eastland reportedly intended to wait until around July 4, when House members would begin feeling real pressure to get back to their home districts to campaign, and then propose a compromise of his own. In fact, the senator did not return to the conference table until July 26.

In the interim, however, Eastland's brand of quiet lobbying never ceased. As former Representative Barbara Jordan recalled, Eastland held individual meetings with her House colleagues on the conference committee in "an effort to syphon off House Judiciary Committee support for his position."[75] "What Senator Eastland did now know," she continued, "is that as soon as they would meet with him they were coming back to me saying, 'This is what happened.' " Jordan explained that although her friends were being counseled by Eastland they maintained positions of support for her. When he failed to make significant headway, Eastland requested a conference with Jordan herself.

When Jordan arrived at the conference room, which the senator had reserved in the middle of the Capitol, she found that Eastland had brought John Stennis (D-MS) with him. Stennis, in his courtly southern manner, complimented Jordan on her accomplishments and especially praised her speech at the 1976 Democratic National Convention. Stennis was clearly present to facilitate a possible reconciliation between the two. Jordan recounted a portion of the conversation:

> *Stennis*: Now, can't we work out this Fifth Circuit business?
> *Jordan*: Well, Senator, what you have to understand is that the reason many people who are black have progressed is because the Fifth Circuit has been a citadel for fairness and that's something we don't want to lose.... Why don't we just leave the circuit as it is because you [Eastland] have announced that you are retiring from Congress after this session, and I have announced that I am retiring from Congress after this session, so why don't we let a subsequent Congress take care of this issue?[76]

---

74. Charles Hayslett, "Eastland's Fight Not Over to Split 5th Circuit Court," *The Atlanta Journal and Constitution*, May 21, 1978, p. 17-C.
75. Jordan interview.
76. Ibid.

"Well, that didn't get anywhere," Jordan remembered. Instead, Eastland left an alternate proposal for Jordan to review, which she found unacceptable. The proposal divided the circuit but created an elaborate scheme for separate and joint en bancs superimposed on intercircuit conflicts that might emerge from the new Fifth and Eleventh circuits. Referred to by some as the "Super Court of Appeals," the proposal allegedly drew not only critical but also comical responses from the conferees.[77]

Amid mounting political tension the conferees met on July 26 to discuss Eastland's proposal. Pressure to break the deadlock was coming from many sources. Two days before the conference session, Chief Justice Burger released a public statement calling for action on the bill. William Spann, president of the American Bar Association, called for President Carter to become personally involved to bring about a conference settlement. Members of the federal judiciary pleaded for a resolution. Congress had set October 7 as a target for adjournment. Time was running terribly short.

The pressure began to have an effect. Although no concrete movement occurred, both camps began to soften their positions somewhat. On the House side, Jordan remained firm, but Representative Brooks, a division supporter, became increasingly active to resolve deadlock. Brooks's role expanded when an illness in Rodino's family forced him to be away from Washington for significant periods of time. As second in seniority among the House conferees, Brooks substituted for Rodino. While presiding over the sessions, he reportedly "attempted to direct discussion toward the plans that would result in a split," much to the dissatisfaction of those House conferees loyal to Jordan.[78] Civil rights leaders began to hint privately that under certain conditions a split of the Fifth Circuit might be acceptable if Mississippi were combined with Texas and Louisiana.[79]

On the Senate side, Eastland was beginning to lose his tight grip. Senators Kennedy and Bayh began arguing that alternatives needed to be considered. Kennedy and DeConcini both developed plans in which the circuit would remain whole but subdivided into administrative units. Even Senator Eastland indicated some willingness to accept less than a full victory, suggesting that a plan providing for two autonomous administrative units (divided according to his 4–2 preferences) should be devised.[80] He realized, of course, that after his retirement Senator Kennedy would assume leadership of the committee and Kennedy would never initiate action to split the circuit. Consequently, Eastland knew that if he were to gain anything, he had to be willing to compromise.

77. Michael York, "Eastland Scheme Reopens Judgeship Bill Hopes," *Legal Times of Washington*, July 24, 1978, p. 5.

78. Cragg Hines, "Jordan Marshals Opponents of Appeals Court Split," *Houston Chronicle*, July 27, 1978, p. 12.

79. York, "Eastland," p. 5.

80. Letter from William James Weller to All Federal Judges, August 16, 1978.

Because of these shifting positions, the staff of the conference committee was instructed to develop a compromise proposal while the Congress took its summer recess—not an easy task, for although the opposing sides had softened somewhat, they still remained far apart. The plan had to be acceptable politically to both House and Senate, and also had to be palatable to the judges affected by it. The Fifth Circuit Council was not at all reluctant to voice its objection to certain specific provisions included in proposed alternatives. In one instance, for example, the judges sent a unanimous statement to the conference opposing plans calling for mandatory cross-assignment of judges or less than full court en bancs.[81]

When Congress returned from its "campaign recess" on September 5, conferees were faced with a four-week adjournment deadline. Action was needed and the conferees were not making sufficient progress.

At this crucial juncture, Griffin Bell seized the initiative to forge a compromise. The attorney general was under considerable pressure to intervene: President Carter regularly consulted him on the status of the bill. Until the new judgeships were officially created, Carter had few opportunities to make good on his promises to diversify the federal bench.[82] Almost two years had passed since his election, and still the judgeships were caught in the jaws of the Fifth Circuit issue. Chief Justice Burger was also in frequent contact with the attorney general, urging that action be taken quickly lest the entire judgeship package die.[83]

Playing the role of peacemaker, Bell stepped up his negotiation efforts, enlisting much of the Justice Department's best legal talent, including Patricia Wald, Michael Egan, and Dan Meador, to assist him. Barely two weeks before adjournment, Bell wrote a single sentence, a compromise that broke the impasse. His wording was ultimately incorporated as section 6 of the Omnibus Judgeship Act: "Any Court of Appeals having more than 15 active judges may constitute itself into administrative units complete with such facilities and staff as may be prescribed by the Administrative Office of the U.S. Courts, and may perform its en banc function by such number of members of its en banc courts as may be prescribed by rule of the Court of Appeals." Bell's proposal was successful because it allowed the warring factions to avoid confrontation on key issues. First, because it applied to all circuits with more than fifteen judges, the provisions could be used by both the Fifth and Ninth circuits. Second, whether the circuits wanted to use administrative units was left up to them. Third, Congress would not be forced to decide the question of geographical boundaries; that, too, was left to the courts. And fourth, the question of en banc procedures was left to circuit discretion. The Ninth could

81. Letter from Judge Gerald B. Tjoflat to Senator James O. Eastland and Representative Peter W. Rodino, Jr., August 25, 1978.

82. Bell interview, October 18, 1982; Carter interview.

83. Bell interview, October 18, 1982.

follow its preference of using less than full-court en bancs, and the Fifth could attempt to administer en bancs with all active judges participating. In other words, it was a compromise that allowed both sides to claim victory. Wisdom, Jordan, and the civil rights groups had maintained the Fifth Circuit as a single entity. Eastland could retire knowing that the Fifth Circuit judges, a majority of whom supported division, had been given authority to devise semiautonomous units.

Nevertheless, negotiating acceptance of the compromise took special care. Bell approached both sides, arguing that this was their last chance to save the judgeship bill. He explained that it was too late to negotiate language; not one word could be changed.[84] If this compromise were not accepted, the entire judgeship bill would likely be lost.

Bell first secured Eastland's agreement. He and the senator had always had a good working relationship, and they had confidence in each other. As Bell described his session with Eastland: "I explained it to Eastland and he said, 'Do you recommend it?' And I said, 'Yes.' And he said, 'Then it's O.K. with me.' He just trusted me."[85] Bell then convinced Kennedy not to oppose the compromise.

Bell's task among House conferees was more difficult. Rodino and the attorney general did not have the close relationship that Bell enjoyed with Eastland. In addition, Representative Jordan was suspicious of Bell, perhaps due in part to his ties to Eastland and to his links to the traditions of the Old South. One observer close to the situation then volunteered the opinion that Jordan probably still thought of Bell as the redneck counsel for Governor Vandiver.[86] So Bell made ample use of his liberal assistant attorney general, Patricia Wald.[87] In a skillful, low-key way, Wald helped to present the compromise to key participants on the House side of the conference committee.[88]

Shortly thereafter, at a cordial meeting between Rodino and Eastland, both agreed to Bell's amendment. Rodino then spoke with Jordan about the proposal. She decided to support it because it would keep the circuit together and break the impasse, even though she had doubts that the plan was workable.[89] When the conferees met for the final session, Griffin Bell had already paved the way, facilitating an agreement between conferees from both chambers. At the meeting, managers reached a nearly unanimous agreement in a matter of minutes. Once again, just as in the last-minute "temporary judgeships" compromise he had negotiated in 1964, Bell's talents as a compromiser had broken a deadlock that was preventing the Fifth Circuit from obtaining desperately needed judges.

84. Ibid.
85. Ibid.
86. Confidential interview.
87. Bell interview, February 14, 1984.
88. Confidential interview.
89. Jordan interview.

Representative McClory was the only manager who refused to sign the conference report. Instead, he issued a blistering dissent denouncing the entire bill and urging the House to reject the report. He claimed that the House managers had lost on every key issue. The House had given the Senate every judgeship it wanted. The House had accepted the Senate's watered-down language on merit selection, permitting members of the upper house to retain their influence over nominations, which McClory likened to "putting the proverbial fox in charge of the chicken coop."[90] As to the compromise on the Fifth Circuit, the Illinois Republican charged:

> But now we have intentionally ambiguous language which will be used by judges who have previously announced that they disagree with the House position on the fifth circuit. How could we delegate to them this undefined power if we have such a difference of opinion? I fear that with section 6 the judges will be able to act faster than we can act to correct their mischief. I do not like to see the House position undercut. But I like it even less when our position is undercut by delegating our legislative role to the judiciary.[91]

Most members of the House were more concerned with adjournment and their own reelection campaigns than they were with McClory's charges. Limited opposition came from Republicans who wanted stronger merit selection provisions and from representatives running on platforms of fiscal austerity who made an issue out of the number of judgeships authorized. Despite these objections, on October 4, 1978, the House passed the Omnibus Judgeship Bill by a vote of 292 to 112. Three days later, with only modest opposition from disgruntled Republicans, the Senate passed the bill by a 67–15 margin. On October 20, President Carter signed H.R. 7843 into law.

While section 6 of the new legislation would not prove to be a permanent solution, adjournment of the Ninety-fifth Congress did mark the last of the more bitter confrontations over the Fifth Circuit. For fifteen years the controversy had been kept alive. Judges, members of Congress, interest-group leaders, and executive branch officials came and went during this period. But the two central antagonists remained the same: John Minor Wisdom and James O. Eastland. The judge and the senator were always involved, pitted against one another both philosophically and personally. "They didn't think much of each other," explained Griffin Bell, who knew both men exceedingly well.[92] The bad political blood between the two had a long history, perhaps dating back to Wisdom's early attempts to help establish a viable Republican party in Eastland's Mississippi.

But now Eastland was leaving the Senate after chairing the Judiciary Committee for twenty-two years. He was respected by his committee members, even those who often found themselves opposing him on specific issues. Ed-

90. *Congressional Record*, September 28, 1978, p. 32339.
91. *Congressional Record*, October 4, 1978, p. 33507.
92. Bell interview, October 18, 1982.

ward Kennedy, Eastland's successor at the helm of the Judiciary Committee, said: "As chairman, he enjoyed the affection and support of all of us, because of the scrupulously fair and evenhanded manner in which he presided over a committee of so many diverse viewpoints with so many complex issues before it. . . . He could say more with a fleeting expression or raised eyebrow or brief comment than others could say in pages of the *Congressional Record*"[93]

Eastland retired to his Sunflower County plantation. Taking senior status after twenty years service on the federal appellate bench, Wisdom maintained both his New Orleans chambers and a rather high profile on the court. Much of the intense political fire fueled for so long by their running battle died down. With the old warriors retired and the central question still unresolved, the final chapter of the Fifth Circuit story had to be written by others.

93. *Congressional Record*, October 14, 1978, p. 38059.

8

A Court
Divided

The final two years of the Fifth Circuit Court of Appeals were filled with extreme swings in the mood of its judges. The court progressed from confusion to indecision to agreement. As a consensus on the future for the court ultimately emerged, delay gave way to committed action. The judges were poised to make their demands on the legislative branch but mindful that successful communication with Congress requires more than submitting facts and logical arguments, methods with which the judiciary is most comfortable. Effective congressional liaison requires meeting the legislature on its own turf, using the language of the political process.

CONFUSION AND DELAY

Following passage of the Omnibus Judgeship Act, federal judges around the country felt a mixture of relief and satisfaction. The much-needed judgeships had not been doomed by the Fifth Circuit deadlock, as many had feared. After years of being denied adequate staff, the federal courts were receiving the largest infusion of new judges in the country's history. The legislation would provide long-awaited assistance to cope with caseloads and jammed dockets.

On the Fifth Circuit Court of Appeals, however, confusion reigned. Although there were feelings of satisfaction that the court's staffing needs were finally being addressed, there was discontent over the enacted statute. Section 6 of the bill did not settle the realignment controversy; it was simply a vehicle to break the legislative standoff. It permitted both sides in the congressional battle to create the needed judgeships without conceding their respective positions on division. As Representative Robert McClory argued on the House floor, "the compromise amendment contains unintelligible and confusing language to resolve the issue of whether to divide the fifth circuit into two new circuits. After this ambiguity was agreed to both sides claimed victory on the issue."[1] In effect, Congress had dodged the controversy, throwing the matter back on the circuit judges. Section 6 was a vague grant of power to the circuit to develop some undefined administrative unit apparatus to solve its own problems.

Unfortunately for the judges, the politicians involved in reaching the compromise held sharply differing views on what it meant, yet all expressed the rather unreasonable belief that the judges would act in concert with congressional intent. Senator Eastland, for example, noted his expectation that the Circuit Council would work out a satisfactory plan.[2] Of course, his confidence was based on the fact that the overwhelming majority of the judges favored a formal division. To Eastland, the administrative units alternative would allow the judges to create semiautonomous departments that would constitute the first step toward reaching that goal.

Now that Eastland was leaving Congress, however, he was of much less concern to the judges than those legislators who would return after the 1978 congressional elections. With the civil rights issue still present, the leaders of the House and Senate judiciary committees were not going to give the Fifth Circuit carte blanche to develop whatever structures and procedures they desired. As Barbara Jordan noted before she left the House, "I think the judges will be persuaded not to split their responsibilities in a manner that would be objectionable to Rodino and Kennedy. If they do something that is either unfair or inequitable, Congress can write a rule or mandate a change."[3] The report of the conference committee agreeing to the compromise embodied in section 6 reinforced this position by declaring that "Congress always has the power to make necessary changes by appropriate legislation" if the judges were to employ an administrative units plan that did not meet congressional approval.[4]

Both Kennedy and Rodino made it quite clear in the congressional debates what their views of the controversial compromise were. Senator Kennedy noted that section 6 authorized the creation of "administrative" not "judicial" units. Under the legislation large circuits were permitted to divide themselves into departments for the purpose of organizing and processing cases. But the senator warned that the language of the statute did not allow a circuit to divide itself so that judges from any state or states would be precluded from hearing cases originating from any other state in the circuit. In fact, Kennedy declared, any attempt to divide judicial power in such a fashion would pose serious constitutional questions.[5]

Representative Rodino spoke even more directly to the potential problem

1. *Congressional Record*, September 28, 1978, p. 32339.
2. Associated Press report, ca. September 21, 1978.
3. Alan Berlow, "Compromise on Fifth Circuit Issue Clears Way for Bill Creating 152 New Judgeships," *Congressional Quarterly Weekly Report*, September 23, 1978, p. 2580.
4. Alan Berlow, "Carter Gets Patronage Plum of 152 Judges," *Congressional Quarterly Weekly Report*, October 14, 1978, p. 2961.
5. *Congressional Record*, October 7, 1978, pp. 34546–47.

hidden in the language of section 6. By authorizing a large court to "perform its en banc function by such number of members of its en banc *courts* as may be prescribed by rule of the Court of Appeals," the new statute could be interpreted to allow a circuit, on its own initiative, to divide into distinct units and have a separate en banc court for each. This, of course, would be tantamount to circuit division, a result opposed by the congressional liberals. To counter such an interpretation, Representative Rodino boldly declared on the floor of the House, "we have not permitted autonomous divisions and we have not authorized anything the Congress may not itself review. We have not authorized more than one en banc court per circuit."[6]

The positions taken by Rodino and Kennedy ran contrary to the understanding of section 6 author Attorney General Griffin Bell. Bell viewed the administrative units compromise not only as a way to break the legislative logjam but also as a viable method for circuits to develop their own solutions for handling caseload problems. He had written section 6 to grant large circuits the authority to perform the en banc function according to their own circuit rules, and had specifically included language referring to a circuit's en banc *courts*, indicating that a circuit might well develop a system of more than one en banc. In negotiating the compromise, Bell had refused to eliminate the plural form. He charged that Rodino and Kennedy purposefully undercut the intent of the legislation. They understood Bell's objectives and both agreed not to oppose the compromise; yet, according to him, they distorted its meaning during congressional debate, fearing that the language contained some trick to allow division without legislative approval.[7]

It was little wonder that judges of the Fifth Circuit were confused about the most appropriate action to take. The Omnibus Judgeship Act granted them flexibility to develop innovative responses to growing caseload levels. Yet it was unclear exactly what that grant entailed. The language of the statute appeared to be in conflict with interpretations of it expressed in Congress.[8] The leaders of the House and Senate Judiciary committees were quite candid in declaring that they would be keeping a watchful eye on how the circuit responded. In a letter to Chief Judge John Brown shortly after passage of the statute, Peter Rodino explained that section 6 was placed in the bill "in lieu of the division of the Fifth Circuit that had been proposed by the Senate bill." He went on to warn the chief judge that "[i]t is important not to construe the language of section 6 as an invitation to the creation of autonomous

6. *Congressional Record*, October 4, 1978, p. 33510.

7. Interview with Griffin B. Bell, Atlanta, Georgia, October 18, 1982.

8. Some of the judges expressed puzzlement over the discrepancy between the statutory language and the interpretations on the floor. Coleman, for example, said, "There wasn't any doubt in my mind, never was, about what the statute meant. It meant just what it said you could have. Up until then it had said c-o-u-r-t; then it said c-o-u-r-t-s. Now I would say that the kid studying eighth-grade English ought to be able to understand the difference." Interview with Judge J. P. Coleman, Jackson, Mississippi, January 26, 1983.

divisions, or as the authorization for a de facto division of the Fifth Circuit. It is neither of these."[9] Just what was allowed under section 6 was not apparent.

It was abundantly clear, however, that Congress had authorized eleven new positions for the Fifth Circuit, expanding its size from fifteen to twenty-six active judges. This action was in direct opposition to the view of the Circuit Council majority that no new judges should be added unless the circuit were split. Nonetheless, the new judges were coming. As 1978 drew to a close, the administration had already activated procedures to nominate individuals to fill the newly created judgeships. According to the merit selection provisions of the law, nominating commissions were to be created for each circuit to recommend qualified individuals to the president. Interestingly, two nominating commissions were established for the Fifth Circuit: one to identify potential judges from the states of Texas and Louisiana; the other, for the states of Florida, Georgia, Alabama, and Mississippi.

The judges on the Fifth Circuit knew that it would not be far into 1979 before new members were confirmed and took their seats. With the prospect of a twenty-six-judge court looming, the judges realized that some action under section 6 was necessary. Consequently, an implementation committee was appointed to make recommendations. By agreement, Chief Judge Brown served on the committee and selected two other members from the two western states, Robert Ainsworth and Irving Goldberg, to participate. Judge Coleman, the senior member from the four eastern states, chose John Godbold and Charles Clark to join him on the committee.[10] Judge Ainsworth was designated as the committee's "Administrative Chairman."

The six-member committee held its initial meeting in New Orleans on November 10, 1978.[11] Before taking any substantive actions it requested opinions from all active and senior judges. The response was overwhelming. Some judges appeared before the committee when it met again on November 27, and others communicated through written reactions or telephone conversations. The only point of agreement was that something had to be done. Judge Gee perhaps expressed the problem best:

> I do not think we should adopt... either the two/four split or no divisions at all. To do the former would risk a confrontation with Congress, which after all must finance whatever we do, and which has indicated an interest in following what we do.... To refuse to try to employ the power we have been given at all to improve our situation would make it appear that, after all our complaints about work load, we were unwilling to work with what we were given....[12]

9. Letter from Representative Peter W. Rodino to Chief Judge John R. Brown, October 26, 1978.

10. Interview with Judge John C. Godbold, Atlanta, Georgia, December 3, 1982.

11. Letter from Judge Robert Ainsworth to all Judges (Active and Senior) November 13, 1978.

12. Letter from Judge Thomas Gibbs Gee to Judge Robert Ainsworth, December 5, 1978.

A number of perplexing questions faced the committee, answers to all of which would have to be found before any workable plan could be implemented. The major issues could be reduced to four: How many administrative units should there be? How were judges to be assigned to the units? How were cases to be assigned to the units: And, what should be done about the en banc function?

Suggestions ranged widely. Most seemed supportive of two units, but proposals for three, four, and even five administrative divisions were also discussed. Many supported the 4–2 configuration that had long been the goal of realignment advocates, but support for a 3–3 division began to increase, largely because of the potential oil and gas problems associated with a Louisiana-Texas circuit. These concerns were emerging because of the energy legislation being enacted by Congress, promising an increase in federal oil and gas litigation. Some members supported the notion that judges should be assigned to the units from throughout the circuit; but others favored unit membership based on the geographic residence of the judge, an alternative that some feared would provoke congressional reaction. Plans were devised to have the units specialize in certain kinds of cases, but other alternatives advanced the idea that cases should be assigned according to the state in which they originated. Ideas for the en banc function varied from a full twenty-six-judge en banc, to nine-judge en bancs with rotating memberships, to the use of several mini–en bancs. No agreement on any of the key questions appeared imminent.

In the end, the committee decided to delay action. This stemmed not only from the fact that consensus would be difficult to achieve but also from a point raised by Senior Judge Elbert Tuttle, who felt that action on the units proposal was premature.[13] The legislation authorized that courts with sixteen or more judges have the option of dividing into administrative units. Tuttle argued that since the Fifth Circuit did not yet have sixteen judges in place, the court should wait until the required number were formally on board. But Tuttle's suggestion actually went even further. He urged the court to wait until perhaps all of the new appointees had been confirmed and sworn in. The respected former chief judge explained that these new members should have a voice in the future of the court on which they would serve; in other words, they should be treated as full members. Collegiality might suffer if eleven new judges joined the court feeling that they had been purposefully left out of key decisions affecting its development. The wisdom of Tuttle's experience and sense of fairness prevailed. The implementation committee continued to conduct a limited study of the problems associated with administrative units, but definitive action was once again placed on hold. The judges

13. Letter from Judge Elbert P. Tuttle to Judge Robert A. Ainsworth, Jr., November 14, 1978. Memorandum from Judge Elbert P. Tuttle to All Fifth Circuit Judges (Active and Senior), November 27, 1978.

agreed that no decisions would be made until after the sixteenth judge was in place.[14] It was almost a full year before the court once again formally considered the division concept.

THE OLD ORDER CHANGETH

Throughout 1979, the executive and legislative branches of the government devoted enormous energies to the staffing of the federal courts. In addition to regularly occurring vacancies, 152 newly created district and circuit court judgeships had to be filled. Because it took so long for the Omnibus Judgeship Bill to be enacted, the Carter administration had only two years left before the next presidential election to complete the task. For each position, potential nominees had to be identified by the Justice Department, members of the Senate, and the various nominating commissions. Candidates meriting serious consideration had to be reviewed by the Federal Bureau of Investigation and the American Bar Association. The president was required to make a final selection for each position and refer the nominee to the Senate for confirmation hearings. For the Carter Democrats to take full advantage of their unusual opportunity to mold the federal judiciary, new federal judges had to complete the entire selection process obstacle course on the average of one every three to four days.

No court was to experience the impact of these rapid changes more than the Fifth Circuit Court of Appeals. During the twelve months of 1979, the court underwent tremendous assimilation and adjustment. Not only did the Omnibus Judgeship Act create eleven new positions for the fifteen-judge court, but two of its more experienced members opted for senior status in the latter part of 1978. Consequently, the Fifth Circuit was staffed by thirteen active judges, with thirteen vacancies awaiting Carter nominees. Such a jarring infusion of new members was bound to create a period of institutional stress.

The two retiring judges were Homer Thornberry of Texas and Lewis Morgan of Georgia. Thornberry took senior status when he reached the age of seventy after having served for more than thirteen years on the court of appeals. Morgan stepped down from active service when he reached his sixty-fifth birthday. He had served for ten years on the court of appeals, and before that, for eight years as a federal trial court judge for the Northern District of Georgia. Both Morgan and Thornberry were supporters of circuit division. Morgan was a strong advocate of realignment, having consistently voted for a split and published an influential article on the concept.[15] Thornberry was a more reluctant supporter. He acknowledged the necessity of division for

14. Letter from Chief Judge John R. Brown to All Active Fifth Circuit Judges, January 29, 1979.
15. Lewis R. Morgan, "The Fifth Circuit: Expand or Divide?" *Mercer Law Review* 29 (1978): 885–97.

the court to keep up with its workload, but he had a distaste for the Eastland 4–2 plan, greatly preferring the placement of Mississippi to the west with Texas and Louisiana.

Between March and July of 1979, nine new judges took their seats on the Fifth Circuit Court of Appeals. As a group they generally reflected Jimmy Carter's stated goals of opening up the bench to women and minorities and selecting nominees on the basis of merit. They also fulfilled his promise to minority groups to appoint judges in the South who were supportive of civil rights claims.

Carter began honoring his commitments by promoting District Judge Frank Johnson, an individual widely recognized as the most activist southern federal judge on civil rights matters. As a thirty-seven-year-old Alabama Republican, Johnson had received Eisenhower's nomination to the trial court bench. Though only sixty years old when he took his seat on the Fifth Circuit, Johnson had already accrued almost a quarter-century of experience as a federal judge. His years on the lower court were highlighted by a long string of precedent-setting civil rights decisions. The tough-minded judge had fully recovered from the illness that had caused him to turn down Carter's request that he head the FBI. Largely because of his judgment that realignment would have an adverse impact on civil rights issues, Johnson was an active member of the Wisdom/Rives campaign to kill Eastland's division plans in the early 1960s.

Among Carter's selections were the court's first two women jurists. Phyllis A. Kravitch took her seat on March 23 at the age of fifty-eight. After receiving her education at Goucher College and the University of Pennsylvania, Kravitch joined her family's firm in Savannah, where she engaged in the private practice of law for thirty-two years. She had served as a state trial court judge for two years when Carter nominated her for the Fifth Circuit vacancy created by Judge Morgan's retirement. In July, Carolyn Dineen Randall of Texas became the second woman on the Fifth Circuit bench. Randall was an unusual nominee for reasons other than gender. Although she had practiced law for seventeen years in Houston, she was not a southerner, born in Syracuse, New York, and educated at Smith College and Yale University. At forty-one she was unusually young for such a prestigious appointment. In addition, the native northerner was both Catholic and Republican.[16] Randall's nomination is one clear example of an appointment that would have been unlikely had President Carter not imposed certain criteria in the selection process that had not been used by earlier administrations.

Two of the president's selections were from minority groups that had not previously been represented on the court. Sixty-four-year-old Reynaldo G. Garza was Carter's choice to fill the vacancy created by Homer Thornberry's retirement. Garza, once Carter's first choice to be attorney general, became

16. Griffin B. Bell, *Taking Care of the Law* (New York: William Morrow, 1982), p. 237.

the first Mexican-American to be elevated to the court of appeals. He had served for eighteen years as a federal district court judge in Brownsville, Texas.

Joseph W. Hatchett of Florida became the first black member of the court. The forty-seven-year-old Hatchett had considerable experience in both federal and state judicial systems, having completed four-year stints as an assistant U.S. attorney, federal magistrate, and justice on the Florida Supreme Court. For Elbert Tuttle and the other judges who had fought the fierce civil rights battles of the 1960s, the Hatchett nomination was of particular significance.[17] It was a fitting tribute to the decisions rendered by the Fifth Circuit that now a black American could be nominated by the president, confirmed by the Senate, and take his seat on the highest court in the South.

Two of Carter's remaining appointees were attorneys in private law practice. In R. Lanier Anderson III of Georgia, the president selected a young man with a distinguished background, whose family had been actively involved in legal practice for several generations. After the Macon-born Anderson had completed his undergraduate work at Yale and his law degree at Harvard, he returned home to join his family's law firm, where he practiced for eighteen years before joining the court of appeals at the age of forty-two. Anderson had been a supporter of Carter since the president's days as governor.

Henry A. Politz received Carter's nod to become one of the nominees for a position created by the Omnibus Judgeship Act after a twenty-year career in private practice in Shreveport, Louisiana. Except for a tour of service in the air force, the forty-seven-year-old Politz had spent his entire life in Louisiana. In 1976 he had been a presidential elector from the state, casting a vote in the Electoral College for candidate Jimmy Carter.

Judges Albert J. Henderson, Jr., and Thomas M. Reavley rounded out the roster of new appointees seated before the end of the 1979 summer months. Both were appointed after years of judicial experience at other levels. Henderson was promoted to the appeals court after serving for eleven years as a federal district court judge in Georgia. Before that he had been a juvenile court and trial court judge in the state system. Thomas Reavley was appointed from his position as an associate justice on the Texas Supreme Court, where he had served for almost a decade. Before that he had been a state trial court judge. Reavley had mixed judicial experience with several years in private practice as well as political activity, having served as secretary of state for Texas during the 1950s.

As eight of the Carter appointees received their commissions during June and July, the court emerged from the summer months of 1979 a very different institution. It now had twenty-two active-status judges. Exactly one-half of the court (the nine 1979 appointees plus Judges Rubin and Vance) had been

17. Jack Bass, "Deep South Breakthrough, Black Judge Marks New Era," *Washington Post*, August 5, 1979, pp. A1 and A10.

appointed by Jimmy Carter. Only four vacancies remained to be filled to bring the court to its full increment of twenty-six authorized positions.

Although still more judges were to come, the personnel changes were already having an impact. It was difficult to initiate the new judges into the ways of the court; there were simply too many new faces. One judge likened the situation to a law school's orientation sessions for the incoming freshman class.[18] When an established court receives a new member or two, the experienced judges are able to take the new appointees under their wings and show them the ropes. The Fifth Circuit had always done an effective job in incorporating new members into the group. In spite of differences in philosophy, divergence of opinion about how to handle specific cases, and even disagreements over the future of the circuit, the judges of the Fifth were fiercely protective of the institution and zealously cultivated an atmosphere of highly valued collegiality. The old guard had survived the test by fire of civil rights days and the burden of coping with crushing caseloads; they had become, in a sense, a brotherhood. But now the old order was changing. The veterans were about to be outnumbered by a new group of judges. Assimilation of the new members would naturally take time.

The settling of the administrative units issue, however, could not wait. In July, the court officially reached and then exceeded the sixteen-judge level, triggering the applicability of section 6 of the Omnibus Judgeship Act. The court postponed its regularly scheduled en banc session and in its place called a Circuit Council meeting for the week of September 10, in New Orleans. The administrative units question was the sole item on the agenda.

One month before the meeting the judges received the final report of the Section 6 Implementation Committee.[19] It recommended the adoption of a plan that included the following essential points:

1. Two administrative units would be created.
2. Each unit would be comprised of contiguous states in such configurations as the council would determine.
3. Each judge would be assigned to an administrative unit based on state of residence.
4. Each case filed would be assigned to the administrative unit of its geographical origin.
5. Each administrative unit would have an en banc court consisting of all judges of the unit. These mini–en bancs would have the authority to review and revise the decisions made by the panels of that unit.
6. There would be an en banc court for the entire circuit. This court would consist of the most senior active judge from each of the six states plus

18. Interview with Judge James C. Hill, Atlanta, Georgia, September 27, 1983.
19. Report and letter from Judge Charles Clark to All Active Judges, August 13, 1979.

seven additional judges selected at random, provided that neither unit would have more than seven members of the en banc. The membership of the en banc would be effective for one year.

The key to the outcome of the issue would be, of course, the new judges. This was their first meeting with the Circuit Council, and they were being asked to cast a very important vote on the future of the court. There was a great deal of speculation as to how the new members would respond, but early signs indicated that there was considerable opposition to the immediate implementation of the plan. Inevitably, there was also a great deal of friendly lobbying. The old members of the court had been dealing with the division issue for years; they all had firm feelings on the matter. The overwhelming majority of experienced hands thought that the units proposal had to be adopted, that there was no way to function effectively with a court membership that would soon reach twenty-six judges. Prospects for a mutually satisfactory outcome were bleak. One judge said he told his secretary to make sure he had a reservation to fly home from New Orleans on Monday evening, because if the judges continued meeting together for the rest of the week there would be "bodies strewn all over New Orleans."[20]

When the twenty-two met on September 10, members of the Implementation Committee, especially Coleman, Clark, Ainsworth, and Godbold, vigorously argued that the units plan was absolutely necessary. Others expressed dissatisfaction with its particulars. Especially criticized were the proposals that both judges and cases be tied to geographical units and that the circuit-wide en banc consist of less than the full membership. By the end of Monday's deliberations, it was obvious that no clear decision was near. According to some recollections, the newly appointed judges unanimously opposed implementation of the units, pleading insufficient experience to cast an informed vote.[21] According to Judge Clark's recollection: "They just said, 'We really don't know. We hear John Wisdom say that we don't need to divide; we hear Tom Gee say we don't need to divide; we hear you say that we do. We need some time.' "[22] By the end of the day, the council was evenly divided.[23]

Members of the court who had long favored division were deeply disappointed by the turn of events. Most of the newly appointed judges had no previous appellate court experience, and some had never before served as judges. Some of the more senior members of the court had hoped that their newly appointed colleagues would accept their own assessment, based on years of experience, that a twenty-six-judge court would not work. There was some

20. Confidential interview.

21. Interview with Judge Peter T. Fay, Atlanta, Georgia, May 23, 1983.

22. Interview with Judge Charles Clark, Jackson, Mississippi, January 26, 1983. A similar account was provided by Judge Randall, one of the new Carter appointees. Interview with Judge Carolyn Dineen Randall, Houston, Texas, March 16, 1983.

23. Interview with Judge Albert J. Henderson, Jr., Atlanta, Georgia, August 9, 1982.

speculation, fueled by the unanimous response of the new judges and intention of the congressional leadership to keep the circuit whole, that during the confirmation process the Carter appointees had made commitments to oppose division.[24] Most of the experienced judges, however, appear to have accepted the point that the Carter judges honestly wanted more experience on the court before they voted on an issue that would so dramatically affect the future of the circuit.

The next morning the judges met again, and a motion was made to table any further consideration of division for a period of one year.[25] Judge Coleman recounts: "Well, then it was agreed that for a year we would go ahead as we had been doing and just try to handle the whole thing in one great mass. A lot of us older guys were greatly disappointed about that, but we'd been on the firing line all the time and we knew [that it wouldn't work]. We didn't have to be told, or to guess, or to speculate. But we wanted to maintain peace and harmony and unity in the court, so we agreed to do that for one year."[26]

The judges left the September meeting without making any structural changes in the court, but as the remaining months of 1979 passed, changes in personnel continued to take place. Three of the final four vacancies were filled by new Carter appointees. In October, two state Supreme Court justices joined the Court of Appeals. Yale-educated Albert Tate, Jr., brought with him a wealth of judicial experience, having served for sixteen years as a state intermediate appellate court judge and for nine years on the Louisiana Supreme Court. Sam Johnson had been a justice on the Texas Supreme Court until his appointment to the federal appeals court. Prior to service on the state's highest court, Johnson had served the Texas judicial system as a district attorney, trial court judge, and intermediate level appellate court judge. In November, Thomas A. Clark joined the Fifth Circuit. Although born and educated in Georgia, the fifty-nine-year-old Clark moved to Florida midway through his legal career and earned a distinguished record as a trial lawyer for a large firm in Tampa. These three appointments brought the court to twenty-five judges, one short of its fully authorized complement. Fourteen of the twenty-five, a clear majority, had been appointed by Jimmy Carter, and twelve had joined the court in a period of less than eight months.

The final staffing change occurred at the top. Chief Judge John Brown, who had guided the court for almost thirteen years, reached the age of seventy and was required by statute to step down from his administrative post. Although his tenure had experienced some turbulence, Brown's devotion to matters of judicial administration had saved the court from crumbling under the weight of its own docket. During his years at the helm, the southern region

24. Confidential interview.
25. Interview with Judge Gerald Tjoflat, Atlanta, Georgia, May 23, 1983.
26. Coleman interview.

experienced unprecedented growth in population and commerce. This development, along with a series of acts of Congress, swelled the region's caseload to unreasonably high levels. Congress failed in its responsibilities to the judiciary by ignoring the need to reform jurisdiction, provide adequate staff, and make other needed improvements in the judicial system. The administrative reforms introduced under John Brown's leadership and the willingness of court members to accept heavy workloads were the only reasons the court stayed afloat. Brown loved his role as chief judge and from an administrative standpoint made more of the rather undefined position that any previous occupant of the office. He knew he would miss the challenge of the post. But Brown did not leave active service as a judge. He continued as a full member of the court for several years before taking senior status.

On December 10, 1979, Judge J. P. Coleman was handed the gavel of the chief judge. Unlike Brown, Coleman did not relish the position.[27] He found it an administrative responsibility without much power. Yet he performed his role well and was especially proud to be the first person from the state of Mississippi to hold the position.[28] Although the change in leadership had little impact on the judicial functions of the court, it made a significant difference in the continuing controversy over Fifth Circuit division. For the first time in the history of the issue, the court had a leader whose personal views corresponded with those of the judges who supported realignment.

THE DECISION TO DIVIDE

January 1980 proved to be a critical month in the history of the Fifth Circuit as it provided the first major test of the feasibility of an appellate court with as many as twenty-six judges. The court had agreed that twelve cases merited hearing en banc, so the full court assembled in New Orleans to take up the issues presented.[29] Over several years one of the recurrent primary arguments had been that an en banc with so many judges would be a nightmare. Because the judges elected not to exercise their authority to use a less than full court en banc, as had the Ninth Circuit, they were now faced with the prospect of making the large en banc workable.

The oral argument session in open court went reasonably well.[30] The

27. Ibid.

28. Hill interview.

29. Although the court had twenty-six authorized positions, only twenty-four judges fully participated in the January en banc session. One position remained vacant. Judge Goldberg, though present at the en banc, took senior status later that month and did not participate in the final voting on the cases argued. Judge Charles Clark was absent and did not participate in several of the cases. Of the twelve cases docketed for that en banc session, several were consolidated with others. The court heard oral arguments in six disputes. Interview with Judge Thomas Reavley, Austin, Texas, March 21, 1983.

30. Randall interview.

twenty-four judges were "perched" (as Judge Coleman described the scene) on a special two-tiered bench to accommodate their number. The court had agreed to limit questioning of the attorneys so that the session would not degenerate into a questioning riot and so that the attorneys would be able to complete at least a portion of their prepared remarks without interruption.[31] Once the judges retired to the conference room, however, the defects in the system became readily apparent. The first case required, by various judges' estimates, a total of four to five hours to go around the table and obtain each judge's initial impressions.[32] "I was climbing the walls," Judge Reavley recalled, describing the deliberations as a "very unsatisfactory judicial experience."[33] To arrive at a decision in one case required two days of deliberations.[34] Peter Fay reported: "The first case took hours and hours. I think it took two hours to decide what questions we were going to vote on. We took the first vote and it was 12–12. From then on it was down-hill.... Right after that en banc you could just feel it. Every judge on the court knew it was not going to work.... We couldn't even decide where to go to lunch."[35]

The quality of the deliberations seemed to be an even greater source of displeasure than the amount of time expended. Judge Godbold noted that the entire dynamics of deliberations changed, that it more closely resembled a legislative session than a judicial conference.[36] All of the judges felt obliged to say something in conference.[37] This led to repetitious discussion and lent an impersonal tone to the debate. Such a large number caused a diffusion of responsibility. Some judges believed that this fact contributed to inadequate preparation on the part of some of the members of the court, who may have felt that they need not be fully schooled on every case prior to oral argument because surely someone else would be.[38] More importantly, moving from a three-judge panel context to being one of two dozen in an en banc session could cause a feeling of loss of efficacy—a feeling that one's power as a judge had been so diluted that participation lost its importance.[39] This, in turn, introduced a silencing factor, a feeling that it was simply not worth pressing a particular point of view. Points that might have been made in a smaller group were not raised.[40]

31. Interview with Judge John R. Brown, Houston, Texas, August 10, 1983.
32. Interview with Judge Robert S. Vance, Birmingham, Alabama, May 18, 1983; Godbold interview.
33. Reavley interview.
34. Henderson interview.
35. Fay interview.
36. Godbold interview.
37. Henderson interview.
38. Confidential interview.
39. Randall interview.
40. Godbold interview; interview with Judge Alvin B. Rubin, New Orleans, Louisiana, May 24, 1983.

Opinion writing for the cases decided en banc also reportedly suffered.[41] Even with conscientious note taking, many of the judges claimed that it was hard to remember all of the positions that had been advocated.[42] Some explained that a judge assigned the task of writing the majority opinion had to reconstruct all of the arguments made in conference and incorporate them into the en banc opinion, a process that might take several months. Circulating opinions among twenty-six judges did not work well either.[43] By the time the draft was circulated, no one remembered what had been said in conference.[44] Other judges complained that there was also a problem in close en banc votes.[45] A judge assigned to write a majority opinion for a court divided 13 to 12, for example, faced the task of drafting a statement that would satisfy twelve other members of the majority. According to several judges, to develop a cohesive, coherent body of law under these circumstances became an almost insurmountable problem. One judge who authored the majority opinion for one of the cases challenged anyone to try to make sense out of the court's ruling.[46]

These problems were evidenced in some of the first decisions. For example, the long period of time required to circulate and approve final opinions could be seen in *Jones v. Diamond*,[47] an appeal from a ruling by District Judge Harold Cox in a Mississippi prison conditions dispute. The majority and dissenting opinions were written by two of the court's fastest-working and productive judges, Rubin and Coleman.[48] Except for Judge Godbold's special concurrence, the court split into two groups, twelve supporting Rubin's majority opinion and nine joining Coleman's dissent. Nonetheless, it took more than a full year for the decision to be issued.

The difficulty in developing coherent law was demonstrated in *Jurek v. Estelle* and *United States v. Williams*.[49] *Jurek* presented issues involving voluntary confessions and jury selection in a capital murder case. Judge Garza was assigned the task of writing the opinion for the majority. In his first footnote, he explained the various floating majorities associated with each of the issues in the case. In addition to Garza's opinion for the court, Judge Godbold (joined by Rubin) concurred specially, Judge Frank Johnson (joined by six others) concurred specially, Judge Brown (supported by ten colleagues) concurred in part and dissented in part, and Judge Reavley (writing for seven others) dissented. The *Williams* case involved exclusionary rule challenges to a charge of heroin possession with intent to distribute. The decision of the court was

41. Interview with Judge Albert Tate, Jr., New Orleans, Louisiana, May 24, 1983.
42. Interview with Judge John R. Brown, Houston, Texas, August 10, 1983.
43. Fay interview.
44. Tate interview.
45. Tjoflat interview.
46. Confidential interview.
47. 636 F.2d 1364 (1981).
48. Interview with Judge John R. Brown, Houston, Texas, August 10, 1983.
49. 623 F.2d 929 (1980); 622 F.2d 830 (1980).

announced in a most unusual per curiam opinion. Normally per curiam opinions do not attribute authorship. In this case, the opinion was divided into two parts. The author of part one was Judge Politz, who was joined by fifteen others. Part two was jointly authored by Gee and Vance and was supported by eleven of their colleagues. Judge Hill wrote a special concurrence that Fay joined, and Judge Rubin wrote a dissenting opinion that attracted the support of ten judges.

Everyone left the January 1980 en banc session convinced that something had to be done.[50] Judge Vance described it as more like a mob than a court.[51] Albert Henderson called it a nightmare, with no capacity to create any kind of definitive law.[52] Judge Hatchett said, "I finally left the en banc session that night and I sat in my hotel room and wondered, 'My goodness, what in the world have we done?' "[53] But perhaps the most reactive of all was Frank Johnson. After calling his own shots for almost a quarter of a century as a district court judge, Johnson now found himself just one voice among twenty-five. His experience in trying to operate on such a large court was a salient factor in the abrupt change of opinion that occurred within the court.[54] In September 1979, the judges had agreed to a year's delay to allow the new judges to gain enough experience to make a proper choice. It did not take a full year: by the end of the first en banc session the judges realized that some form of division was necessary.

But other problems besides the en banc considerations were beginning to emerge. One was workload. The court was now receiving more than 4,200 cases per year. These appeals were being decided by a corps of twenty-five active judges and eight to ten senior judges. Though the Omnibus Judgeship Act had increased total judge power to levels sufficient to process the cases, it had become quite difficult for them to keep pace with what their colleagues were doing. Since the opinion of any three-judge panel sets binding precedent for all judges in the circuit, it is obligatory that every judge read the opinions written by all members of the court. The resulting number of opinions being circulated was tremendous. Just keeping up with the changing law of the circuit as it developed in the opinions of the other judges was demanding more and more time. According to one estimate, in the last year the Fifth Circuit remained intact, in addition to deciding cases and writing their own decisions, the judges read more opinions than a law student reads in an entire three-year course of study.[55] Similar problems were being faced by the judges at the district court level, who were also bound by the decisions of every circuit court panel.

50. Godbold interview.
51. Vance interview.
52. Henderson interview.
53. Telephone interview with Judge Joseph W. Hatchett, June 17, 1983.
54. Charles Clark interview.
55. Vance interview.

A final problem that was beginning to concern the judges was the decrease in court collegiality. In a smaller court the judges knew each other intimately. They understood each other's philosophies, interests, and work habits. They were personally close enough to have frank and open deliberations without worrying about offending each other or causing serious and possibly permanent intracourt divisions. In a court of fifteen or less, each judge has an opportunity, within a reasonable period of time, to sit on panels with every other judge. This is essential to developing strong internal cohesion. But with a court of twenty-six, there are 2,600 possible three-judge panel combinations. With a typical schedule of seven sittings per year, a judge could expect to participate on a panel with any other given judge about once every two years. When the participation of senior and visiting judges are added into the process, the probability of close interaction between any two active judges dwindles considerably. In consequence, increased numbers of judgeships made the development and maintenance of close ties and effective working relationships quite difficult.[56] Obviously, interactions on the twenty-six-judge court were much more impersonal than they had been in the earlier years. Judge Hill commented that at times he felt as if he had to introduce himself.[57]

By March 1980, informal discussions among the judges revealed substantial sentiment to reconsider the matter even before the previously agreed-upon one-year moratorium expired. Of the newer judges, Robert Vance, Frank Johnson, and Thomas Reavley were particularly active in trying to forge a new consensus on the issue. Given the most pressing problems, the administrative units alternative did not seem viable: under that system, judges would still have to keep abreast of all opinions written in the entire circuit; collegiality among members of the same unit would improve, but relations of judges in the other unit would be even more distant. Still, the judges remained reluctant to adopt less than full-court en bancs, which would have alleviated some of the problems. The new judges, in particular, did not want to serve on a court where the en banc function was dominated by senior members. More and more judges were reaching the conclusion that splitting the court into two separate circuits was the only workable alternative.

At this point, Judge Robert Vance of Alabama played a crucial role. He had had years of political experience as head of the Alabama Democratic party. Success in that position requires the ability to identify political problems and create solutions acceptable to diverse intraparty factions. Vance knew that unless the court was united behind a particular alternative, Congress would not respond to its problems. With his political experience, he was able to isolate the following factors that stood in the way of achieving the needed consensus: (1) With Judge Goldberg's decision to take senior status in January, only two active judges, John Brown and Thomas Gee, remained committed

56. Interviews with Judges Goldberg, Thomas A. Clark, Rubin, and Hatchett.
57. Hill interview.

to keeping the circuit whole. (2) The Mississippi judges, J. P. Coleman and Charles Clark, supported division but were firm in their desire that Mississippi join her three sister states to the east. (3) Louisiana interests opposed a two-state western circuit, fearing their state would be dominated by Texas. Others opposed a two-state western circuit for fear that it would be beset with excessive parochialism associated with oil and gas interests. (4) Proposing a 4–2 division would reactivate opposition from civil rights groups. Senator Kennedy and Representative Rodino could be counted on to champion the civil rights cause in Congress and block enactment. Opposition in Congress to a 4–2 split was so fixed as to make it politically impossible to achieve.

Given these political realities, Vance concluded that the best, and perhaps only viable, option was a 3–3 split, with Mississippi joining Louisiana and Texas to the west. Before Senator Eastland's retirement this alternative had been politically unfeasible. The first challenge would be to reorient the judges' thinking to consider a 3–3 rather than a 4–2 alignment. In Vance's estimation, the key to that challenge was J. P. Coleman. If Chief Judge Coleman could be convinced to align Mississippi with the western states, the rest of the judges would fall into line. Conversely, if Coleman refused to accept the 3–3 option, his friend and political ally, Senator John Stennis, probably had enough clout in Congress to kill it.[58]

To facilitate action on the issue, the Alabama judges, Robert Vance, Frank Johnson, and John Godbold, met with Chief Judge Coleman in Vance's Birmingham chambers in the early spring. Vance described the gathering as a "prayer meeting" to thrash out the issue.[59] Godbold's opinion was also important because he was a strong influence among the judges and next in line to be chief judge. Godbold had been a longtime supporter of division and had represented the court in the congressional battles of 1977–78. In spite of this, Godbold refused to back a 3–3 split unless Coleman agreed, a position based on his deep respect for Coleman. He also faced possible accusations of conflict of interest, since a 3–3 split would result in his immediately becoming chief judge of the new eastern circuit.

The condition of the court and the political realities of the situation were laid out before Judge Coleman. He did not like what he heard. Judge Vance described it as a "very bitter pill" for Coleman to swallow.[60] His deep sense of history, culture, and legal tradition predisposed the chief judge to a strong desire to be with the eastern states. Yet he did understand the situation and wanted to do what was best for the court. He said he would think it over and consult with Judge Clark upon his return to Mississippi, which was as much as Vance and the others could ask. Coleman was "heartbroken," explained

58. Reavley interview.
59. Vance interview.
60. Ibid.

Vance; but he was "a giant of a man" and responded in a very statesmanlike fashion.[61]

Shortly thereafter, Coleman and Clark met in Clark's chambers in Jackson to review the situation. Coleman was still disappointed; he understood that his desire to link Mississippi to the east was not going to materialize. Although all the judges agreed that civil rights was no longer a relevant issue, Mississippi was being forced to go to the west so that civil rights advocates in Congress would not balk at circuit division. To Coleman, this meant that the wishes of Mississippi were being rejected for essentially cosmetic purposes. Yet the two Mississippi judges knew they had to face political reality. As Coleman explained, "I would say as a matter of unwritten history that the 3–3 split took place here in this office...when Judge Clark and I said we are no longer going to contend to stay east of the Mississippi River, as much as we want to, because that will not get the unanimous support of the court."[62] When Coleman and Clark made known to the other judges that, in the best interests of the court, they were willing to be placed to the west, rapid steps toward realignment began.

On May 5, 1980, the twenty-four judges assembled in New Orleans to discuss dividing the circuit.[63] John Brown and Thomas Gee, the last of the active judges to oppose a split, announced that they were withdrawing their opposition. They did so reluctantly.[64] Brown explained that the general dissatisfaction with the large en banc and the change in opinion of the new judges left the opponents to division without support to continue the fight.[65] As long as Mississippi was placed to the west, Brown and Gee were willing to vote in favor of division.[66] The active judges were now unanimous. Only Senior Judge John Wisdom remained unconvinced, but he was no longer a voting member of the council.[67]

The Circuit Council unanimously signed a petition to Congress requesting that legislation be passed to divide the Fifth into two completely autonomous circuits. As a personal tribute to Judge Wisdom and as a mark of respect to the history and tradition of the Fifth Circuit, the council recommended that

61. Ibid.

62. Coleman interview.

63. The court had two vacancies at this time. Confirmation of the final Omnibus Judgeship Act nominee had been delayed and the replacement for the retired Judge Goldberg had not yet been named.

64. Vance interview.

65. Interview with John R. Brown, Houston, Texas, August 10, 1983. Similar views were expressed by Judge Gee. Interview with Judge Thomas Gibbs Gee, Austin, Texas, March 18, 1983.

66. Interview with Charles Alan Wright, Austin, Texas, March 21, 1983.

67. Senior Judges Goldberg and Rives, who had previously opposed division, agreed to the proposal (Godbold interview). Judge Tuttle, who continued to be emotionally opposed to the split, finally reached the conclusion that division was necessary. Interview with Judge Elbert P. Tuttle, Atlanta, Georgia, August 9, 1982.

the western three states retain the designation as the Fifth Circuit and keep its headquarters in New Orleans. The states of Alabama, Florida, and Georgia would become the Eleventh Circuit, with headquarters in Atlanta.

After more than a decade and a half of debate, the judges of the Fifth Circuit were united for the first time. The key to the resolution of the issue was the willingness of Judges Coleman and Clark to forgo their personal preferences for the good of the court, a concession described by those close to the situation as "magnanimous" and made at "great sacrifice" of their own wishes.[68]

SWINGING FROM THE LEFT

Now that the court was united, the final obstacle to division was convincing Congress to enact the appropriate legislation. Having decided to build as much support as possible for the proposal, demonstrating to Congress a show of great strength, the judges set about to gather the endorsement of as many key individuals and groups as possible. It was imperative that every interest affected by the division support its implementation. The court wanted no margin of error; once and for all, the issue had to be brought to a close.

The civil rights issue remained the greatest threat to passage. Fear that the recommendation for division was a plot to subvert the progress made by minorities in the South continued to linger among those who had been active during the early years of the controversy. Although Senator Eastland was no longer involved as the primary advocate of division, the memory of his previous campaigns had not died. Kennedy and Rodino had to be convinced that the fears for civil rights were not justified. If the major civil rights organizations opposed division, Rodino and Kennedy would support them. Both had promised Barbara Jordan that they would not allow the judges of the Fifth Circuit to use section 6 of the Omnibus Judgeship Act as a means to split the circuit de facto. So the judges had to face the challenge of convincing the congressional leaders that the rationale for division was administrative and not political.

Events since 1978 had weakened the civil rights argument. The addition of liberal judges like Frank Johnson, Phyllis Kravitch, Joseph Hatchett, and others to the eastern side of the circuit made claims of a conservative "Deep South" court obsolete. The 3–3 proposal reduced some of the effectiveness of the objections based on federalizing function and parochialization. Civil rights groups could no longer protest that J. P. Coleman would become chief judge of an eastern circuit, as he was now the leader of the entire court. If the judges' division proposal were enacted, John Godbold, a sturdy defender of civil rights, would become chief judge of the eastern half of the circuit.

Although the conditions in 1980 were a far cry from those of the early

68. Bell interview, October 18, 1982; Godbold interview.

1960s, assertions alone might not be enough to convince key members of Congress that something sinister was not afoot. Simply too much political baggage remained from years past. The politically astute Robert Vance realized full well what obstacles the judges faced, but he also knew the best strategy to overcome them. He explained that to deal with Congress you have to "swing from the left."[69] By this he meant that to counter civil rights objections the court had to designate as its representatives judges with established and widely recognized civil rights credentials. This political symbolism would build more credibility for the court's cause than all of the facts and logical arguments the judges could muster.

As a result of this reasoning, Chief Judge Coleman appointed a Legislative Liaison Committee to speak for the court in ushering the proposal through Congress. To head the committee, and thus act as chief advocate for the court's resolution, Coleman appointed the circuit's most liberal civil rights activist, Frank M. Johnson. It was a masterful choice. Johnson spoke with great authority to those committed to the civil rights movement. As Griffin Bell noted, "Even Kennedy and Rodino would have trouble standing up to [Frank Johnson]."[70]

To fend off any lingering civil rights arguments, Joseph Hatchett, the circuit's first black appellate court judge, and Reynaldo Garza, the first Mexican-American judge, were enlisted to help argue the court's position with members of Congress.[71] It would be very difficult for anyone to contend seriously that the division proposal would be damaging to civil rights interests with Judges Johnson, Hatchett, and Garza advocating its adoption.

As well as members appointed to defuse the civil rights issue, three other judges contributed to liaison efforts. Each appealed to slightly different interests in Congress. Robert Ainsworth was appointed by Coleman because he was widely respected as an expert in administrative affairs and had excellent relations with members of the Senate and House Judiciary committees, having testified before them on numerous occasions as head of the Court Administration Committee of the Judicial Conference of the United States.[72] Thomas Gee appealed to more conservative elements in Congress, and his willingness to drop his previous opposition made the court's plea particularly effective. Robert Vance, of course, had strong political ties to southern Democrats and could speak with some influence in those circles.

The mission of these judges was to describe to Congress the problems facing the circuit and to respond to any questions the legislators might have.[73] As a group, they appealed to a wide spectrum of interests. They presented

69. Vance interview.
70. Bell interview, October 18, 1982.
71. Vance interview.
72. Coleman interview.
73. Hatchett interview.

a united front, from the very conservative to the very liberal, from white southerners to members of minority groups. The message was clear: active judges of every stripe supported circuit division.

The strategy of the court was quite effective but insufficient to eliminate the civil rights question altogether. Through its chief lobbyist, Althea T. L. Simmons, the Washington bureau of the NAACP registered opposition to the split.[74] Other civil rights groups, according to Simmons, agreed not to oppose the legislation because they would be bringing cases before the judges who were requesting realignment.[75] The NAACP argued that circuit division was premature. There were too many unknowns: two vacancies remained on the circuit court and several more at the district court level; black nominees were facing obstacles in the confirmation process and the NAACP wanted some assurances that they would be approved. Simmons preferred to see all the Carter judges confirmed, in order to evaluate the contours of the southern judiciary, before deciding whether to drop opposition to division. "As you know from Supreme Court appointments," Simmons explained, "one person can make a difference."[76]

The Fifth Circuit judges tried to convince Simmons to drop her opposition. She recalled that Frank Johnson, Joseph Hatchett, and a number of other judges contacted her.[77] Some even sent her copies of their civil rights rulings. Griffin Bell, although no longer attorney general at this time, also attempted to sway Simmons. The NAACP's position was difficult to maintain in the face of Frank Johnson's support for realignment. Judge Johnson enjoyed great credibility. When he maintained that circuit division would not have an adverse effect on civil rights, his argument was effective.[78] Having endured so many years of turbulence in the South, however, the NAACP was leery of any changes on the southern federal bench, remained unmoved, and stood as the lone organization opposing division.[79]

The judges also persuaded several members of Congress to join their campaign. Especially effective were Judges Coleman and Clark, who were able to

74. For a discussion of Simmons's background and career, see Lena Williams, "Black and Female, and Now Deemed Effective," *New York Times*, June 30, 1987.

75. Telephone interview with Althea T. L. Simmons, April 25, 1983.

76. Ibid.

77. Ibid.

78. Judge Johnson explained, "... we had reached a point in the disposition of these very sensitive civil rights cases where, in my judgment, it wouldn't make any difference in the disposition of those cases if we had a circuit split divided as we did divide it, with Alabama, Georgia, and Florida in one circuit and Mississippi, Louisiana, and Texas in the other circuit. So the legislation I supported [in 1980] had a different complexion completely from the legislation I opposed [in 1964]." Telephone interview with Judge Frank M. Johnson, Jr., October 25, 1982.

79. Judge Johnson thought that the NAACP opposition to the 1980 realignment legislation was based primarily on feelings that carried over from the 1964 proposal. Johnson interview.

enlist the help of Senators Stennis and Cochran, as well as every member of the Mississippi House delegation. Other members of the court also secured the assistance of members of their respective state delegations. One of the most useful legislators on the issue was Senator Howell Heflin of Alabama, recruited to the cause by Frank Johnson. Although Heflin was a first-term senator, he had considerable influence in judicial matters, owing largely to the fact that he had served as chief justice of the Alabama Supreme Court from 1970 to 1977 and had led the movement to reform that state's judicial system. He had a particular interest in the Fifth Circuit and took responsibility for guiding the realignment legislation through the upper house.[80]

On June 13, 1980, just five weeks after the judges voted to petition Congress, Senator Heflin introduced S. 2830, proposing to divide the circuit according to the plan proposed by the court, with the new Fifth Circuit having fourteen authorized judgeships and the new Eleventh, twelve. Cosponsors of the bill included Senator Kennedy (D-MA), who chaired the Judiciary Committee; Senator DeConcini (D-AZ), head of the Subcommittee on Improvements in Judicial Machinery; Senator Thurmond (R-SC), ranking minority member of the Judiciary Committee; and every senator from the six affected states.[81] Five days later, having bypassed the normal committee process, the Senate passed the bill without opposition.[82] According to the Senate version, the old Fifth Circuit would cease to exist on October 1, 1980.

In the House, Peter Rodino and several cosponsors introduced a companion bill, H.R. 7665, on June 25.[83] Unlike the Senate, however, the House Judiciary Committee scheduled hearings on the measure. On August 22, 1980, Robert Kastenmeier (D-WI) presided over hearings of his Subcommittee on Courts, Civil Liberties, and the Administration of Justice.[84] Led by Frank Johnson and supported by the testimony of Robert Ainsworth and J. P. Coleman, the court representatives presented their case for division. Also giving testimony was Griffin Bell, former Fifth Circuit judge and attorney general, who appeared before the subcommittee representing the American Bar Association. Formal letters of support from Judges John Brown, Joseph Hatchett, and Alabama's first black district court judge, U. W. Clemon, who had so vigorously opposed division in the previous Congress, were introduced. In addition, statements urging division were registered by the bar associations of each of the six states, the magistrates of the Fifth Circuit, the district judges of the Fifth Circuit, the bankruptcy judges of the Fifth Circuit, the Federal

80. Howell Heflin, "Fifth Circuit Court of Appeals Reorganization Act of 1980—Overdue Relief for an Overworked Court," *Cumberland Law Review* 11 (1980): 597–617.

81. *Congressional Record*, June 13, 1980, p. S6912.

82. *Congressional Record*, June 18, 1980, p. S7320–23.

83. *Congressional Record*, June 25, 1980, p. H5680.

84. U.S. Congress, House, Committee on the Judiciary, Subcommittee on Courts, Civil Liberties, and the Administration of Justice, *Hearings on Federal Court Organization and Fifth Circuit Division*, 96th Cong., 2d sess., 1980, pp. 1–463.

Bar Association, and the Justice Department. Chief Justice Warren Burger and Fifth Circuit Justice Lewis Powell urged passage. The Judicial Conference, deferring to the wishes of the Circuit Council, endorsed the proposal. Statements withdrawing opposition to realignment were submitted by the American Civil Liberties Union, the Lawyers Committee for Civil Rights Under Law, the Alabama Black Lawyers Association, and the NAACP Legal Defense Fund. A long list of public officials from the South and black political leaders, including Coretta Scott King, also expressed support.[85] The lone opposing voice was that of Althea Simmons on behalf of the NAACP, who appeared before the subcommittee to urge Congress not to act until all appellate and trial court vacancies were filled.

After it had been favorably reported by the Judiciary Committee, the House passed H.R. 7665 on October 1, 1980.[86] The House version of the reorganization differed from the Senate bill in only two ways. First, the Senate bill had mistakenly placed the Canal Zone in the new Eleventh Circuit instead of the new Fifth Circuit. What little judicial work had been necessary before the Canal Zone was fully transferred to the nation of Panama was being administered by a district judge in the Fifth Circuit, and consequently the Canal Zone had to be officially placed under the appellate jurisdiction of the new Fifth. Second, the House bill designated the effective date of realignment to be October 1, 1981. This date, twelve months later than the Senate had proposed, was a concession to the opposition registered by the NAACP and also a recognition of the time necessary to implement the transition. That same day the United States Senate concurred in the House amendments.[87] Two weeks later, with President Carter's signature, The Fifth Circuit Court of Appeals Reorganization Act of 1980 became Public Law 96–452.

Throughout the final year of activity on the division of the circuit, Judge John Minor Wisdom remained relatively quiet. He realized that his long fight to preserve the venerable Fifth Circuit was drawing to a close. Although Wisdom was still convinced that his view of the proper organization of the judiciary was correct, he did not make a last stand at the House subcommittee hearings. Instead, he wrote an article entitled "Requiem for a Great Court," which was published in the *Loyola Law Review*.[88] It began with the following words: "For many lawyers and some federal judges, Wednesday, October 15, 1980, was a day of mourning.... On that day Congress sliced a great court in two."

85. Memorandum from Joseph L. Nellis, General Counsel to Peter W. Rodino, Jr., September 15, 1980.

86. U.S. Congress, House, Committee on the Judiciary, *Report on the Fifth Circuit Court of Appeals Reorganization Act of 1980*, 96th Cong., 2d sess., 1980; *Congressional Record*, October 1, 1980, pp. H10187–88.

87. *Congressional Record*, October 1, 1980, pp. S14209–10.

88. John Minor Wisdom, "Requiem for a Great Court," *Loyola Law Review* 26 (1980): 787–92.

A COURT IN TRANSITION

In anticipation of a favorable congressional response to their petition for division, the judges of the Fifth Circuit invoked the administrative units option available to them under section 6 of the Omnibus Judgeship Act.[89] Effective July 1, 1980, three months before the realignment statute was passed by Congress and fifteen months prior to the effective date of the actual split, the court broke itself into two administrative units. Unit A consisted of the states of Texas, Louisiana, and Mississippi; and Unit B was composed of Florida, Alabama, and Georgia. Judges were assigned to the units based on the state of their residence. Cases were referred to the units for processing and disposition based upon the state of their origin. In keeping with the spirit of the Omnibus Judgeship Act, the court acknowledged that all judges retained their authority throughout the entire circuit, and that there would be only one body of law, one judicial council, and one judicial conference for the entire circuit.

The unit system was adopted only as a precursor to the split. It was not intended to be used as a permanent solution to the circuit's problems, although that might have been tried if Congress had turned down the court's petition to divide. Section 6 provided a convenient medium of transition; by establishing Unit B's headquarters in Atlanta the preliminary groundwork for permanent Eleventh Circuit offices was laid.

In the midst of the activity surrounding congressional consideration of realignment and subsequent transition plans, two personnel changes occurred. The first was the addition of the twenty-fifth judge, a replacement for the seat left vacant by the retirement of Irving Goldberg. President Carter selected sixty-four-year-old Jerre S. Williams. Although Judge Williams was born in Colorado and received his law degree from Columbia University, he had been a resident of the region since 1946, when he accepted a teaching position at the School of Law of the University of Texas. Williams, who held the John B. Connally Chair of Civil Jurisprudence, became the first person ever appointed to the Fifth Circuit Court of Appeals after having devoted an entire career to university-level teaching and research. William's appointment left the court with only one vacancy. As fate would have it, though, the Court never achieved its full strength of twenty-six judges. The circuit was officially divided before a final judge could be confirmed.

The second personnel matter was of greater immediate significance. J. P. Coleman announced that, effective February 2, 1981, he was stepping down as chief judge of the circuit. Although he had occupied the center chair for only slightly more than a full year, the court had undergone dramatic change during his tenure. Most importantly, Coleman had led the judges in their final attempts to secure congressional approval for circuit realignment. Had

89. By resolution of the Judicial Council of the Fifth Circuit, May 5, 1980.

it not been for his agreement to allow Mississippi to be placed to the west and his implementation of a congressional liaison strategy, the division of the circuit would certainly not have occurred as soon as it did. Although his views were more conservative than those of many of his colleagues, Coleman dissented in relatively few civil rights and voting rights decisions.[90] Members of the court regarded him as an effective judge and a delightful colleague. Even the more liberal judges acknowledged that Coleman never used his position as chief judge to impose his will on the rest of the court.[91]

Although it was true that Coleman did not particularly enjoy the administrative aspects of the position, his decision to step down as chief judge, like that to drop his opposition to Mississippi joining the western states, was made for the good of the court. Coleman was not required by statute to give up his leadership; he was only sixty-seven years old and could have served until seventy. But he realized that the transition from one large court to two new circuits would be much more effectively accomplished if he stepped aside. His decision cleared the way for John Godbold to assume the chief judgeship. Godbold had both good administrative skills and, as he would eventually become chief judge of the new Eleventh Circuit, significant personal incentive to make the transition an effective one. By dropping out of the leadership structure, Coleman also made it possible for his fellow Mississippian, Charles Clark, to become the first chief judge of the new Fifth Circuit and, during the transition period under the administrative units system, to head Unit A. In sum, Coleman's action, described by Judge Clark as "a magnanimous gesture,"[92] made it possible for the future chief judges of the new Fifth and Eleventh circuits to orchestrate the transition, organize their respective units, and move into the postrealignment period with experience and confidence.

The mechanics of the division were complex.[93] The judges, assisted by Circuit Executive Thomas Reese and administrative staff personnel, had to establish an entirely new operation in Atlanta while maintaining a smoothly functioning apparatus in New Orleans. A building for courtrooms and offices had to be made ready in Atlanta, furniture and equipment purchased, employees hired and trained, a library established, case files and personnel records transferred to the new location, clerks, librarians, and staff attorneys secured. All these things had to be done before the final transition on October 1. During this hectic period, of course, case filings did not cease; and the last months of the old Fifth Circuit broke all previous caseload records. In the year ending on June 30, 1981, 4,907 new cases were filed with the court— 2,508 in Unit A and 2,399 in Unit B.[94] In spite of the burdens of that difficult

90. Interview with Judge John R. Brown, Houston, Texas, August 10, 1983.
91. Goldberg interview.
92. Charles Clark interview.
93. Interview with Circuit Executive Thomas Reese, Atlanta, Georgia, October 25, 1982.
94. Harvey C. Couch, *A History of the Fifth Circuit 1891–1981* (Washington, D.C.: U.S.

transition year, the judges did not let other matters interfere with their primary responsibility of efficiently deciding appeals brought before them for resolution.

On Thursday, October 1, 1981, the judges of the Fifth Circuit Court of Appeals assembled en banc in New Orleans for the official closing ceremonies. Almost all the court's eleven senior and twenty-four active judges[95] were there. Noticeably absent was Judge John Minor Wisdom, the longtime opponent of realignment. Although Wisdom had attended a special dinner for the judges the night before, he left town before the final ceremonies to conduct business on the special federal Railroad Reorganization Court.[96] The closing event would have been extremely difficult for the New Orleans judge. His emotional attachment to the Old Fifth had never flagged, nor had his degree of opposition to the split of the circuit.

In front of a huge American flag, with such dignitaries as Chief Justice Warren Burger and Griffin Bell along with five hundred spectators looking on, Chief Judge Godbold passed the gavel to new Chief Judge Charles Clark. "In return Godbold received the last American flag to fly over the Camp Street courthouse to be taken with him to Atlanta."[97] Members of the new Eleventh Circuit, led by Chief Judge Godbold, filed from the platform, symbolizing the final division. The Old Fifth Circuit was no more. It was an emotional moment for the judges; some compared the break to the pain of divorce.

The judges of the new Eleventh Circuit then flew to Atlanta for the next day's opening ceremonies for the nation's first new circuit in more than fifty years. In New Orleans, trucks were being loaded with the last of the records that had to be transferred to Atlanta. On Monday morning, October 5, the Court of Appeals for the Eleventh Circuit was open for business.

When the days of the Old Fifth Circuit came to an end, a significant chapter in judicial history closed. The old court had held jurisdiction over a huge expanse—from El Paso to Savannah to Key West and the Canal Zone, a territory encompassing forty million people. It had developed significant areas of the law, such as admiralty, and had earned the respect of the nation with its civil rights rulings. The judges had grappled with George Wallace, Bull Connor, and Ross Barnett. They had protected and extended the right of black citizens to vote, desegregated public schools and facilities, enhanced the

---

Government Printing Office under the Auspices of the Bicentennial Committee of the Judicial Conference of the United States, 1984), p. 192.

95. On May 31, 1981, four months after he had given up his position as chief judge, J. P. Coleman took senior status, reducing the number of judges in active status to twenty-four.

96. Interview with Judge John Minor Wisdom, New Orleans, Louisiana, May 28, 1985.

97. Ed Anderson, "Federal Court Is Split," *New Orleans Times-Picayune*, October 1, 1981, p. 1.

fairness of the criminal trial, and enforced the Constitution in a reluctant region. The old Fifth Circuit was gone. But the traditions of the old court survive. The Fifth and Eleventh circuits both agreed to accept the precedents of the former Fifth as their own. And so, though the old Fifth Circuit expired, its rulings live on, continuing to bind the judges who sit on its successor courts.

9

Cooperative Oversight
and the Principles
of Judicial Politics

The saga of the Fifth Circuit Court of Appeals is more than just an interesting chapter in the history of the federal judiciary. The events leading to its division provide instructive propositions for comprehending how judicial institutions function within the American governmental system and how problems facing other appellate courts may be effectively addressed. In this chapter we offer some closing comments on the realignment controversy and provide a more general schema for understanding the web of interinstitutional politics within which policies for the judiciary are determined.

CONSEQUENCES FOR REFORM

On March 7, 1984, Charles Clark and John Godbold, chief judges of the former Fifth Circuit's successor courts, appeared before the Senate Subcommittee on Courts to discuss the effects of realignment. After two and a half years of experience under the new structure, both were very satisfied with the results. According to Godbold, the judges of the Eleventh Circuit considered its creation an "unqualified success."[1] His evaluation of the impact of realignment read like the litany of advantages the proponents of division had recited throughout the years of the controversy: more stable circuit law, a better functioning en banc court, reduced backlog, increased productivity,

1. U.S. Congress, Senate, Subcommittee on Courts of the Committee on the Judiciary, *Oversight on the Federal Court of Appeals*, 98th Cong., 2d sess., 1984. Interestingly, at the same hearing Chief Judge James Browning of the Ninth Circuit argued just as persuasively that the Ninth Circuit was functioning quite well as a large court under the provisions of section 6 of the Omnibus Judgeship Act. Browning appeared before the subcommittee in part to argue against a bill (S. 1156) introduced by Slade Gorton (R-WA) to split the Ninth Circuit.

improved collegiality, less travel, more efficient administration, and improved capacity of the judges to keep up with the law of the circuit. In spite of these generally acknowledged and statistically supported benefits, the process that led to the decision to divide the circuit must be placed in proper perspective.

The core problem plaguing the former Fifth Circuit was ever-increasing caseload. Fueled by an expanding regional population, more commerce, and congressional actions that expanded the jurisdiction of the federal courts, the cases filed in New Orleans rapidly outstripped the decision-making capacity of the court. Noticeably absent from the congressional response to conditions in the Fifth Circuit was any attempt whatsoever to confront the caseload issue through systematic study or experimentation with alternatives. From its inception, the debate centered on ways to handle caseload rather than on the source of the problem itself. The Fifth Circuit's original preference was to devise a means of accommodating the burden while keeping the court intact. Once the discussion of alternatives had become politicized, leaving no chance for legislative enactment of any reform, the court and Congress grappled with the caseload problem in the most politically and administratively expedient manner. Consequently, both the source of the problem and possible long-term solutions to it were excluded from consideration.

Many Fifth Circuit judges, joined by other prominent federal jurists, hurled criticism at Congress for not addressing the problems associated with federal jurisdiction. Congress, they argued, had been entirely too prone to pass legislation affecting the federal courts without considering the consequences of increased caseloads. Chief Judge Brown, for example, presented the House Subcommittee on Monopolies and Commercial Law with a list of forty-one pieces of recently passed legislation that had contributed significantly to the caseload problems of the federal courts. In 1984, Chief Judge Clark submitted to the Senate Subcommittee on Courts a list of 316 statutes, most passed within the previous fifteen years, which vested special jurisdiction in the federal judiciary. Even judges who disagreed on realignment were in accord that the federal courts should not be devoting their resources to deciding controversies arising under statutes such as the Motor Vehicle Information and Cost Savings Act (commonly referred to as the Odometer Act), the Apple Barrel Standards Act, the Egg Products Inspection Act, the Horse Protection Act, or the Small Loan Act. The impact of congressional actions such as these prompted Chief Justice Burger repeatedly to demand that Congress compile a judicial impact statement before passing any legislation expanding federal jurisdiction. Witnesses urged Congress to find alternative methods of resolving Social Security benefit appeals and similar matters arising from administrative determinations. The legislature was asked to consider revising diversity jurisdiction, a major source of litigation, which requires federal courts to determine disputes controlled by state law. Also a target of judicial criticism was the tendency of Congress to designate certain disputes as preference cases, mandating that they be heard before more important issues, such as civil rights. But pleas for a comprehensive assessment of the caseload explosion fell on deaf ears.

Rather than through serious consideration of long-term solutions, the caseload crisis had to be managed in other ways. For the courts this meant a streamlining of the decision-making process through summary decisions, non-published opinions, and reduced use of oral argument. Although these measures alleviated some of the pressure of a heavy docket, they did so only by expediting the handling of the cases, not by solving the workload problem. The congressional solution was to authorize additional judgeships, a remedy particularly dear to legislators because of its political patronage benefits. Adding judges provided immediate, if temporary, relief. In the long run, however, this method created more problems than it solved. Too much reliance on additional judgeships placed the en banc decision-making process in jeopardy, thus creating the pressure that led to the ultimate decision to divide.

Although the solution eventually adopted for the Fifth Circuit did bring the benefits cited in Judge Godbold's testimony, these positive results of circuit division can be considered only temporary. The jurisdictional problem has yet to be confronted. Realignment did not remove a single case from the court's docket; it merely split the circuit ranking first in caseload and, as a result, created two new circuits that immediately ranked second and third in number of appeals filed. As cases continue to mount nationwide, Congress will most likely respond by increasing the number of judges until other courts reach the same breaking point as did the former Fifth. Realignment was not the answer to the caseload problem; it was a political rather than an administrative solution, owing primarily to the nature of the process of which it was a product.

Circuit division, then, cannot be considered a long-term solution. Even strong advocates of realignment realize that it is a stop-gap remedy. Charles Clark, for example, estimated that circuit division would confer its benefits for ten to fifteen years before caseload growth would once again outstrip court capacity.[2] Repeated reliance on realignment as a response to increases in caseload will only result in ever-smaller circuits, inevitably leading to the dangers of excessive parochialism about which John Wisdom so cogently warned. Sooner or later, those responsible for policies affecting the federal judiciary must confront the fundamental causes of caseload increase.

COOPERATIVE OVERSIGHT

In addition to the issues specifically related to caseloads and realignment, the Fifth Circuit controversy is instructive concerning the more general subject of policy-making for the federal courts. Through our study of background

2. Interview with Judge Charles Clark, Jackson, Mississippi, January 26, 1983.

activities, personalities, and relationships, we extrapolate a model of politics from this event which can provide us with a better understanding of influence in this area of politics. Our concept outlines the interinstitutional political relationships that determine government responses to judicial problems. In this vein, our approach is similar to that taken by David J. Danelski in his classic study of the judicial selection process.[3] After describing in rich historical detail the activities and influences that led to the appointment of Justice Pierce Butler, Danelski was able to develop theoretical propositions that helped us better understand the politics of the nomination process.

Unlike the executive and legislative branches, which possess a degree of authority to implement intrabranch reorganizations without external approval, the judiciary must obtain legislative authorization for all significant structural alterations. The Founders so dictated in the first section of Article III of the Constitution. This constitutional requirement means that all reforms of the federal court system will necessarily be the result of interinstitutional politics. Scholars have become accustomed to the fact that, in reality, politics quite often takes on a convenient, xenogenic form. But decisions concerning the structure and process of the lower federal courts are made within the constitutional framework of the separation of powers doctrine. The doctrine is more prevalent in the minds of politicians than one might expect. Controversies over changes in the federal courts are played out with representatives of both branches keenly aware that excessive interference by one branch in the affairs of the other can reduce the latter's ability to exercise its primary functions.

Because of these realities, decisions governing the federal judiciary are arrived at through a process of cooperative oversight, a pragmatic policy arrangement that accommodates the constitutional responsibility of Congress to oversee the lower courts while supporting the integrity and independence of the judiciary. It facilitates the legislative process by permitting the judiciary to aid Congress in making well-informed, and on occasion, timely decisions. The process legitimizes and institutionalizes the flow of necessary communication between both branches for the development of legislation applicable to the courts. Figure 1 outlines the major participants and their relative positions in the cooperative oversight system.

At the most fundamental level, policy formulation begins with the identification of a problem needing correction or a condition requiring improvement. The primary responsibility for identifying such situations lies with members of the judicial branch, as federal judges clearly are in the best position to detect institutional problems that warrant attention. Although members of Congress or their staffs may also isolate areas worthy of legislation,

---

3. David J. Danelski, *A Supreme Court Justice Is Appointed* (New York: Random House, 1964).

JUDICIAL LEGISLATION AND THE POLICY MAKING PROCESS

Cooperative Oversight

Critical Policy Formulation Among Experts   Formal Policy Adoption

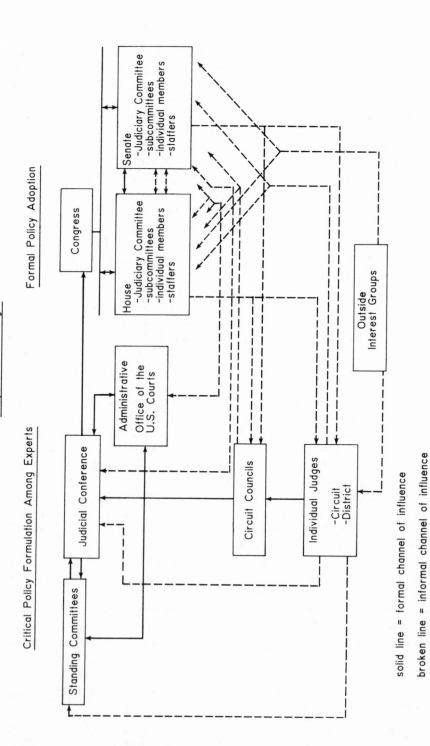

solid line = formal channel of influence

broken line = informal channel of influence

Fig. 1. Diagram of cooperative oversight model. (Illustration by the authors.)

they are less likely to do so unless such situations are brought to their attention by constituents or organized interests.

Key participants in this process are the circuit councils, whose responsibilities include monitoring the condition of all federal courts within their regional jurisdiction. The ability of these largely autonomous councils to identify and seek solutions for administrative problems was improved in 1980 when district-judge representation was added. Problems brought to the attention of the circuit councils are discussed, and when agreement on a suggested remedy is reached, a recommendation is forwarded to the Judicial Conference. The formal rules of the conference, which is generally supportive of the decentralized nature of the federal judiciary, give great deference to the recommendations of the circuit councils, especially if the problem and recommended solution affect only a single circuit.

The standing committees of the Judicial Conference constitute another critical stage in the policy-making process. These committees are organized according to substantive jurisdiction and are staffed by individuals with considerable expertise in the area. They are assisted by the personnel and resources of the Administrative Office of the United States Courts. When a circuit council sends a matter to the Judicial Conference, it is normally referred to the appropriate standing committee for additional study. The committees also conduct independent analyses of conditions facing the federal judiciary within their substantive purview and examine the potential impact on the courts of legislation pending in Congress. These activities result in a recommendation to the parent Judicial Conference, which then determines the official policy position of the federal court system. The entire process to this point takes place within a closed community of legal experts.

Once the Judicial Conference has arrived at a position requiring legislative action, arrangements are made with a member of Congress (or legislative staff) for an appropriate bill to be introduced. From that point, the legislative process works in its normal manner. The bill is referred to the appropriate committee (usually the Judiciary), where hearings are customarily held. This provides an opportunity for selected conference members to testify on behalf of the judiciary's official position. Only at this point may dissenting federal judges and outside interests affected by the legislation participate in the process. Substantial interaction occurs between House and Senate staffs during legislative deliberations, as well as between congressional and Administrative Office staff. If a favorable result is reached in the congressional committee, the bill is sent to the chamber floor for final approval.

Normally, then, maintaining an effectively functioning court system is a responsibility shared by the legislative and judicial branches. It is usual for the judiciary first to identify a problem and recommend a solution and for the legislative branch to consider the recommendation and make a final determination. This procedure, of course, does not preclude the possibility that Congress may act independently of the judiciary or even against the expressed preferences of the nation's judges. This can and does occasionally occur. Congress, however, is not likely to do so unless pressured by politically important, outside interest groups such as the organized bar or civil rights organizations.

Noticeably absent from the cooperative oversight process is the executive branch. For the most part, the president's active interest in judicial matters is confined to the selection process. Rarely does the chief executive become involved in the administrative matters of the Third Branch. This avoidance is dictated by the practical demands of more pressing matters of state, as well as by the more general proscriptions of the separation of powers doctrine. In the history of the Fifth Circuit controversy, for example, there is relatively little evidence of presidential participation. Only Jimmy Carter became even moderately involved in the issue; and his concern was based, not on any particular interest in judicial administration, but on the need to obtain additional judgeships in order to fulfill his pledge of diversifying the federal bench. Any executive influence is more likely to be exerted through the offices of the attorney general, although even at this level involvement is likely to be limited. Griffin Bell's participation in the congressional battle over realignment, for example, was due primarily to his own interest in the Fifth Circuit and the administration's urgent need for passage of the Omnibus Judgeship Act.

CONGRESSIONAL DISINTEREST

Studies of the congressional process have repeatedly concluded that the driving force behind the behavior of legislators is the desire to be reelected.[4] Understandably, members of Congress are keenly interested in maintaining the support of broad-based electoral groups and are preoccupied with matters of constituent service. The area of judicial reform does not contain issues likely to contribute to a legislator's reelection. Nor are federal judges, the primary advocates of court-related policy, able to provide tangible reelection benefits to members of Congress.[5] They do not represent substantial numbers of voters, nor can they activate armies of campaign workers. For most voters issues of judicial administration have no salience. Given these realities, it is not surprising that legislators are disinclined to expend time and energy familiarizing themselves with court issues. To emphasize this point, a former Senate aide explained that: "Courts issues in the Congress are not by and large intrinsically interesting issues.... They certainly don't have a landed

4. See, for example, Morris P. Fiorina, *Congress: Keystone of the Washington Establishment* (New Haven: Yale University Press, 1977); David R. Mayhew, *Congress: The Electoral Connection* (New Haven: Yale University Press, 1974).

5. Thomas G. Walker and Deborah J. Barrow, "Funding the Federal Judiciary: The Congressional Connection," *Judicature* 69 (June–July, 1985): 43–50.

constituency that can make campaign contributions. The public doesn't view courts issues as something important for them."[6]

As a consequence, problems facing the courts tend to take a backseat to issues either considered more important or promising greater reelection benefits. Service on the Judiciary committees of Congress, while conferring moderate prestige, ranks substantially lower in a legislator's preferences than membership on committees dealing with foreign affairs, taxation, appropriations, and armed services.[7] Even within the Judiciary committees themselves there are greater reelection benefits attached to working on legislation dealing with immigration, crime, civil liberties, and commercial law than with the nuts and bolts of court operations.

Members of Congress, of course, are well aware of their responsibility to insure that the courts operate in a satisfactory manner. Because the political payoff for fulfilling this responsibility is relatively low, however, they tend to accommodate the needs of the judiciary with as little effort as possible. Historically, Congress has responded to the need for court administration by providing the judiciary with its own administrative structures. Substantial discretion has been delegated to the Judicial Conference and the Administrative Office. Where legislation is required in order to respond to a judicial need, Congress is likely to respond favorably to reasonable requests that do not generate significant opposition. To a certain extent this attitude is also based on separation of powers considerations. As one Senate aide explained: "For most people in the Congress there is an institutional separation of powers concern which is, it is not our place to be forcing upon the judicial branch things the judicial branch does not want or can't handle. On the other hand, when they have a problem and propose a solution and agree upon it, then institutionally we probably should, to the best extent possible, grant them what they are asking."[8] This arrangement serves the needs of both institutions. The courts are given primary authority to identify problems and recommend solutions. This gives the judges substantial control over the issues of judicial administration that affect them directly. Congress is able to enact policy with a minimal expenditure of time and effort. From this politically convenient "partnership,"[9] the legislative and judicial branches cooperate in overseeing the operations of the federal courts, and in the process federal judges derive

6. Interview with Thomas M. Susman, Washington, D.C., April 26, 1983.

7. See Lynette P. Perkins, "Member Recruitment to a Mixed Goal Committee: The House Judiciary Commitee," *Journal of Politics* 43 (May 1981): 348–64; Steven S. Smith and Christopher J. Deering, *Committees in Congress* (Washington, D.C.: Congressional Quarterly Press, 1984).

8. Interview with Guy P. Land, Washington, D.C., April 27, 1983.

9. See Carl Baar, "Federal Judicial Administration: Political Strategies and Organizational Change," in *Judicial Administration: Text and Readings*, ed. Russell R. Wheeler and Howard R. Witcomb (Englewood Cliffs, N.J.: Prentice-Hall, 1977), pp. 97–109.

a good bit of discretion and autonomy over judicial administrative policy-making.

The general lack of legislative interest in the intracacies of judicial policy was apparent throughout the public record on the Fifth Circuit issue and was reinforced in our interviews with the participants. One member of Congress who had played a key role on the issue for years but changed committee assignments prior to the issue's final resolution was even unaware that Congress had divided the Fifth Circuit. Staff members candidly admitted that they handled the legislation, with scant attention from their "bosses." This has two implications for the process through which court reform is considered. First, federal judges have great latitude as policy advisers to Congress. Representatives of the judiciary normally come before Congress armed with an impressive array of their own statistics to plead their case and, in this respect, have "absolute expertise."[10] In addition, they derive influence as experts ("relative expertise")[11] because they are received with respect owing to their judicial role and bring advice that is the product of institutional arrangements established by Congress. Thus, on administrative matters, members of the federal bench are formidable advocates.

ACCOMMODATIONIST POLITICS

Nevertheless, judges make an important trade-off for this discretionary authority. Members of Congress demand nearly unanimous endorsement of proposals as a prerequisite for approval. Among the circuit judges interviewed for this study, there was overwhelming agreement on the necessity to speak to Congress with unanimity in order to persuade it to respond favorably on judicial matters. Congress is reluctant to act as an umpire to settle internal judicial disputes. Dissent within the judiciary's own ranks means that legislators must devote resources to studying the relative merits of the opposing sides; when there is unanimity, on the other hand, members of Congress feel more comfortable in ratifying the judges' request. This position was succinctly described by a Senate staff member:

> Until the judicial branch speaks almost with one voice, the Congress is unlikely to do anything legislatively. There is no incentive for Congress to do anything; the constituency is far too small. You just don't gain anything by dealing with the judicial branch that way. Once they all agree this is what needs to be done, here is a problem, here is a solution, we're all going to be happy, nobody outside is going to be upset, it's not going to cost that much money, then fine.[12]

10. Francis E. Rourke, *Bureaucracy, Politics, and Public Policy* (Boston: Little, Brown, 1976).

11. Ibid.

12. Interview with Guy P. Land, Washington, D.C., April 27, 1983.

This position was reinforced by Michael Remington, counsel to a House Judiciary subcommittee, who explained that judicial policies are much more likely to be enacted if those directly affected—federal judges, in this instance— have reached an agreement, thereby eliminating controversy before entering the congressional arena.[13] The congressional preference for unanimity became clearly evident during the Fifth Circuit controversy. Members of the Judiciary committees of both houses of Congress frequently displayed aggravation during the hearings over the judges' failure to reach a consensus.

The congressional demand that judges speak with one voice has an important ripple effect on the judiciary's internal politics. A unified position among federal judges can be achieved only if a high premium is placed on consensus-building. The result is accommodationist politics.[14] Members of the U.S. Judicial Conference, for example, place a high priority on supporting the requests of the circuit councils.

This strong adherence to accommodationist politics explains much of the political maneuvering during the early battles over realignment. The original decision of the United States Judicial Conference to endorse realignment was in no small measure based on the representatives' desire to accommodate what they perceived to be the preferences of the Judicial Council of the Fifth Circuit. Once that consensus-building process had begun it was extremely difficult to reverse. The strong value placed on regionalism and deference to circuit preferences also explain the high priority Judges Wisdom and Rives gave to changing the votes of their council. Only if the opponents of realignment could demonstrate that the circuit's judges were not in agreement on its advisability could they hope to derail the natural tendency of the conference to ratify the earlier resolution of the Circuit Council. It was only after Rives and Wisdom were able to deadlock the council's vote and expose the extent of internal disagreement publicly that the move to ratify the realignment recommendation of the powerful Biggs Committee was stopped.

Because of the intensity of the 1964 battle, the Judicial Conference decided it would no longer consider realignment proposals that did not have the unanimous support of the affected circuit. Congress only reluctantly, and at the insistence of Senator Eastland, was willing to discuss the issue but was repeatedly unable to resolve it. Therefore, until those key decisionmakers who were injecting dissension into the policy process either left the scene (as did Rives, Wisdom, Jordan, and Eastland) or changed their positions (as did Brown, Gee, Goldberg, and, most importantly, Mississippi's Coleman and Clark), the threshold for congressional action could not be reached. This was

13. Interview with Michael Remington, Washington, D.C., April 25, 1983.
14. For a thorough discussion of the accommodationist politics of the U.S. Judicial Conference, see Jerry Goldman, "Jurisdictional Politics and the Federal Courts," (Ph.D. diss., Johns Hopkins University, 1974).

why circuit division, though for many years supported by a significant majority of the Fifth Circuit's active judges, was not passed by Congress, and why five short months after unanimity was reached the reform was enacted into law.

AGENDA ACCESS

Unanimously endorsed proposals, however, do not automatically evoke favorable congressional attention. Though consensus support from the judiciary may be a necessary condition for policy adoption, it is certainly not a sufficient one. It may not even be enough to guarantee access to the congressional agenda, let alone a priority position on that agenda.

Interviews with the judges involved in the Fifth Circuit odyssey revealed a common complaint that court problems had to reach crisis proportions before eliciting congressional attention. Judicial legislation, like any other, is the result of a successfully built coalition among members of Congress. Rallying support within the legislature for changes is a time-consuming and tedious process. Building a congressional coalition for judicial change is particularly arduous, as policies of court reform have little to offer members in terms of logrolling, constituency service, or reelection benefits. Furthermore, even relatively serious problems affecting the judiciary do not have the urgency of such competing issues as war and peace, economic development, taxation, or appropriations. So policy adoption depends to a great extent on the sponsorship of an interested and influential legislator who is trusted on relevant matters by other members of Congress. In the final stages of the Fifth Circuit realignment effort, for example, Senator Heflin (D-AL) and Representative Kastenmeier (D-WI) and their respective staffs took responsibility for successfully shepherding the proposal through the legislative process.

Occasionally when Congress considers court-related policy proposals, political factors and outside interests supersede the immediate concerns of judicial administration.[15] Court reform proposals may die or be postponed at this stage, as was the realignment legislation when the House and Senate conferees played chicken in 1978. Whichever political demands members of Congress perceive as being the most pressing will largely determine the legislative outcome; and rarely are matters pertaining to the court system considered so urgent as to outweigh political considerations. If a judiciary-endorsed proposal evokes active opposition from powerful interests, such as

15. That the administrative merits of court reform proposals often play a secondary role to political concerns has been documented in studies of federal and state court systems. See Peter G. Fish, *The Politics of Federal Judicial Administration* (Princeton, N.J.: Princeton University Press, 1973); Joel A. Thompson and Robert T. Roper, "The Determinants of Legislators' Support for Judicial Reorganization," *American Politics Quarterly* 8 (April 1980): 221–36.

labor unions, civil rights groups, or the organized bar, it has little chance of legislative success.

As decisionmakers completely immersed in electoral politics, members of Congress have their antennae tuned to their constituencies, relevant interest groups, and the politics of compromise, logrolling, and reciprocity that mark their policy-making process. In short, representatives are politicians who respond to political demands and require answers to political questions. One House Judiciary Committee counsel assessed the situation in the following terms: "If you are going to get into the sophisticated nature of an issue of court administration, you will lose them [members of Congress] very quickly. They will start to yawn and forget about that issue very quickly. If you are talking about something more dramatic or intense, like civil rights problems, they get very attentive. But court administration is just not something they are going to bother with."[16] So, while judges may expect considerable deference on the more technical issues of court administration, they may be bombarded with political questions such as: Are any outside groups affected? If so, is there strong opposition? Is my constituency affected?

Fifth Circuit judges were openly frustrated throughout the commission and congressional hearings from 1974 to 1980 by repeatedly being forced to answer what they considered to be nongermane political questions concerning civil rights. They were in agreement that the civil rights issue did not have the same relevance in the 1970s as it had had in the first stages of the realignment saga. Nonetheless, members of Congress had permanently locked their focus on the political issue rather than on the administrative needs of the court. In 1977, when Chief Judge Brown inadvertently neglected to denounce the relevance of the civil rights argument, he elicited criticism from his Fifth Circuit colleagues, who were well aware of the importance Congress placed on the issue. Because of the way in which Congress perceives court-related matters, every time the reform proposal was submitted to Congress it was transformed into a political issue. Only after the circuit achieved unanimity and employed the "swinging from the left" strategy was it able to refocus congressional attention on the more immediately relevant administrative issues.

JUDICIAL LOBBYING

Underlying the model of cooperative oversight is a communications network, the heart of which is judicial lobbying. Once policy preferences are agreed upon within the political processes of the judiciary itself, judges must turn their attention to Congress in order to secure policy adoption. Despite the limitations inherent in the legislature's consideration of court administration questions, the recognized expertise of judges prompts members of Con-

16. Confidential interview.

gress to pay heed. One knowledgeable observer summed it up in this way: "When it comes to money and organization, they can't hold a candle to the oil industry. But when federal judges lobby Congress, members usually listen."[17]

The idea of judicial lobbying is anathema to many. It somehow seems inappropriate for federal judges, whose adjudicative role requires neutrality rather than advocacy, to urge the passage or defeat of proposed legislation. In spite of its unfortunate negative connotations, however, lobbying is nothing more than communicating information and considered opinion to the appropriate decisionmakers. No one has more accurate information on matters of judicial administration or is in a better position to comment on conditions facing the courts than the federal judge. In fact, the Canons of Judicial Ethics admonishes judges to use their expertise to advise lawmakers on ways to improve the judicial process. Without such communication, members of Congress would have great difficulty enacting legislation relating to the courts in an intelligent way. It is both proper and essential for this communications process to function effectively. Thus federal judges press their cases before Congress both through regular, formal channels and through sporadic, informal means of communication. The partisan nature of the recruitment and selection process assures that many judges have a fairly good rapport with some senator, guaranteeing them a point of access inside the system.

The formal communications process of lobbying relies on established institutional mechanisms. Usually this takes place through the Judicial Conference of the United States and the Administrative Office of the United States Courts. Representatives of these organizations regularly appear before appropriate congressional committees to provide relevant information and to communicate the official preferences of the organized judiciary. Such appearances may be invited by the congressional panel concerned or may be initiated by the judiciary itself. In order to insure that the judges maintain access to the legislative process, the Administrative Office has established a legislative affairs department whose officers monitor congressional activity and act as liaison for the judiciary.

It is also common for judges who have expertise in special areas of the judicial process to be relied upon heavily by lawmakers. This expert knowledge may have been accumulated by a judge prior to taking his position on the bench or acquired through service on one of the standing committees of the Judicial Conference. For example, the head of the Conference Committee on Court Administration, John Biggs and Robert Ainsworth during the years of the Fifth Circuit controversy and District Judge Elmo Hunter in the 1980s, is regularly consulted. So, too, are judges with expertise in substantive areas

17. Nadine Cohodas, "When Federal Judges Lobby, Congressman Usually Listen," *Congressional Quarterly Weekly Report*, October 18, 1980, p. 3167.

of the law. Gerald Tjoflat, for example, frequently provides congressional panels with expert opinions on the criminal process.

On circuit-specific matters, such as the Fifth Circuit controversy, the Circuit Council may be the institution through which formal legislative liaison is conducted. Unlike the Judicial Conference and Administrative Office, which deal with Congress regularly, the councils do so more sporadically and therefore are less likely to have well-honed liaison skills. The degree of influence of a circuit council depends largely on the knowledge of its judges. The Fifth Circuit Council was very effective in 1980, for example, largely because the politically savvy Robert Vance was able to suggest ways of dealing with Congress in terms the legislators would understand.

The formal communications process serves a number of functions. First, it allows the judiciary to speak to the legislature with one official voice. Second, it establishes an ongoing communications network that can respond with relative speed when the need arises. Third, it places the responsibility for communications in the hands of those who, through experience in dealing with Congress, have developed skills in representing the views of the judges. And fourth, it permits the individual members of the federal bench to concentrate on their adjudicative duties while having their views communicated to Congress through established representative channels. While not all judges or congressional staff members evaluate the effectiveness of the formal process positively, most, especially the more senior judges who have been active in such affairs,[18] prefer its advantages over exclusive reliance on individual judges contacting Congress.

Informal lobbying occurs outside the official institutional channels. For the most part, it involves individual judges communicating with members of Congress or congressional staff personnel. As a means of influencing the policy-making process, it can be very effective.

The extent to which judges engage in informal legislative liaison varies considerably depending upon their individual concepts of the judicial role and the kind of legislative contacts they may have. Some, like the Fifth Circuit's Irving Goldberg, prefer to abstain from such efforts altogether.[19] Others are willing to become involved when the issue is one in which they are deeply interested or has an especially important impact on their court. Judge Frank Johnson, for example, was extremely active in the Fifth Circuit controversy in both 1964 and 1980. Yet he acknowledges that in twenty-five years of judicial service splitting the Fifth Circuit was the only issue over which he called upon Congress.[20] Still others, as previous parts of this book have doc-

18. Interview with Judge Charles Clark, Jackson, Mississippi, January 26, 1983; interview with Judge Clement Haynsworth, Jr., Greenville, South Carolina, July 7, 1983.
19. Interview with Judge Irving L. Goldberg, Dallas, Texas, December 14, 1983.
20. Cohodas, "When Federal Judges Lobby," p. 3168.

umented, are not at all hesitant to make individual contact with members of Congress.

Many federal judges have well-developed relationships with one or more legislators. After all, most judges were active politically prior to assuming a position on the federal bench. A large proportion of them would not have received their appointments if they had not had close ties with a senator from their home state; many were classmates, political allies, and even law partners. Consequently, many judges are quite comfortable expressing their views to members of their state's congressional delegation. Conversely, when a member of Congress has a question regarding proposed legislation affecting the courts, the legislator without hesitation may contact a federal judge from his or her constituency. For a legislator who serves on the Judiciary Committee, such communications take place on a regular basis.

At key points in a political deadlock these relationships can be crucial. For example, in 1965 when the Fifth Circuit was having difficulties obtaining the four temporary judgeships endorsed by the Judicial Conference, personal contacts made the difference. Griffin Bell was able to use his influence with Georgia Senator Herman Talmadge to intercede with Eastland. This, coupled with Judge Haynsworth's use of intermediary Gordon McCabe, was crucial to breaking the standoff. Fifteen years later, the ability of Judges Coleman and Clark to mobilize the entire Mississippi congressional delegation in support of the previously opposed 3–3 division greatly facilitated passage of the legislation that ultimately divided the circuit.

Another interesting communications network through which judges lobby the legislative branch involves the relationship between federal judges and congressional staff. The history of the Fifth Circuit debate revealed several instances in which judges were able to contact and activate support from former law clerks who held key staff positions in Washington. However, for any federal judge to have, as one aide stated, as many "working troops" in Congress as did Judge Wisdom is rather unusual. At one point, four key staff members in the Senate could be identified as former Wisdom clerks. This influence was most notably manifest when a former clerk organized, drafted, and then sent to Wisdom for editing a copy of the dissenting views of the committee's liberal minority. In another instance, a key House staff member submitted the final 1980 Judiciary Committee report to Judge Frank Johnson for revision. Even as members were commenting on the final legislation, this clerkship phenomenon was acknowledged by Senator Howard J. Baker, Jr. (R-TN), who expressed a "personal devotion" to the Fifth Circuit because one of his former staff members and later Tennessee governor, Lamar Alexander, "was a law clerk for one of the Fifth Circuit's most outstanding and exemplary members, the Honorable John Wisdom."[21]

21. U.S. Congress, Senate, 96th Cong., 2d sess., 18 June 1980 *Congressional Record*, p. 7323.

Law clerks, of course, are not placed in Washington in any systematic or conspiratorial manner, but a surprising proportion of congressional staffers have had prior experience working for federal judges. It is certainly not uncommon to find in Congress bright legal talents whose career paths have included prestigious federal court clerkships. Wisdom's clerk connection to Washington, while more extensive than most, was not unusual. Former clerks of Judges Brown, Rives, Goldberg, Coleman, and others were also in evidence during the Fifth Circuit affair. Because the congressional staff is so critical to the legislative process, both substantively and procedurally, any influence with them gives an individual the opportunity to shape policy. The relationship between a law clerk and a judge is often quite intimate. Although the length of service is customarily one year, the bond often lasts a lifetime, with the clerks feeling great allegiance to "their judge." The judges active in the Fifth Circuit controversy certainly did not hesitate to express their opinions to their former clerks.

As Charles O. Jones explained, staff members lend continuity and stability to the legislative process, especially in light of the generally high turnover of legislators and the constant shifting among committees in the Senate. They also form an important bridge between individual chambers within the same institution.[22] It is an acknowledged fact of Washington life that congressional staffers exercise considerable influence over the substance of public policy by drafting the particulars of legislation (and sometimes a good bit more). That the Senate and House conferees during the 1978 Omnibus Judgeship Bill deadlock delegated to staffers the task of fashioning a compromise proposal speaks of their importance.

Occasionally, informal lobbying by judges escalates beyond communication with a member of Congress or a staff member. The 1964 campaign waged by Richard Rives and John Wisdom to kill the original realignment proposal is such an example. Even Judge Wisdom described the extensiveness of the effort as "unusual."[23] No point of potential influence was neglected. Every possible means of communication was explored. The judges used the press, the academic community, the bar, fellow judges, outside interest groups, legislative and executive branch officials, and a host of political contacts, in a well-orchestrated and effectively executed strategy to block adoption of what they considered to be a most pernicious alteration of their court.

The activities of Wisdom and Rives highlight the position in which dissenters within the judicial politics arena find themselves. When the official decisionmakers of the judicial branch, the circuit councils and the Judicial Conference, arrive at policy conclusions and are prepared to recommend legislation to Congress, there is little recourse for those judges who do not

22. Charles O. Jones, *Congress: People, Process, Policy* (Homewood, Ill.: Dorsey Press, 1981).

23. Interview with Judge John Minor Wisdom, New Orleans, Louisiana, May 28, 1985.

agree. In 1964, Wisdom and Rives could not in good conscience accept division of their circuit. For them the consequences were too dire. Instead, they initiated the campaign to reverse the tide. Theirs was a classic political strategy adapted to the judicial arena. They politicized the issue by changing the terms of the debate, thus broadening the scope of conflict and expanding the number of participants.[24] By this strategy, the minority increased its chances of becoming the majority.

CONCLUSION

The cooperative oversight model illustrates that a mutual relationship exists between Congress and the judiciary as they jointly formulate, adopt, and implement policies pertaining to the administration of the federal court system. For pragmatic political reasons, the legislature relies heavily on federal judges to participate in identifying court problems and formulating proposed solutions to them. As policy advisers, the judges wield influence over administrative issues. Therefore, Congress is able to take advantage of the expertise of federal judges and delegate to the judiciary a substantial share of the responsibility for monitoring the nation's court system. Congress tends to focus almost entirely on the political aspect of court reform issues, whether or not such a side exists. This cooperative effort, however, should not be seen as an abdication by Congress of either its oversight responsibility or its legislative powers over the court system. On the contrary, legislators are jealous of their prerogatives and adamant about the fact that theirs is the final word. Congress sets policies not in accord with the wishes of the judiciary often enough to show that it is far from a rubber stamp for the judges. However, when the key elements are present—unanimity among the judges, effective political communication among the institutions, legislative sponsorship, and political neutrality—the process runs smoothly.

The political realities surrounding policy-making for the federal courts make it very unlikely that fundamental reform will be adopted until the judiciary finds itself mired in problems of catastrophic proportions. In several important ways the system is biased against significant change. First, there is little incentive for Congress to engage in the systematic analysis necessary to devise a plan for comprehensive change. Competing legislative demands and the lack of political payoff for such efforts preclude such extensive congressional activity.

Second, there is little interest among scholars, the organized bar, or citizens' groups to initiate such a process. Because court reform issues are bound up with fundamental questions concerning the litigation explosion and social policy, they require complex public policies. For this reason, they deserve the systematic study and experimentation that other important social problems

24. E. E. Schattschneider, *The Semisovereign People* (Hinsdale, Ill.: Dryden Press, 1960).

receive. Effectively addressing the problems facing the federal court system goes far beyond collecting and presenting court statistics. Even with all the necessary information they possess, the responsibility for change in the federal courts should not fall to federal judges alone.

Third, the internal politics of the judiciary is not conducive to wholesale change. The strong norms of decentralization and accommodation virtually assure that the unanimity needed for such change will not be present. When nationwide realignment was suggested, for example, federal judges indicated general support for the concept—as long as their own circuit boundaries were left untouched. If and when consensus does exist, the policy is likely to reflect agreement on the least common denominator.

Fourth, significant organized interests are likely to oppose, and consequently politicize, any substantial alteration in the judicial system. The courts decide issues affecting the exercise of political power, the extent to which civil liberties are guaranteed, and the control of vast economic assets. Any suggested change that might have an impact on those outcomes will arouse opposition. The civil rights issue during the Fifth Circuit battles is a case in point. So, too, is the opposition posted by the organized bar whenever jurisdictional changes, such as the elimination of diversity jurisdiction from the federal courts, are proposed.

As a consequence of the cooperative oversight arrangement and the reigning political realities, judicial reform will doubtless continue to take place on a piecemeal basis. If a court reform policy is administratively but not politically feasible, then the judges probably will have the discretion to attack the problems in at least a stopgap fashion. If the change is politically feasible, it may be of little consequence for improving the overall machinery of justice. What remains from the process, then, are two institutions that do not speak the same language but are trying to communicate and understand each other. Problems will be identified, however, and specific solutions adopted through shared judicial and legislative responsibility. In fact, some major reforms have already been implemented, but without the benefit of sufficient careful analysis. The system would undoubtedly profit from extensive study of alternatives. Where disagreements arise, the building of consensus and the processes of interinstitutional politics will, over time, lead to politically acceptable solutions for specific needs. The system does not operate with great efficiency, but in the end it produces a workable, if not perfect, federal judiciary. As Arthur T. Vanderbilt, former chief justice of the New Jersey Supreme Court, prophetically remarked decades ago, "Judicial reform is not a sport for the short-winded."

Interviewed Participants

Judicial Branch:

Fifth Circuit Court of Appeals
Judge John R. Brown (Houston, Texas), August 10–11, 1983
Judge J. P. Coleman (Ackerman, Mississippi), January 26, 1983
Judge Charles Clark (Jackson, Mississippi), January 26, 1983
Judge John Minor Wisdom (New Orleans, Louisiana), March 23, 1983;
    May 28, 1985
Judge Alvin B. Rubin (Baton Rouge, Louisiana), May 24, 1983
Judge Albert Tate, Jr. (New Orleans, Louisiana), May 24, 1983
Judge Jere Williams (Austin, Texas), March 22, 1983
Judge Thomas M. Reavley (Austin, Texas), March 21, 1983
Judge Carolyn Dineen Randall (Houston, Texas), March 16, 1983
Judge Joe MacDonald Ingraham (Houston, Texas), March 16, 1983
Judge Irving L. Goldberg (Dallas, Texas), December 14, 1983
Judge Thomas G. Gee (Austin, Texas), March 18, 1983

Eleventh Circuit Court of Appeals
Judge Elbert P. Tuttle (Atlanta, Georgia), August 9, 1982; October 2, 1982
Judge John C. Godbold (Montgomery, Alabama), December 3, 1983
Judge Joseph W. Hatchett (Tallahassee, Florida), June 17, 1983
Judge Frank M. Johnson, Jr. (Montgomery, Alabama), October 25, 1982
Judge Robert S. Vance (Birmingham, Alabama), May 18, 1983
Judge R. Lanier Anderson III (Macon, Georgia), October 20, 1982
Judge Albert J. Henderson (Atlanta, Georgia), August 9, 1982
Judge Gerald B. Tjoflat (Jacksonville, Florida), May 23, 1983
Judge Peter T. Fay (Miami, Florida), May 23, 1983
Judge Warren L. Jones (Jacksonville, Florida), June, 1983
Judge James C. Hill (Atlanta, Georgia), September 27, 1983
Judge Thomas A. Clark (Atlanta, Georgia), July 12, 1983

Judge David W. Dyer (Miami, Florida), June 14, 1983
Judge Lewis R. Morgan (Newnan, Georgia), May 3, 1983
Former Circuit Executive Thomas H. Reese (Atlanta, Georgia), October 25, 1982

Fourth Circuit Court of Appeals
Judge Clement F. Haynsworth, Jr. (Greenville, South Carolina), August 9, 1983

Ninth Circuit Court of Appeals
Judge James R. Browning (San Francisco, California), March 8, 1984

Court of Appeals for the District of Columbia
Judge J. Skelly Wright (Washington, D.C.), May 22, 1985

Federal Judicial Center
Former Director A. Leo Levin (Washington, D.C.), October 27, 1983

Legislative Branch:

United States Senators
Quentin N. Burdick (Democrat, North Dakota), May 5, 1983
Roman L. Hruska (Republican, Nebraska), July 29, 1983

Senate Staff
Guy P. Land (Stennis; Democrat, Mississippi), April 27, 1983
Francis E. Rosenberger (Eastland; Democrat, Mississippi), April 26, 1983
Thomas M. Susman (Kennedy; Democrat, Massachusetts), April 26, 1983
Kenneth R. Feinberg (Kennedy; Democrat, Massachusetts), April 27, 1983
William P. Westphal (Senate Judiciary Committee), May 12, 1983

United States House of Representatives
Barbara Jordan (Democrat, Texas), March 22, 1983

House Staff
Alan A. Parker (Rodino; Democrat, New Jersey), April 29, 1983
Michael J. Remington (Kastenmeier; Democrat, Wisconsin) April 25, 1982

Executive Branch:
Former President Jimmy Carter (Atlanta, Georgia) April 13, 1983
Former Attorney General Griffin B. Bell (Atlanta, Georgia), October 18, 1982; February 14, 1984
Former Attorney General Nicholas deB. Katzenbach (Armonk, New York), May 8, 1985
Former Assistant Attorney General Burke Marshall (New Haven, Connecticut), April 26, 1985
Former U.S. Civil Rights Commission Chairman John Hannah (East Lansing, Michigan), April, 1985

Interest Groups:
  Althea T. L. Simmons (Washington Bureau, NAACP), April 25, 1983
  Judge U. W. Clemon (Alabama Black Lawyers Association, Birmingham, Alabama), November 4, 1983
  Frank R. Parker (Lawyers Committee for Civil Rights under Law, Washington, D.C.), April 28, 1983
  Neil Bradley (American Civil Liberties Union, Southern Region, Atlanta, Georgia), August 2, 1983

Scholars:
  Jack Bass (Columbia, South Carolina), June 29, 1982
  Charles Alan Wright (Austin, Texas), March 21, 1983

Index